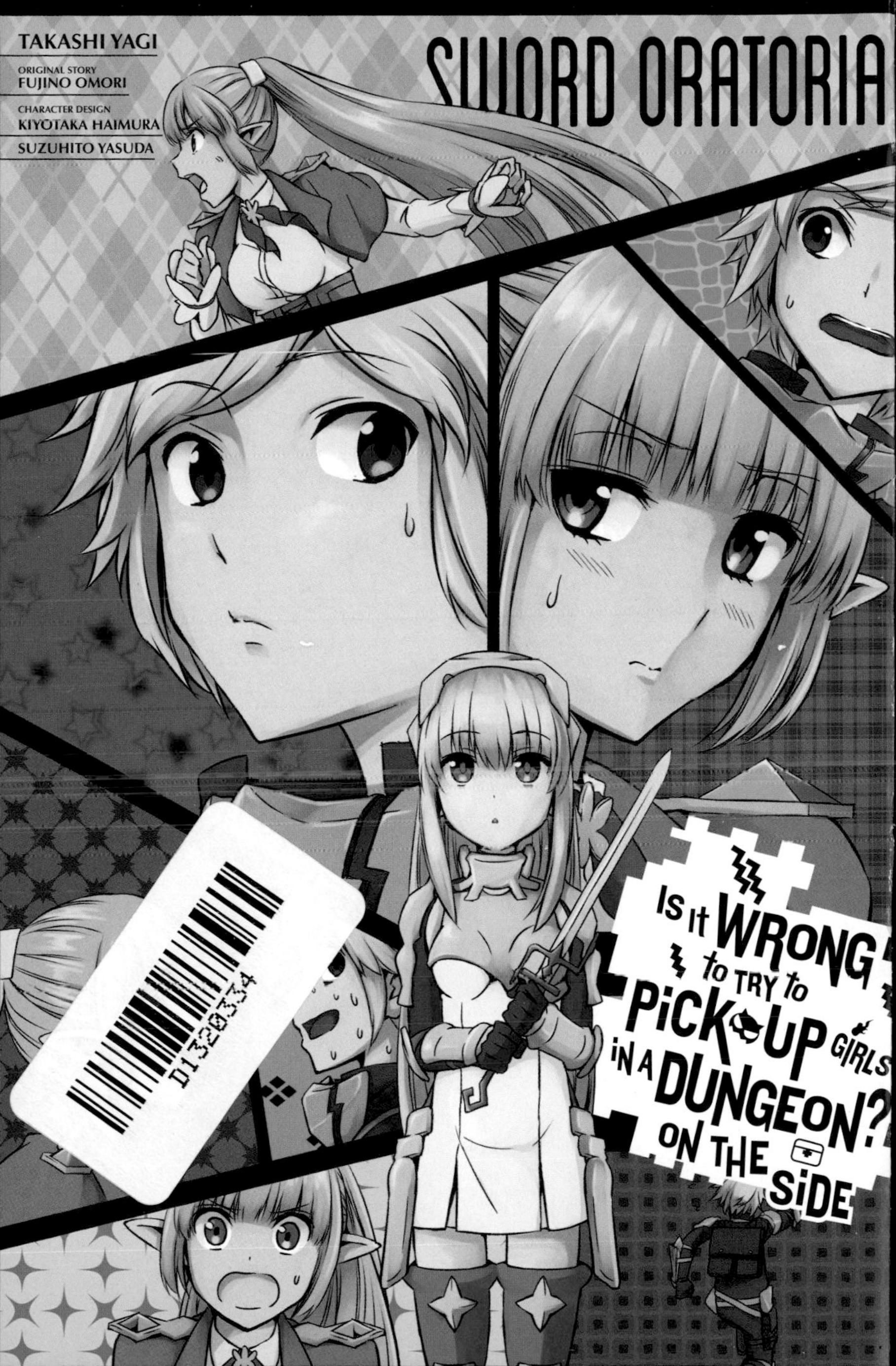
TAKASHI YAGI
ORIGINAL STORY
FUJINO OMORI
CHARACTER DESIGN
KIYOTAKA HAIMURA
SUZUHITO YASUDA
SWORD ORATORIA
IS IT WRONG TO TRY TO PICK UP GIRLS IN A DUNGEON? ON THE SIDE

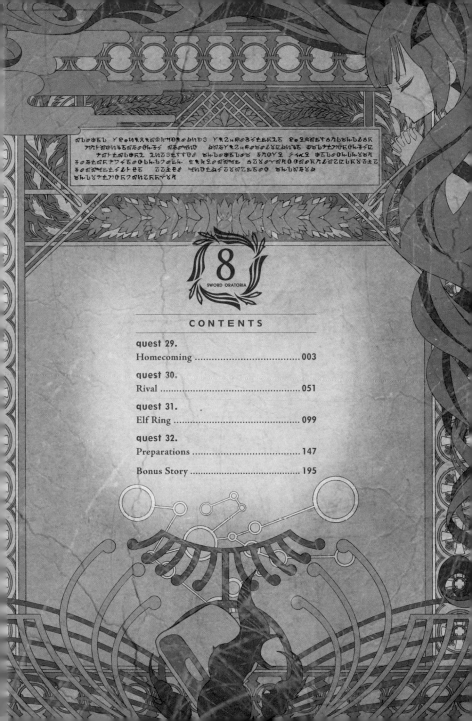

8

SWORD ORATORIA

CONTENTS

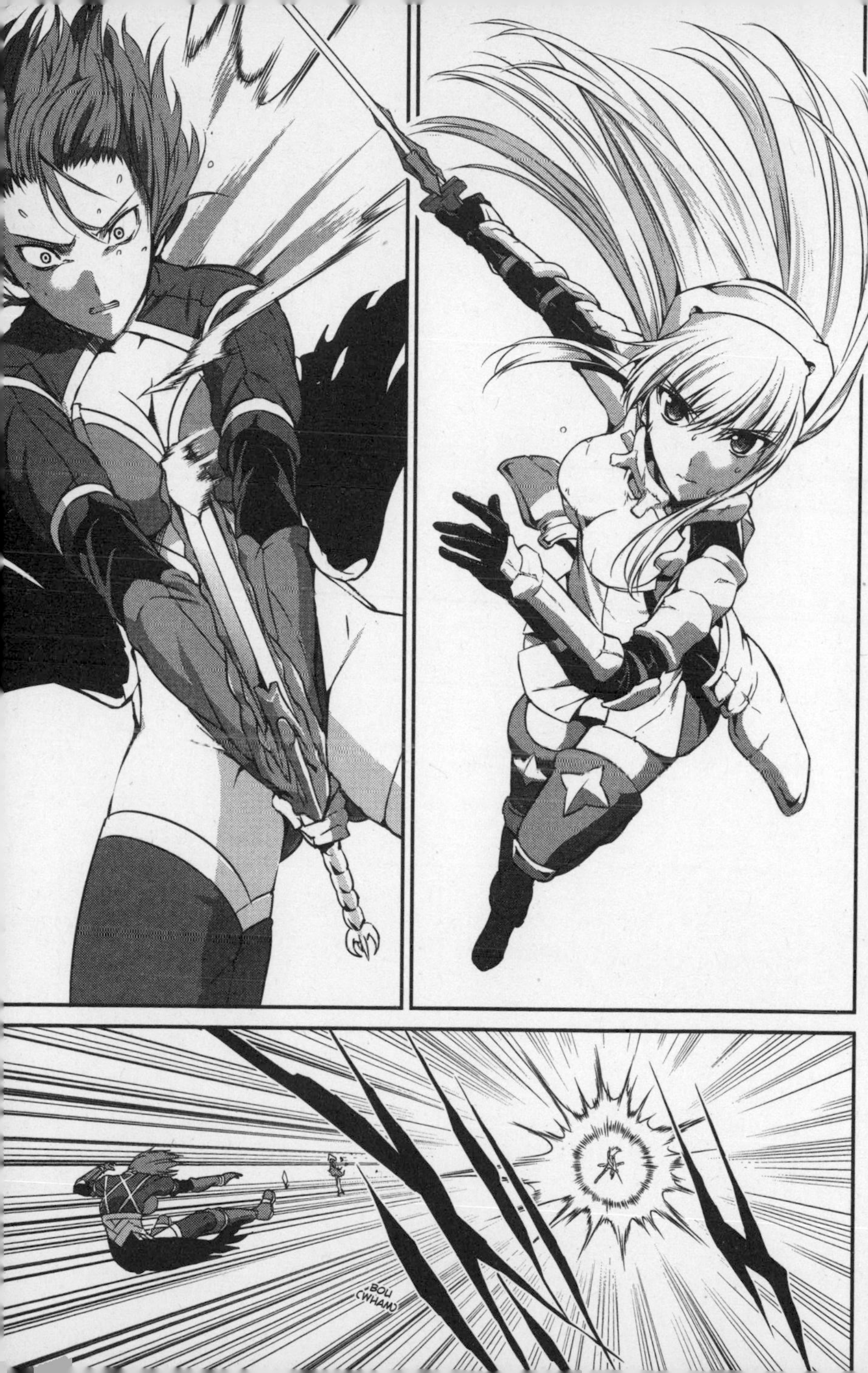
BOU (WHAM)

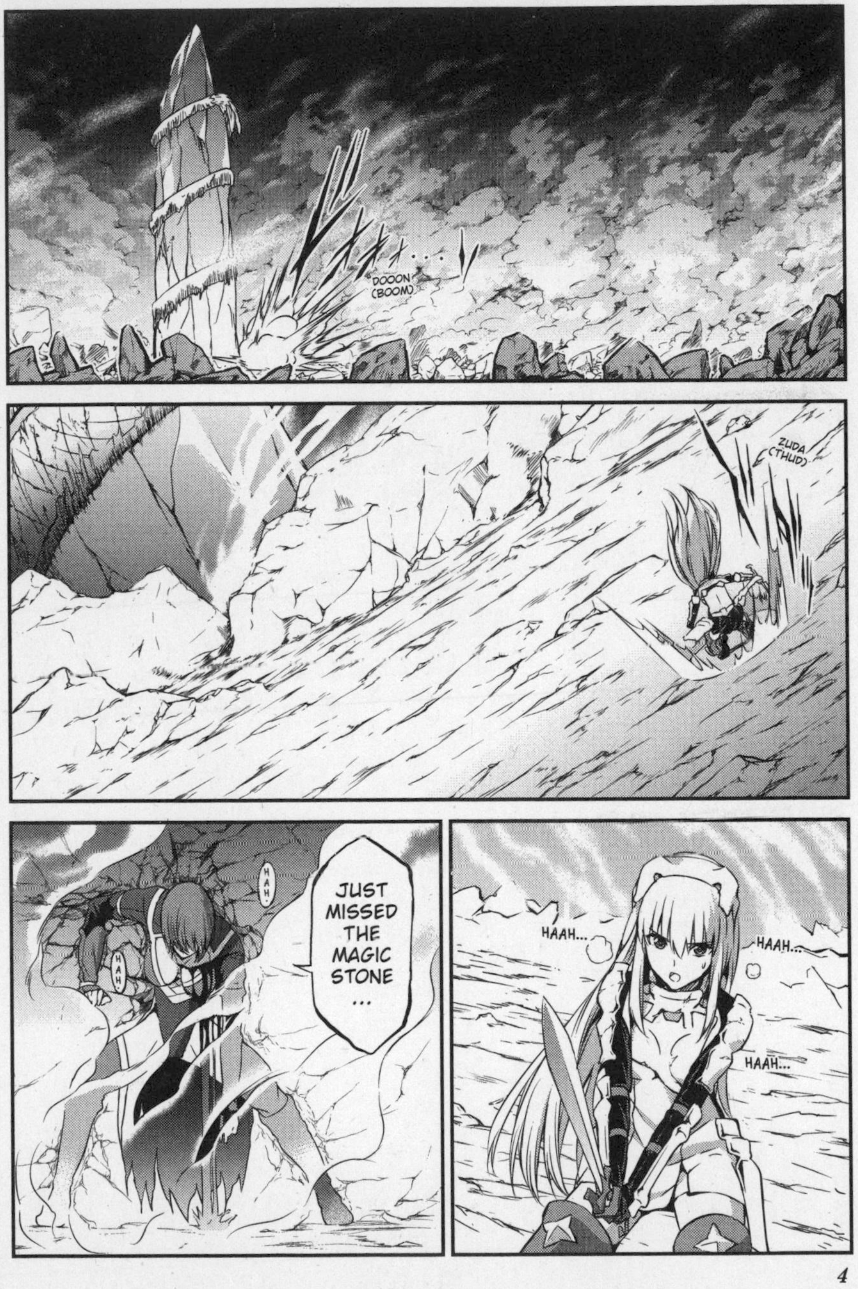
DOOON (BOOM)
ZUDA (THUD)
HAAH...
HAAH...
HAAH...
JUST MISSED THE MAGIC STONE ...
HAH.
HAH.

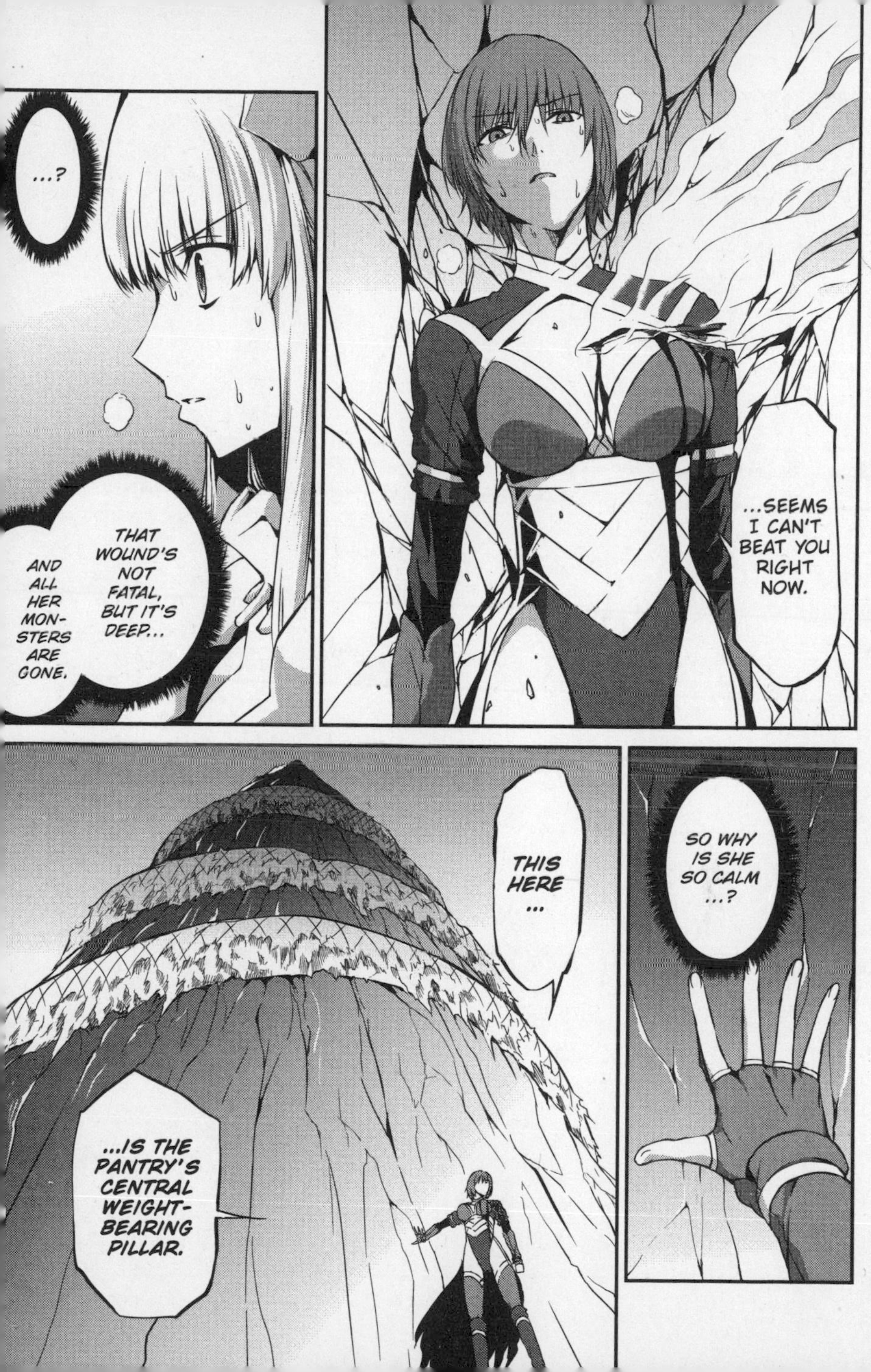
...SEEMS I CAN'T BEAT YOU RIGHT NOW.
...?
THAT WOUND'S NOT FATAL, BUT IT'S DEEP...
AND ALL HER MONSTERS ARE GONE.
SO WHY IS SHE SO CALM ...?
THIS HERE ...
...IS THE PANTRY'S CENTRAL WEIGHT-BEARING PILLAR.

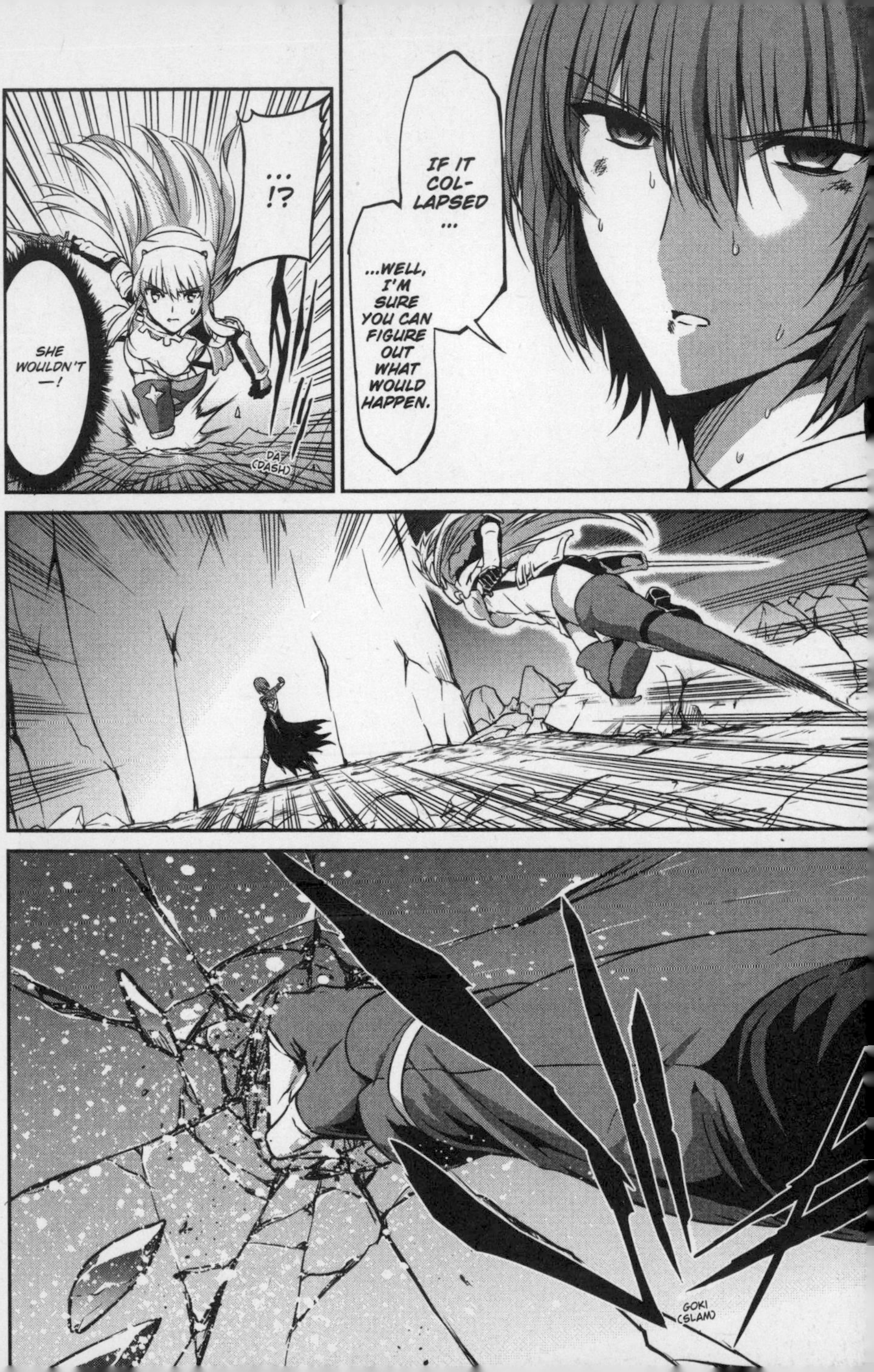
IF IT COL-LAPSED ...
...WELL, I'M SURE YOU CAN FIGURE OUT WHAT WOULD HAPPEN.
...!?
SHE WOULDN'T —!
DA (DASH)
GOKI (SLAM)

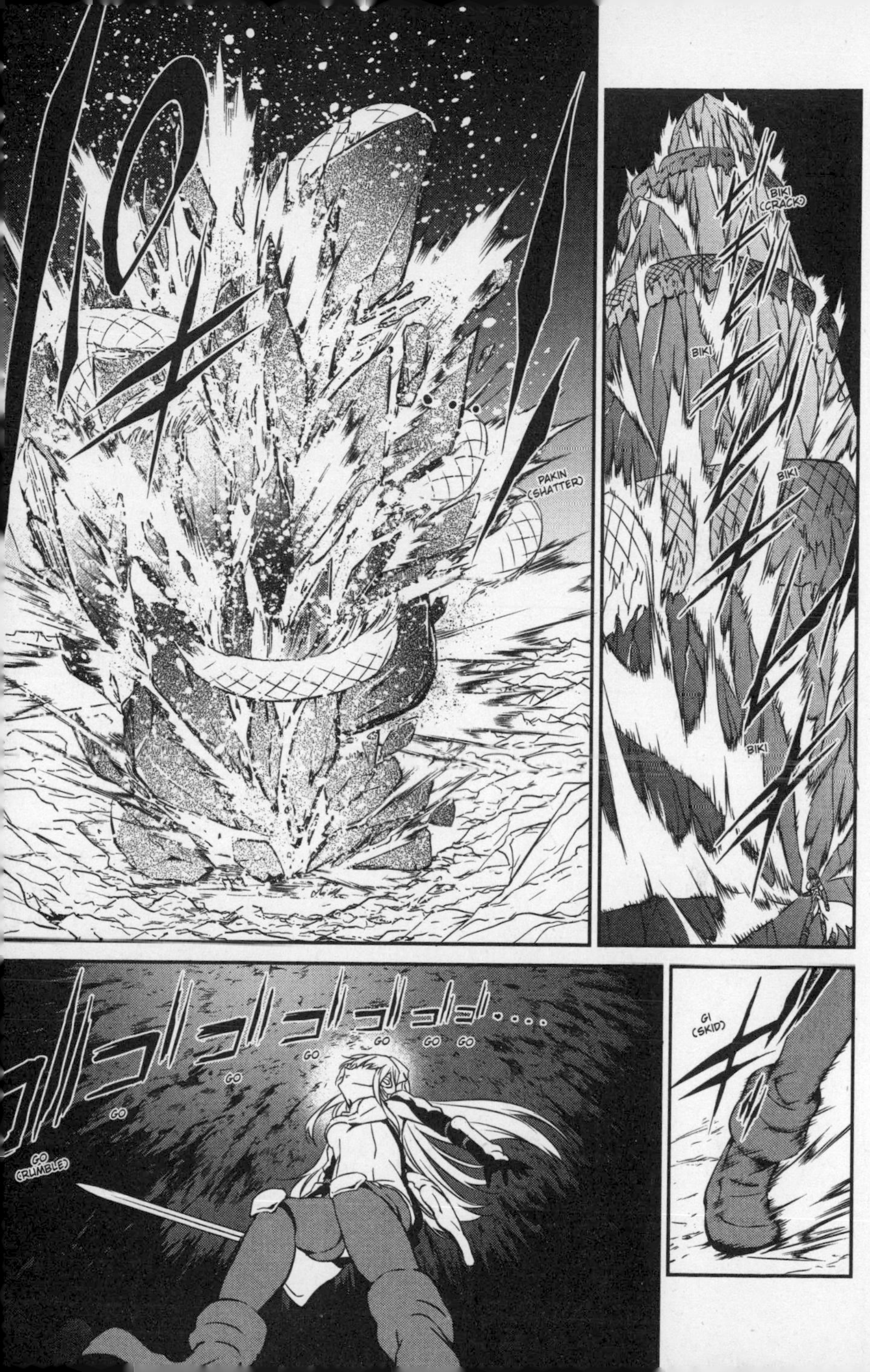
BIKI (CRACK)
BIKI
BIKI
BIKI
PAKIN (SHATTER)
GI (SKID)
GO GO GO
GO
GO
GO
GO (RUMBLE)

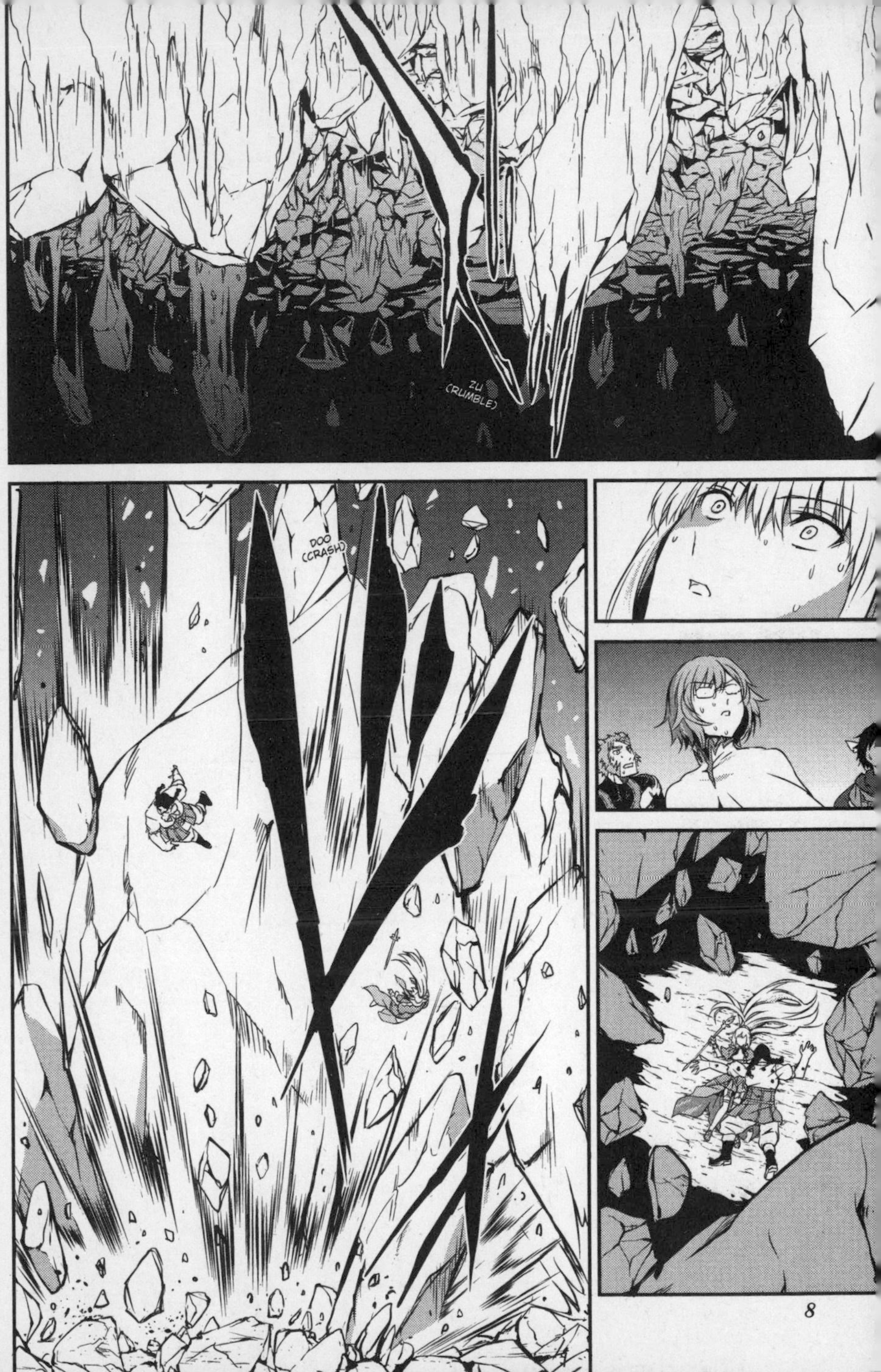
ZU
(RUMBLE)
DOO
(CRASH)

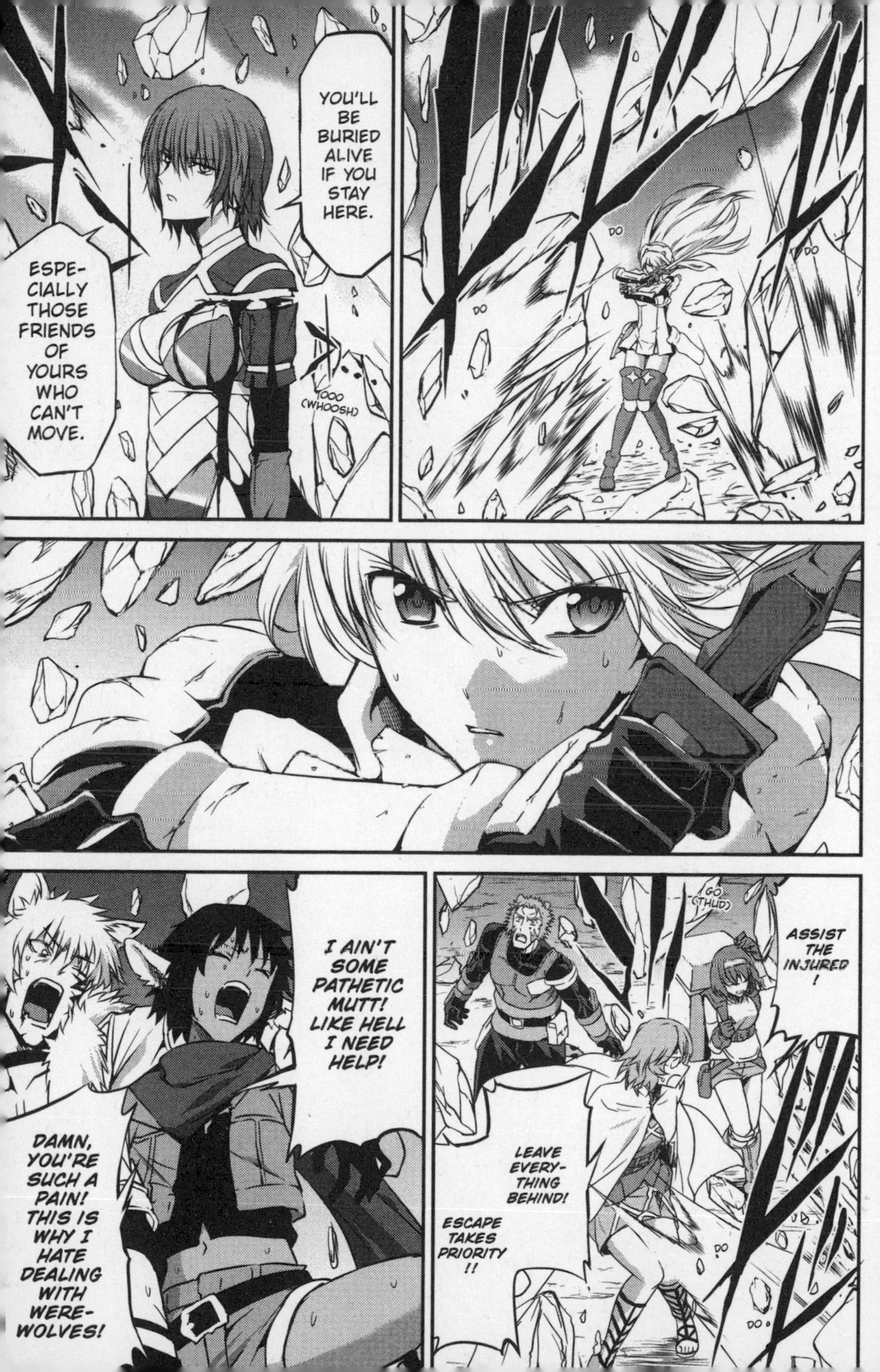
DO
DO
DO
YOU'LL BE BURIED ALIVE IF YOU STAY HERE.
ESPE-CIALLY THOSE FRIENDS OF YOURS WHO CAN'T MOVE.
OOO (WHOOSH)
GO (THUD)
ASSIST THE INJURED!
LEAVE EVERY-THING BEHIND!
ESCAPE TAKES PRIORITY!!
DO
DO
I AIN'T SOME PATHETIC MUTT! LIKE HELL I NEED HELP!
DAMN, YOU'RE SUCH A PAIN! THIS IS WHY I HATE DEALING WITH WERE-WOLVES!

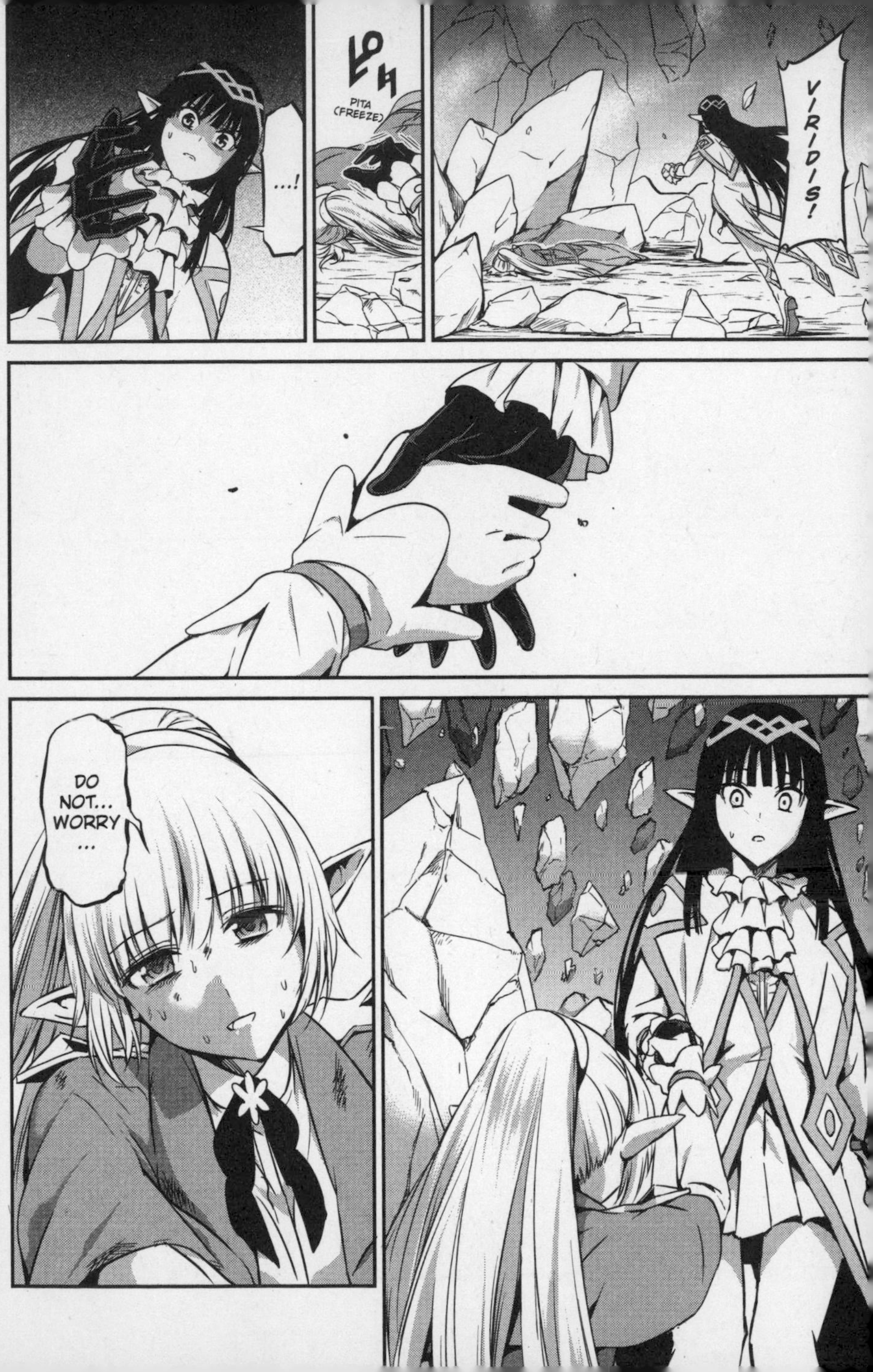
VIRIDIS!
ピタ
PITA (FREEZE)
...!
DO NOT... WORRY ...

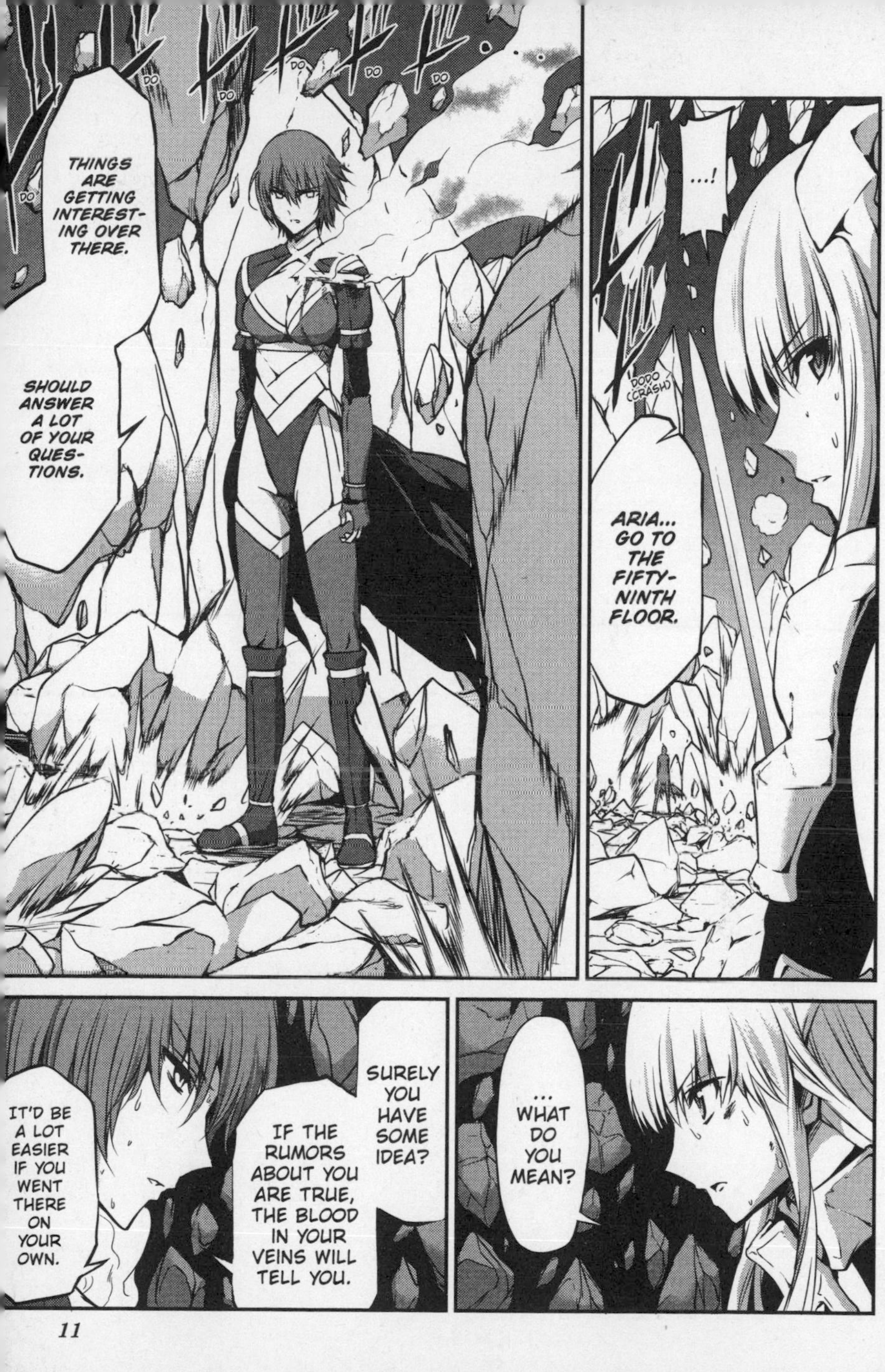
...!
DODO (CRASH)
ARIA... GO TO THE FIFTY-NINTH FLOOR.
DO DO DO DO DO DO
THINGS ARE GETTING INTEREST-ING OVER THERE.
SHOULD ANSWER A LOT OF YOUR QUES-TIONS.
... WHAT DO YOU MEAN?
SURELY YOU HAVE SOME IDEA?
IF THE RUMORS ABOUT YOU ARE TRUE, THE BLOOD IN YOUR VEINS WILL TELL YOU.
IT'D BE A LOT EASIER IF YOU WENT THERE ON YOUR OWN.

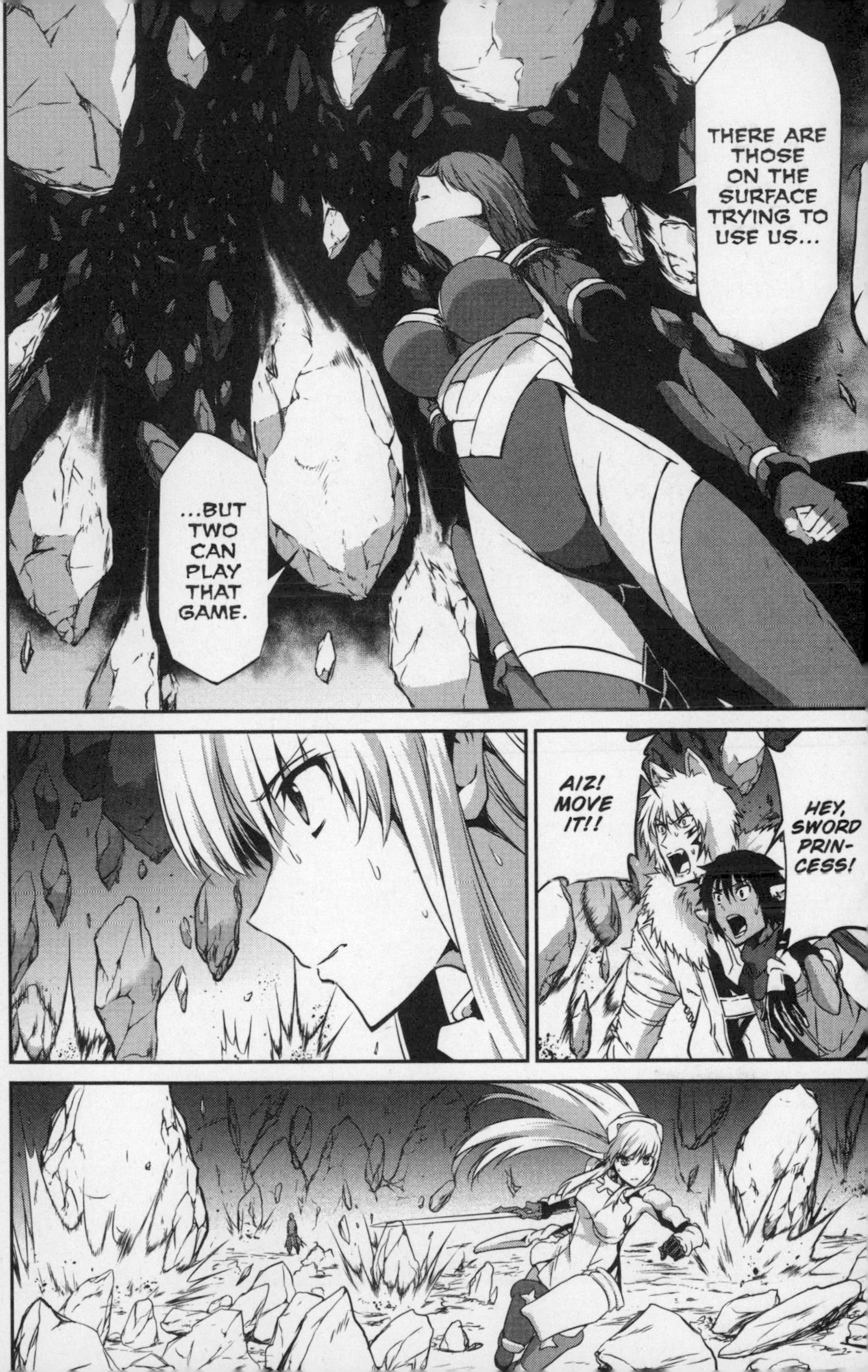
THERE ARE THOSE ON THE SURFACE TRYING TO USE US...
...BUT TWO CAN PLAY THAT GAME.
HEY, SWORD PRIN-CESS!
AIZ! MOVE IT!!

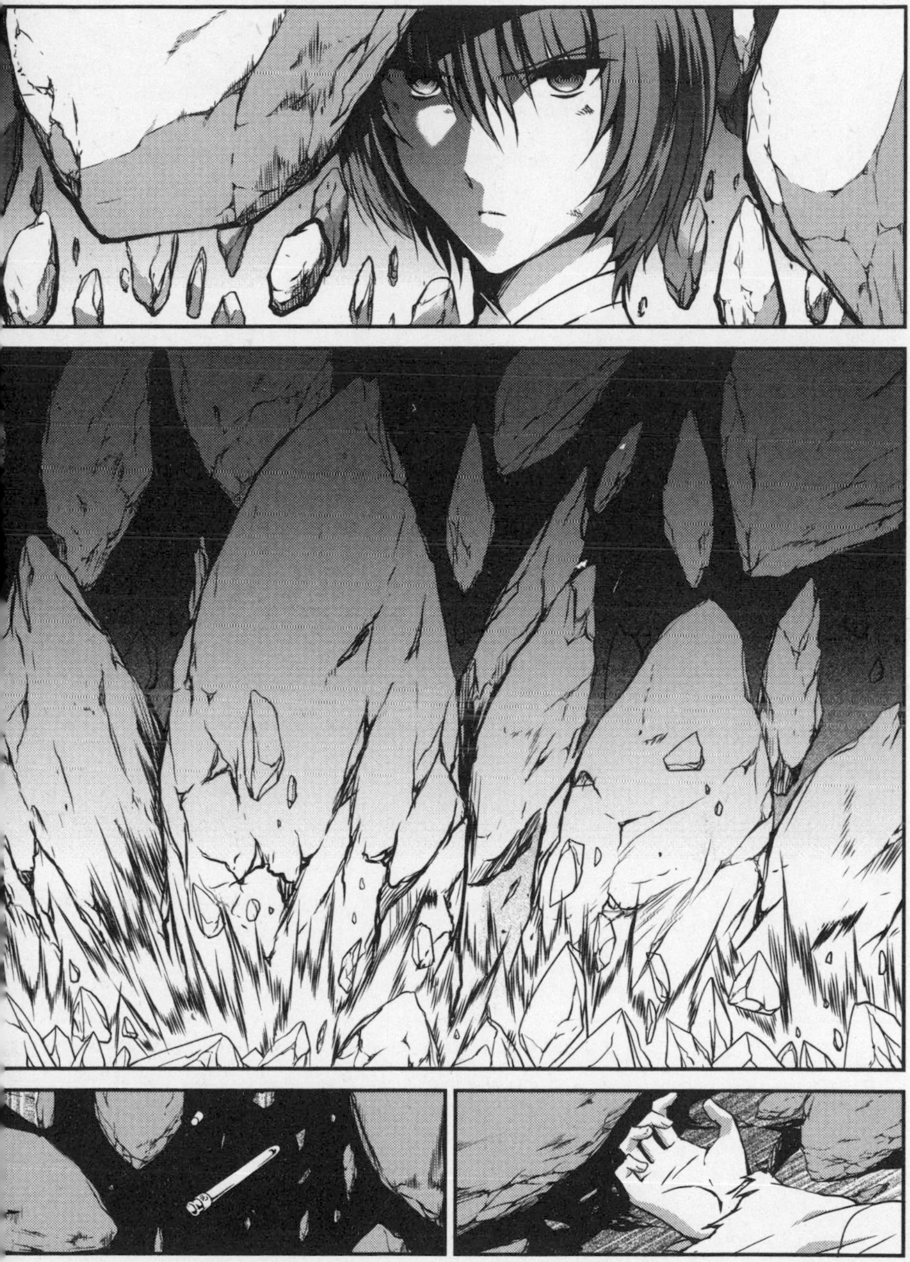

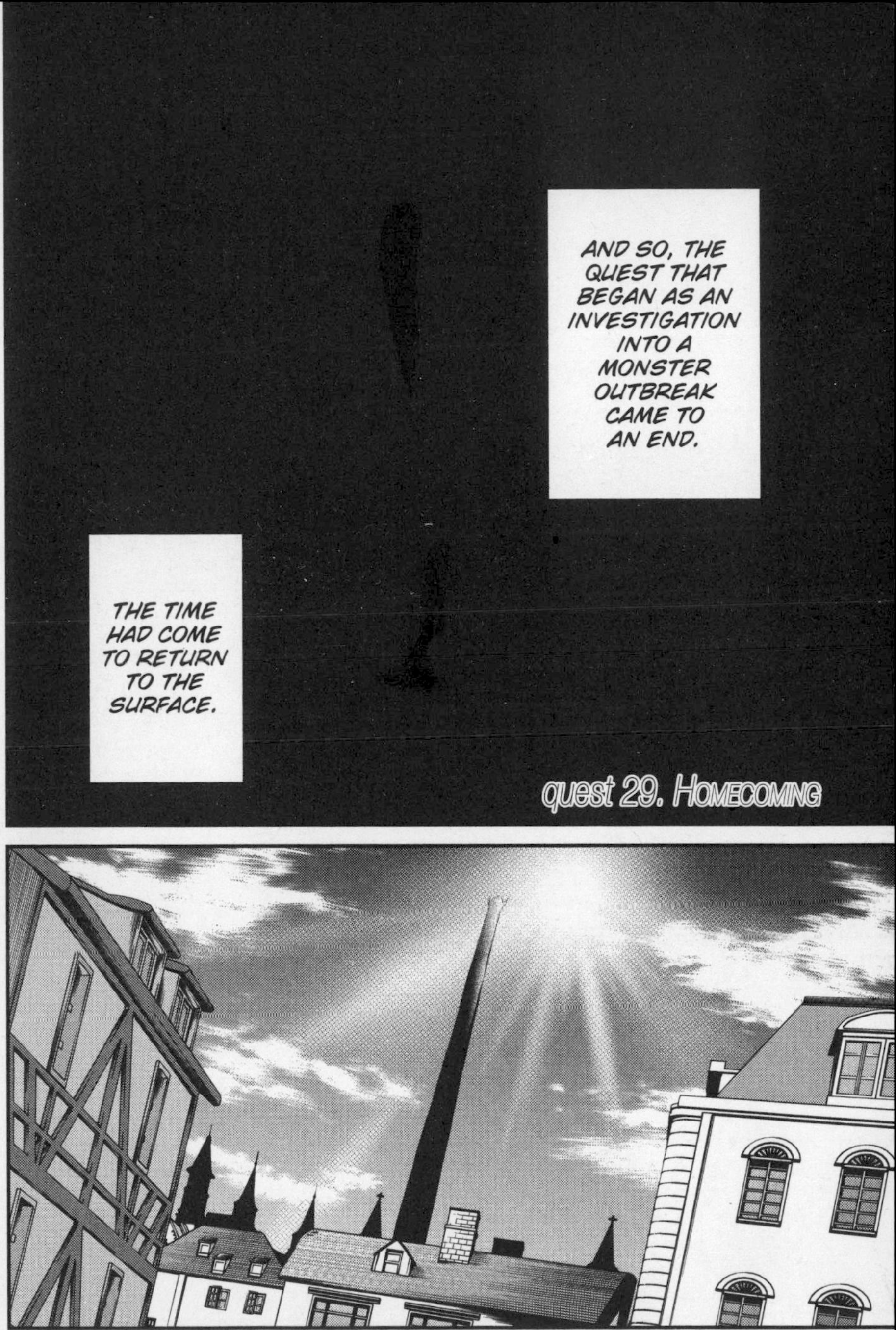
AND SO, THE QUEST THAT BEGAN AS AN INVESTIGATION INTO A MONSTER OUTBREAK CAME TO AN END.
THE TIME HAD COME TO RETURN TO THE SURFACE.
quest 29. HOMECOMING

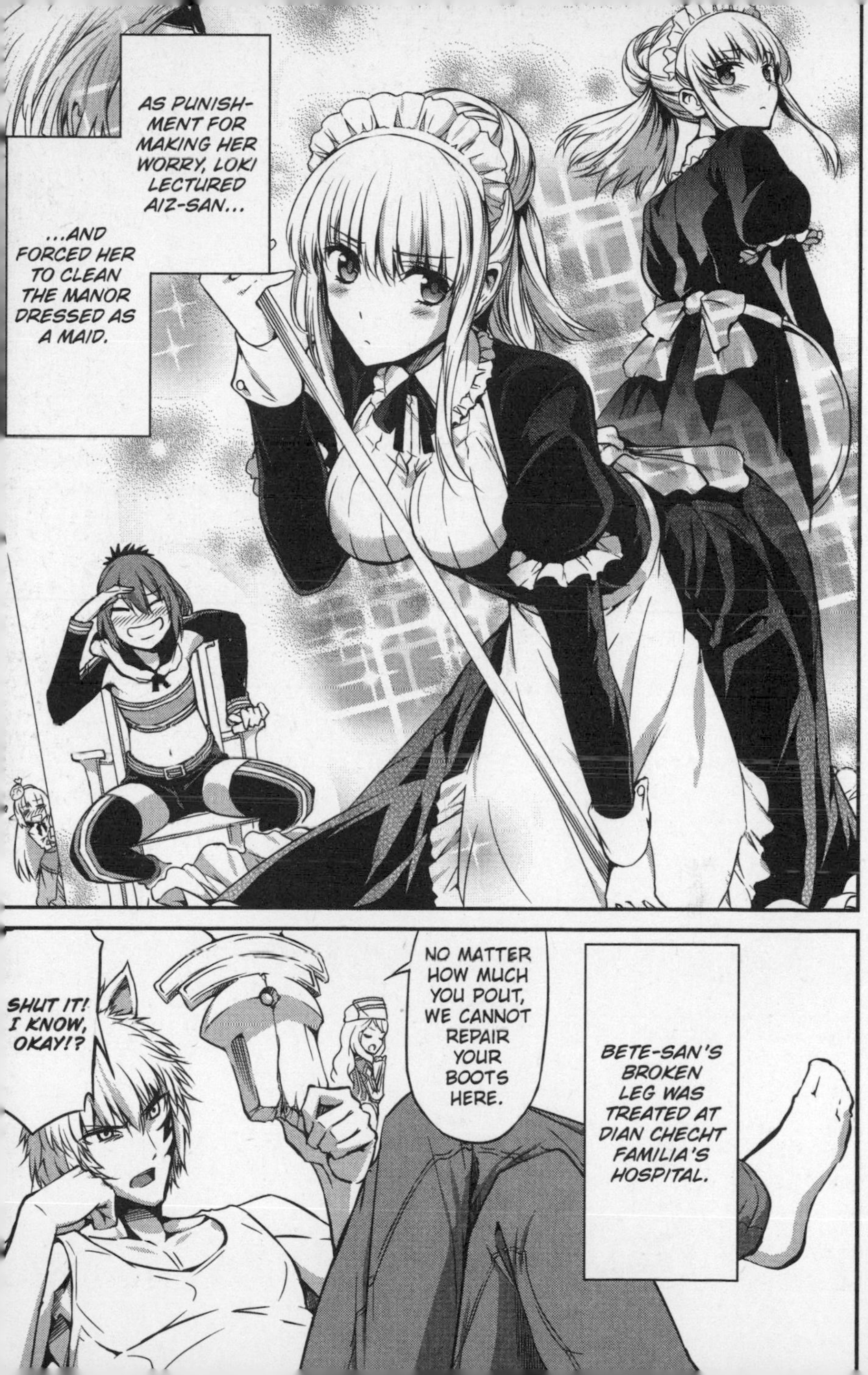
AS PUNISH-MENT FOR MAKING HER WORRY, LOKI LECTURED AIZ-SAN...
...AND FORCED HER TO CLEAN THE MANOR DRESSED AS A MAID.
BETE-SAN'S BROKEN LEG WAS TREATED AT DIAN CHECHT FAMILIA'S HOSPITAL.
NO MATTER HOW MUCH YOU POUT, WE CANNOT REPAIR YOUR BOOTS HERE.
SHUT IT! I KNOW, OKAY!?

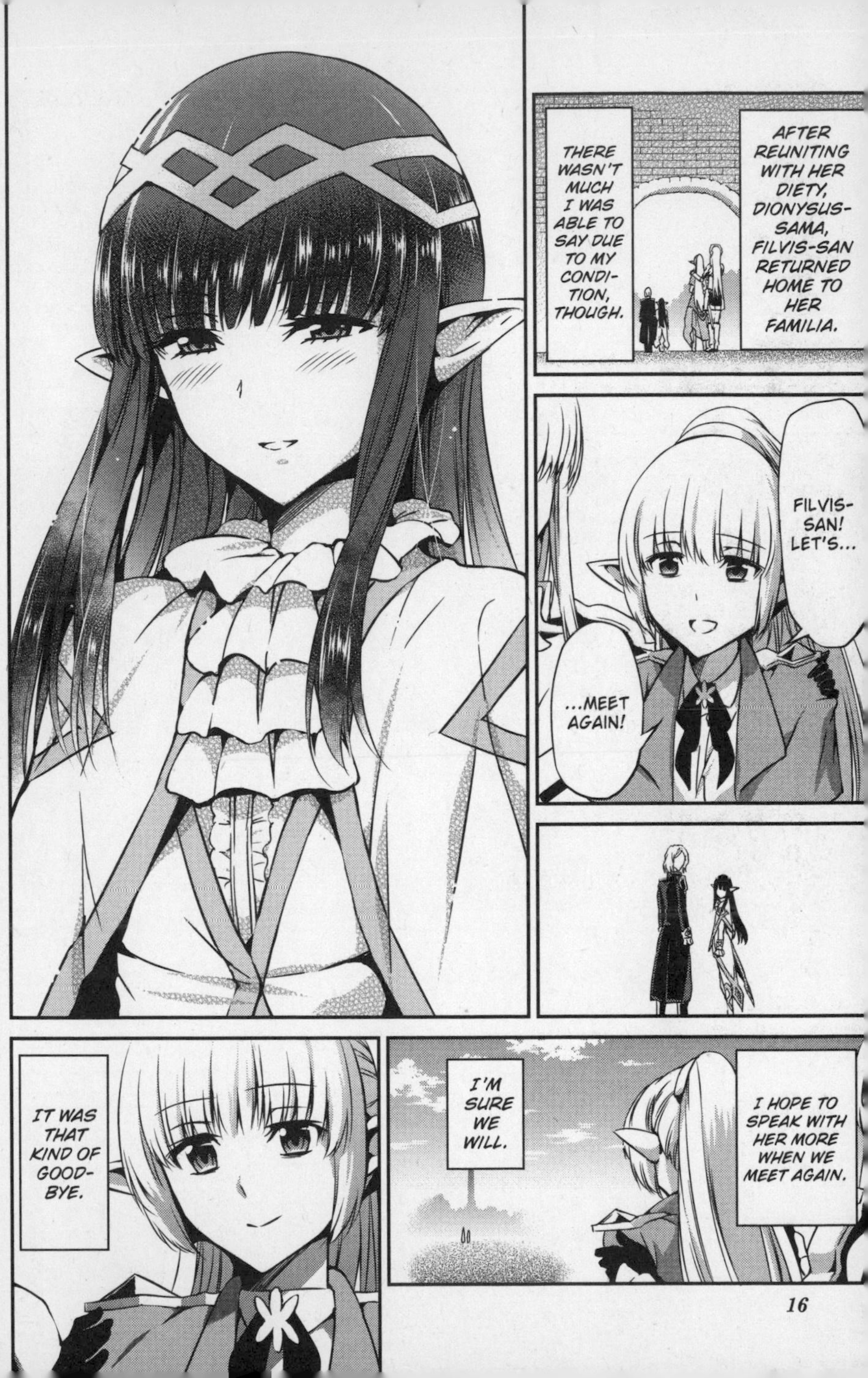
AFTER REUNITING WITH HER DIETY, DIONYSUS-SAMA, FILVIS-SAN RETURNED HOME TO HER FAMILIA.
THERE WASN'T MUCH I WAS ABLE TO SAY DUE TO MY CONDITION, THOUGH.
FILVIS-SAN! LET'S...
...MEET AGAIN!
I HOPE TO SPEAK WITH HER MORE WHEN WE MEET AGAIN.
I'M SURE WE WILL.
IT WAS THAT KIND OF GOOD-BYE.

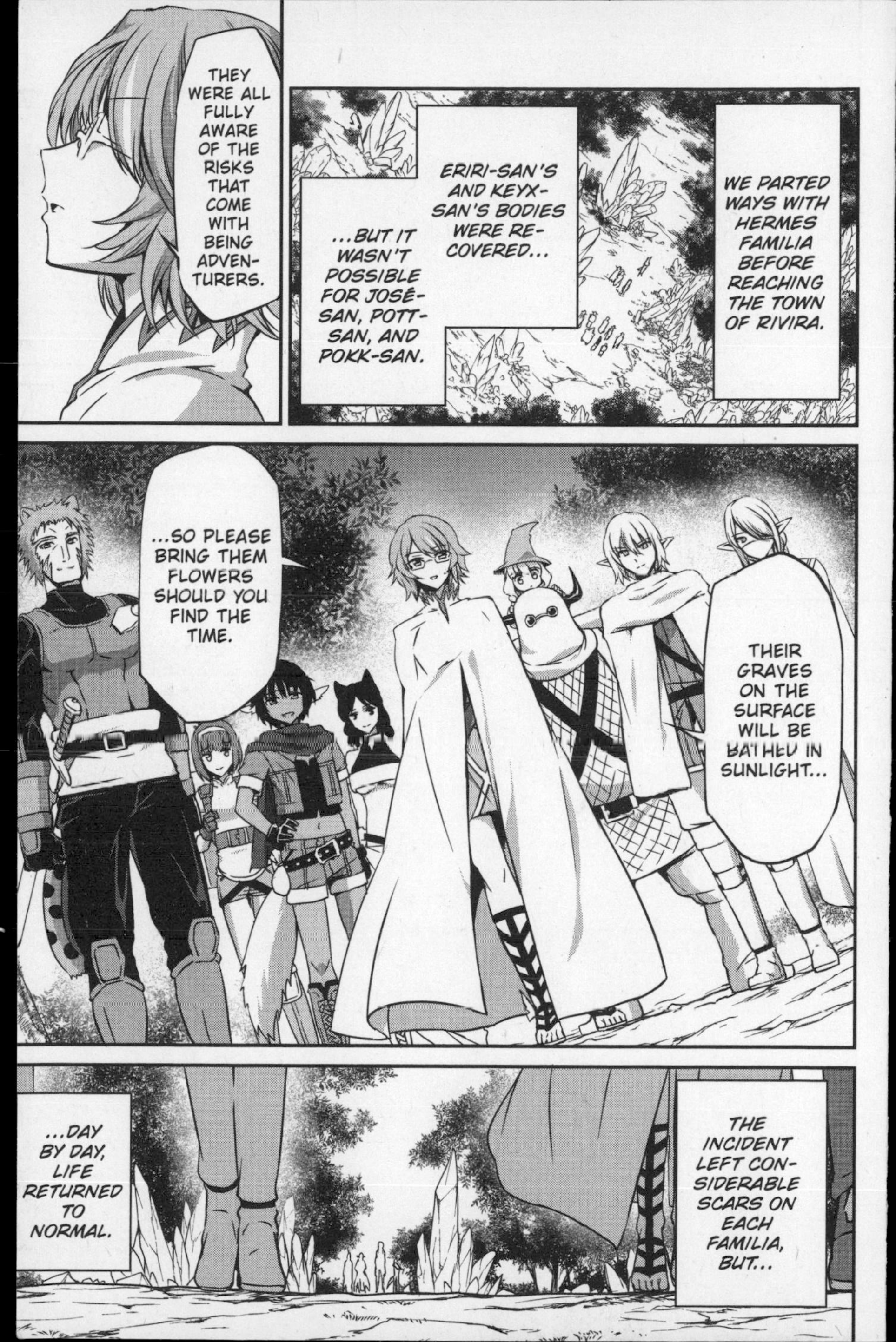
WE PARTED WAYS WITH HERMES FAMILIA BEFORE REACHING THE TOWN OF RIVIRA.
ERIRI-SAN'S AND KEYX-SAN'S BODIES WERE RECOVERED...
...BUT IT WASN'T POSSIBLE FOR JOSÉ-SAN, POTT-SAN, AND POKK-SAN.
THEY WERE ALL FULLY AWARE OF THE RISKS THAT COME WITH BEING ADVENTURERS.
THEIR GRAVES ON THE SURFACE WILL BE BATHED IN SUNLIGHT...
...SO PLEASE BRING THEM FLOWERS SHOULD YOU FIND THE TIME.
THE INCIDENT LEFT CONSIDERABLE SCARS ON EACH FAMILIA, BUT...
...DAY BY DAY, LIFE RETURNED TO NORMAL.

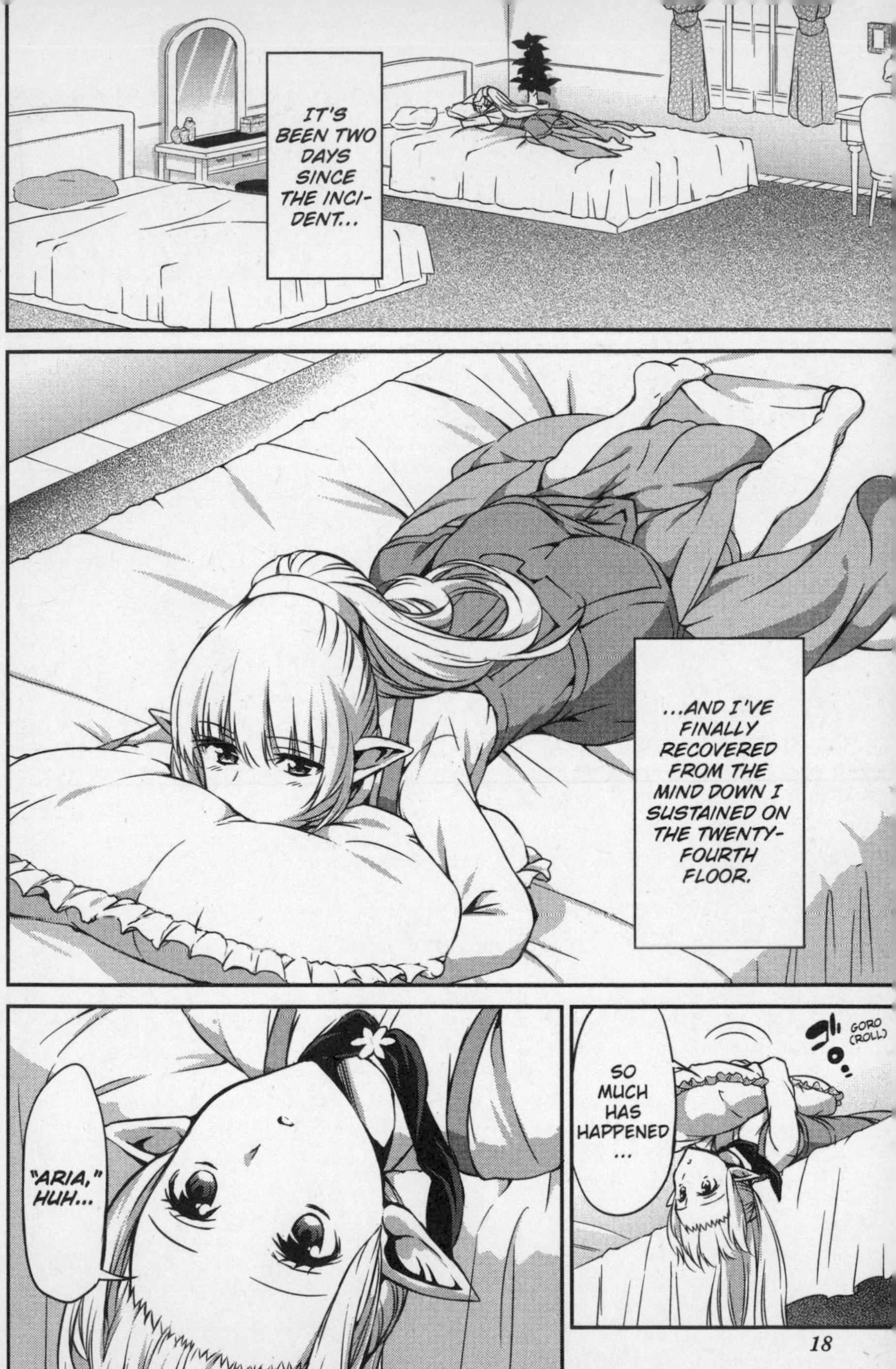
IT'S BEEN TWO DAYS SINCE THE INCI-DENT...
...AND I'VE FINALLY RECOVERED FROM THE MIND DOWN I SUSTAINED ON THE TWENTY-FOURTH FLOOR.
GORO (ROLL)
SO MUCH HAS HAPPENED ...
"ARIA," HUH...

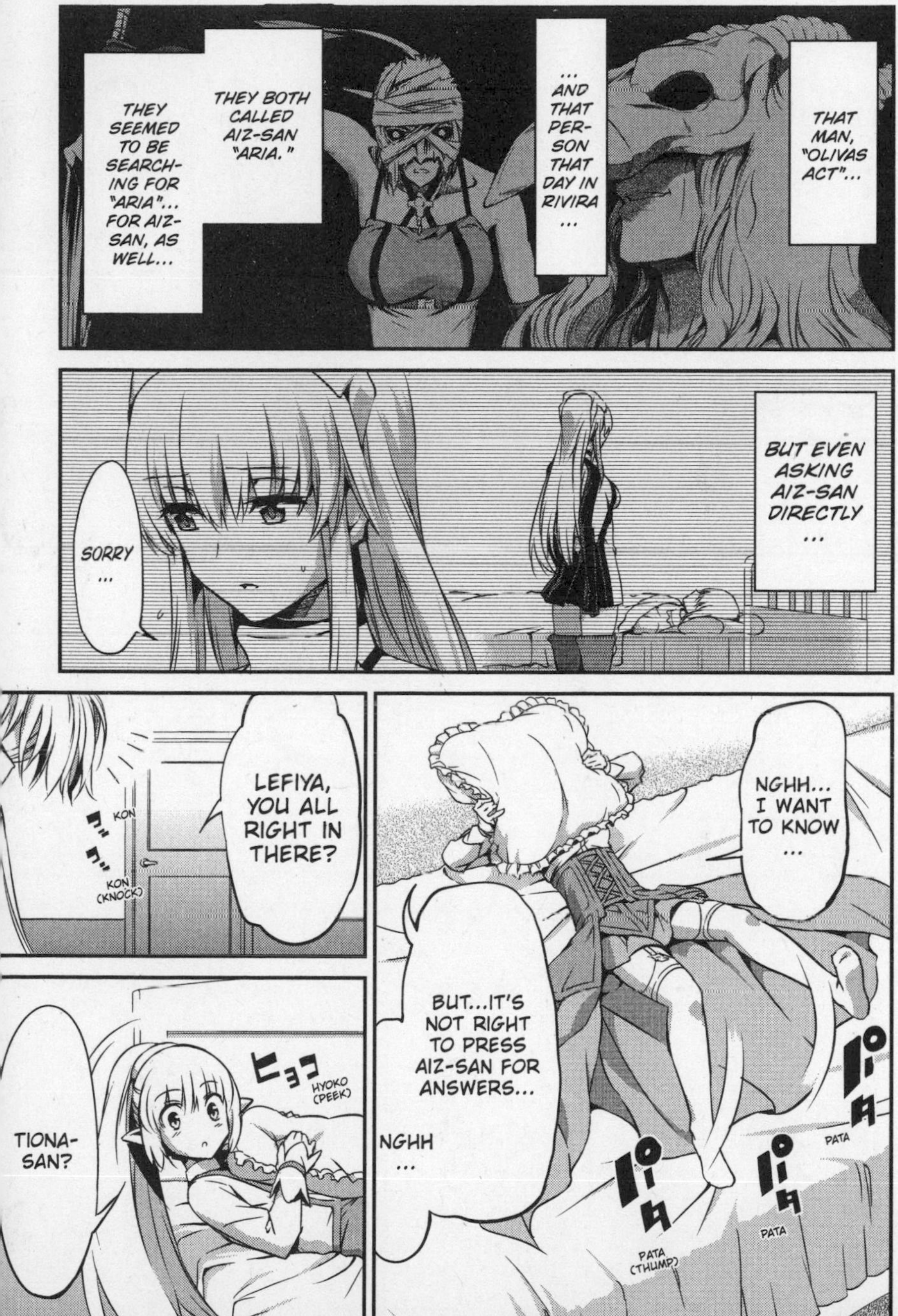
THAT MAN, "OLIVAS ACT"...
...AND THAT PERSON THAT DAY IN RIVIRA...
THEY BOTH CALLED AIZ-SAN "ARIA."
THEY SEEMED TO BE SEARCHING FOR "ARIA"... FOR AIZ-SAN, AS WELL...
BUT EVEN ASKING AIZ-SAN DIRECTLY...
SORRY...
NGHH... I WANT TO KNOW...
BUT...IT'S NOT RIGHT TO PRESS AIZ-SAN FOR ANSWERS...
NGHH...
PATA
PATA
PATA (THUMP)
LEFIYA, YOU ALL RIGHT IN THERE?
KON
KON (KNOCK)
HYOKO (PEEK)
TIONA-SAN?

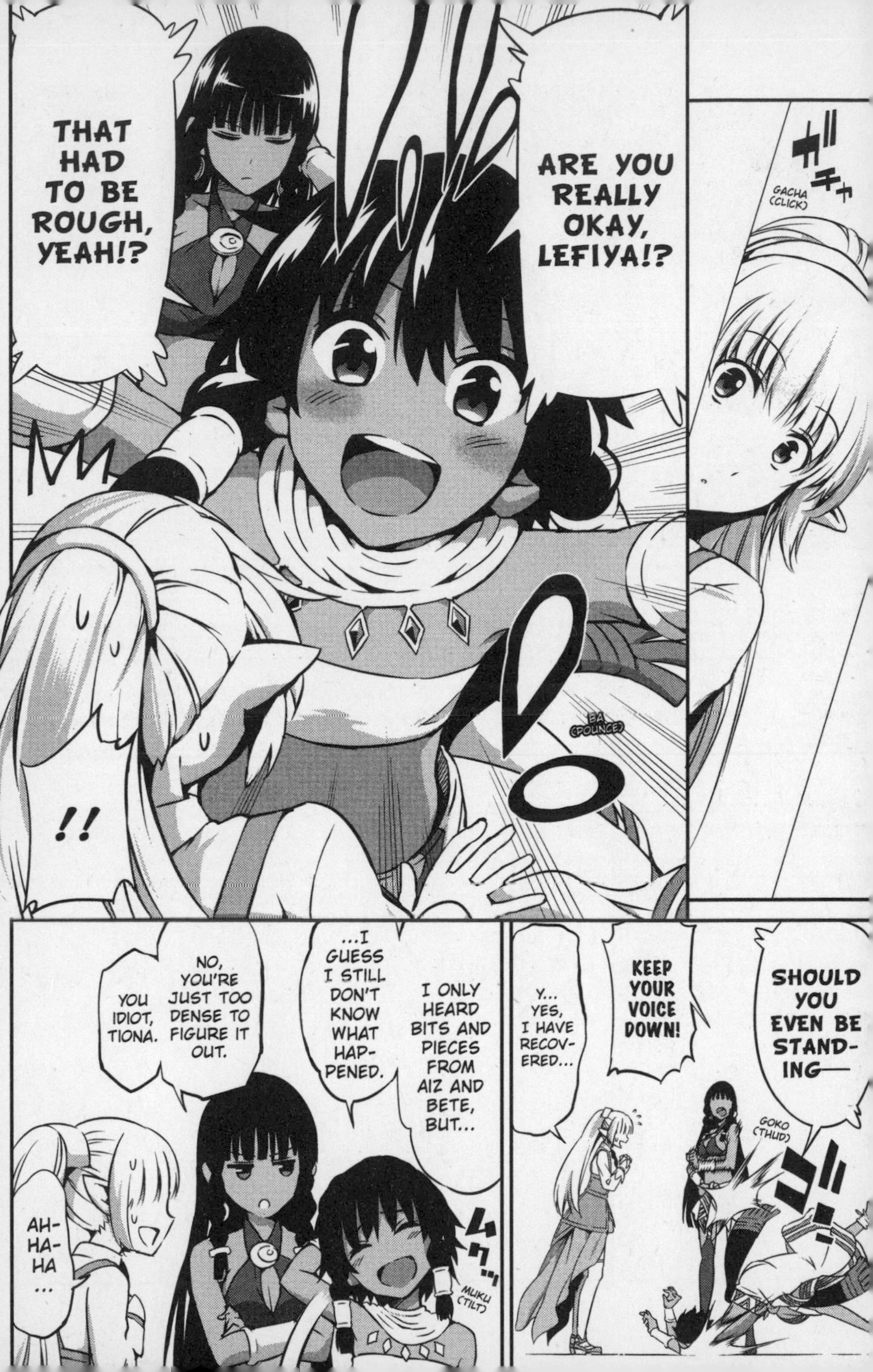
GACHA (CLICK)
ARE YOU REALLY OKAY, LEFIYA!?
BA (POUNCE)
THAT HAD TO BE ROUGH, YEAH!?
!!
SHOULD YOU EVEN BE STANDING—
GOKO (THUD)
KEEP YOUR VOICE DOWN!
Y... YES, I HAVE RECOVERED...
I ONLY HEARD BITS AND PIECES FROM AIZ AND BETE, BUT...
...I GUESS I STILL DON'T KNOW WHAT HAPPENED.
NO, YOU'RE JUST TOO DENSE TO FIGURE IT OUT.
YOU IDIOT, TIONA.
MUKU (TILT)
AH-HA-HA...

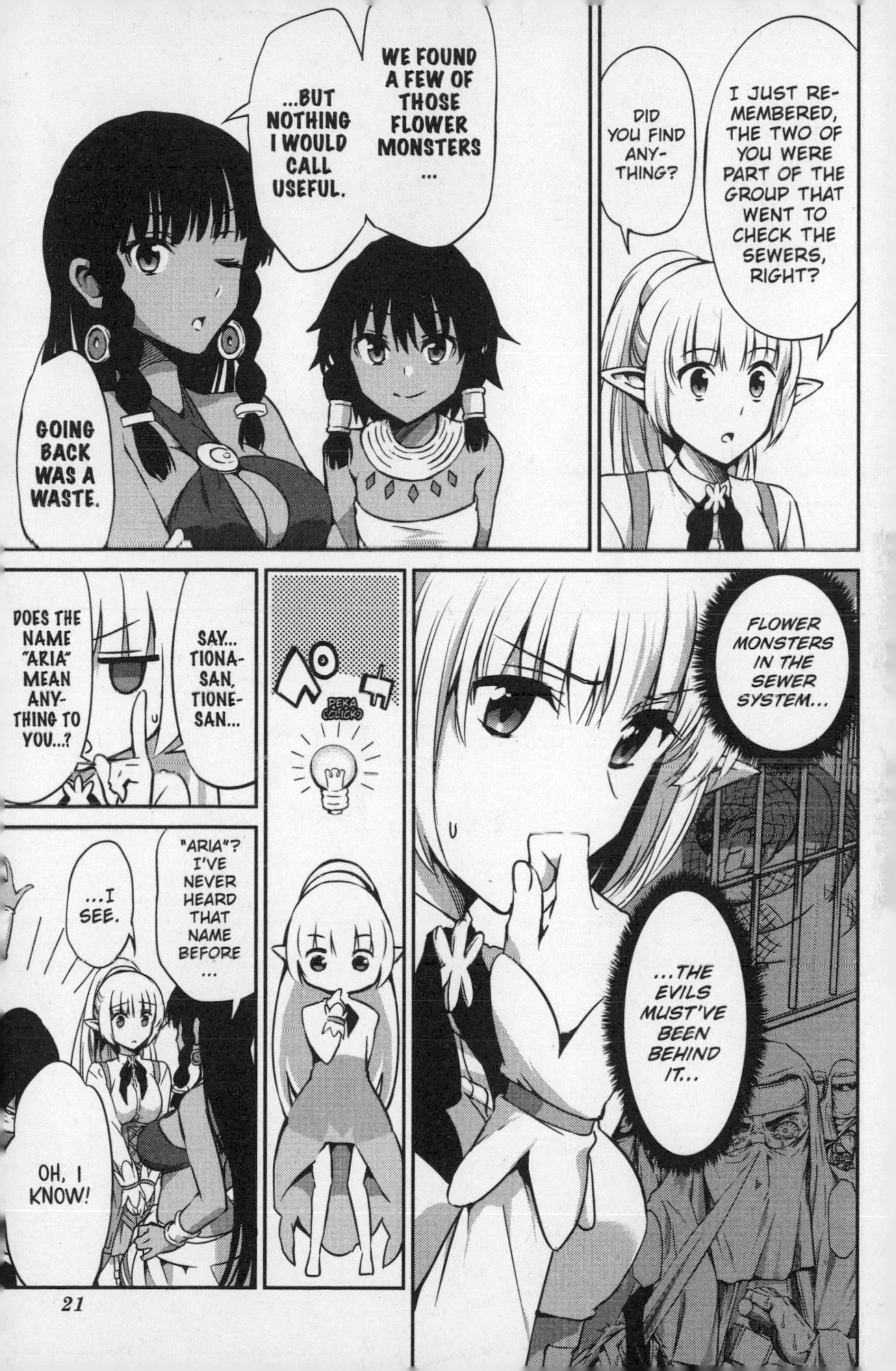
I JUST RE-MEMBERED, THE TWO OF YOU WERE PART OF THE GROUP THAT WENT TO CHECK THE SEWERS, RIGHT?
DID YOU FIND ANY-THING?
WE FOUND A FEW OF THOSE FLOWER MONSTERS...
...BUT NOTHING I WOULD CALL USEFUL.
GOING BACK WAS A WASTE.
FLOWER MONSTERS IN THE SEWER SYSTEM...
...THE EVILS MUST'VE BEEN BEHIND IT...
PEKA (CLICK)
SAY... TIONA-SAN, TIONE-SAN...
DOES THE NAME "ARIA" MEAN ANY-THING TO YOU...?
"ARIA"? I'VE NEVER HEARD THAT NAME BEFORE...
...I SEE.
OH, I KNOW!

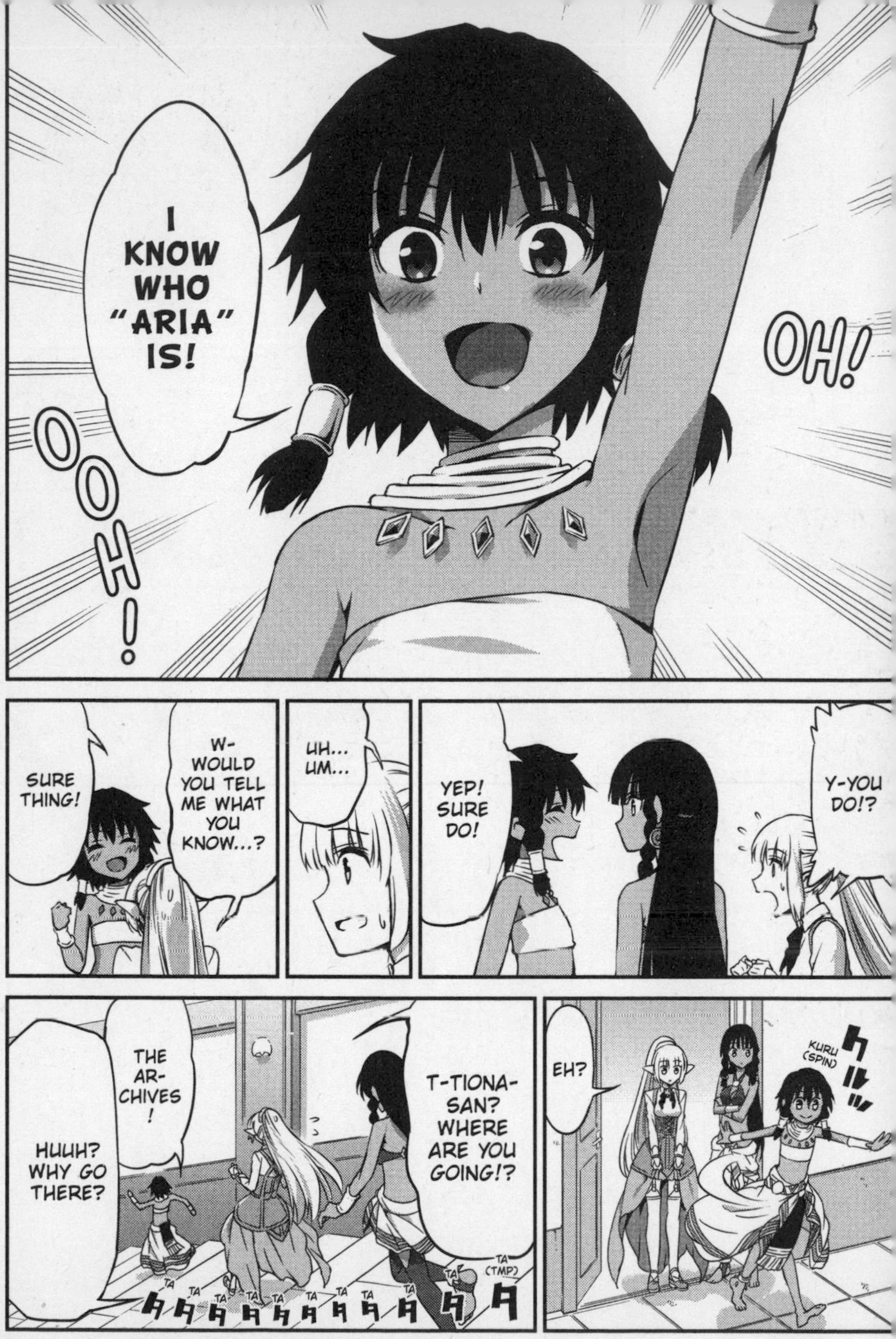
I KNOW WHO "ARIA" IS!
OH!
OOOH!
Y-YOU DO!?
YEP! SURE DO!
UH... UM...
W-WOULD YOU TELL ME WHAT YOU KNOW...?
SURE THING!
KURU (SPIN)
EH?
T-TIONA-SAN? WHERE ARE YOU GOING!?
THE ARCHIVES!
HUUH? WHY GO THERE?
TA (TMP)
TA TA TA TA TA TA TA TA TA TA

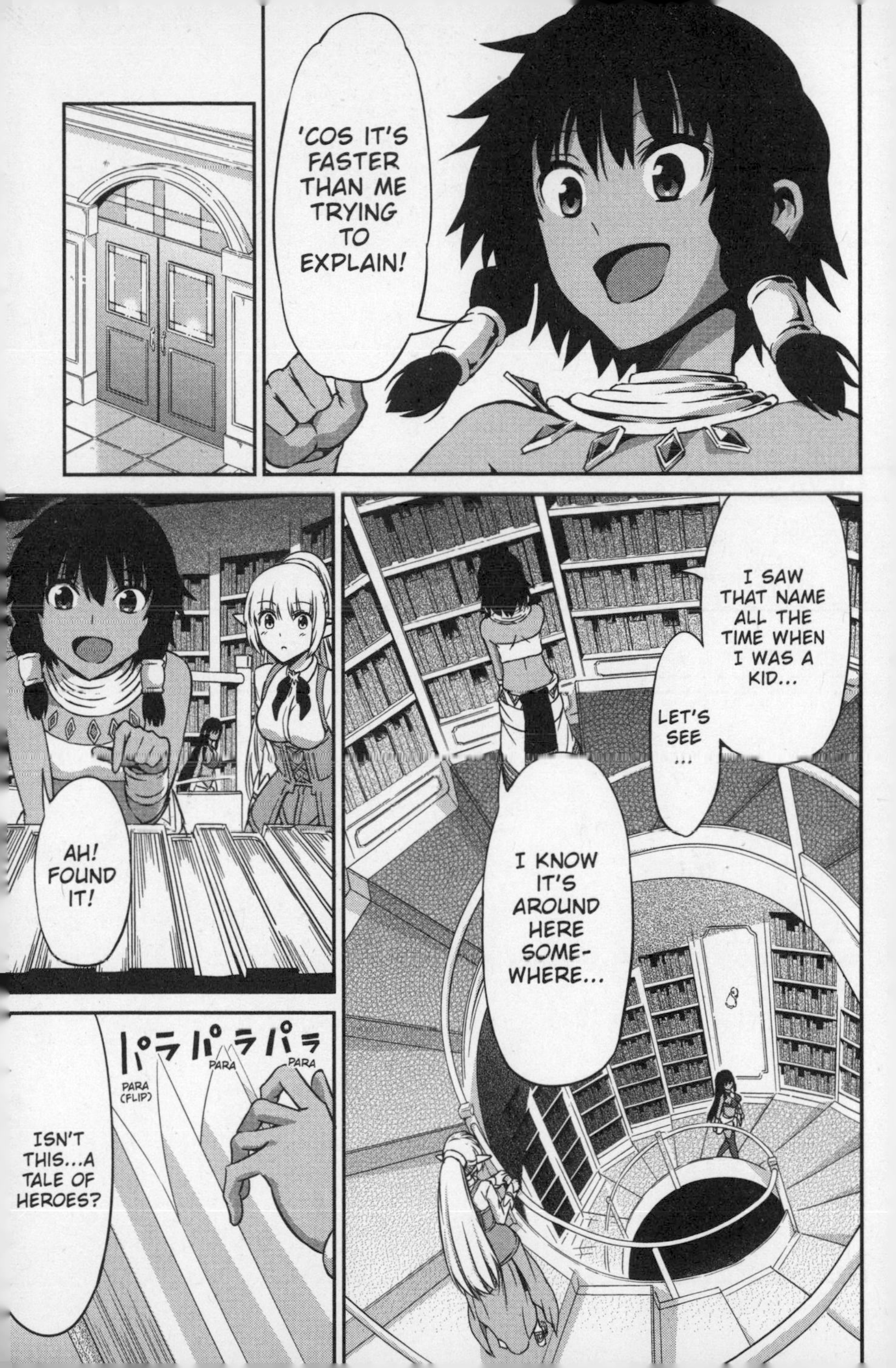
'COS IT'S FASTER THAN ME TRYING TO EXPLAIN!
I SAW THAT NAME ALL THE TIME WHEN I WAS A KID...
LET'S SEE ...
I KNOW IT'S AROUND HERE SOME-WHERE...
AH! FOUND IT!
パラパラパラ
PARA (FLIP)
PARA
PARA
ISN'T THIS...A TALE OF HEROES?

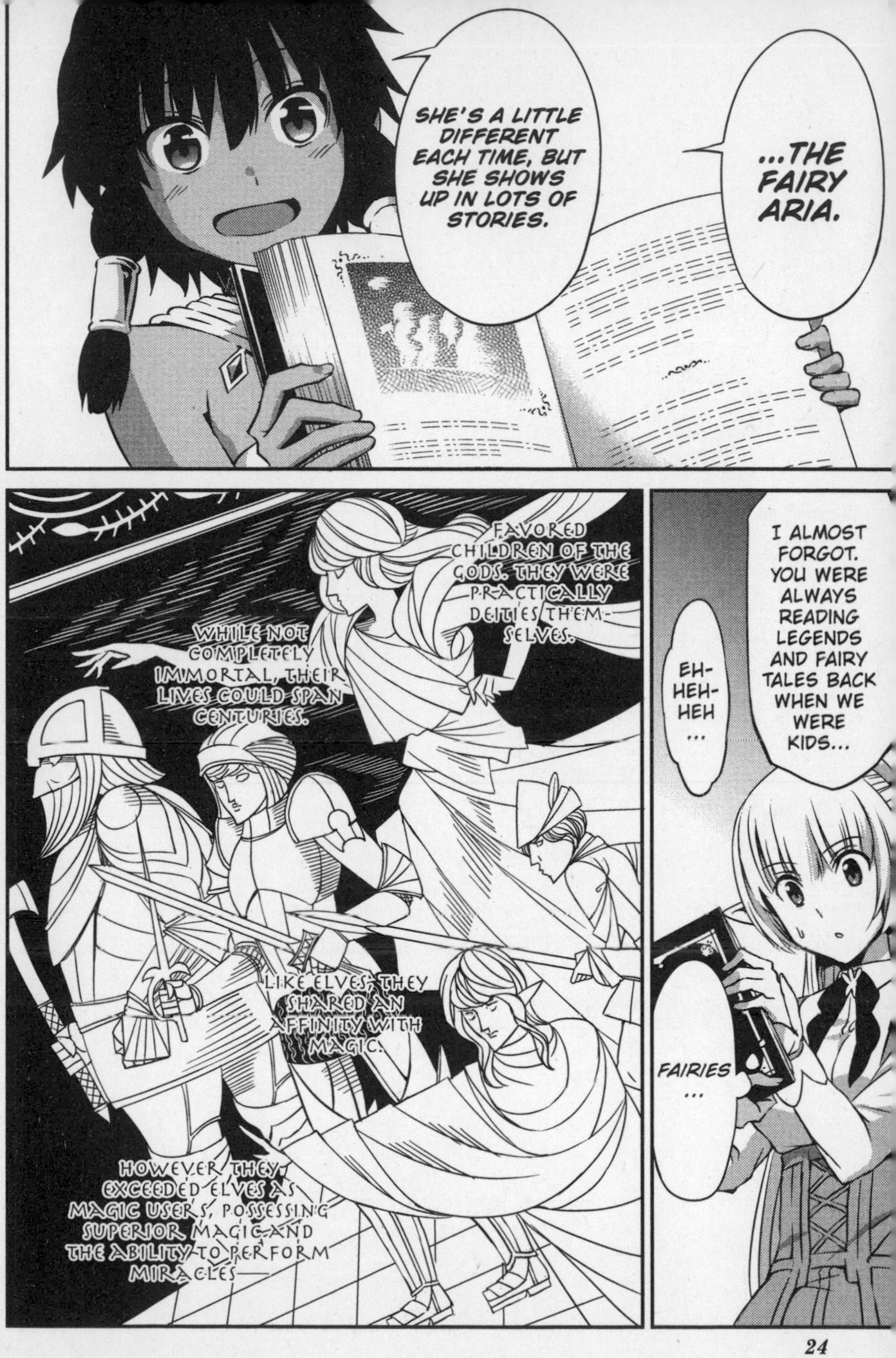
...THE FAIRY ARIA.
SHE'S A LITTLE DIFFERENT EACH TIME, BUT SHE SHOWS UP IN LOTS OF STORIES.
I ALMOST FORGOT. YOU WERE ALWAYS READING LEGENDS AND FAIRY TALES BACK WHEN WE WERE KIDS...
EH-HEH-HEH...
FAIRIES...
FAVORED CHILDREN OF THE GODS. THEY WERE PRACTICALLY DEITIES THEM-SELVES.
WHILE NOT COMPLETELY IMMORTAL, THEIR LIVES COULD SPAN CENTURIES.
LIKE ELVES, THEY SHARED AN AFFINITY WITH MAGIC.
HOWEVER THEY EXCEEDED ELVES AS MAGIC USERS, POSSESSING SUPERIOR MAGIC AND THE ABILITY TO PERFORM MIRACLES—

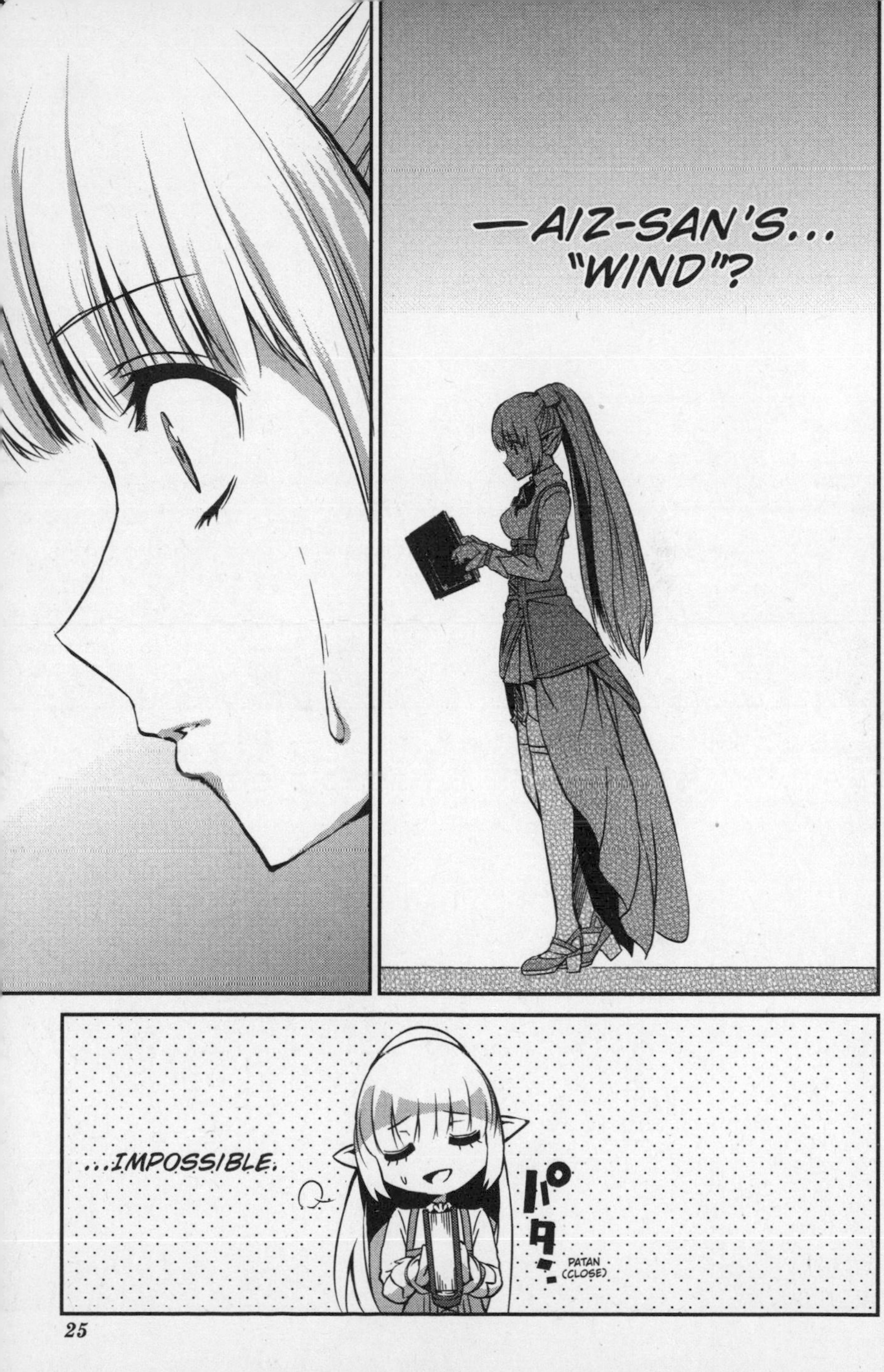
—AIZ-SAN'S... "WIND"?
...IMPOSSIBLE.
PATAN (CLOSE)

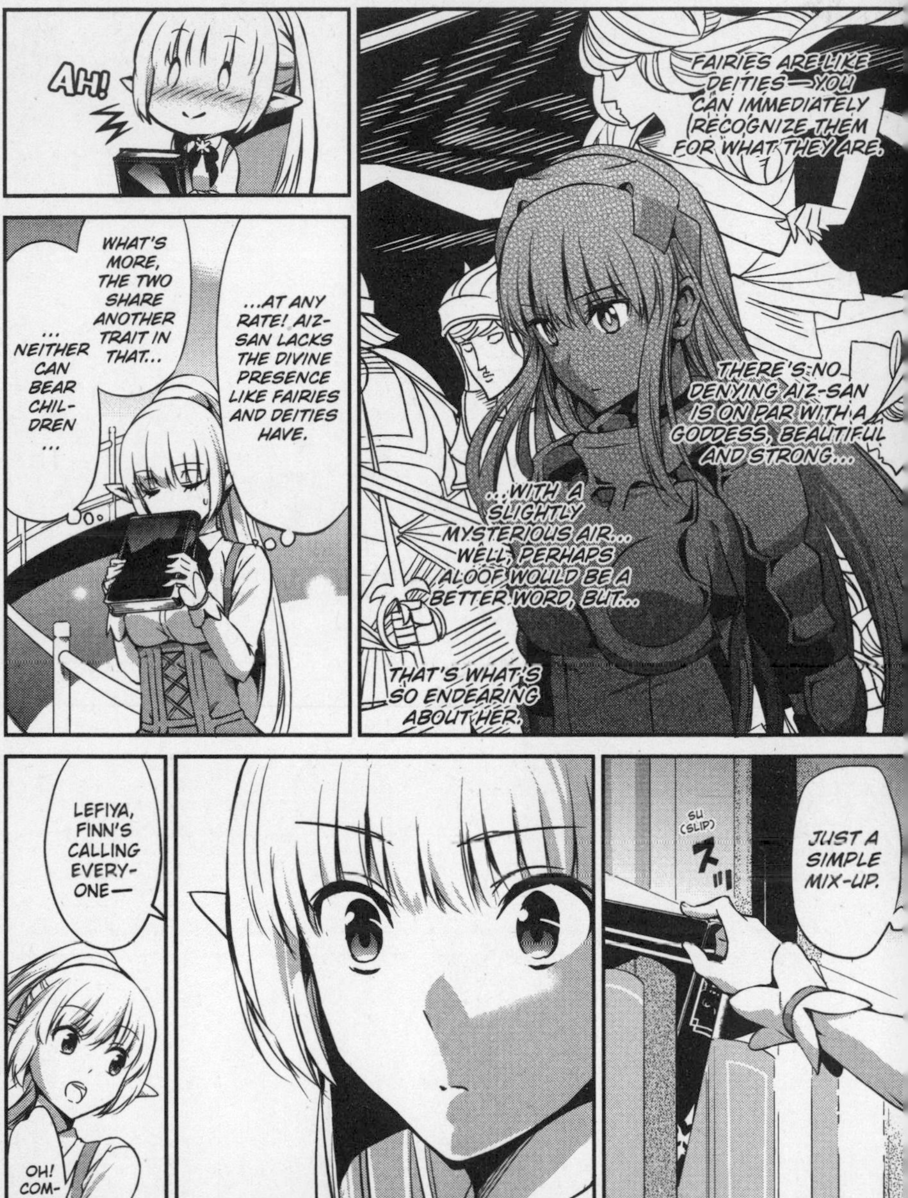
FAIRIES ARE LIKE DEITIES—YOU CAN IMMEDIATELY RECOGNIZE THEM FOR WHAT THEY ARE.
THERE'S NO DENYING AIZ-SAN IS ON PAR WITH A GODDESS, BEAUTIFUL AND STRONG...
...WITH A SLIGHTLY MYSTERIOUS AIR... WELL, PERHAPS ALOOF WOULD BE A BETTER WORD, BUT...
THAT'S WHAT'S SO ENDEARING ABOUT HER.
AH!
...AT ANY RATE! AIZ-SAN LACKS THE DIVINE PRESENCE LIKE FAIRIES AND DEITIES HAVE.
WHAT'S MORE, THE TWO SHARE ANOTHER TRAIT IN THAT...
...NEITHER CAN BEAR CHILDREN...
JUST A SIMPLE MIX-UP.
SU (SLIP)
LEFIYA, FINN'S CALLING EVERYONE—
OH! COMING!

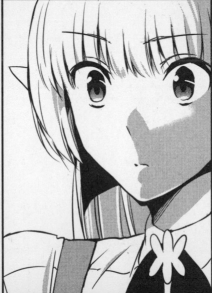

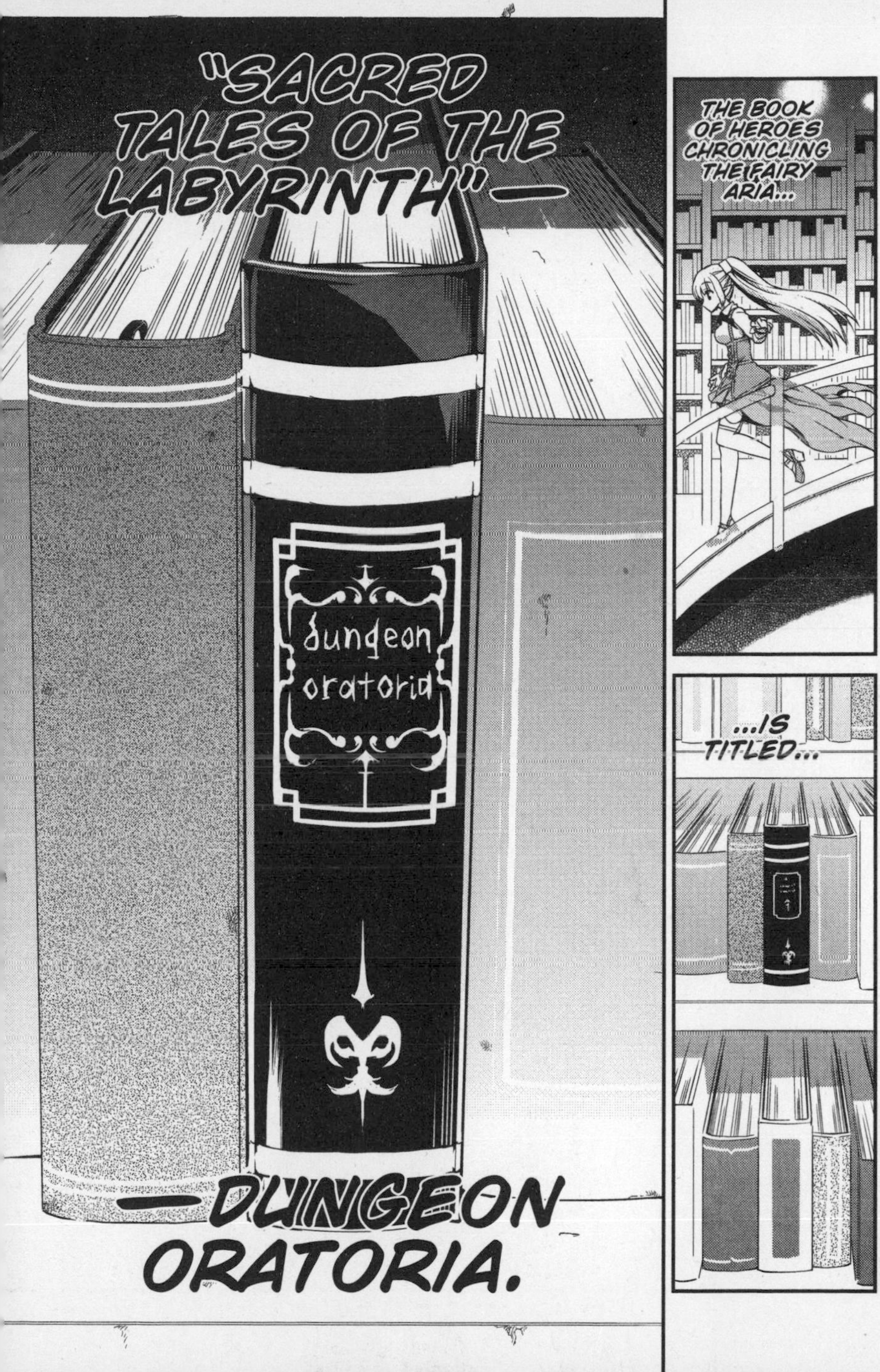
THE BOOK OF HEROES CHRONICLING THE FAIRY ARIA...
...IS TITLED...
"SACRED TALES OF THE LABYRINTH"—
dungeon oratoria
—DUNGEON ORATORIA.

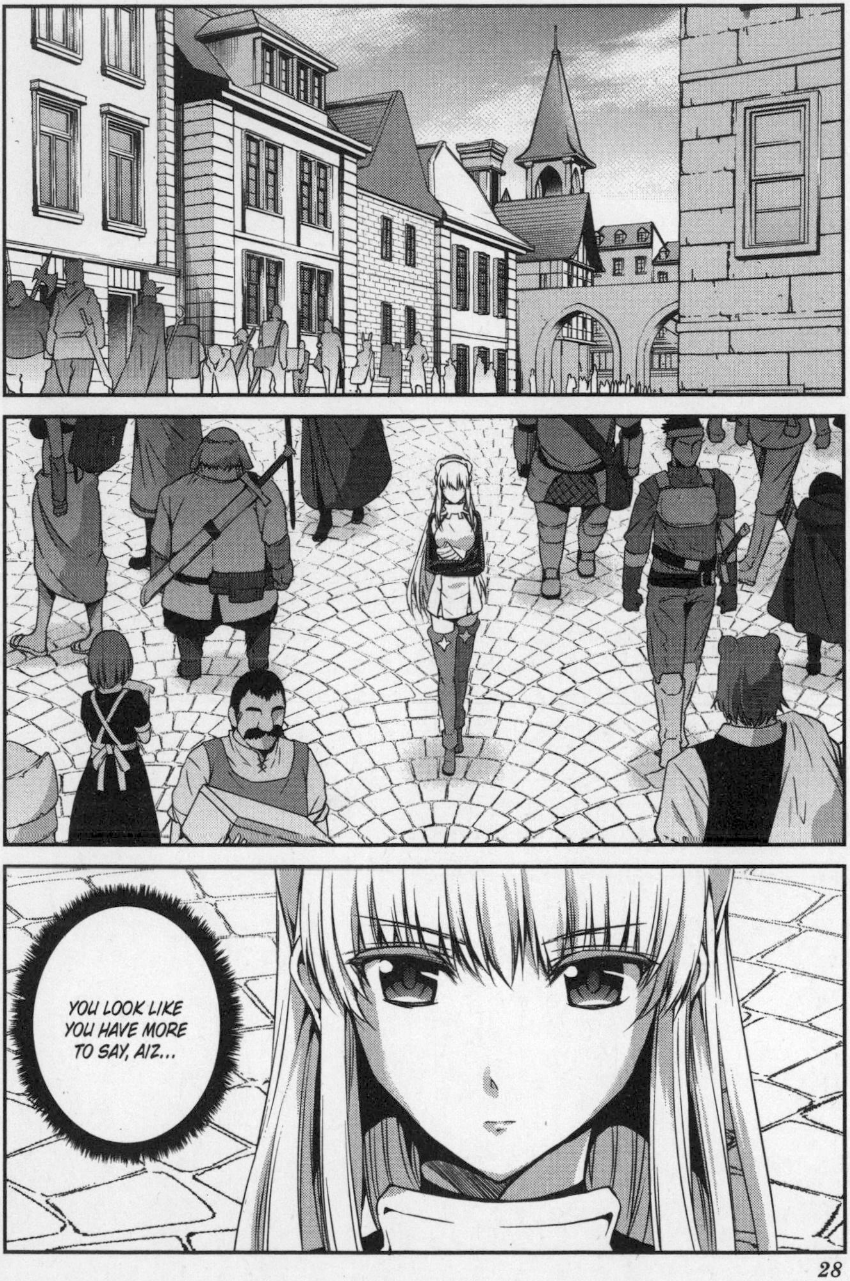
YOU LOOK LIKE YOU HAVE MORE TO SAY, AIZ...

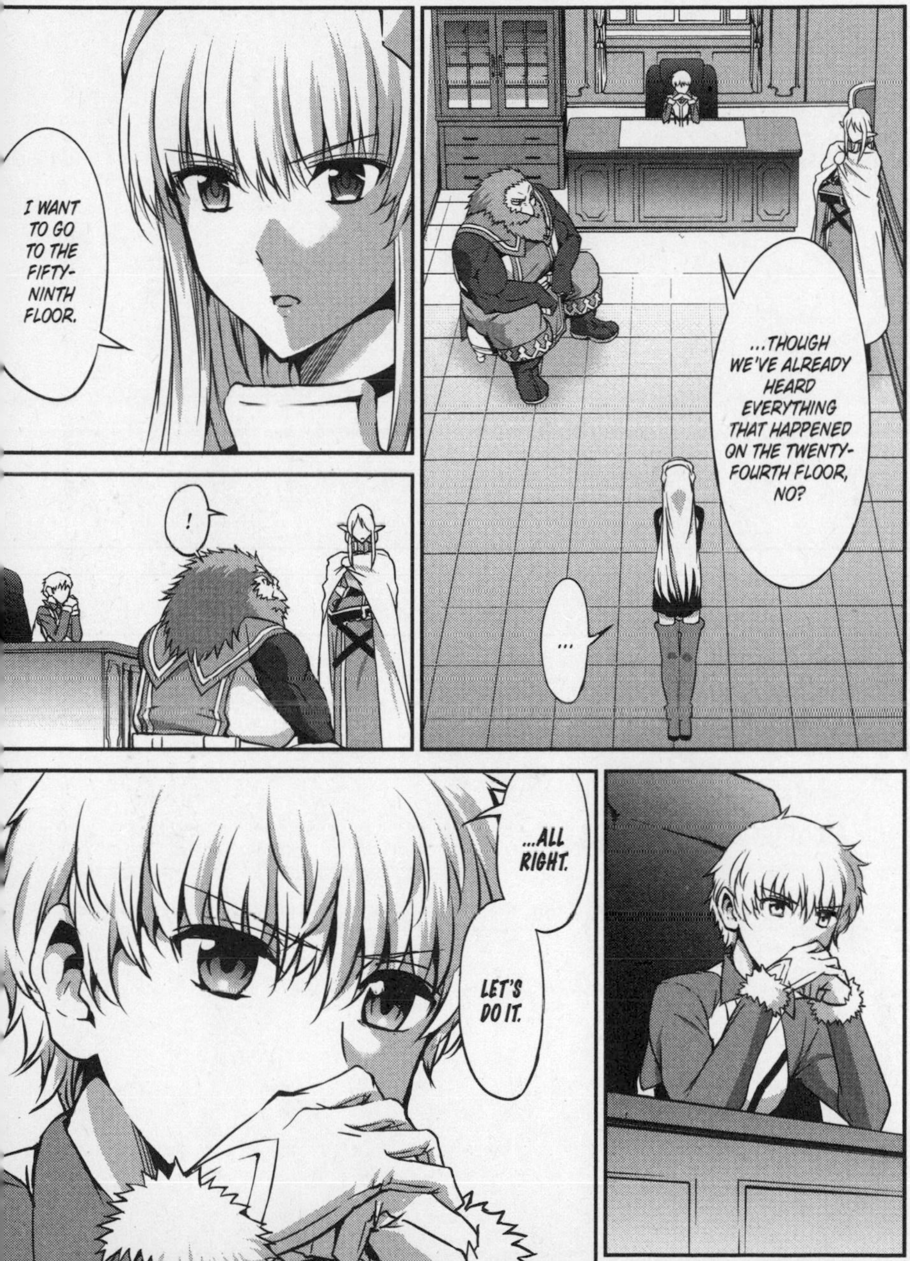
...THOUGH WE'VE ALREADY HEARD EVERYTHING THAT HAPPENED ON THE TWENTY-FOURTH FLOOR, NO?
...
I WANT TO GO TO THE FIFTY-NINTH FLOOR.
!
...ALL RIGHT.
LET'S DO IT.

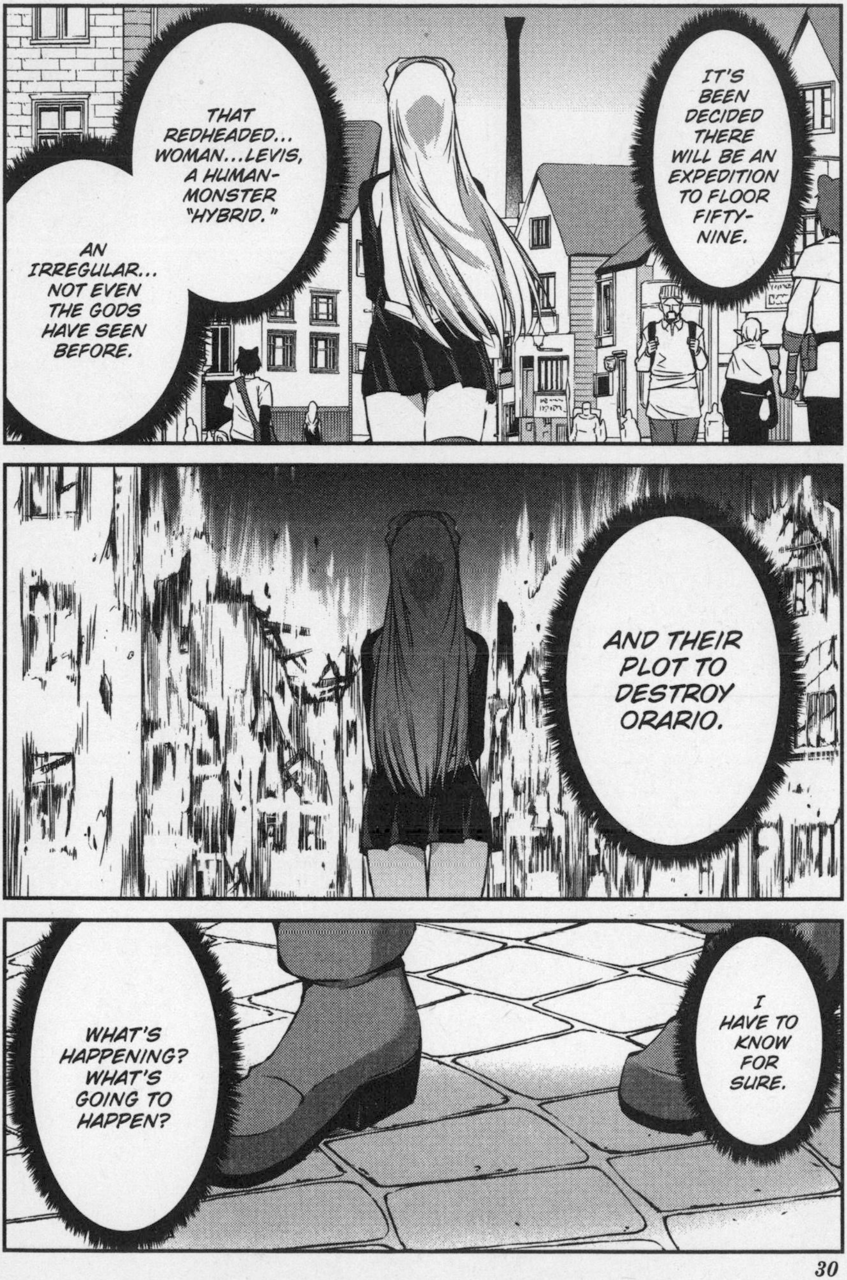
IT'S BEEN DECIDED THERE WILL BE AN EXPEDITION TO FLOOR FIFTY-NINE.
THAT REDHEADED... WOMAN...LEVIS, A HUMAN-MONSTER "HYBRID."
AN IRREGULAR... NOT EVEN THE GODS HAVE SEEN BEFORE.
AND THEIR PLOT TO DESTROY ORARIO.
I HAVE TO KNOW FOR SURE.
WHAT'S HAPPENING? WHAT'S GOING TO HAPPEN?

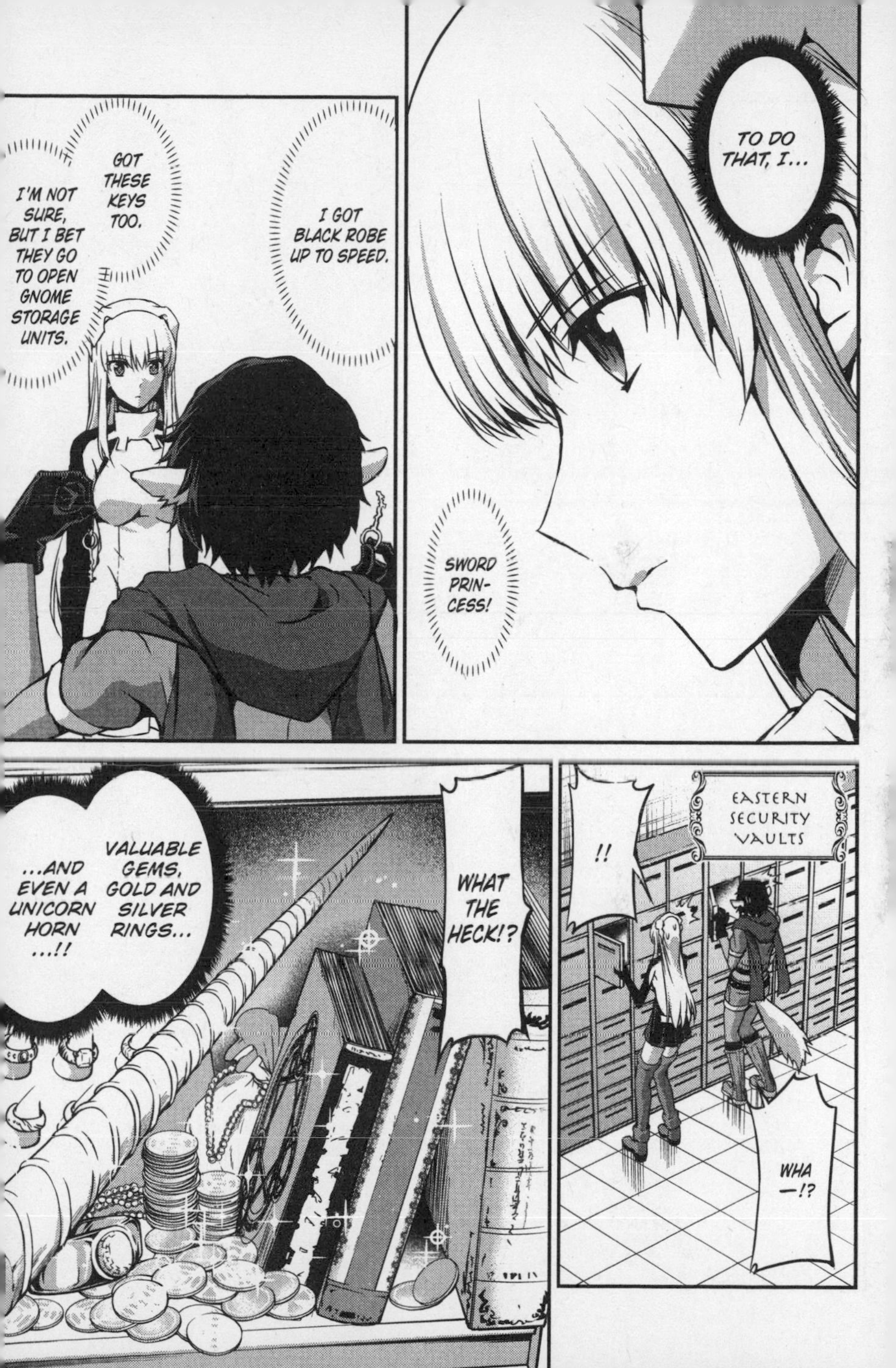
TO DO THAT, I...
SWORD PRINCESS!
I GOT BLACK ROBE UP TO SPEED.
GOT THESE KEYS TOO.
I'M NOT SURE, BUT I BET THEY GO TO OPEN GNOME STORAGE UNITS.
EASTERN SECURITY VAULTS
!!
WHA—!?
WHAT THE HECK!?
VALUABLE GEMS, GOLD AND SILVER RINGS...
...AND EVEN A UNICORN HORN...!!

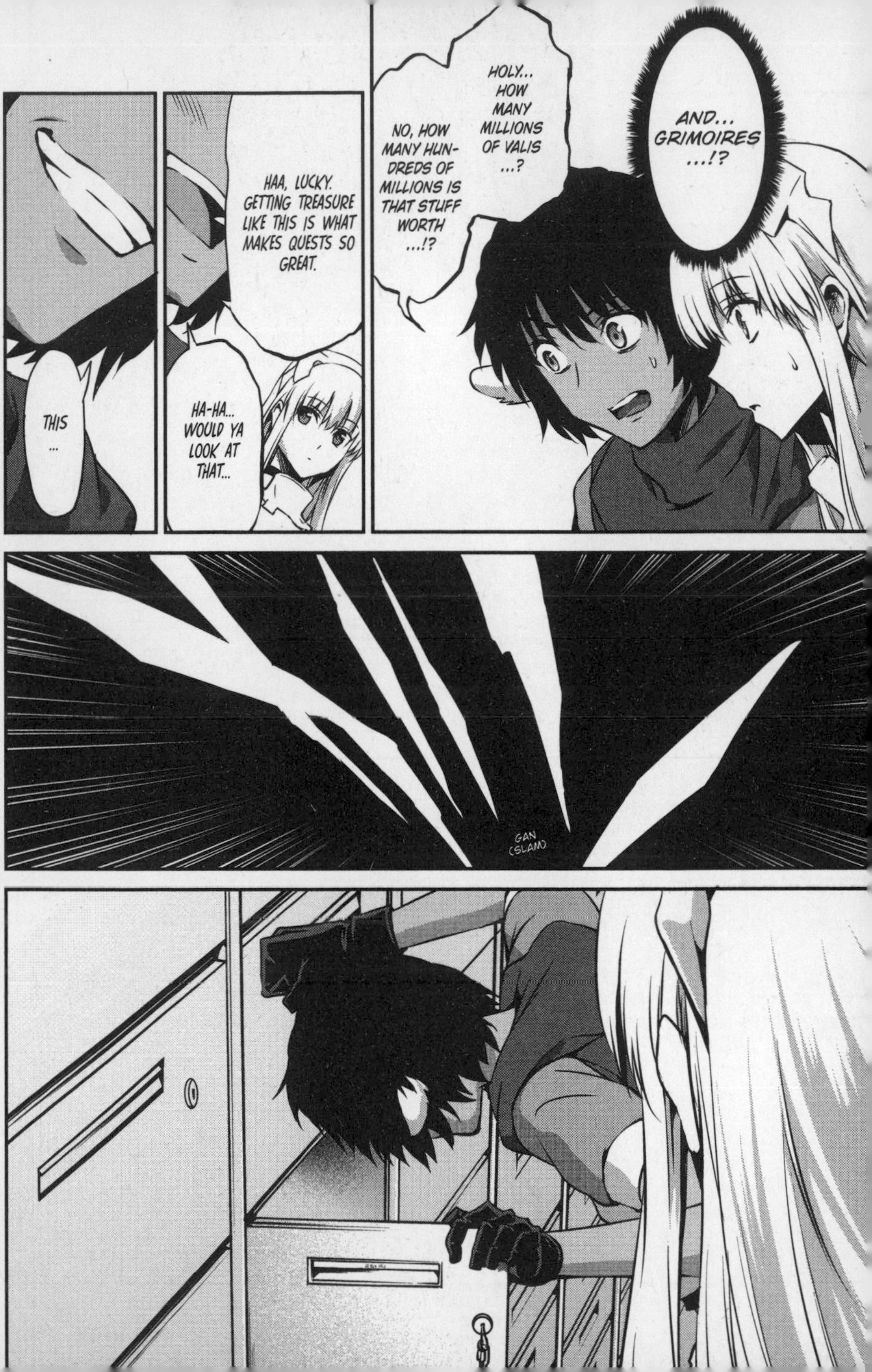
AND... GRIMOIRES ...!?
HOLY... HOW MANY MILLIONS OF VALIS ...?
NO, HOW MANY HUN-DREDS OF MILLIONS IS THAT STUFF WORTH ...!?
HAA, LUCKY. GETTING TREASURE LIKE THIS IS WHAT MAKES QUESTS SO GREAT.
HA-HA... WOULD YA LOOK AT THAT...
THIS ...
GAN (SLAM)

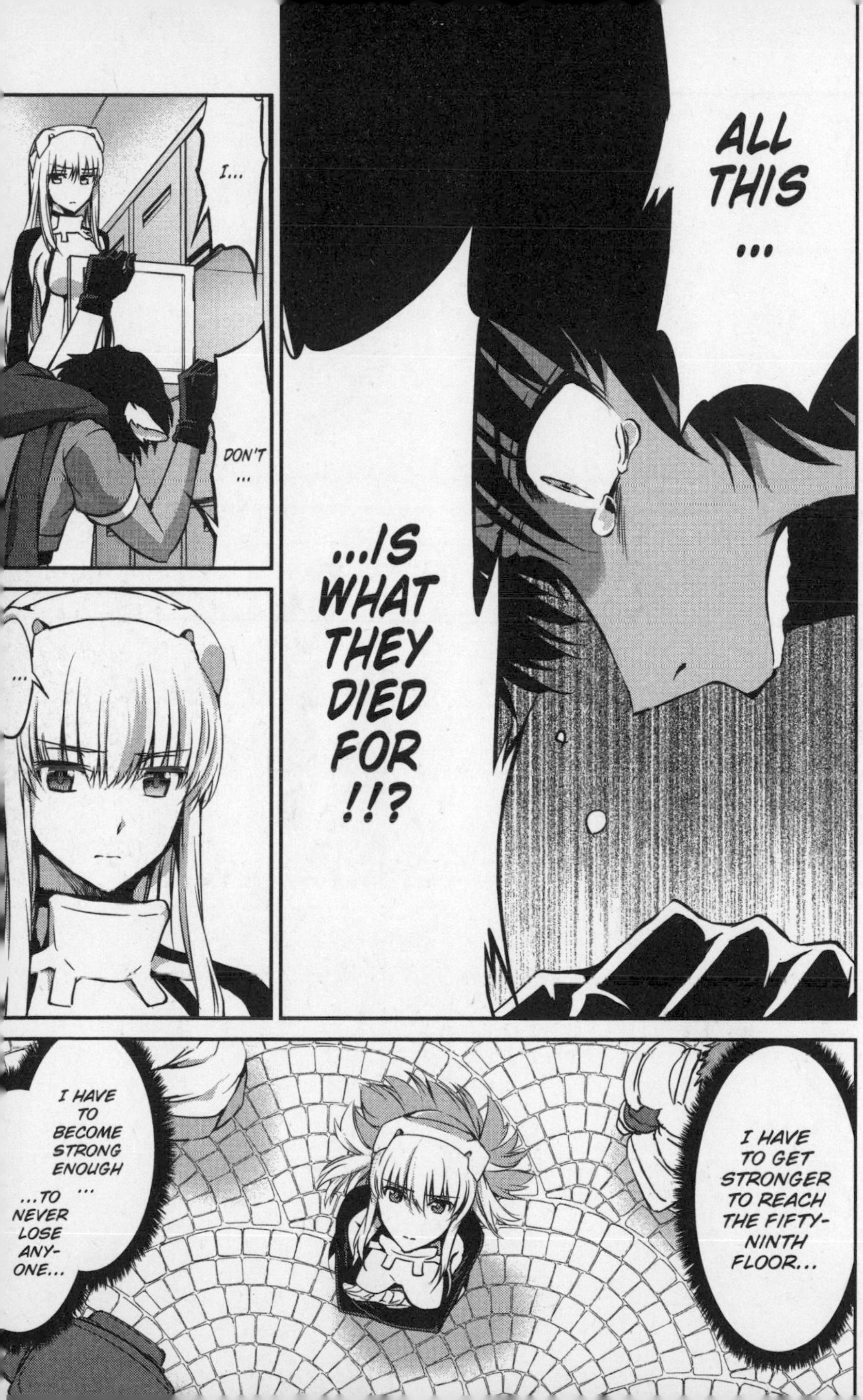
ALL THIS ...
...IS WHAT THEY DIED FOR !!?
I...
DON'T ...
...
I HAVE TO GET STRONGER TO REACH THE FIFTY-NINTH FLOOR...
I HAVE TO BECOME STRONG ENOUGH ...
...TO NEVER LOSE ANY-ONE...

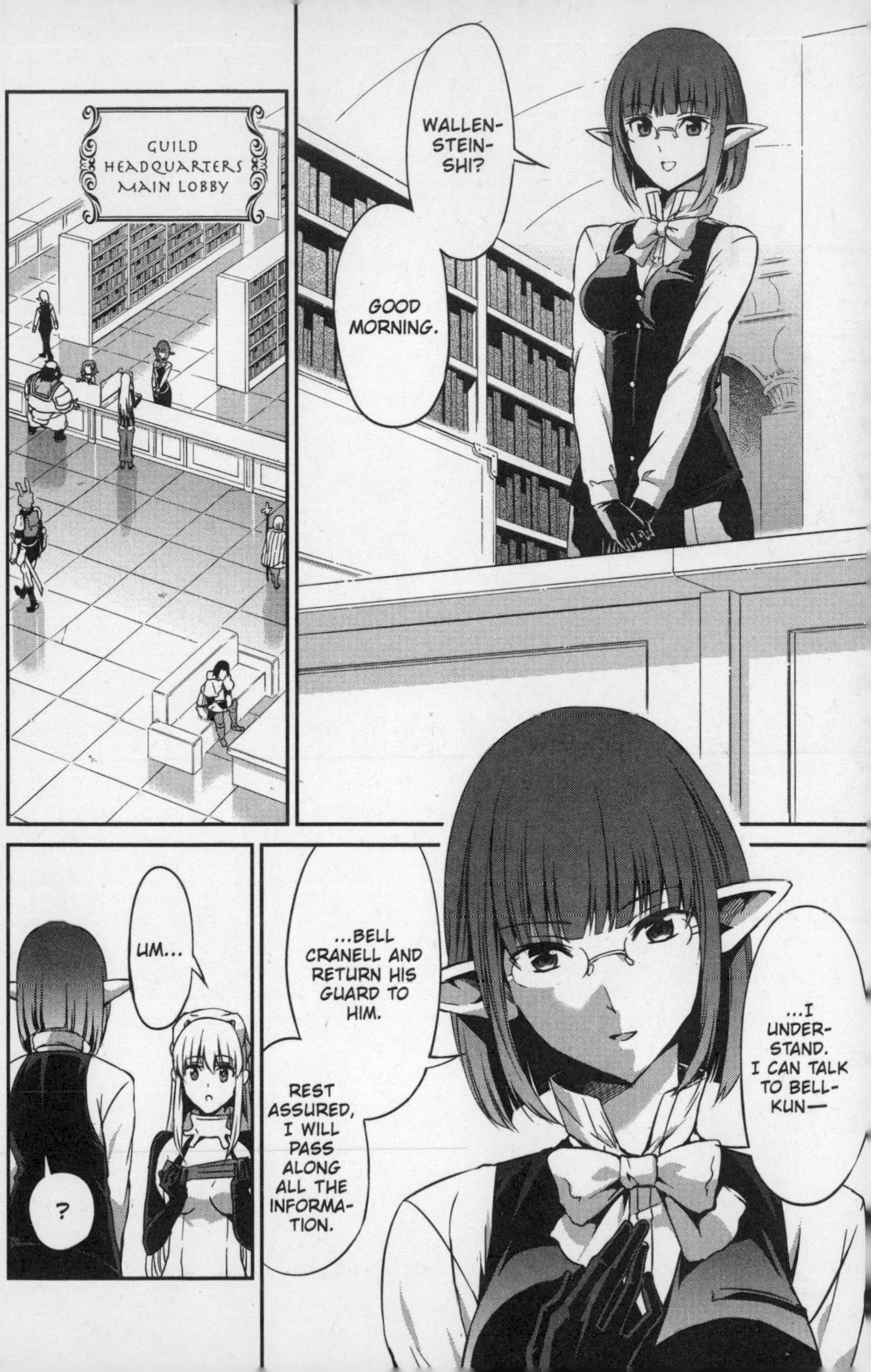
WALLEN-STEIN-SHI?
GOOD MORNING.
GUILD HEADQUARTERS MAIN LOBBY
...I UNDER-STAND. I CAN TALK TO BELL-KUN—
...BELL CRANELL AND RETURN HIS GUARD TO HIM.
REST ASSURED, I WILL PASS ALONG ALL THE INFORMA-TION.
UM...
?

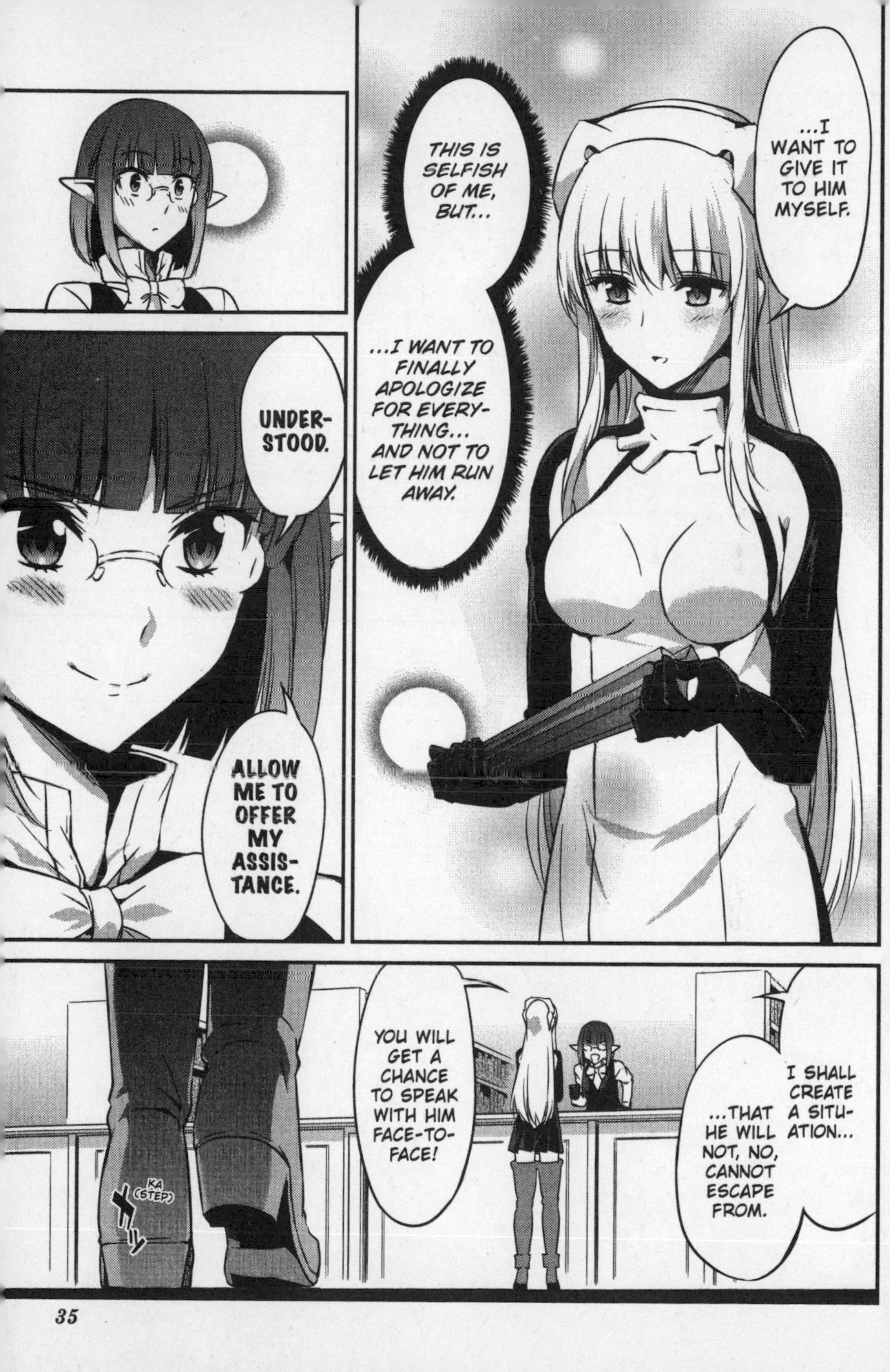
...I WANT TO GIVE IT TO HIM MYSELF.
THIS IS SELFISH OF ME, BUT...
...I WANT TO FINALLY APOLOGIZE FOR EVERYTHING... AND NOT TO LET HIM RUN AWAY.
UNDERSTOOD.
ALLOW ME TO OFFER MY ASSISTANCE.
I SHALL CREATE A SITUATION...
...THAT HE WILL NOT, NO, CANNOT ESCAPE FROM.
YOU WILL GET A CHANCE TO SPEAK WITH HIM FACE-TO-FACE!
KA (STEP)

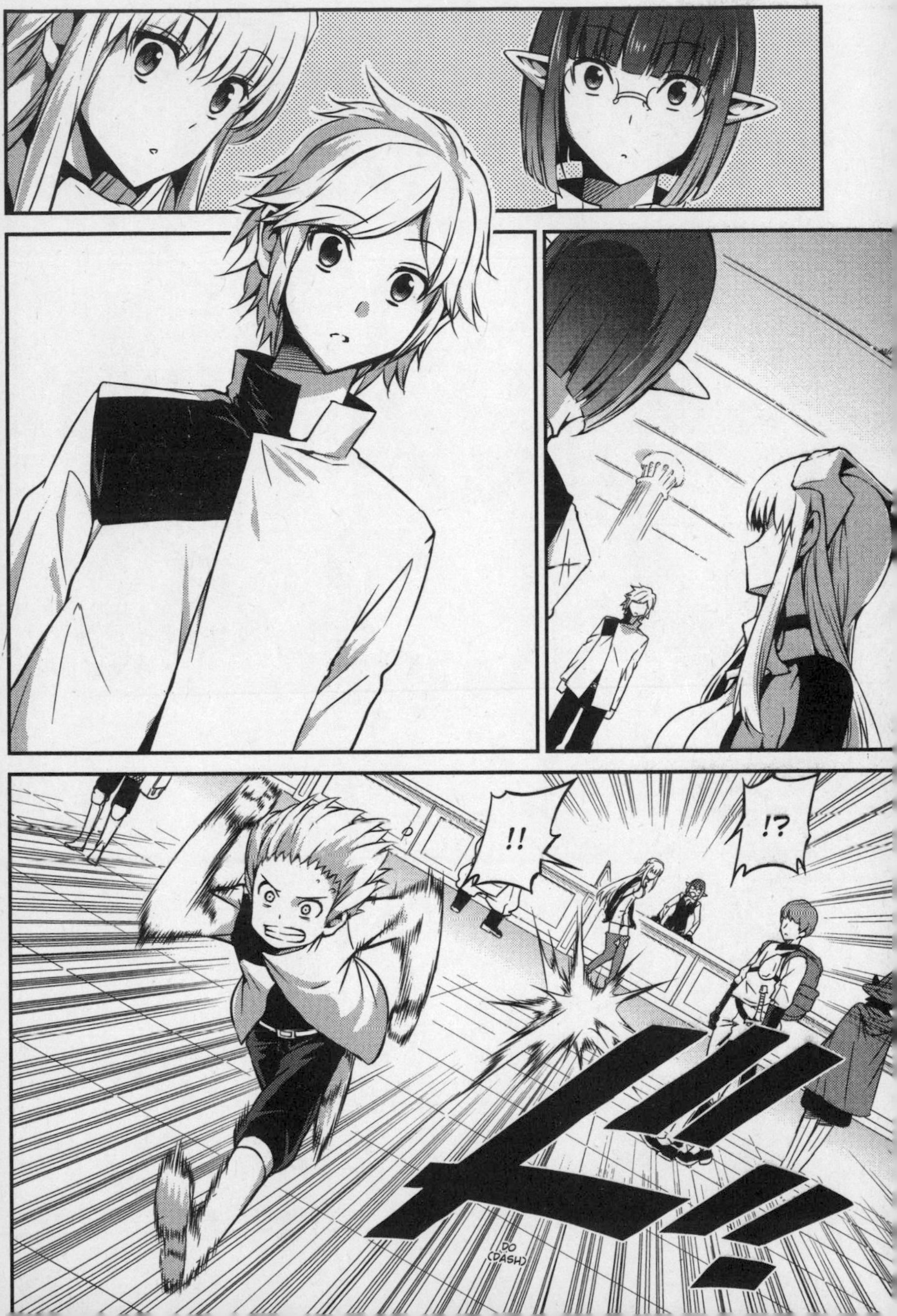
!?
!!
DO
(DASH)

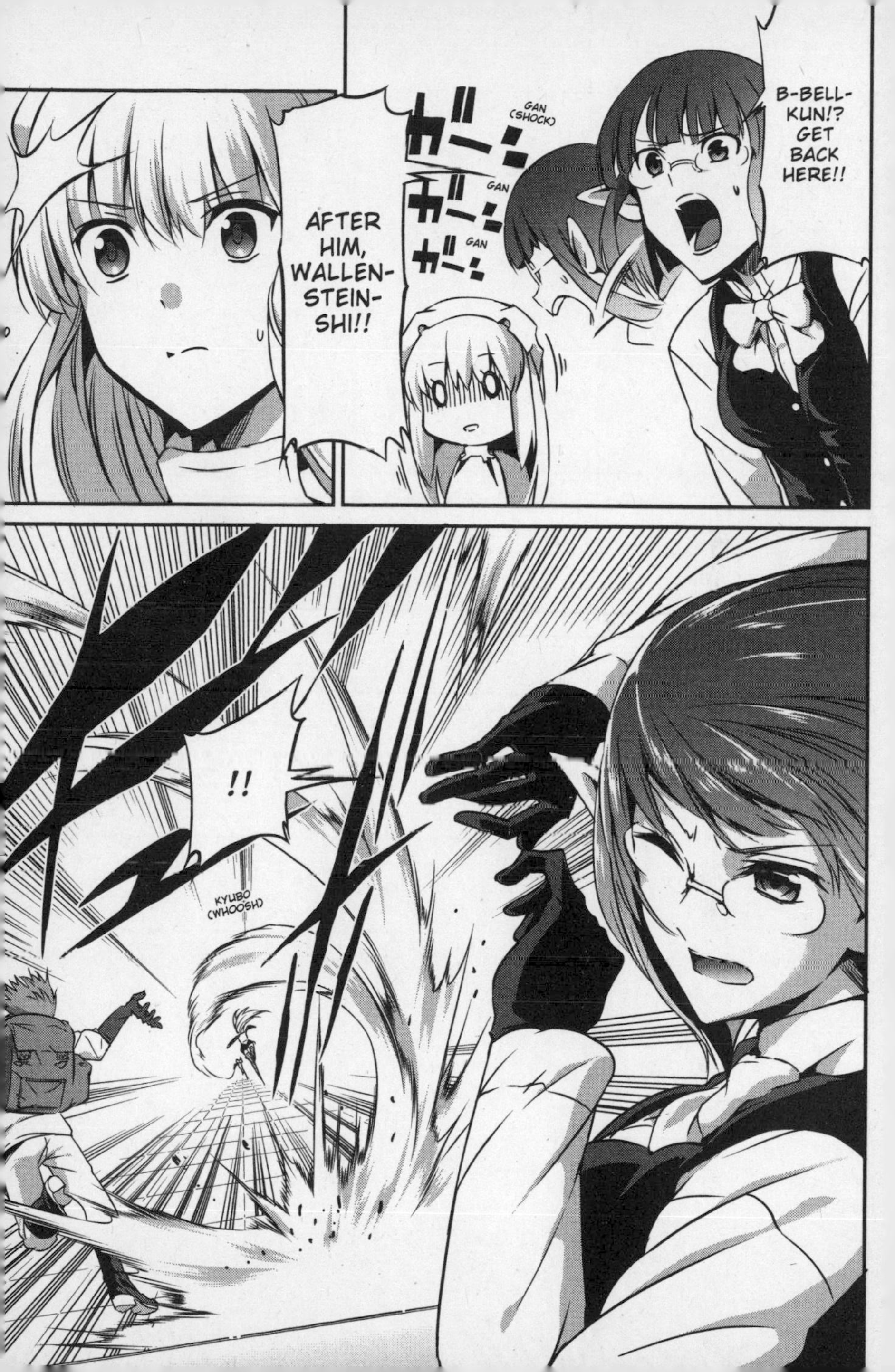
B-BELL-KUN!? GET BACK HERE!!
ガーン
GAN (SHOCK)
ガーン
GAN
ガーン
GAN
AFTER HIM, WALLEN-STEIN-SHI!!
!!
KYUBO (WHOOSH)

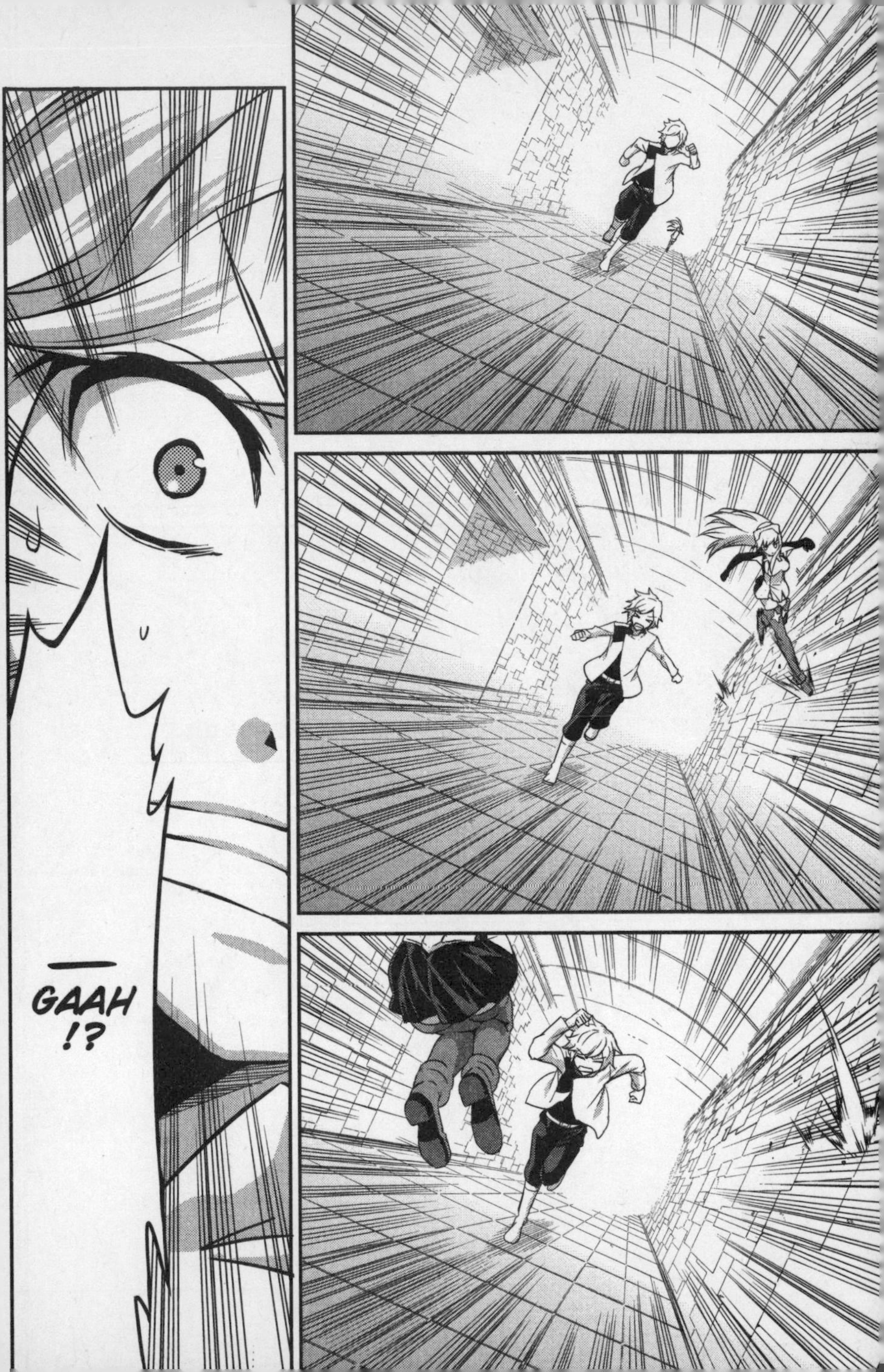
—GAAH !?

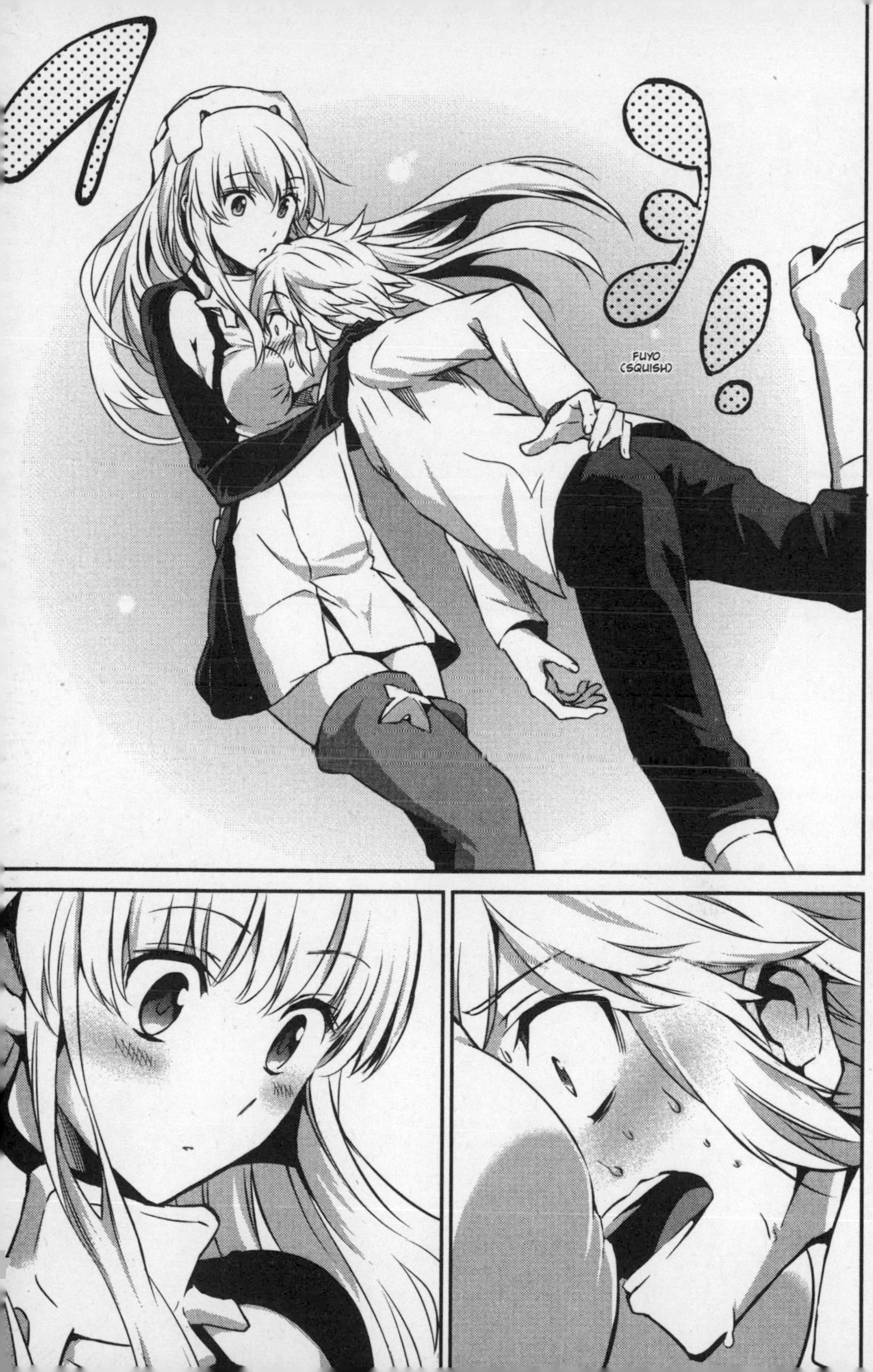
FUYO
(SQUISH)

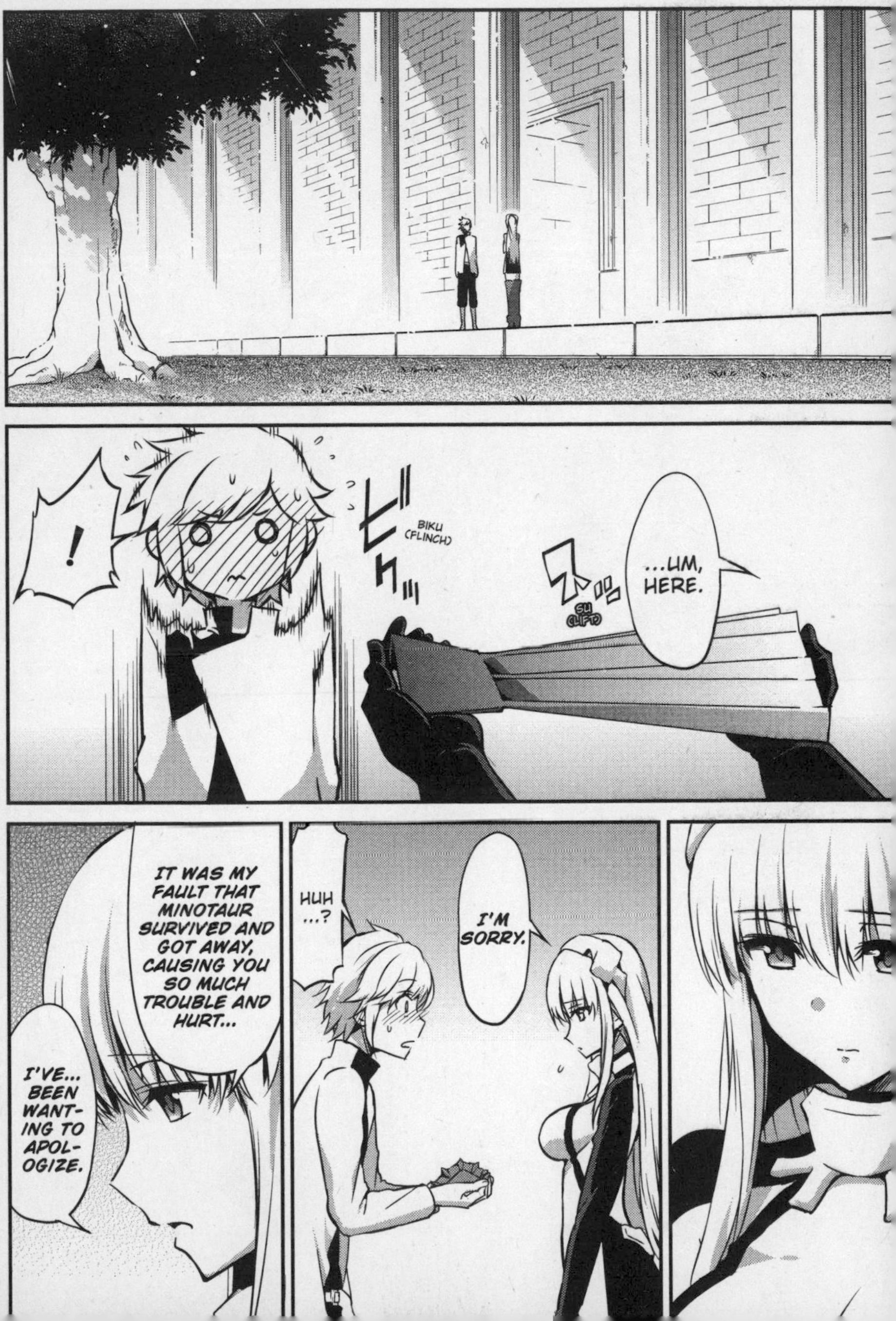
...UM, HERE.
SU (LIFT)
BIKU (FLINCH)
!
I'M SORRY.
HUH ...?
IT WAS MY FAULT THAT MINOTAUR SURVIVED AND GOT AWAY, CAUSING YOU SO MUCH TROUBLE AND HURT...
I'VE... BEEN WANTING TO APOLOGIZE.

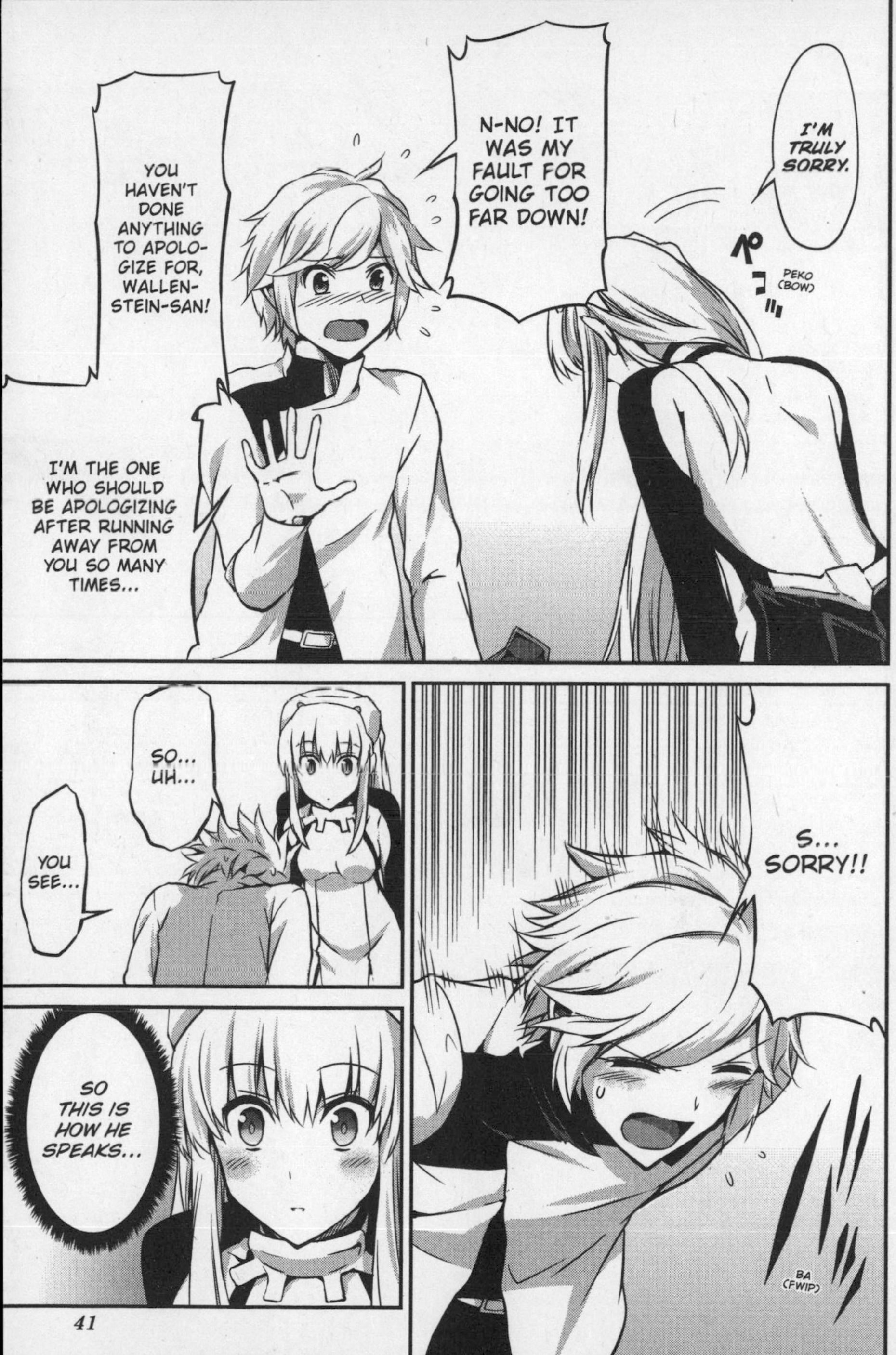
I'M TRULY SORRY.
PEKO (BOW)
N-NO! IT WAS MY FAULT FOR GOING TOO FAR DOWN!
YOU HAVEN'T DONE ANYTHING TO APOLOGIZE FOR, WALLENSTEIN-SAN!
I'M THE ONE WHO SHOULD BE APOLOGIZING AFTER RUNNING AWAY FROM YOU SO MANY TIMES...
S... SORRY!!
BA (FWIP)
SO... UH...
YOU SEE...
SO THIS IS HOW HE SPEAKS...

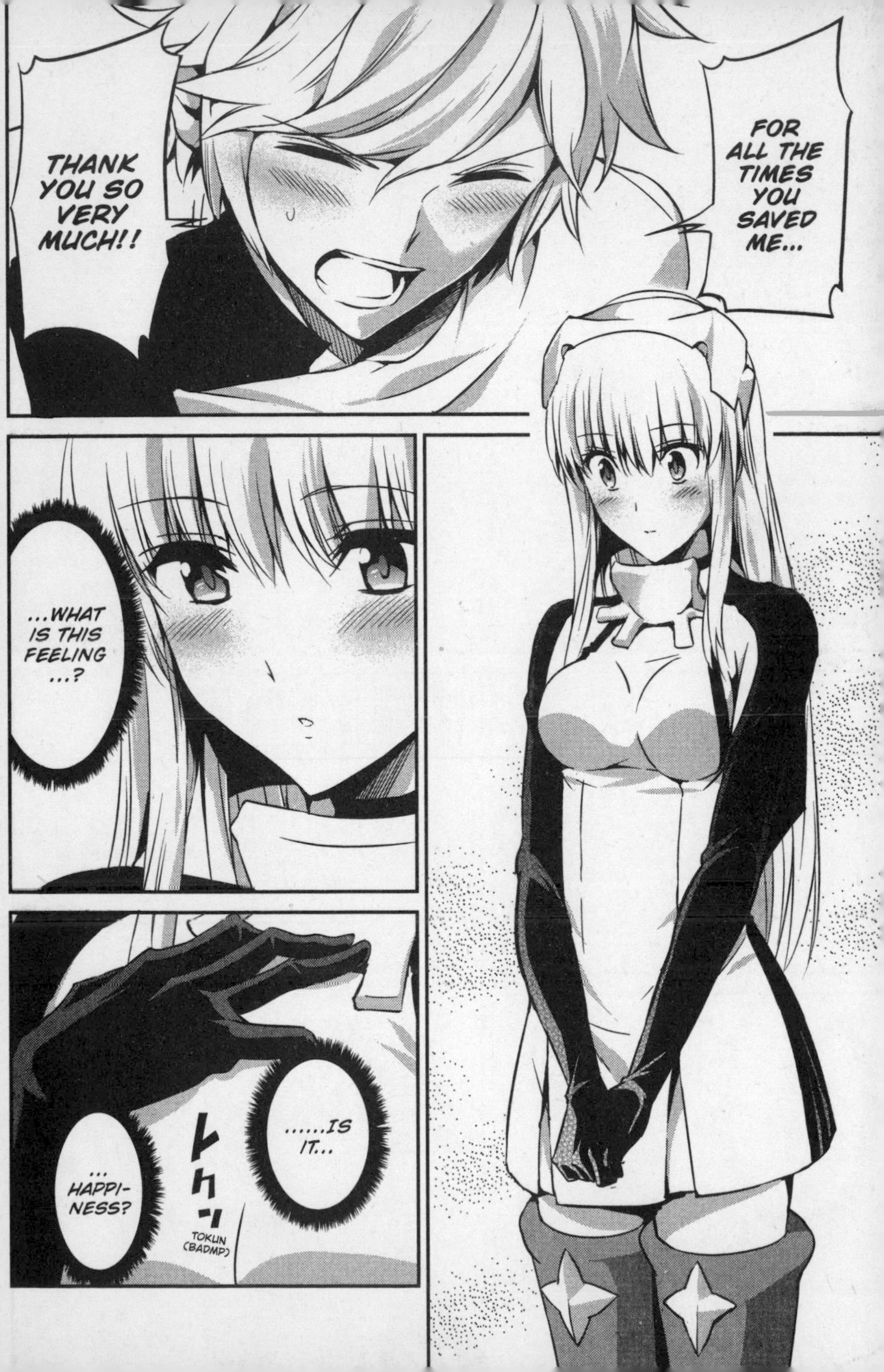
FOR ALL THE TIMES YOU SAVED ME...
THANK YOU SO VERY MUCH!!
...WHAT IS THIS FEELING ...?
......IS IT...
トクッ
TOKUN (BADMP)
... HAPPI-NESS?

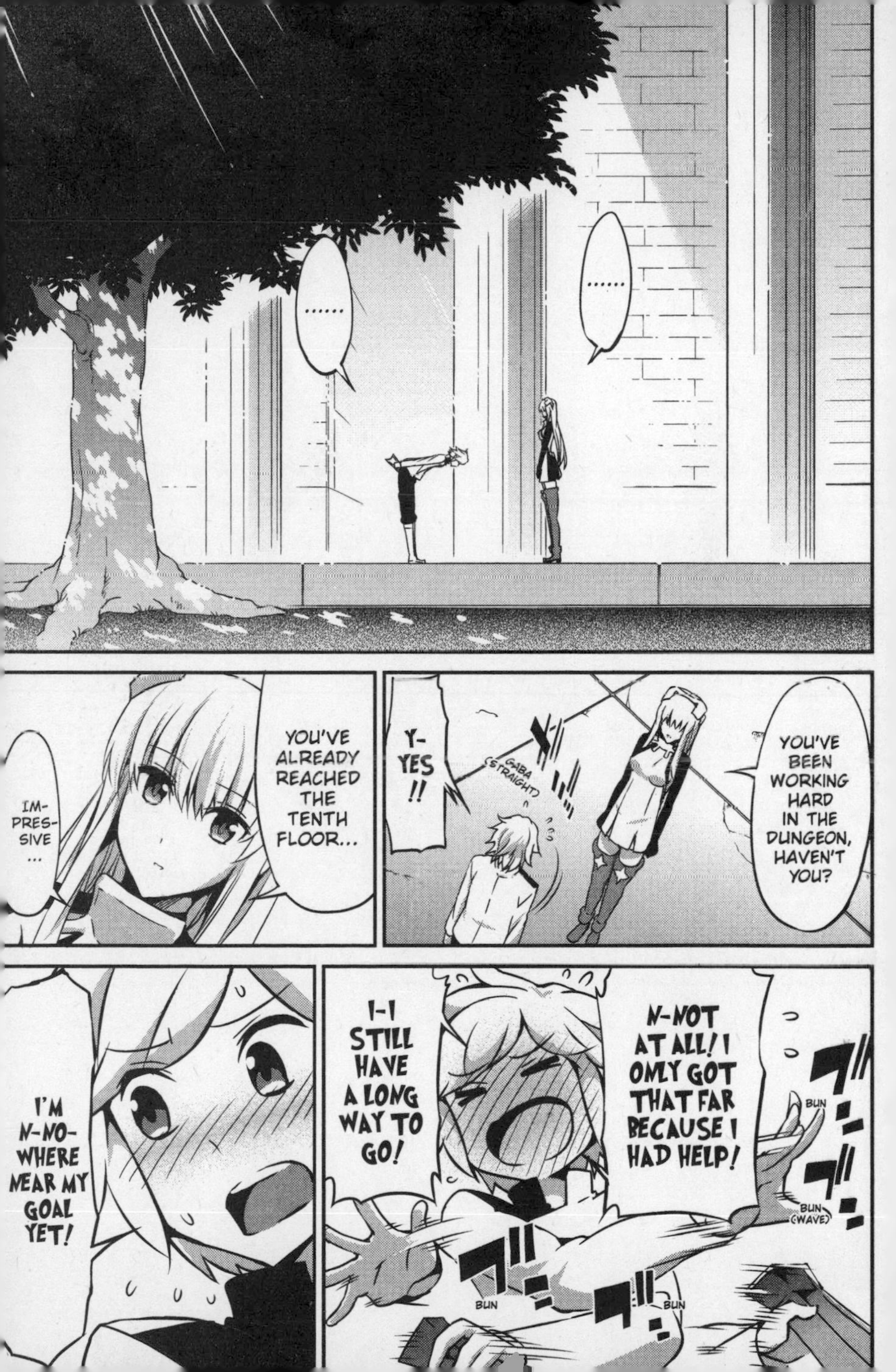

....
....
YOU'VE BEEN WORKING HARD IN THE DUNGEON, HAVEN'T YOU?
GABA (STRAIGHT)
Y-YES!!
YOU'VE ALREADY REACHED THE TENTH FLOOR...
IM-PRESSIVE...
N-NOT AT ALL! I ONLY GOT THAT FAR BECAUSE I HAD HELP!
BUN
BUN (WAVE)
I-I STILL HAVE A LONG WAY TO GO!
BUN
BUN
I'M N-NOWHERE NEAR MY GOAL YET!

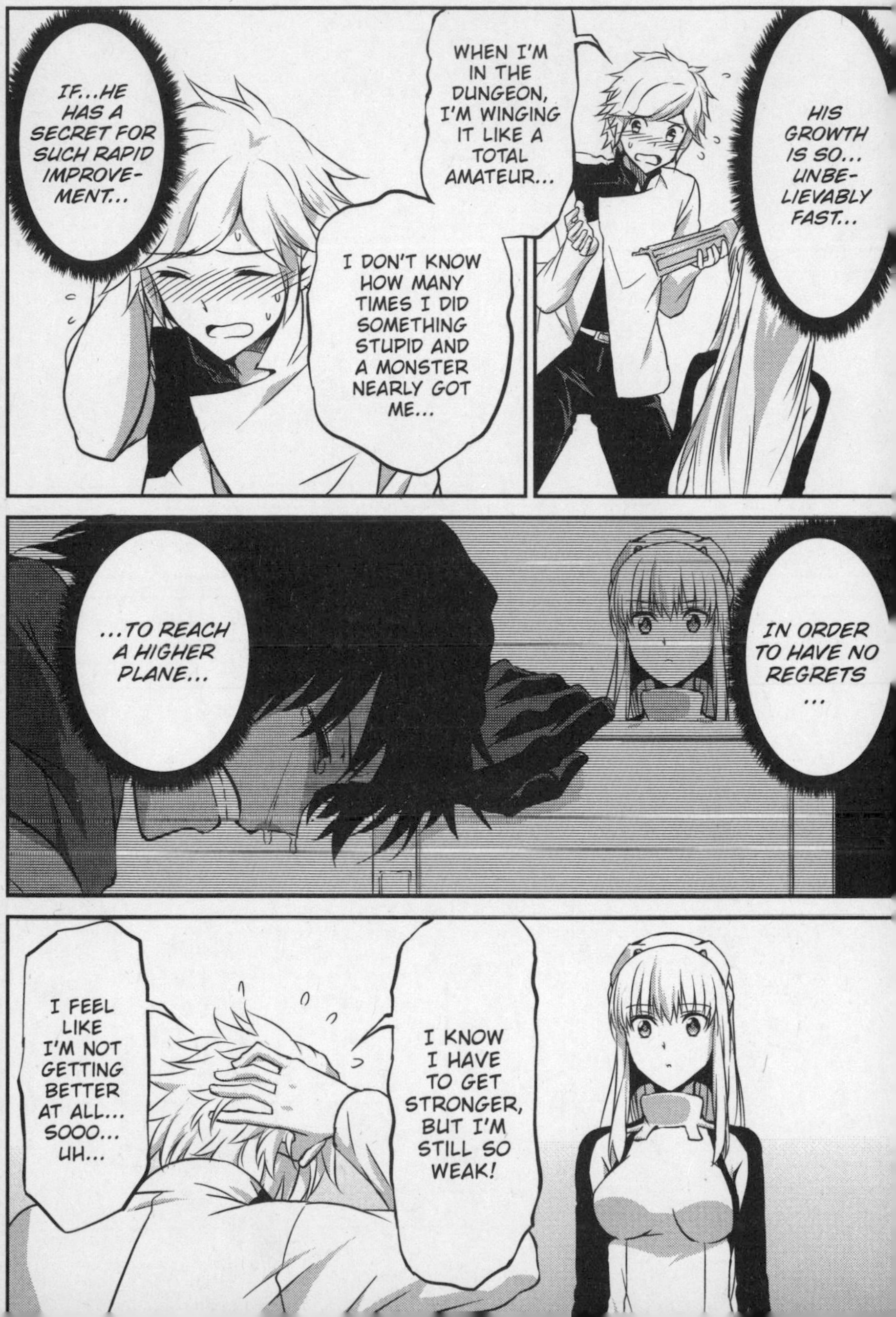
HIS GROWTH IS SO... UNBELIEVABLY FAST...
WHEN I'M IN THE DUNGEON, I'M WINGING IT LIKE A TOTAL AMATEUR...
I DON'T KNOW HOW MANY TIMES I DID SOMETHING STUPID AND A MONSTER NEARLY GOT ME...
IF...HE HAS A SECRET FOR SUCH RAPID IMPROVEMENT...
IN ORDER TO HAVE NO REGRETS ...
...TO REACH A HIGHER PLANE...
I KNOW I HAVE TO GET STRONGER, BUT I'M STILL SO WEAK!
I FEEL LIKE I'M NOT GETTING BETTER AT ALL... SOOO... UH...

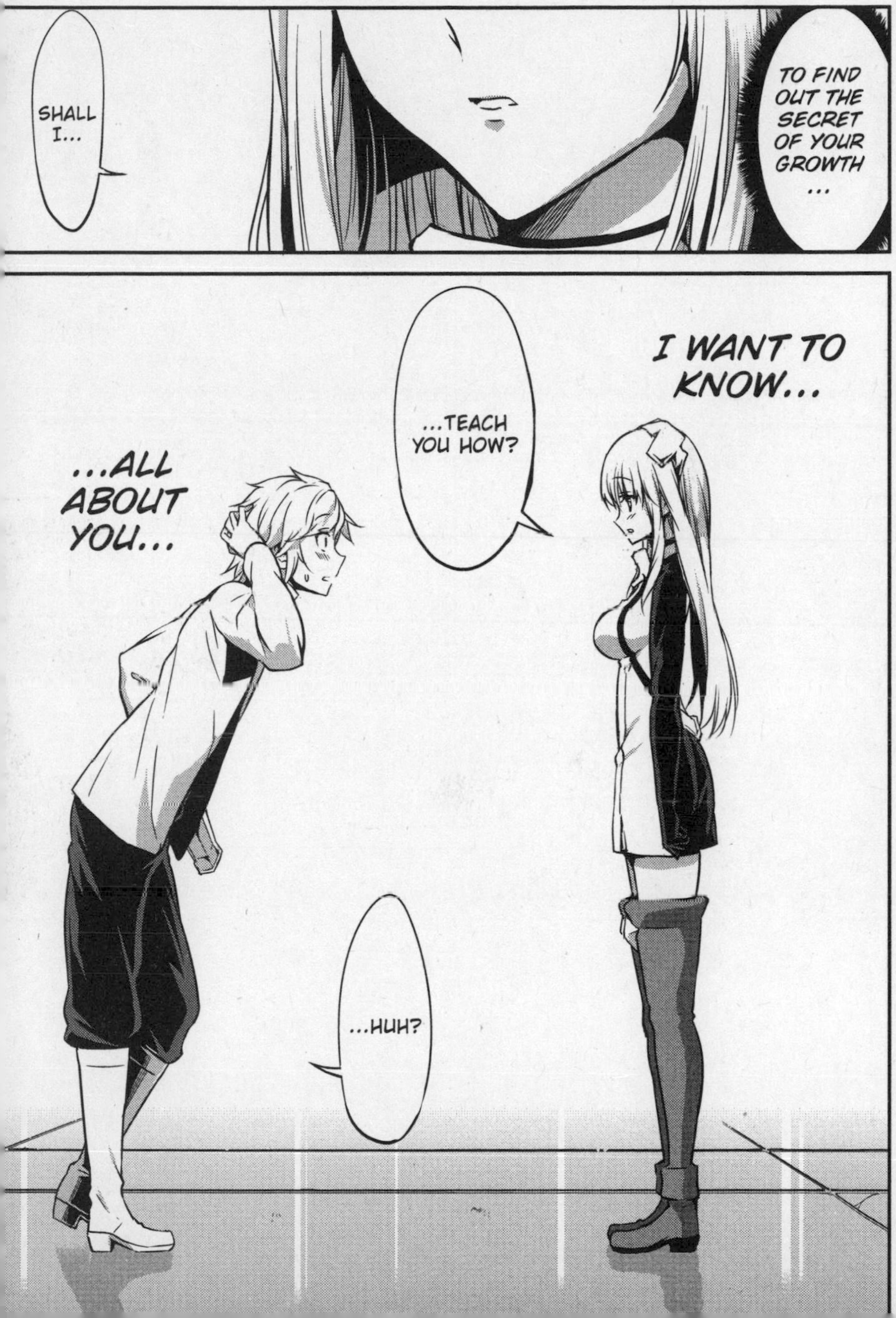
TO FIND OUT THE SECRET OF YOUR GROWTH...
SHALL I...
I WANT TO KNOW...
...TEACH YOU HOW?
...ALL ABOUT YOU...
...HUH?

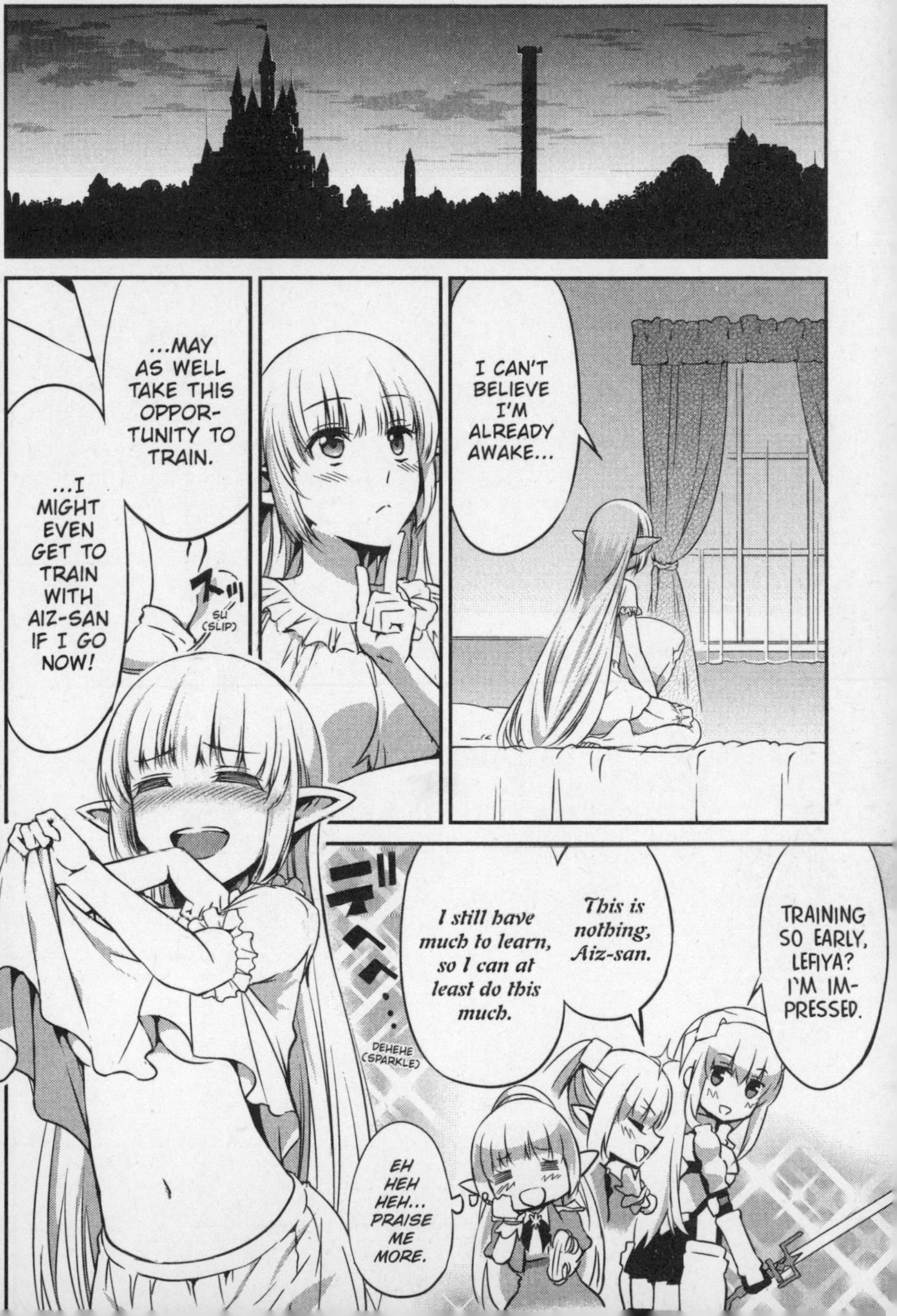
I CAN'T BELIEVE I'M ALREADY AWAKE...
...MAY AS WELL TAKE THIS OPPOR-TUNITY TO TRAIN.
...I MIGHT EVEN GET TO TRAIN WITH AIZ-SAN IF I GO NOW!
SU (SLIP)
TRAINING SO EARLY, LEFIYA? I'M IM-PRESSED.
This is nothing, Aiz-san.
I still have much to learn, so I can at least do this much.
EH HEH HEH... PRAISE ME MORE.
DEHEHE (SPARKLE)

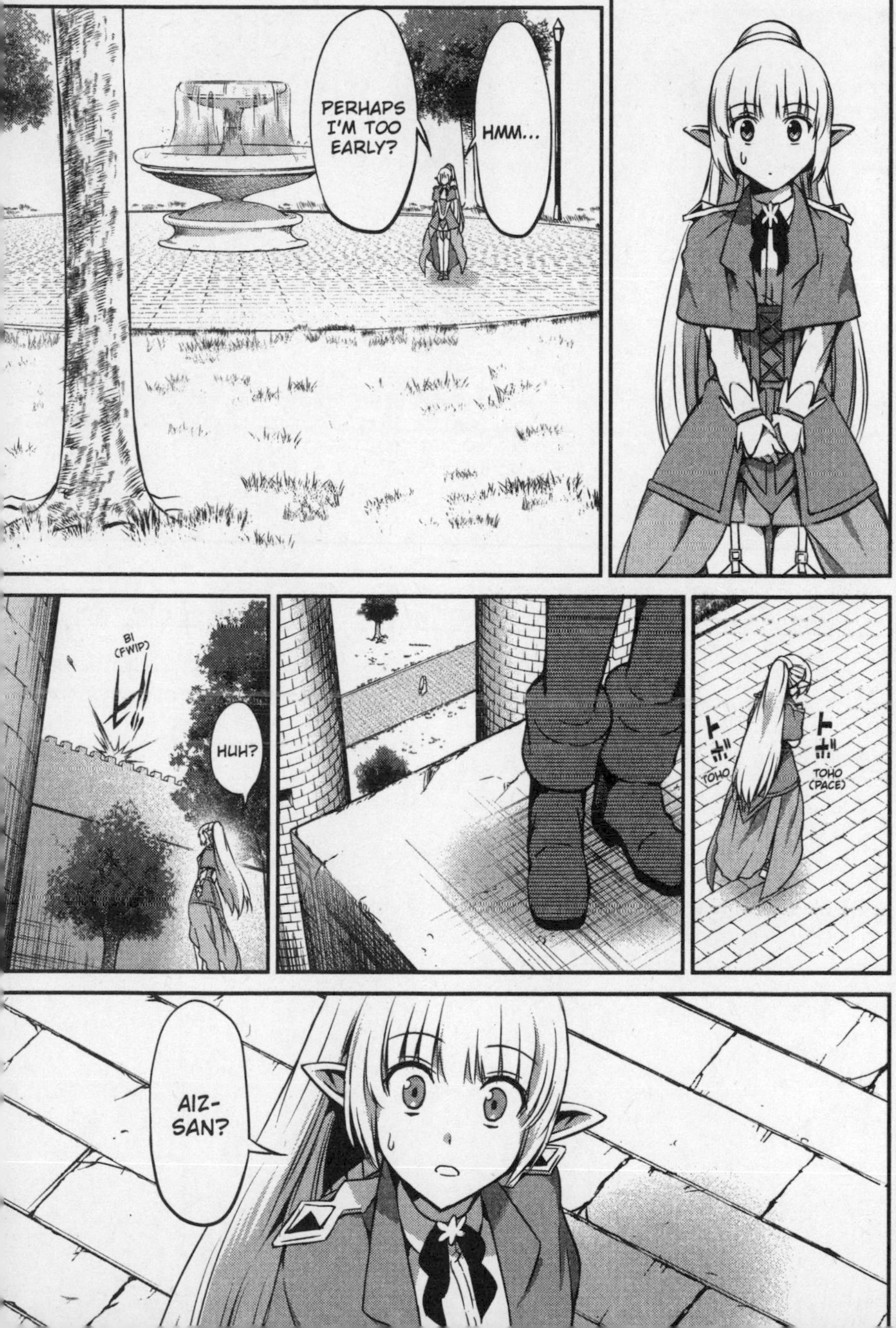
HMM...
PERHAPS I'M TOO EARLY?
TOHO
TOHO (PACE)
BI (FWIP)
HUH?
AIZ-SAN?

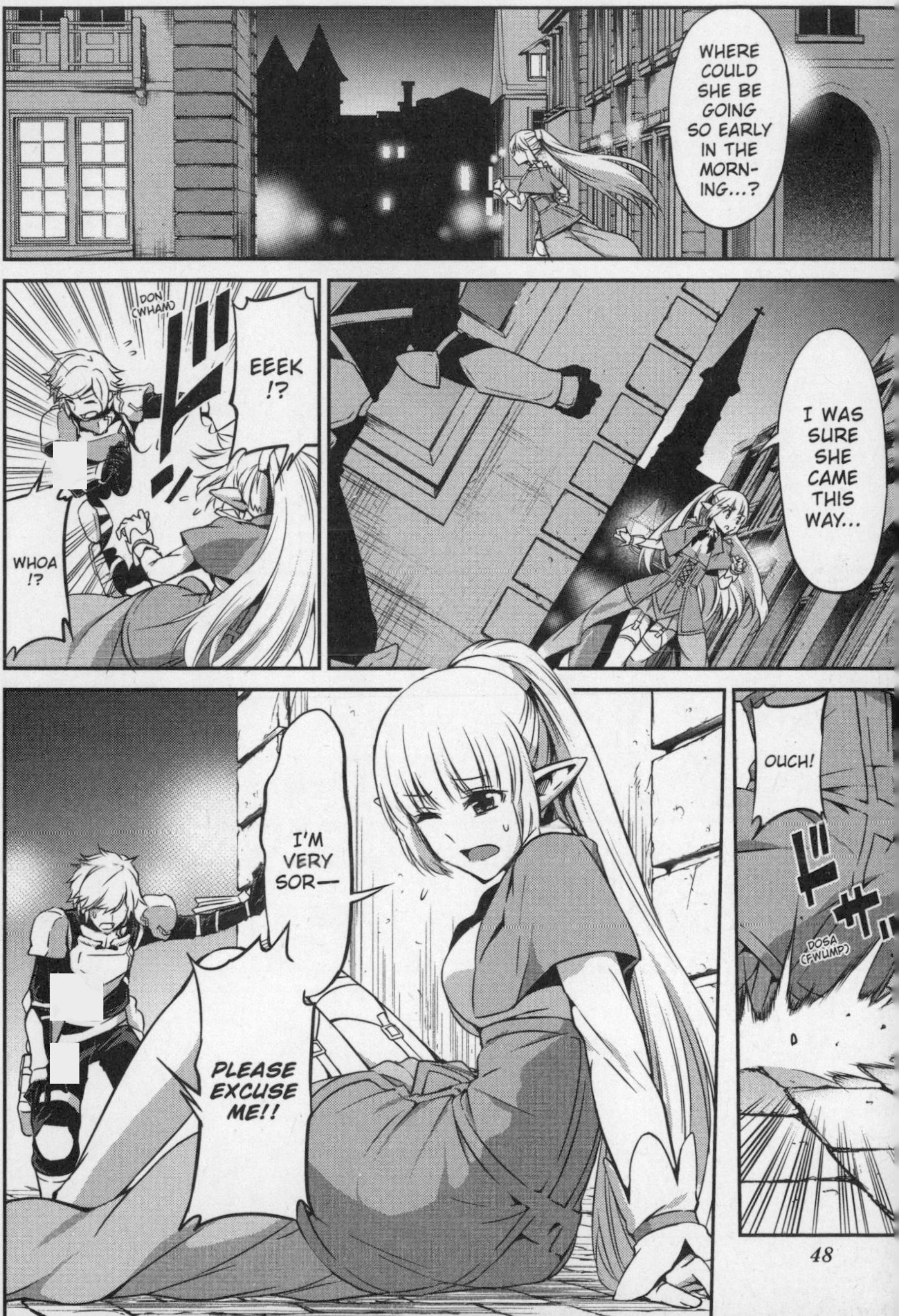
WHERE COULD SHE BE GOING SO EARLY IN THE MORN-ING...?
I WAS SURE SHE CAME THIS WAY...
DON (WHAM)
EEEK !?
WHOA !?
OUCH!
DOSA (FWUMP)
I'M VERY SOR—
PLEASE EXCUSE ME!!

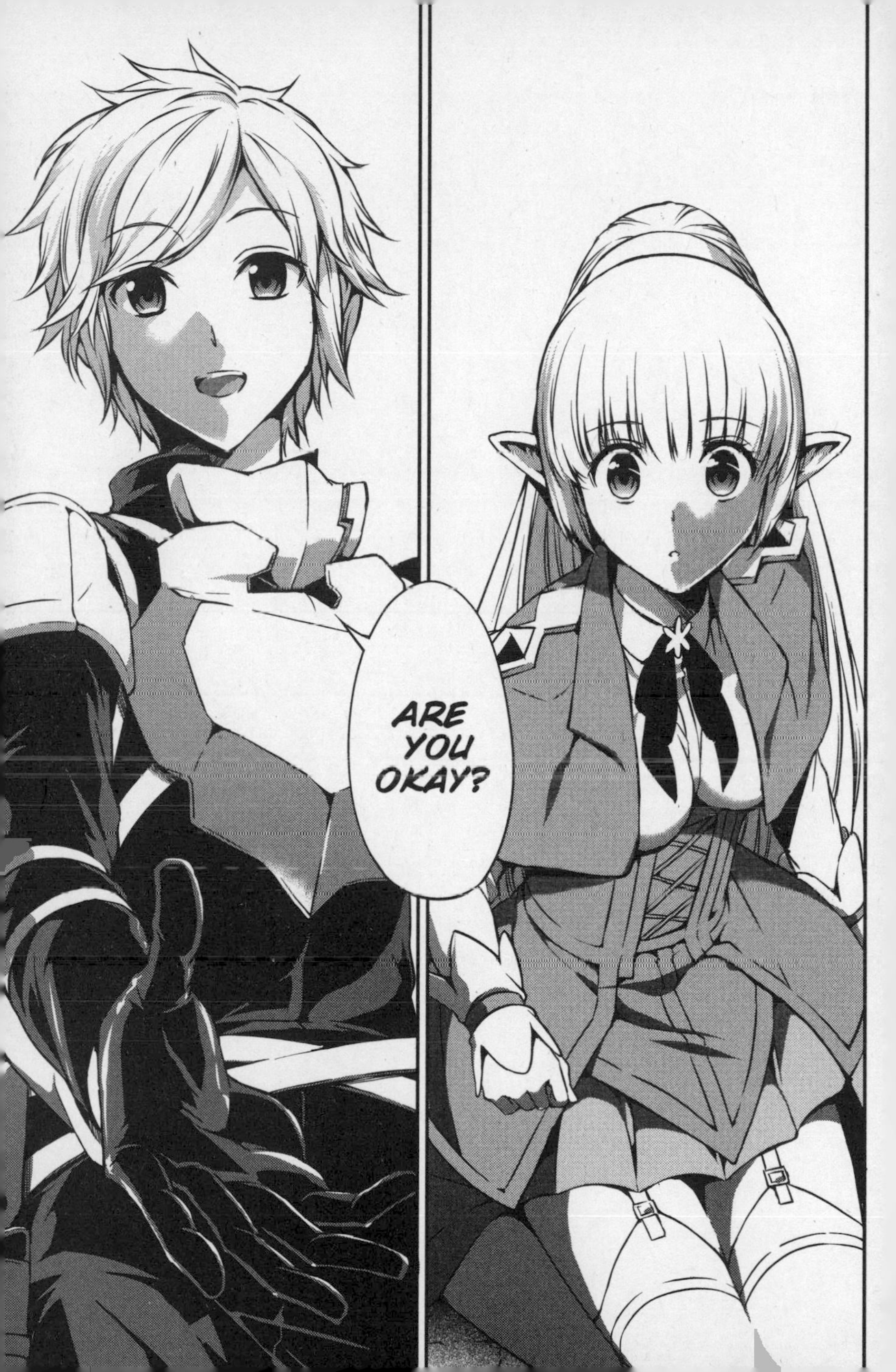
ARE YOU OKAY?

Is It WRONG to Try to PICK-UP GIRLS IN A DUNGEON? ON THE SIDE

Sword Oratoria

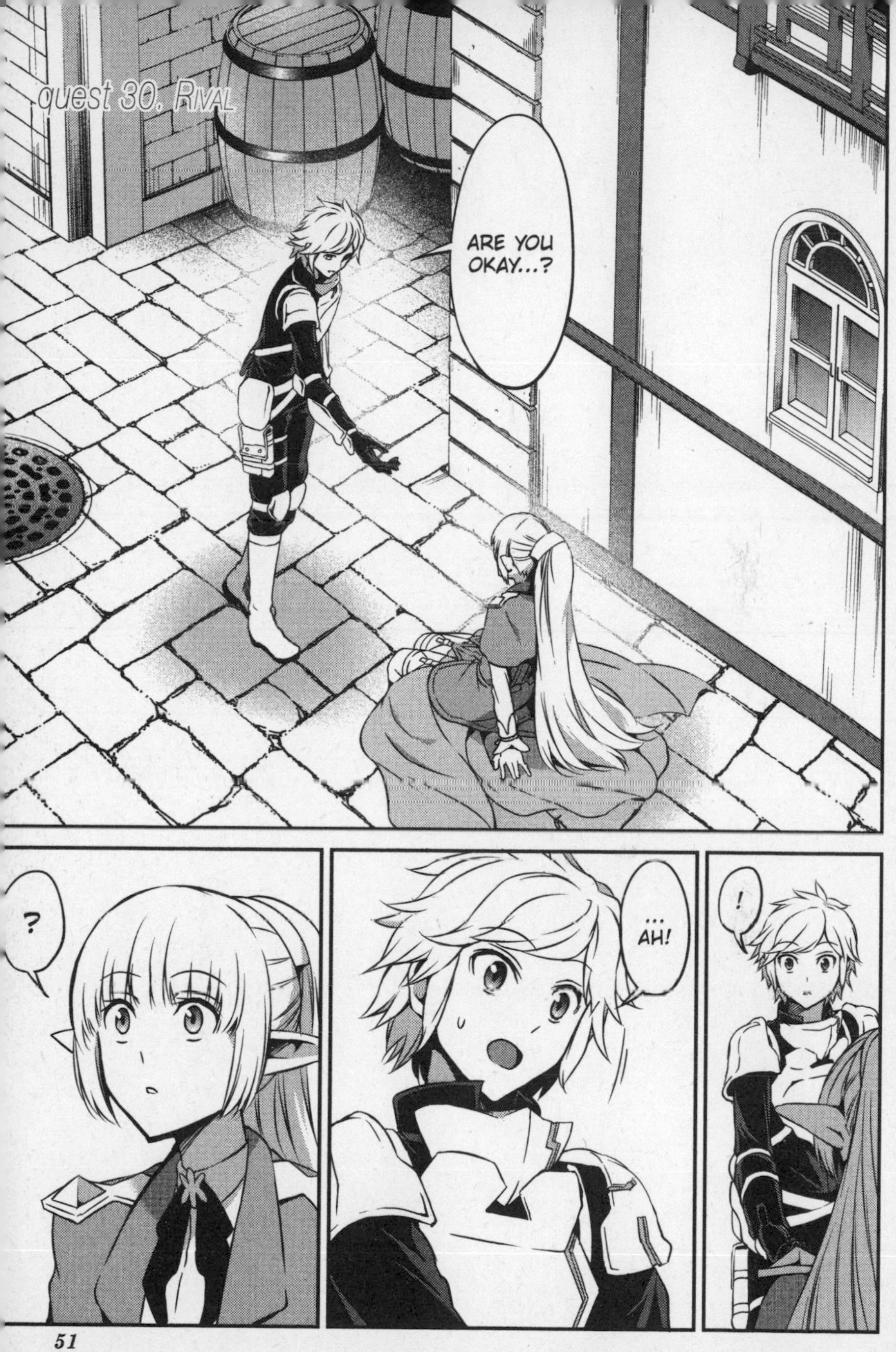
quest 30. RIVAL
ARE YOU OKAY...?
!
... AH!
?

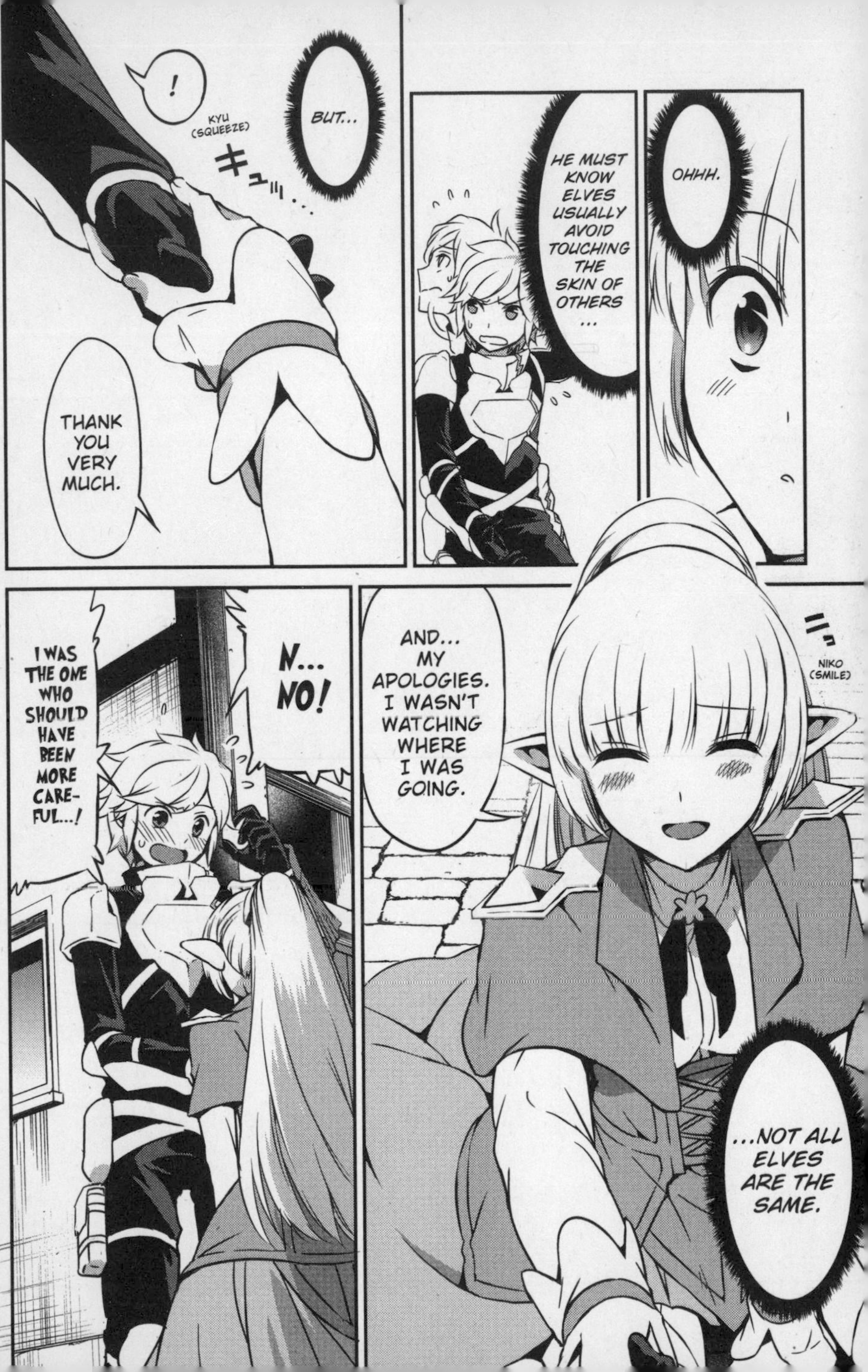
OHHH.
HE MUST KNOW ELVES USUALLY AVOID TOUCHING THE SKIN OF OTHERS...
BUT...
!
KYU (SQUEEZE)
キュッ...
THANK YOU VERY MUCH.
ニコ
NIKO (SMILE)
AND... MY APOLOGIES. I WASN'T WATCHING WHERE I WAS GOING.
...NOT ALL ELVES ARE THE SAME.
N... NO!
I WAS THE ONE WHO SHOULD HAVE BEEN MORE CARE-FUL...!

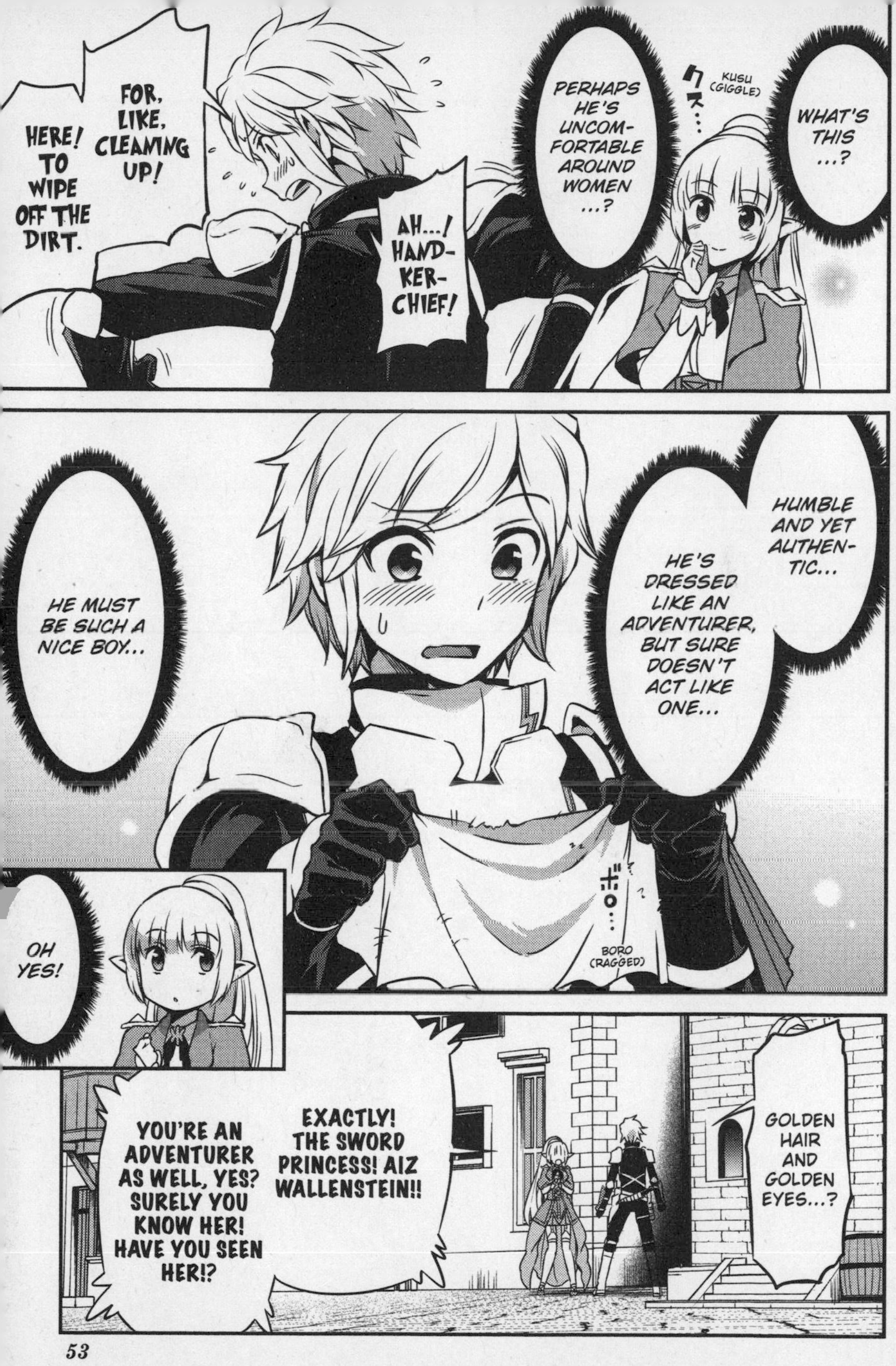
WHAT'S THIS ...?
KUSU (GIGGLE)
PERHAPS HE'S UNCOM-FORTABLE AROUND WOMEN ...?
AH...! HAND-KER-CHIEF!
FOR, LIKE, CLEANING UP!
HERE! TO WIPE OFF THE DIRT.
HUMBLE AND YET AUTHEN-TIC...
HE'S DRESSED LIKE AN ADVENTURER, BUT SURE DOESN'T ACT LIKE ONE...
HE MUST BE SUCH A NICE BOY...
BORO (RAGGED)
OH YES!
GOLDEN HAIR AND GOLDEN EYES...?
EXACTLY! THE SWORD PRINCESS! AIZ WALLENSTEIN!!
YOU'RE AN ADVENTURER AS WELL, YES? SURELY YOU KNOW HER! HAVE YOU SEEN HER!?

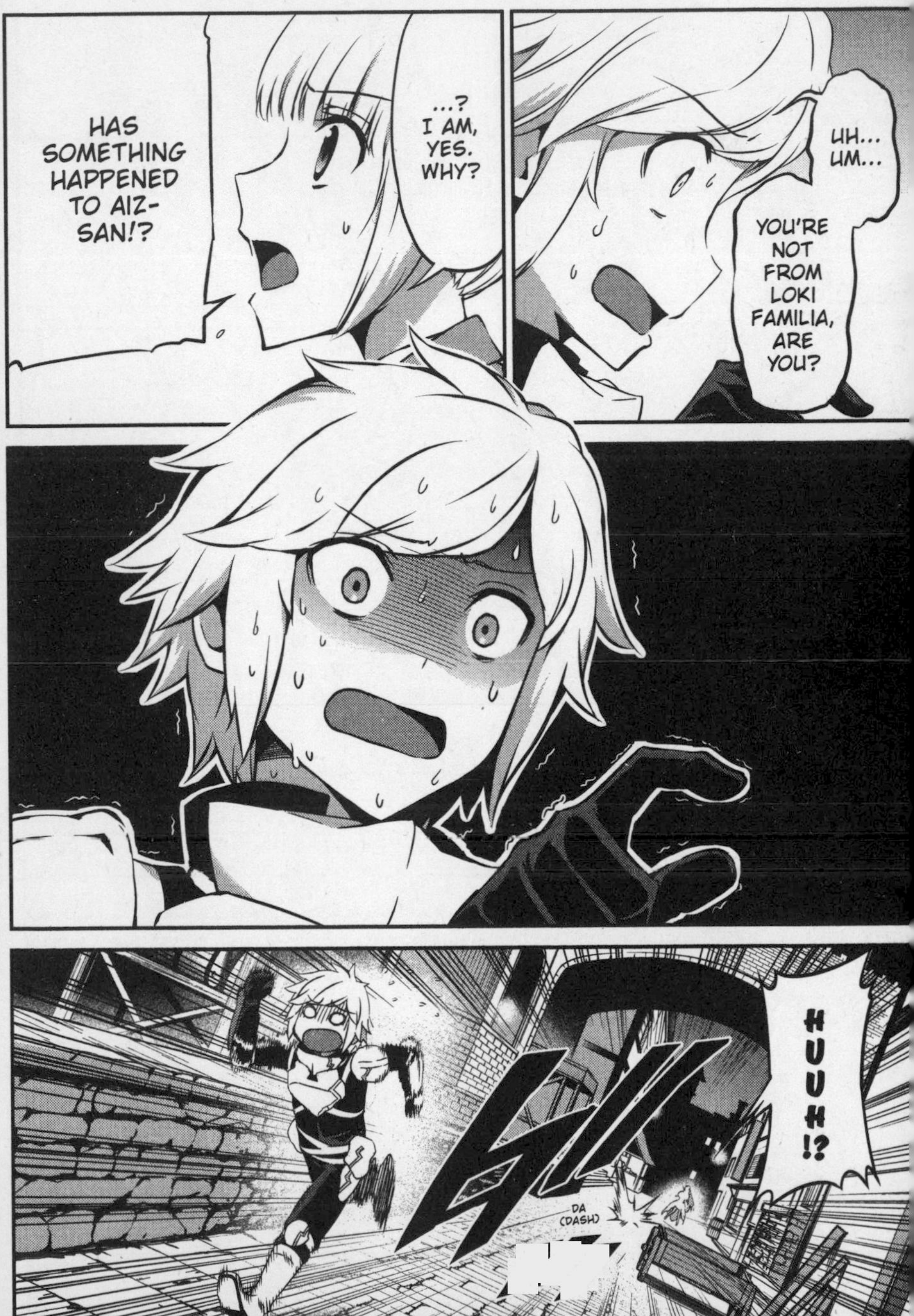
UH... UM...
YOU'RE NOT FROM LOKI FAMILIA, ARE YOU?
...? I AM, YES. WHY?
HAS SOMETHING HAPPENED TO AIZ-SAN!?
HUUUH!?
DA (DASH)

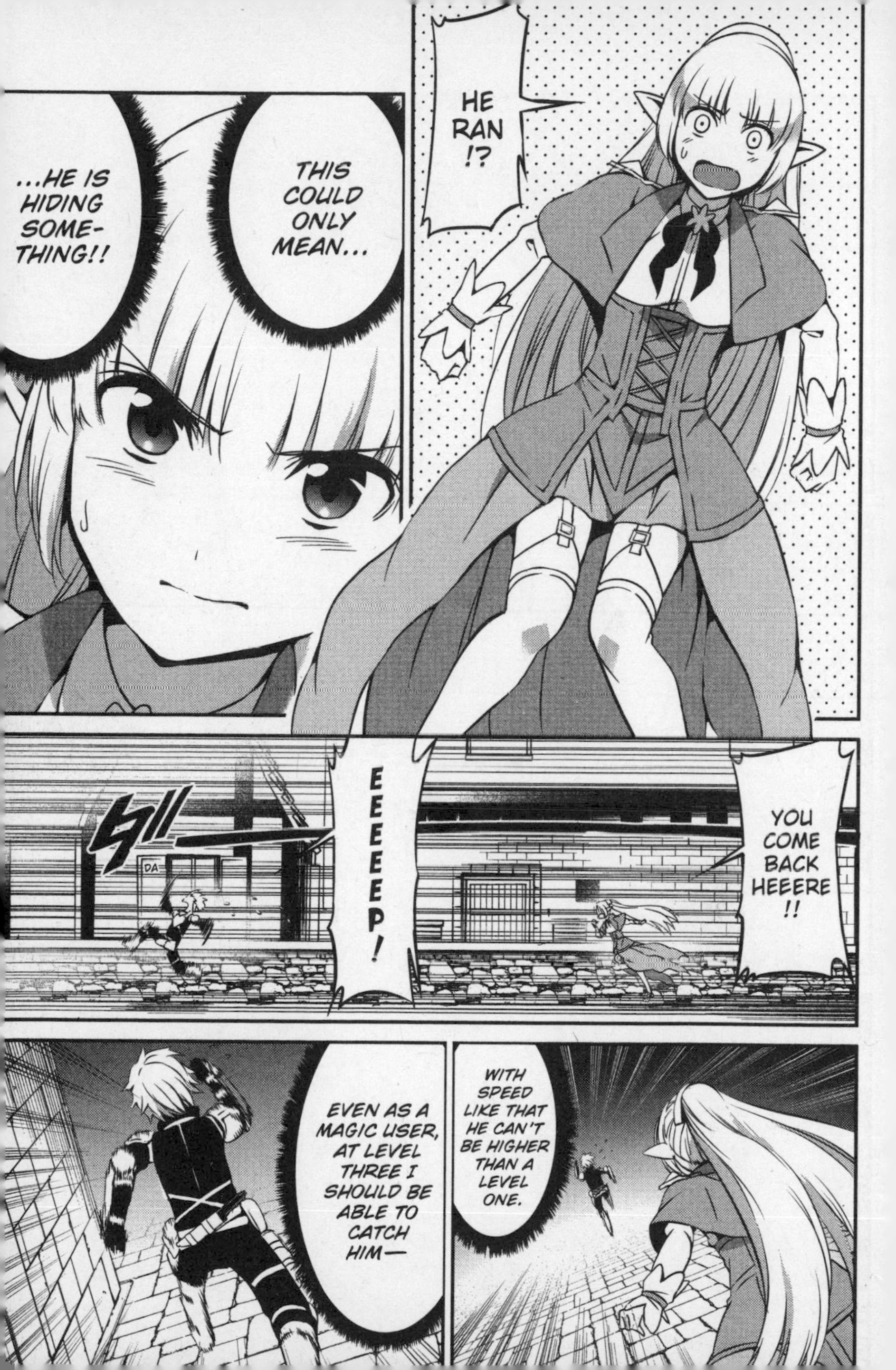
HE RAN !?
THIS COULD ONLY MEAN...
...HE IS HIDING SOME-THING!!
YOU COME BACK HEEERE !!
EEEEEP!
DA
WITH SPEED LIKE THAT HE CAN'T BE HIGHER THAN A LEVEL ONE.
EVEN AS A MAGIC USER, AT LEVEL THREE I SHOULD BE ABLE TO CATCH HIM—

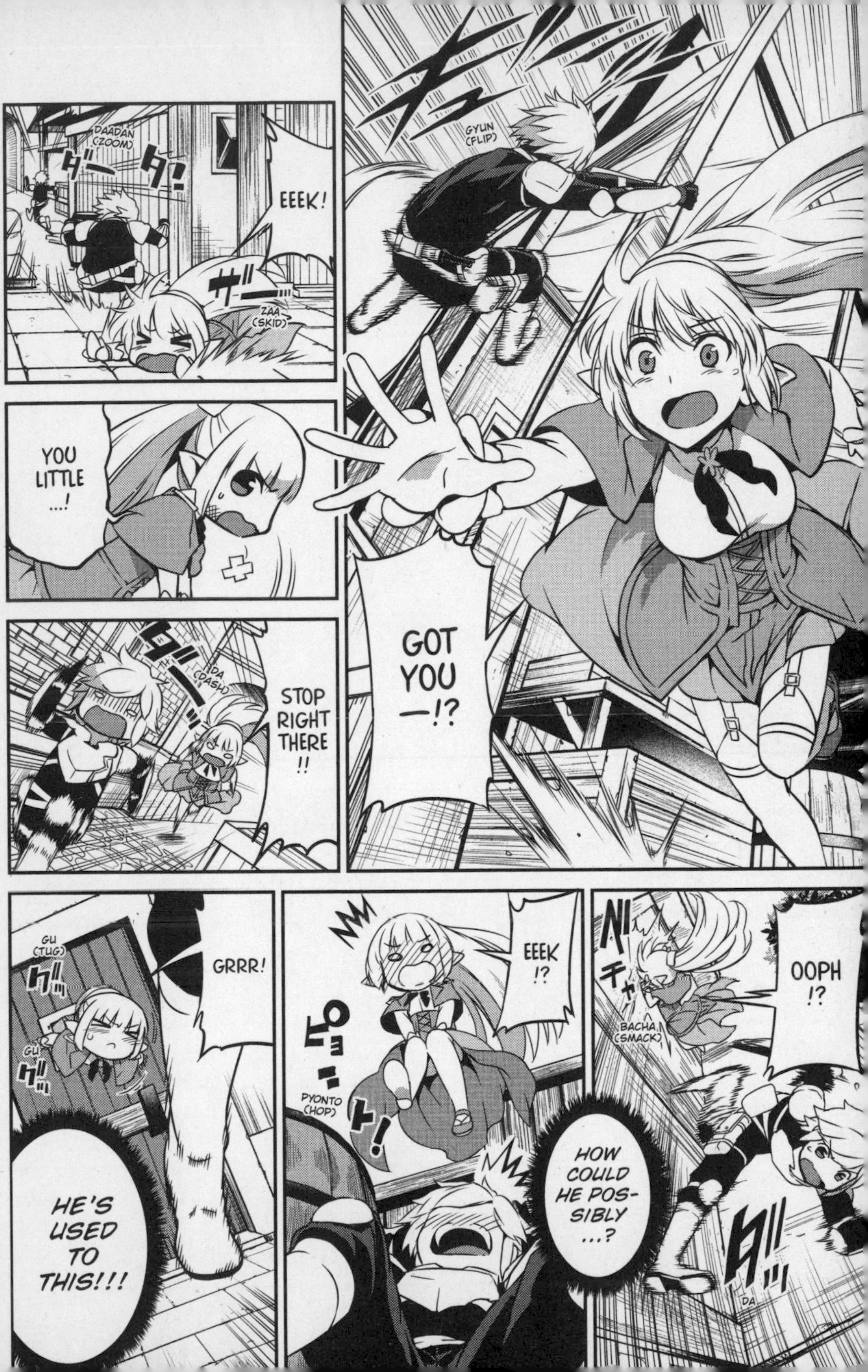
GYUN (FLIP)
GOT YOU—!?
DAADAN (ZOOM)
EEEK!
ZAA (SKID)
YOU LITTLE ...!
DA (DASH)
STOP RIGHT THERE!!
OOPH!?
BACHA (SMACK)
DA
EEEK!?
PYONTO (HOP)
HOW COULD HE POSSIBLY ...?
GRRR!
GU (TUG)
GU
HE'S USED TO THIS!!!

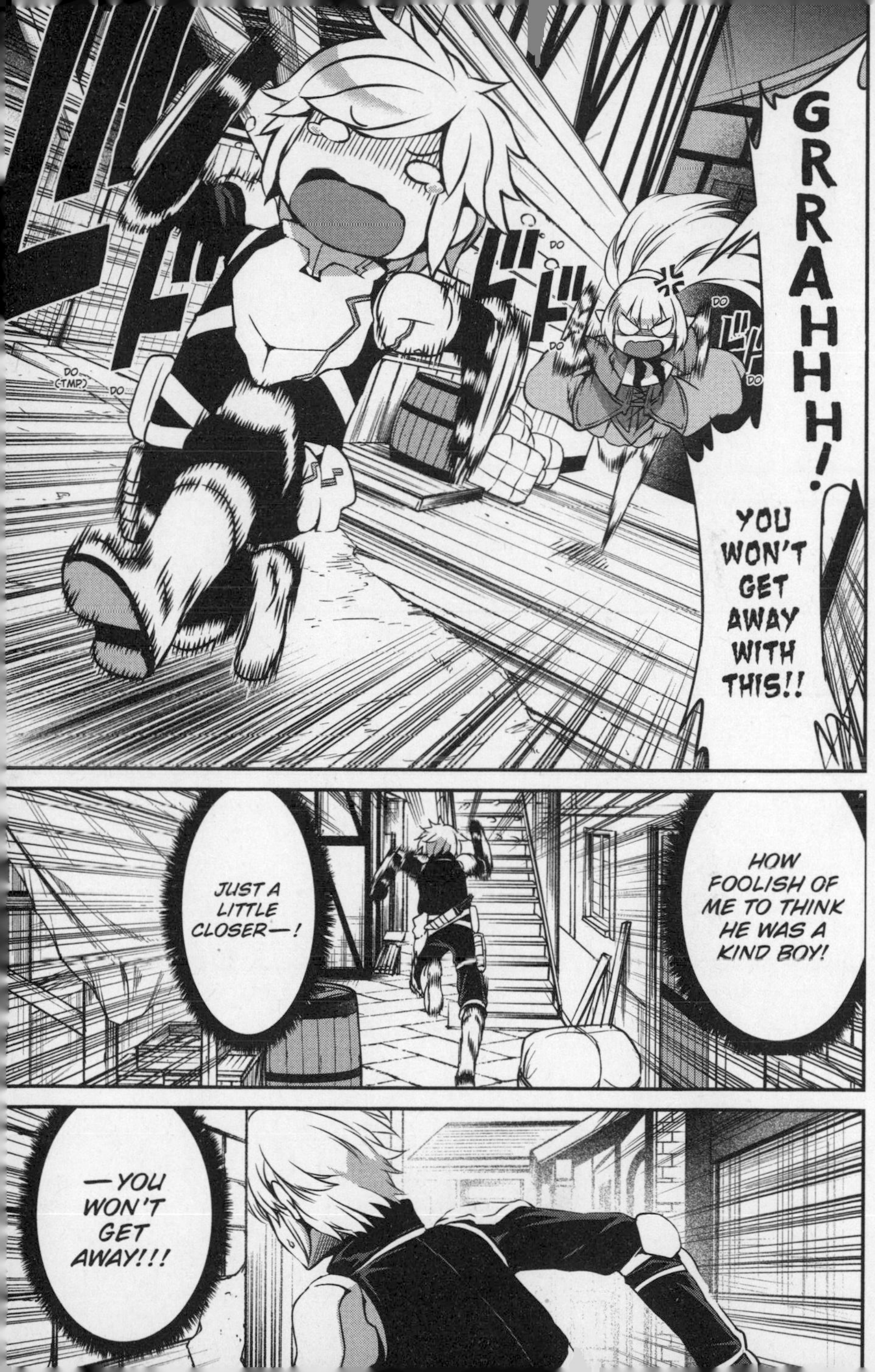

GRRAHHH!
YOU WON'T GET AWAY WITH THIS!!
DO
DO
DO
DO
DO (TMP)
DO
HOW FOOLISH OF ME TO THINK HE WAS A KIND BOY!
JUST A LITTLE CLOSER—!
—YOU WON'T GET AWAY!!!

HUH !?

HE... HE'S GONE!?

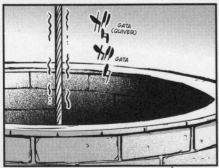

GATA (QUIVER)

GATA

WHERE COULD HE HAVE GONE!?

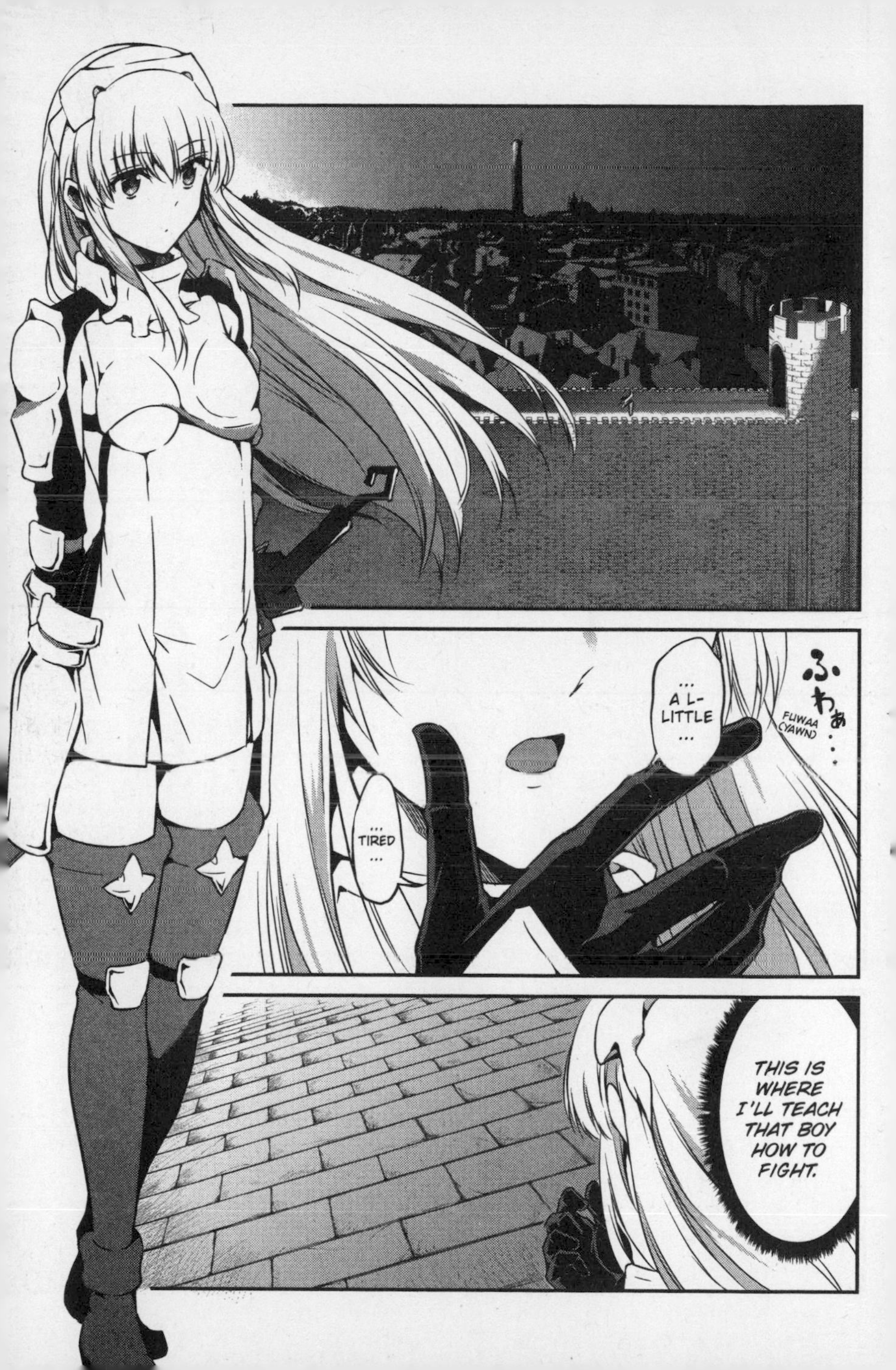

ふわぁ…
FUWAA (YAWN)
...A L-LITTLE...
...TIRED...
THIS IS WHERE I'LL TEACH THAT BOY HOW TO FIGHT.

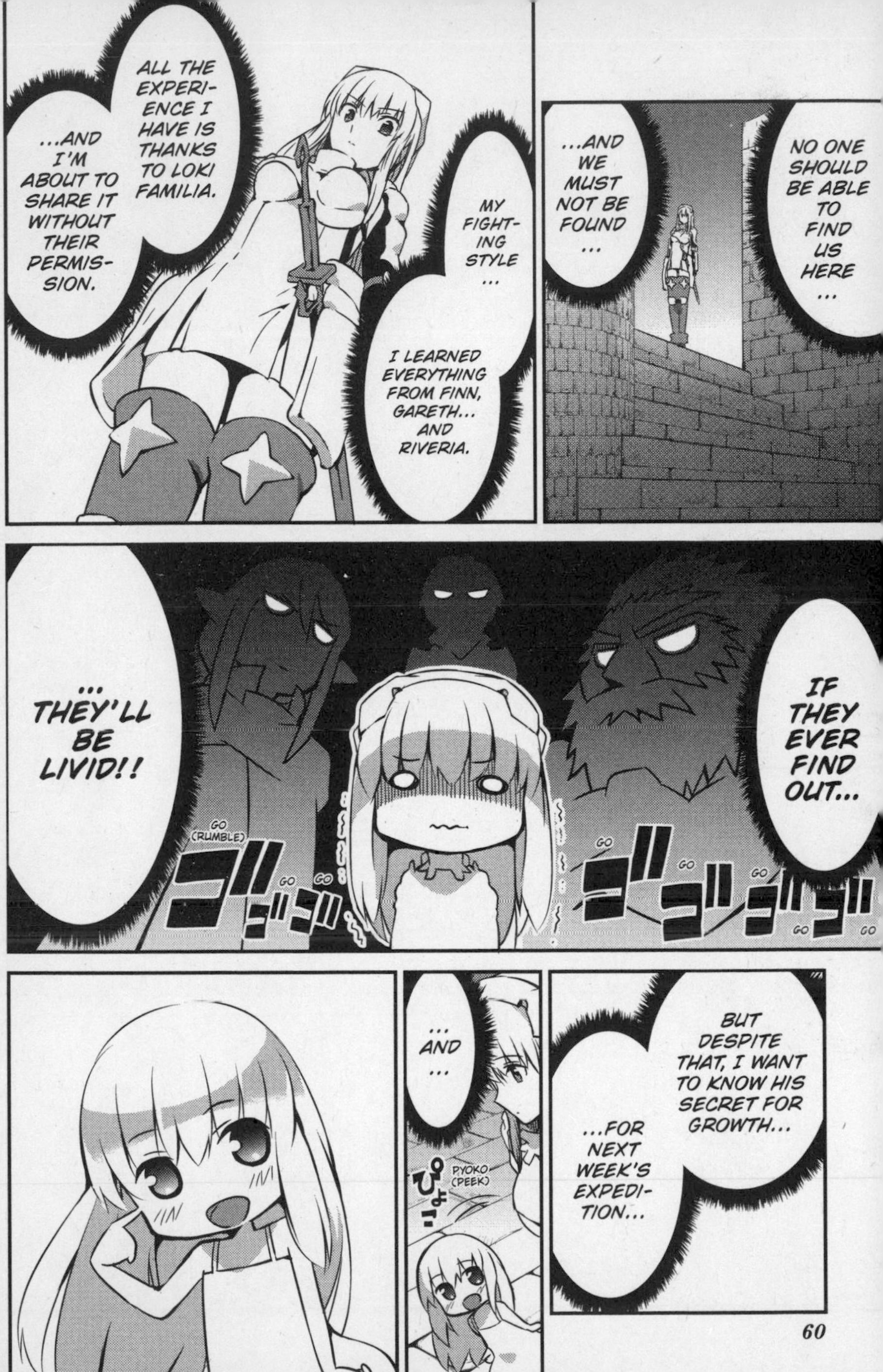

NO ONE SHOULD BE ABLE TO FIND US HERE...
...AND WE MUST NOT BE FOUND...
MY FIGHTING-STYLE...
I LEARNED EVERYTHING FROM FINN, GARETH... AND RIVERIA.
ALL THE EXPERIENCE I HAVE IS THANKS TO LOKI FAMILIA.
...AND I'M ABOUT TO SHARE IT WITHOUT THEIR PERMISSION.
IF THEY EVER FIND OUT...
GO GO GO GO GO
...THEY'LL BE LIVID!!
GO (RUMBLE) GO GO
BUT DESPITE THAT, I WANT TO KNOW HIS SECRET FOR GROWTH...
...FOR NEXT WEEK'S EXPEDITION...
...AND...
PYOKO (PEEK)

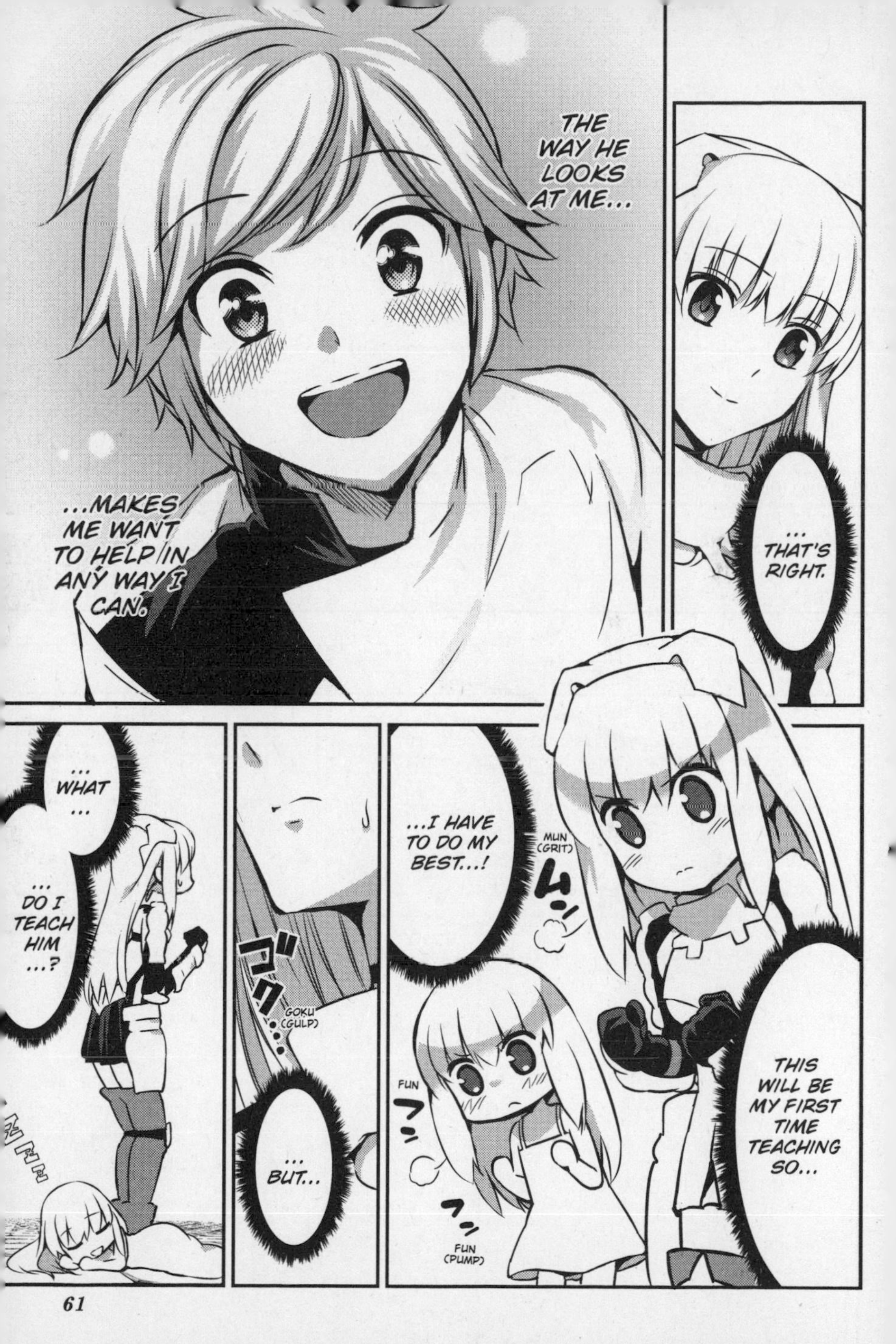

...THAT'S RIGHT.
THE WAY HE LOOKS AT ME...
...MAKES ME WANT TO HELP IN ANY WAY I CAN.
THIS WILL BE MY FIRST TIME TEACHING SO...
...I HAVE TO DO MY BEST...!
MUN (GRIT)
FUN
FUN (PUMP)
GOKU (GULP)
...BUT...
...WHAT...
...DO I TEACH HIM...?

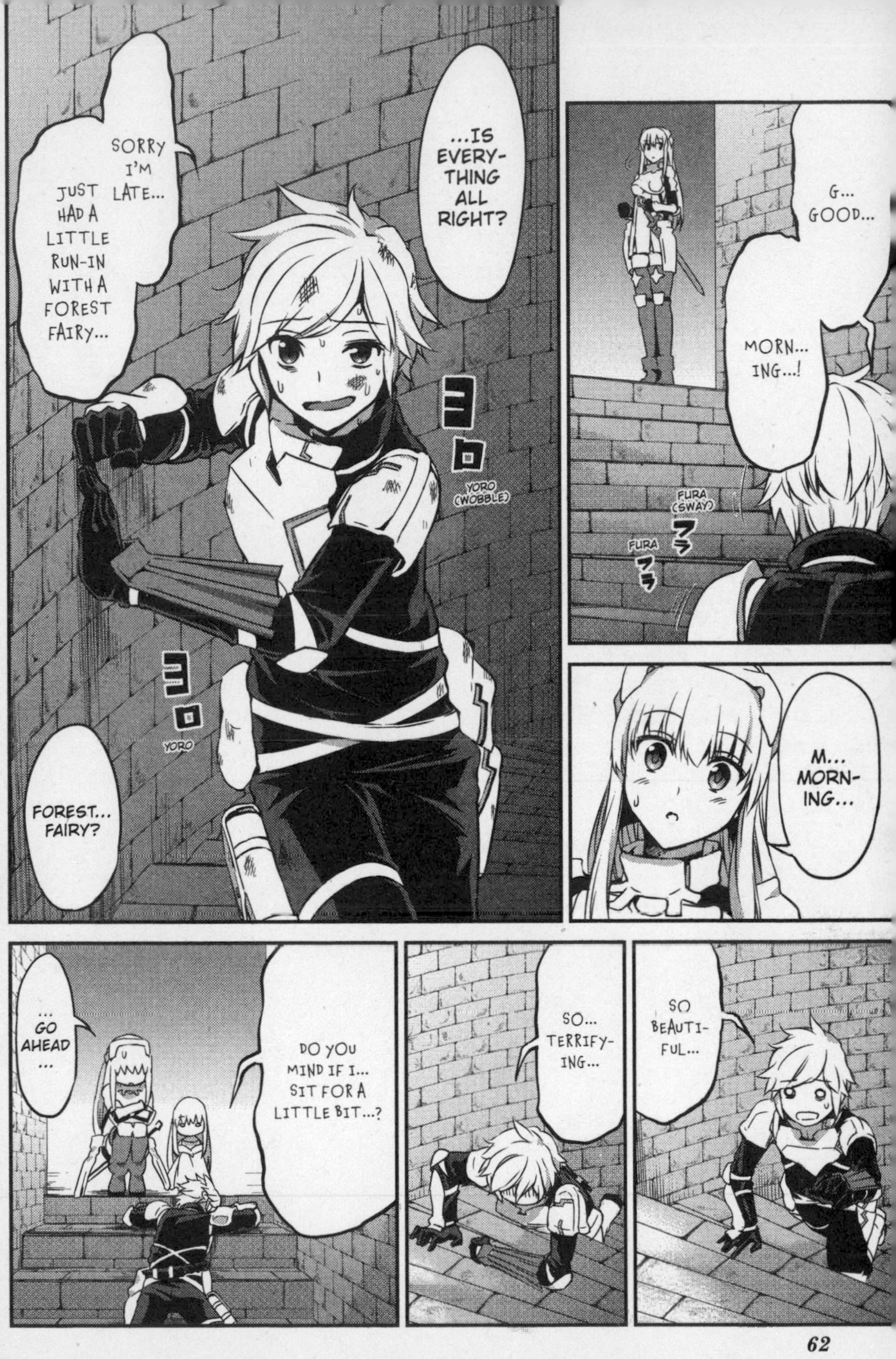
G... GOOD... MORNING...!
FURA (SWAY)
フラ
FURA
フラ
M... MORNING...
...IS EVERYTHING ALL RIGHT?
SORRY I'M LATE... JUST HAD A LITTLE RUN-IN WITH A FOREST FAIRY...
ヨロ
YORO (WOBBLE)
ヨロ
YORO
FOREST... FAIRY?
SO BEAUTIFUL...
SO... TERRIFYING...
DO YOU MIND IF I... SIT FOR A LITTLE BIT...?
...GO AHEAD...

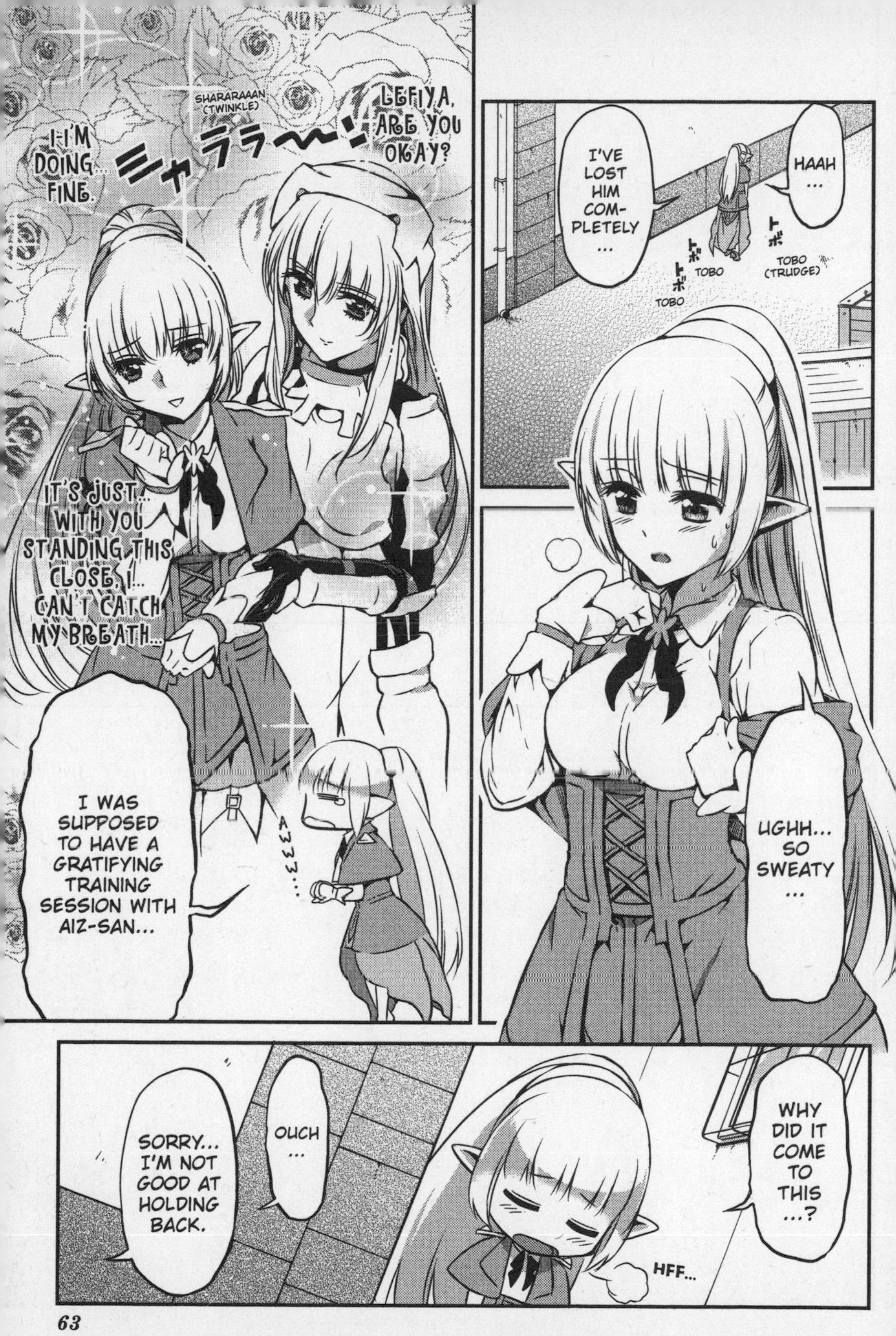

HAAH...
トボ
TOBO (TRUDGE)
トボ
TOBO
トボ
TOBO
I'VE LOST HIM COMPLETELY...
UGHH... SO SWEATY...
LEFIYA, ARE YOU OKAY?
シャララ〜ン
SHARARAAAN (TWINKLE)
I-I'M DOING... FINE.
IT'S JUST... WITH YOU STANDING THIS CLOSE, I... CAN'T CATCH MY BREATH...
AWWW...
I WAS SUPPOSED TO HAVE A GRATIFYING TRAINING SESSION WITH AIZ-SAN...
WHY DID IT COME TO THIS...?
HFF...
OUCH...
SORRY... I'M NOT GOOD AT HOLDING BACK.

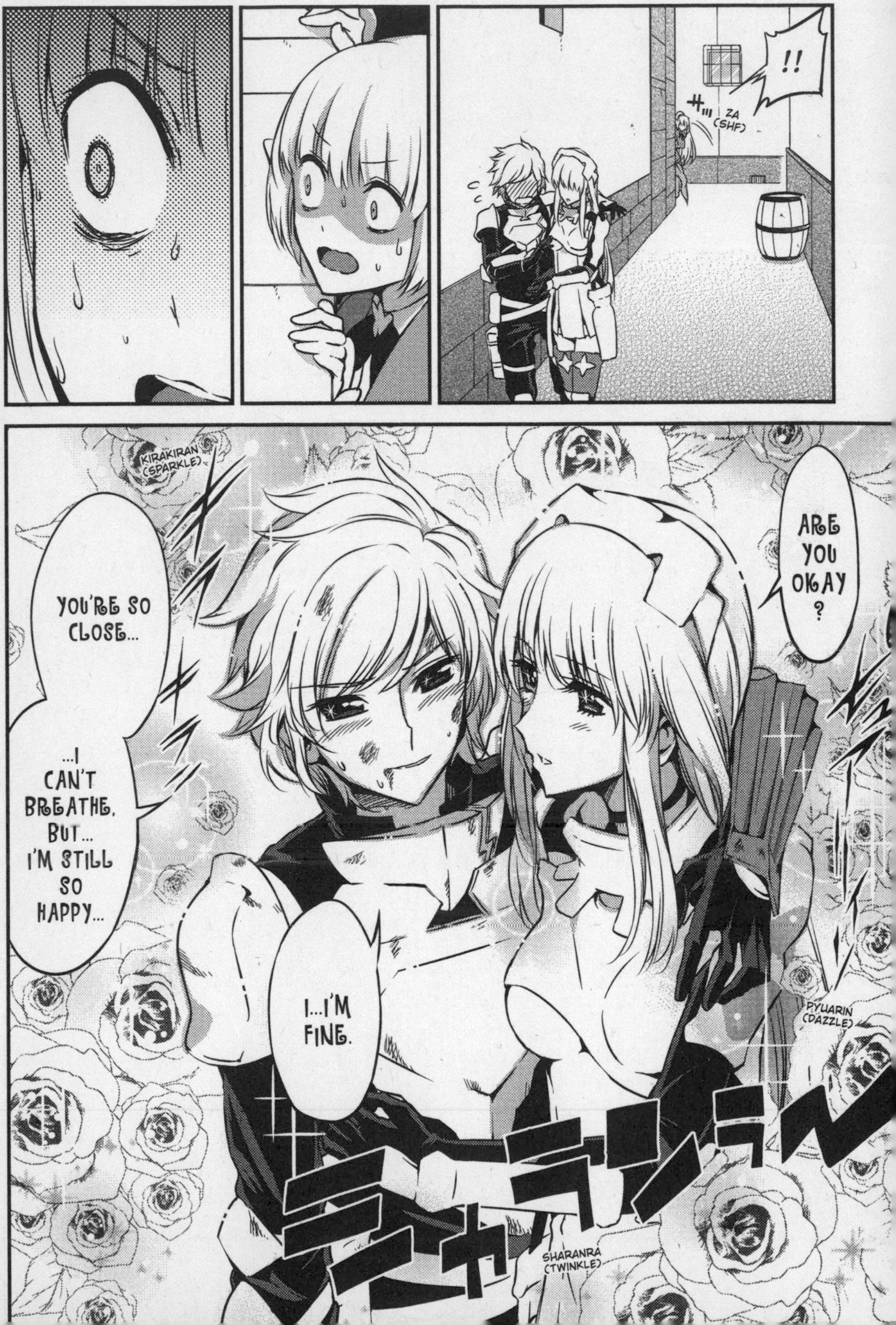
!!
ZA (SHF)
ARE YOU OKAY ?
KIRAKIRAN (SPARKLE)
YOU'RE SO CLOSE...
...I CAN'T BREATHE, BUT... I'M STILL SO HAPPY...
PYUARIN (DAZZLE)
I...I'M FINE.
SHARANRA (TWINKLE)

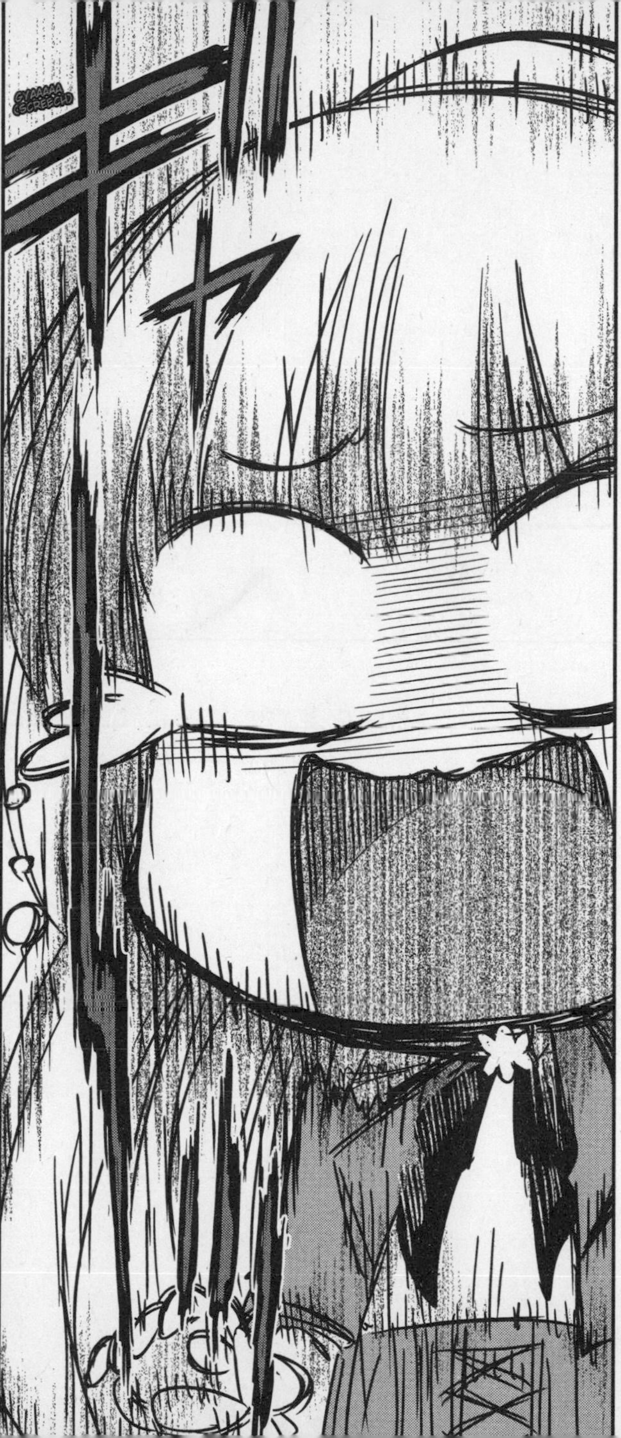
GYAAAAA
(SCREECH)
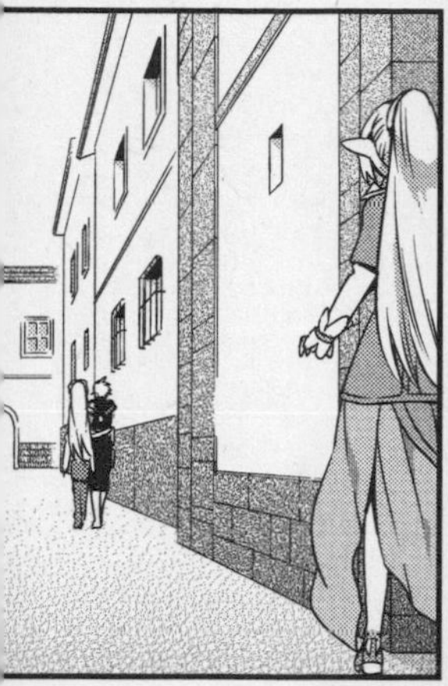
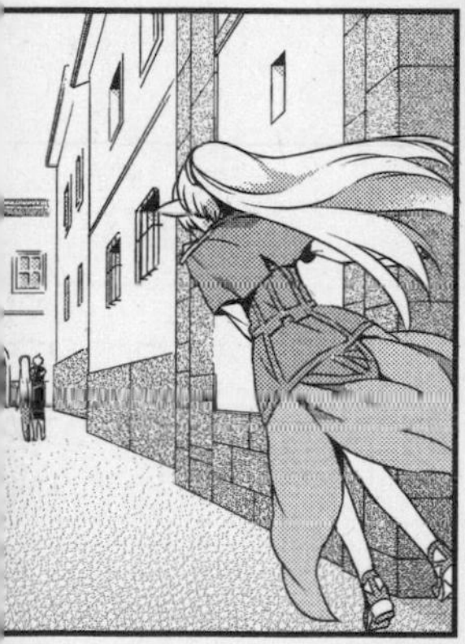
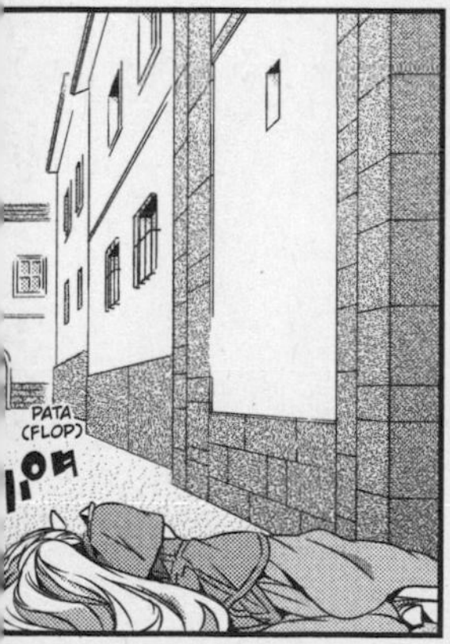
PATA
(FLOP)

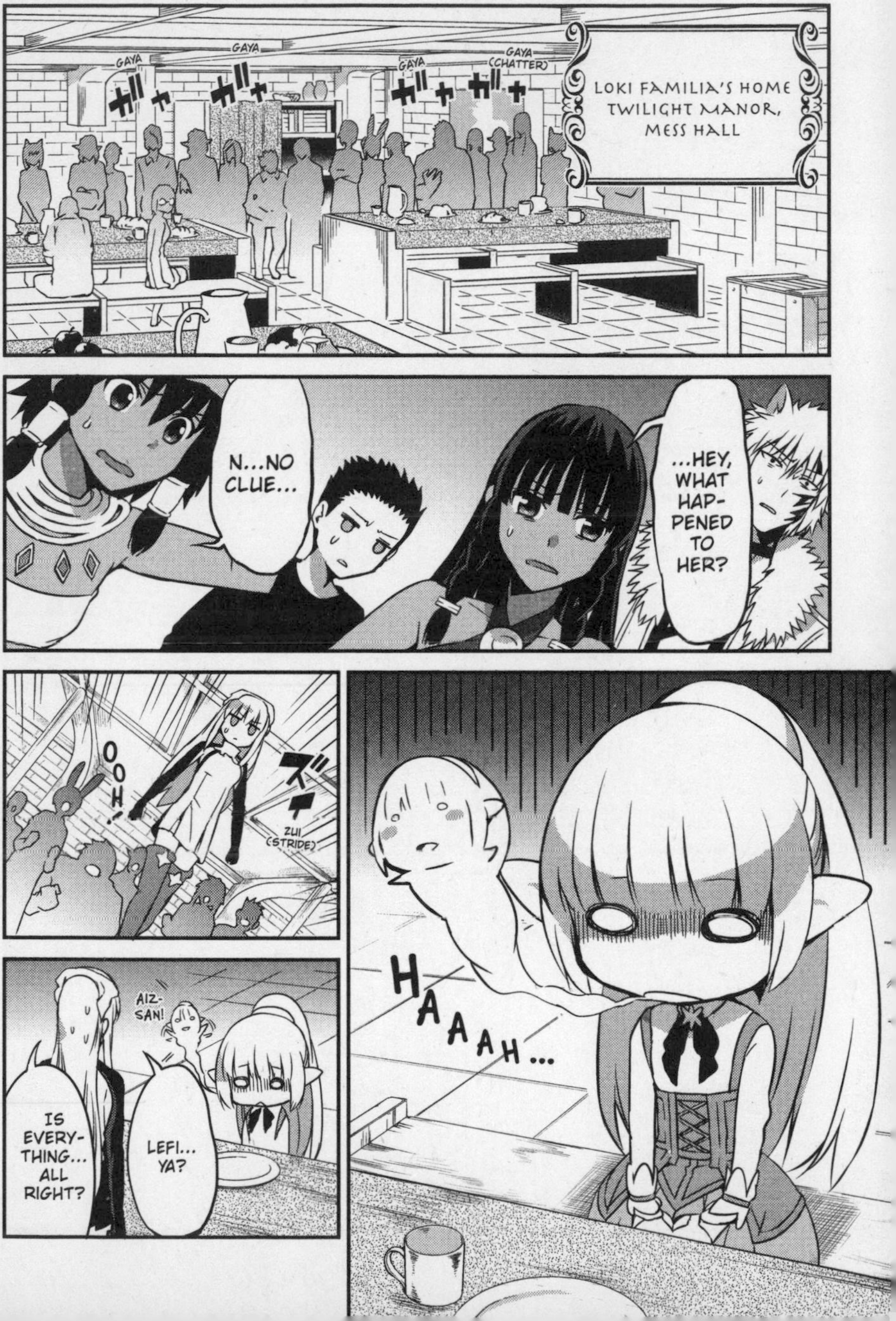

LOKI FAMILIA'S HOME TWILIGHT MANOR, MESS HALL
GAYA (CHATTER)
GAYA
GAYA
GAYA
...HEY, WHAT HAPPENED TO HER?
N...NO CLUE...
HAAAAH...
ZUI (STRIDE)
OOH!
AIZ-SAN!
LEFI... YA?
IS EVERYTHING... ALL RIGHT?

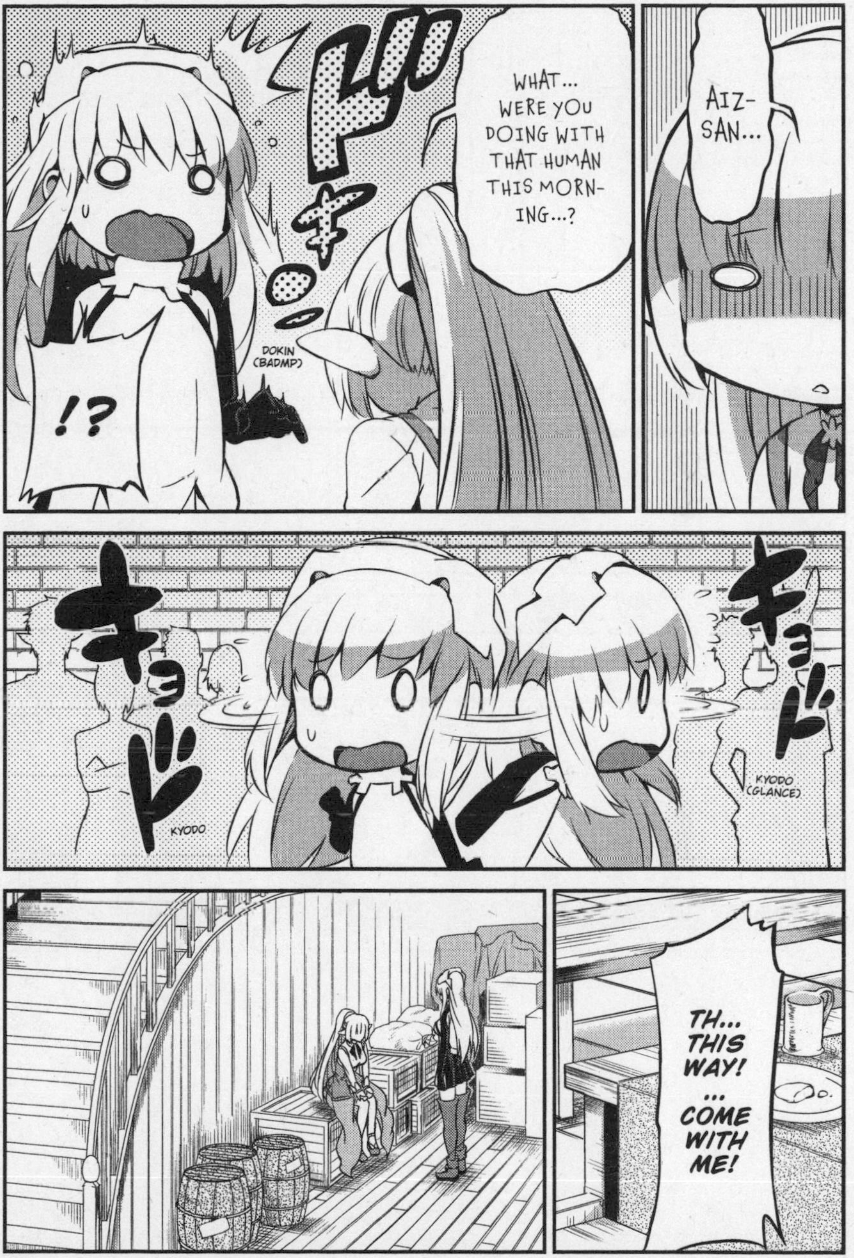
AIZ-SAN...
WHAT... WERE YOU DOING WITH THAT HUMAN THIS MORNING...?
ドキッ
DOKIN (BADMP)
!?
キョド
KYODO (GLANCE)
キョド
KYODO
TH... THIS WAY! ... COME WITH ME!

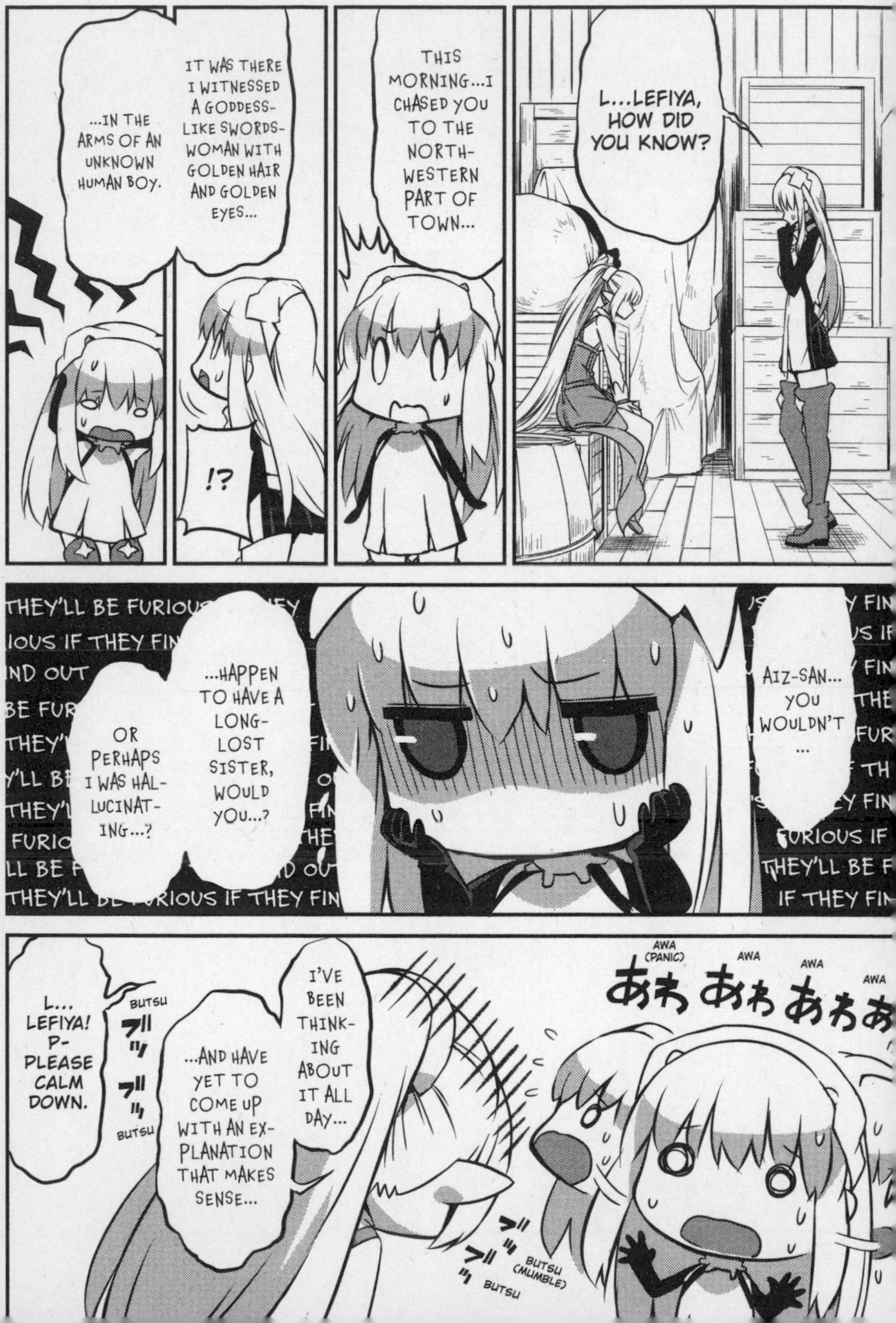
L...LEFIYA, HOW DID YOU KNOW?
THIS MORNING...I CHASED YOU TO THE NORTH-WESTERN PART OF TOWN...
IT WAS THERE I WITNESSED A GODDESS-LIKE SWORDSWOMAN WITH GOLDEN HAIR AND GOLDEN EYES...
!?
...IN THE ARMS OF AN UNKNOWN HUMAN BOY.
THEY'LL BE FURIOUS IF THEY FIN
AIZ-SAN... YOU WOULDN'T ...
...HAPPEN TO HAVE A LONG-LOST SISTER, WOULD YOU...?
OR PERHAPS I WAS HALLUCINATING...?
あわ あわ あわ あ
AWA (PANIC) AWA AWA AWA
I'VE BEEN THINKING ABOUT IT ALL DAY...
...AND HAVE YET TO COME UP WITH AN EXPLANATION THAT MAKES SENSE...
ブツ ブツ
BUTSU (MUMBLE) BUTSU
ブツ ブツ
BUTSU BUTSU
L... LEFIYA! P-PLEASE CALM DOWN.

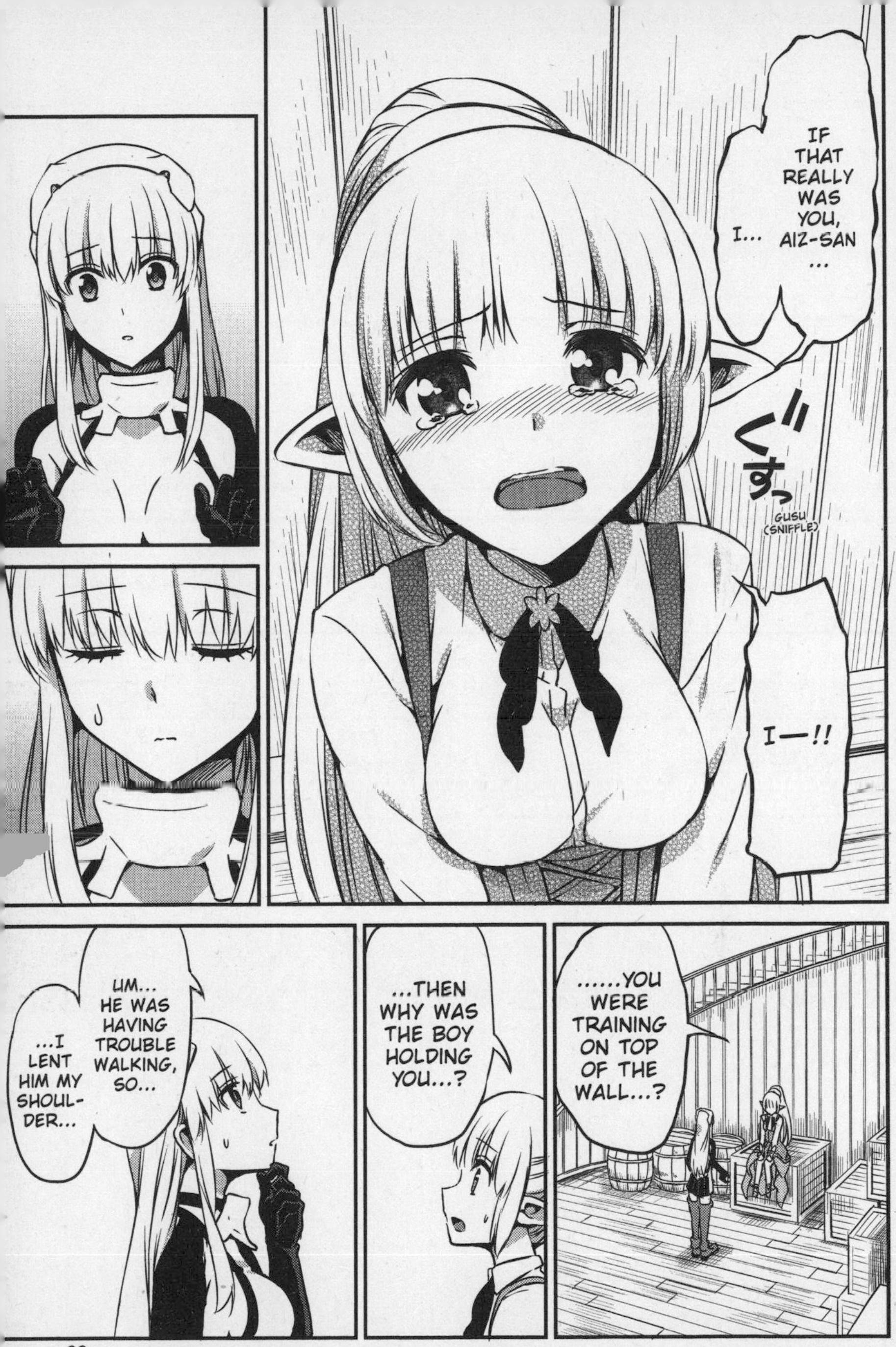
IF THAT REALLY WAS YOU, AIZ-SAN ... I...
ぐすっ
GUSU (SNIFFLE)
I—!!
......YOU WERE TRAINING ON TOP OF THE WALL...?
...THEN WHY WAS THE BOY HOLDING YOU...?
UM... HE WAS HAVING TROUBLE WALKING, SO... ...I LENT HIM MY SHOUL-DER...

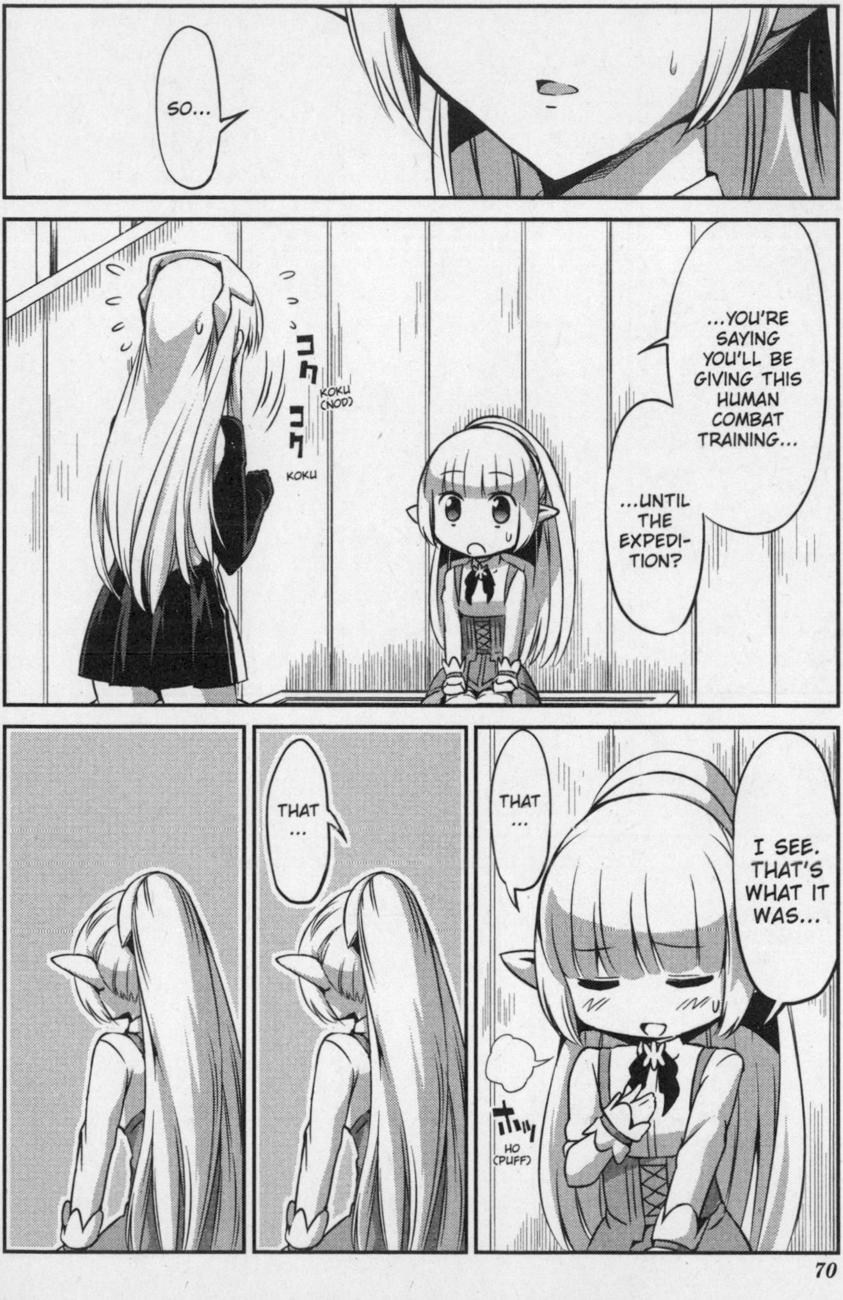
SO...
...YOU'RE SAYING YOU'LL BE GIVING THIS HUMAN COMBAT TRAINING...
...UNTIL THE EXPEDITION?
コク
KOKU (NOD)
コク
KOKU
I SEE. THAT'S WHAT IT WAS...
ホッ
HO (PUFF)
THAT...
THAT...

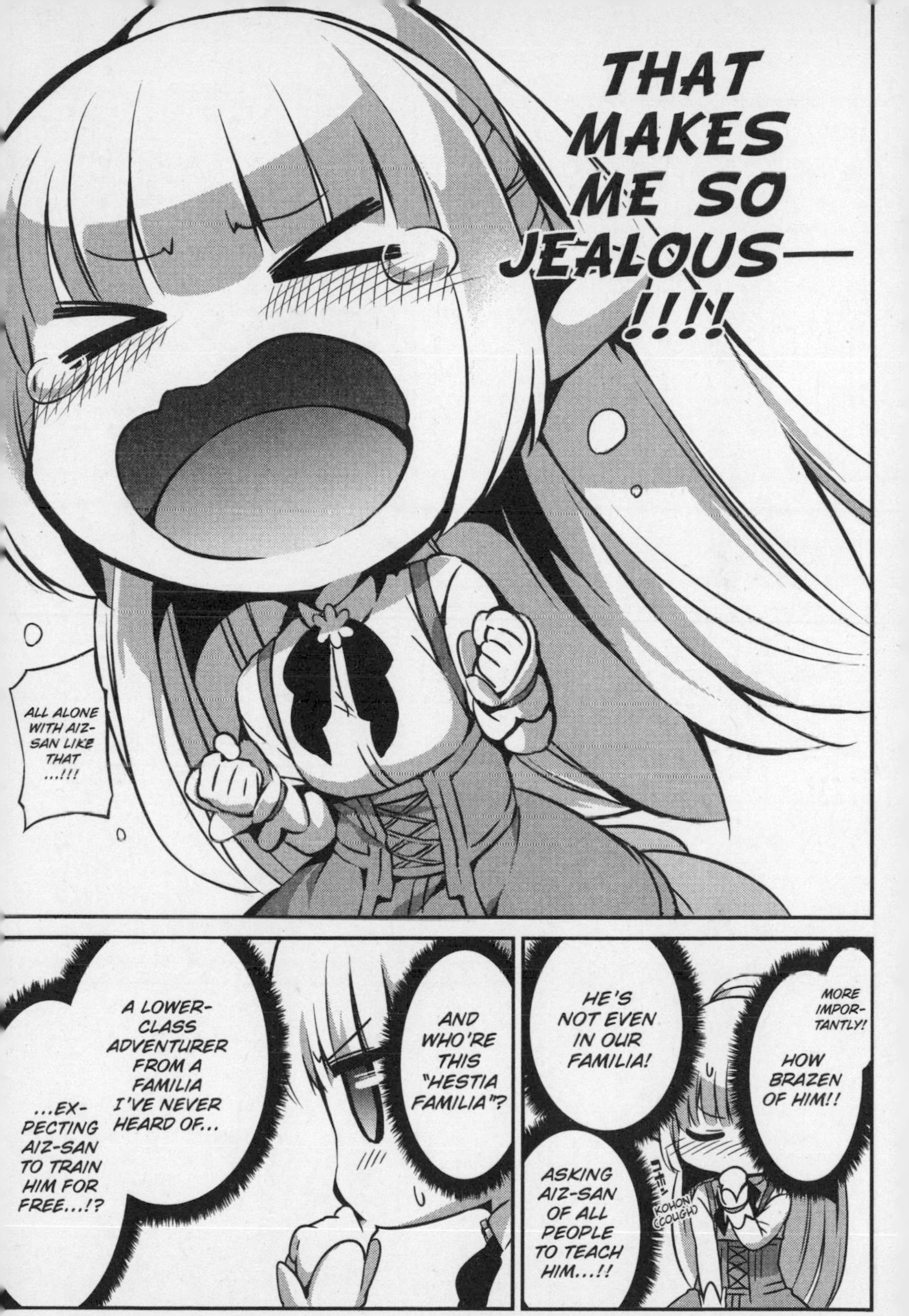
THAT MAKES ME SO JEALOUS—!!!!
ALL ALONE WITH AIZ-SAN LIKE THAT ...!!!
MORE IMPORTANTLY!
HOW BRAZEN OF HIM!!
HE'S NOT EVEN IN OUR FAMILIA!
KOHON (COUGH)
ASKING AIZ-SAN OF ALL PEOPLE TO TEACH HIM...!!
AND WHO'RE THIS "HESTIA FAMILIA"?
A LOWER-CLASS ADVENTURER FROM A FAMILIA I'VE NEVER HEARD OF...
...EXPECTING AIZ-SAN TO TRAIN HIM FOR FREE...!?

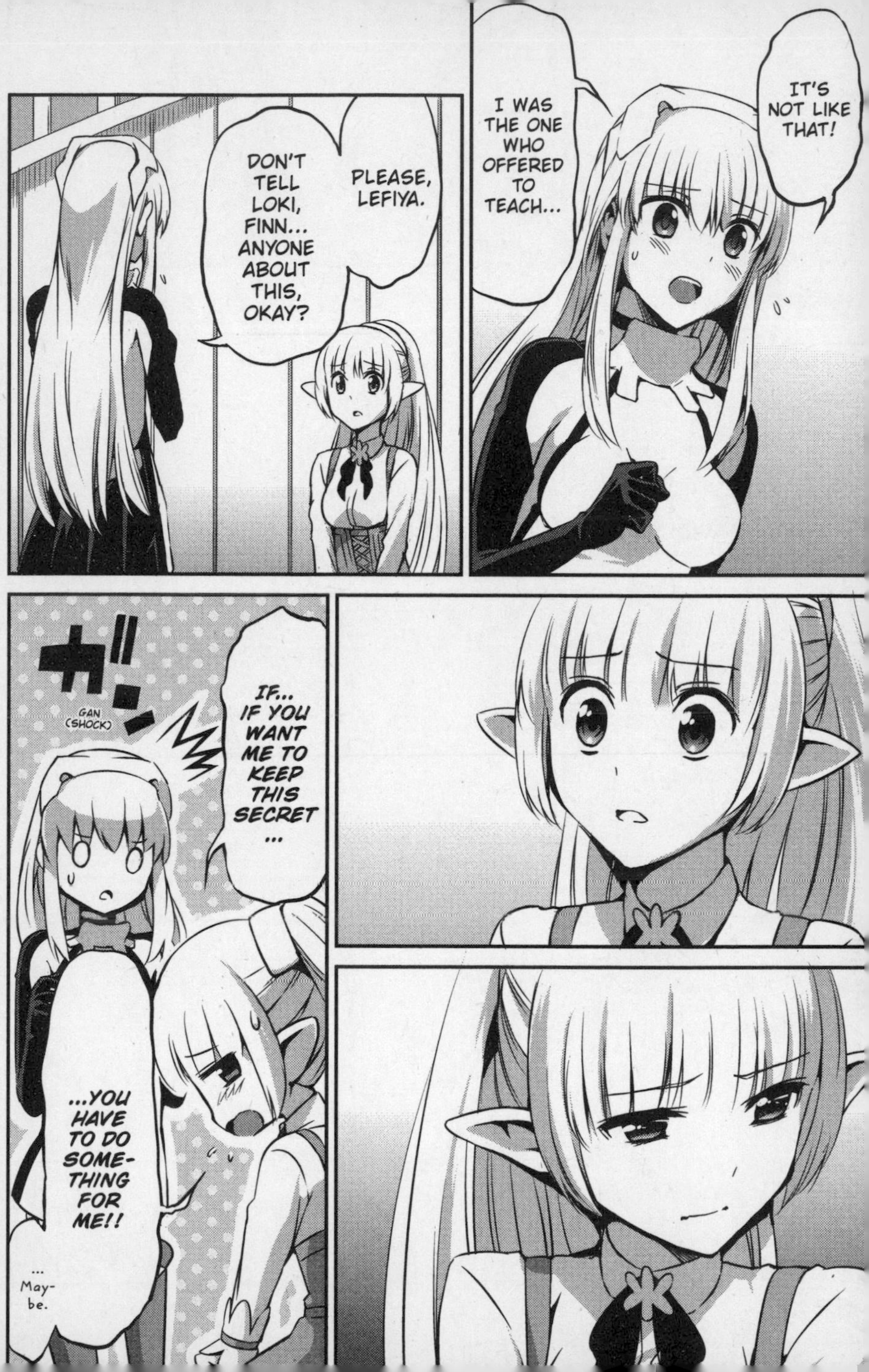
IT'S NOT LIKE THAT!
I WAS THE ONE WHO OFFERED TO TEACH...
PLEASE, LEFIYA.
DON'T TELL LOKI, FINN... ANYONE ABOUT THIS, OKAY?
IF... IF YOU WANT ME TO KEEP THIS SECRET ...
GAN (SHOCK)
...YOU HAVE TO DO SOME-THING FOR ME!!
... May-be.

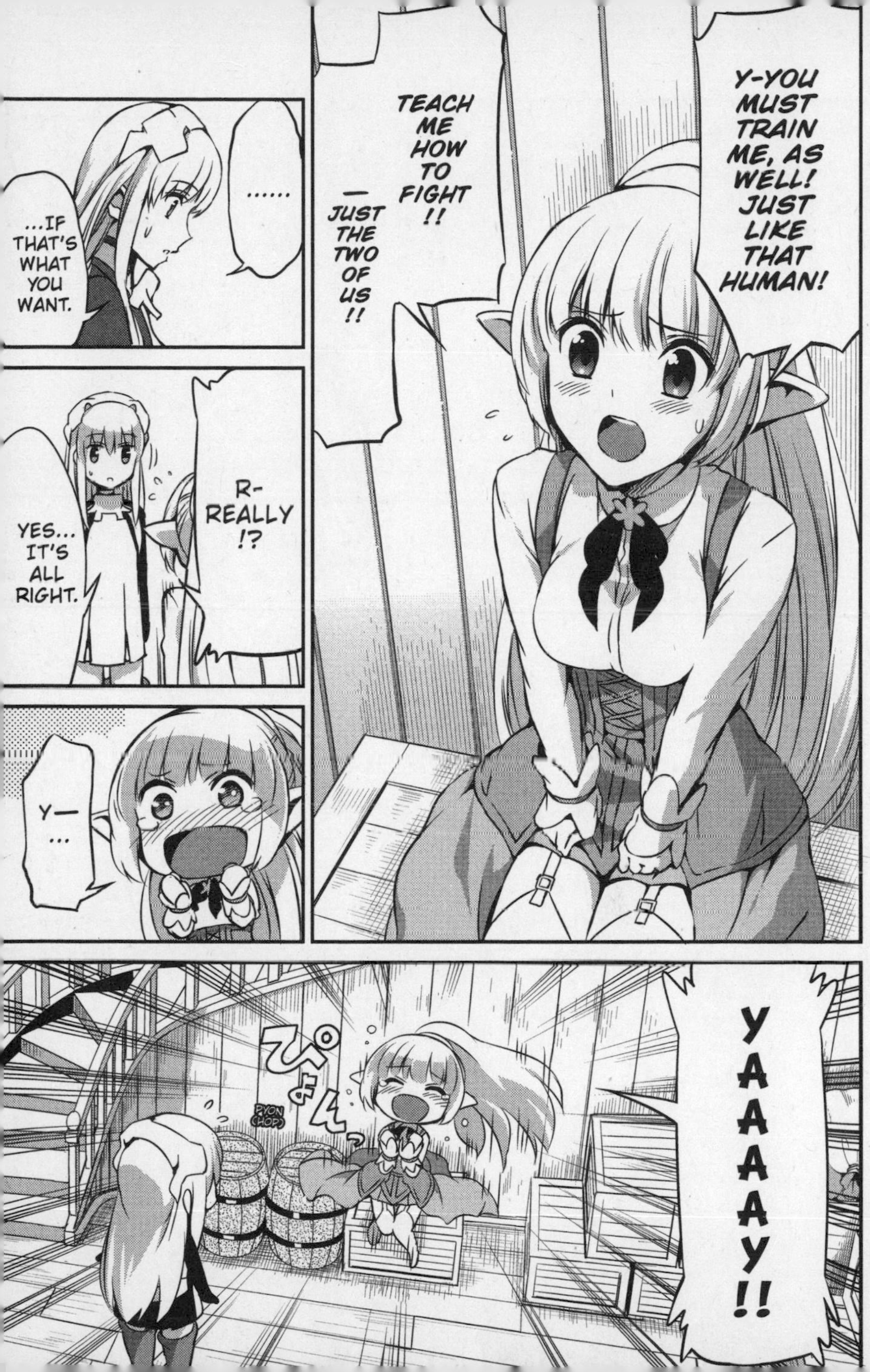
Y-YOU MUST TRAIN ME, AS WELL! JUST LIKE THAT HUMAN!
TEACH ME HOW TO FIGHT!!
—JUST THE TWO OF US!!
......
...IF THAT'S WHAT YOU WANT.
R-REALLY!?
YES... IT'S ALL RIGHT.
Y— ...
YAAAAAY!!
ぴょんっ
PYON (HOP)

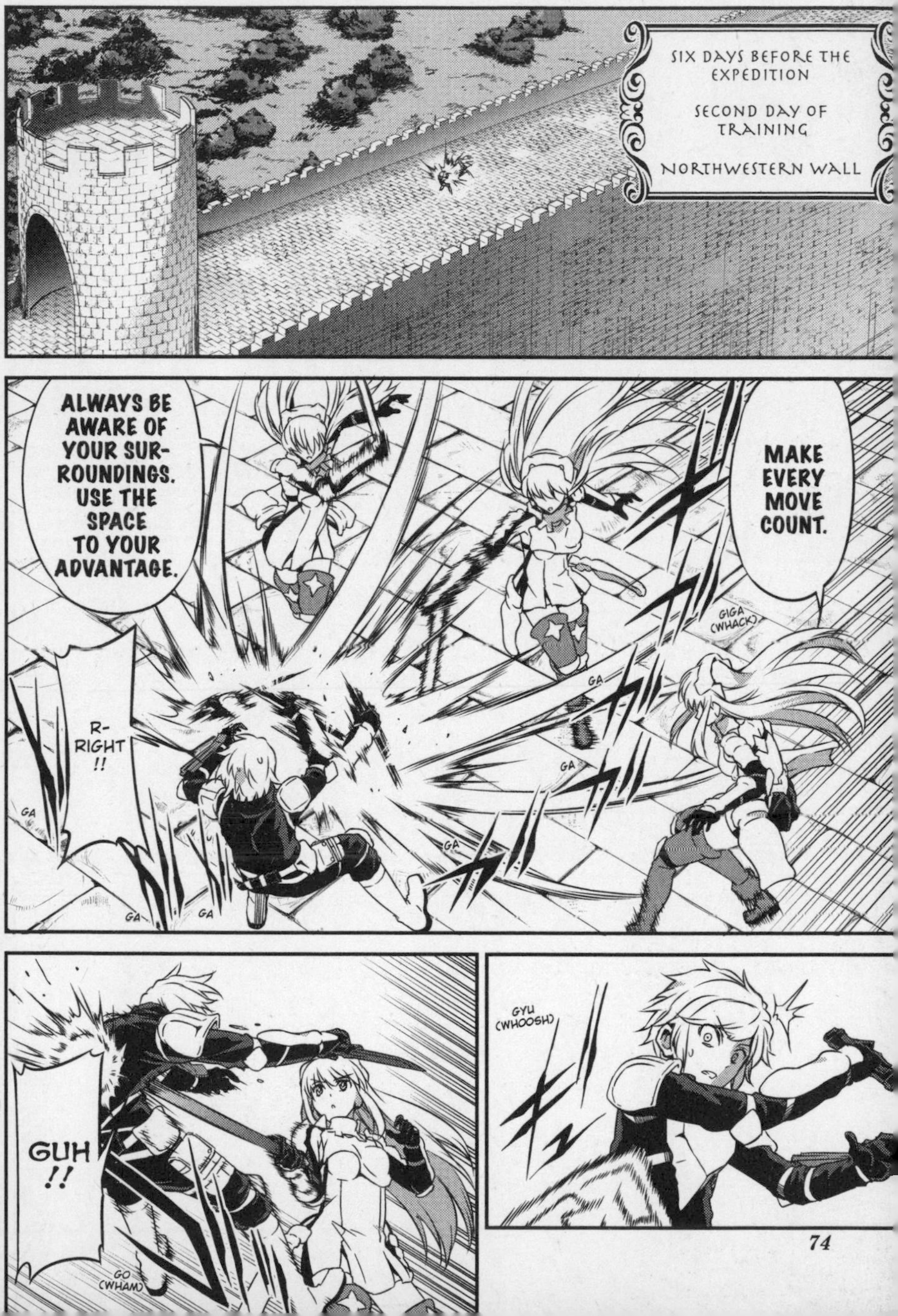

SIX DAYS BEFORE THE EXPEDITION
SECOND DAY OF TRAINING
NORTHWESTERN WALL
MAKE EVERY MOVE COUNT.
GIGA (WHACK)
ALWAYS BE AWARE OF YOUR SURROUNDINGS. USE THE SPACE TO YOUR ADVANTAGE.
GA
GA
R-RIGHT!!
GA
GA
GA
GA
GYU (WHOOSH)
GUH!!
GO (WHAM)

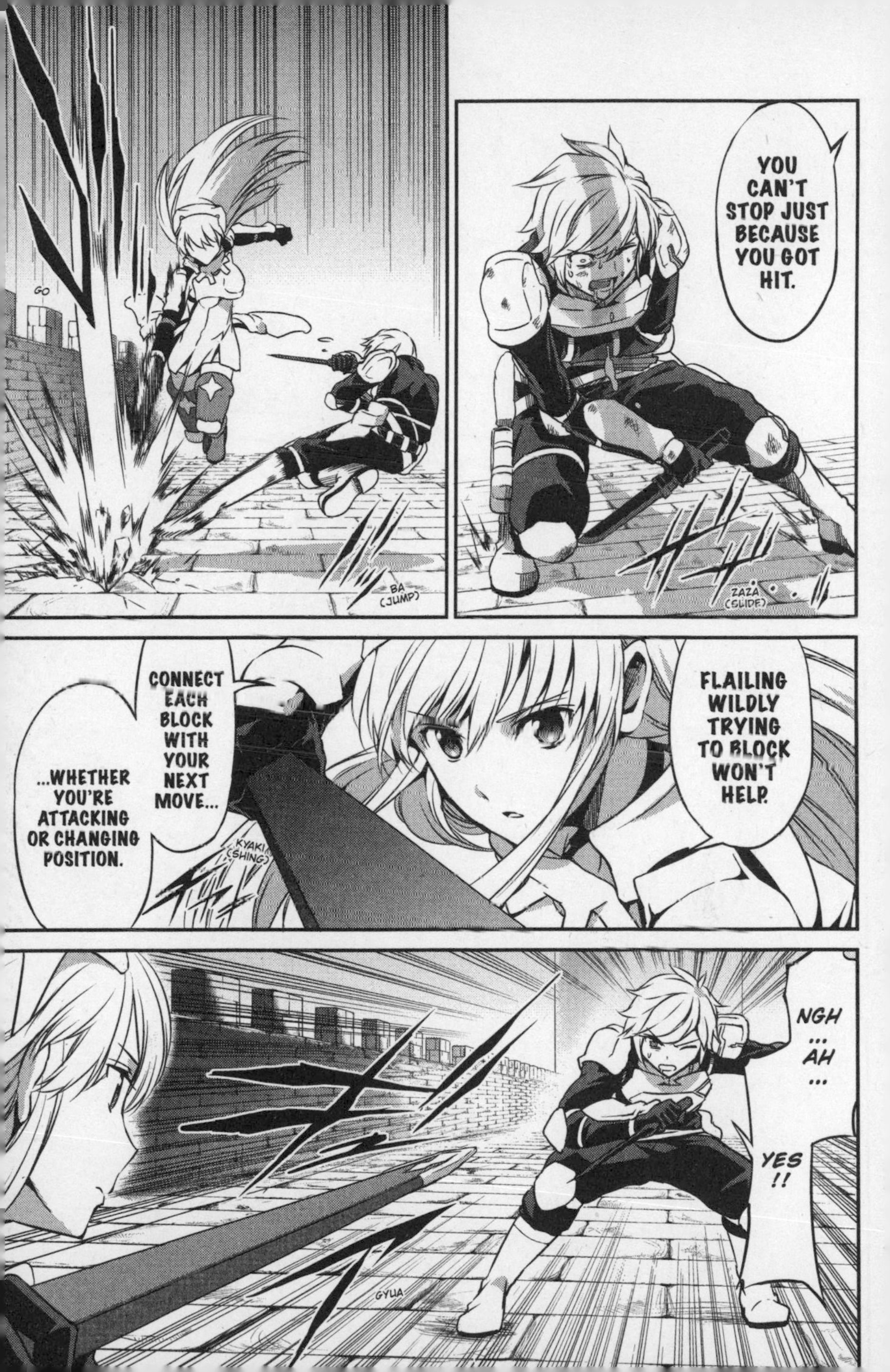
YOU CAN'T STOP JUST BECAUSE YOU GOT HIT.
ZAZA (SLIDE)
GO
BA (JUMP)
FLAILING WILDLY TRYING TO BLOCK WON'T HELP.
CONNECT EACH BLOCK WITH YOUR NEXT MOVE...
...WHETHER YOU'RE ATTACKING OR CHANGING POSITION.
KYAKI (SHING)
NGH... AH...
YES!!
GYUA

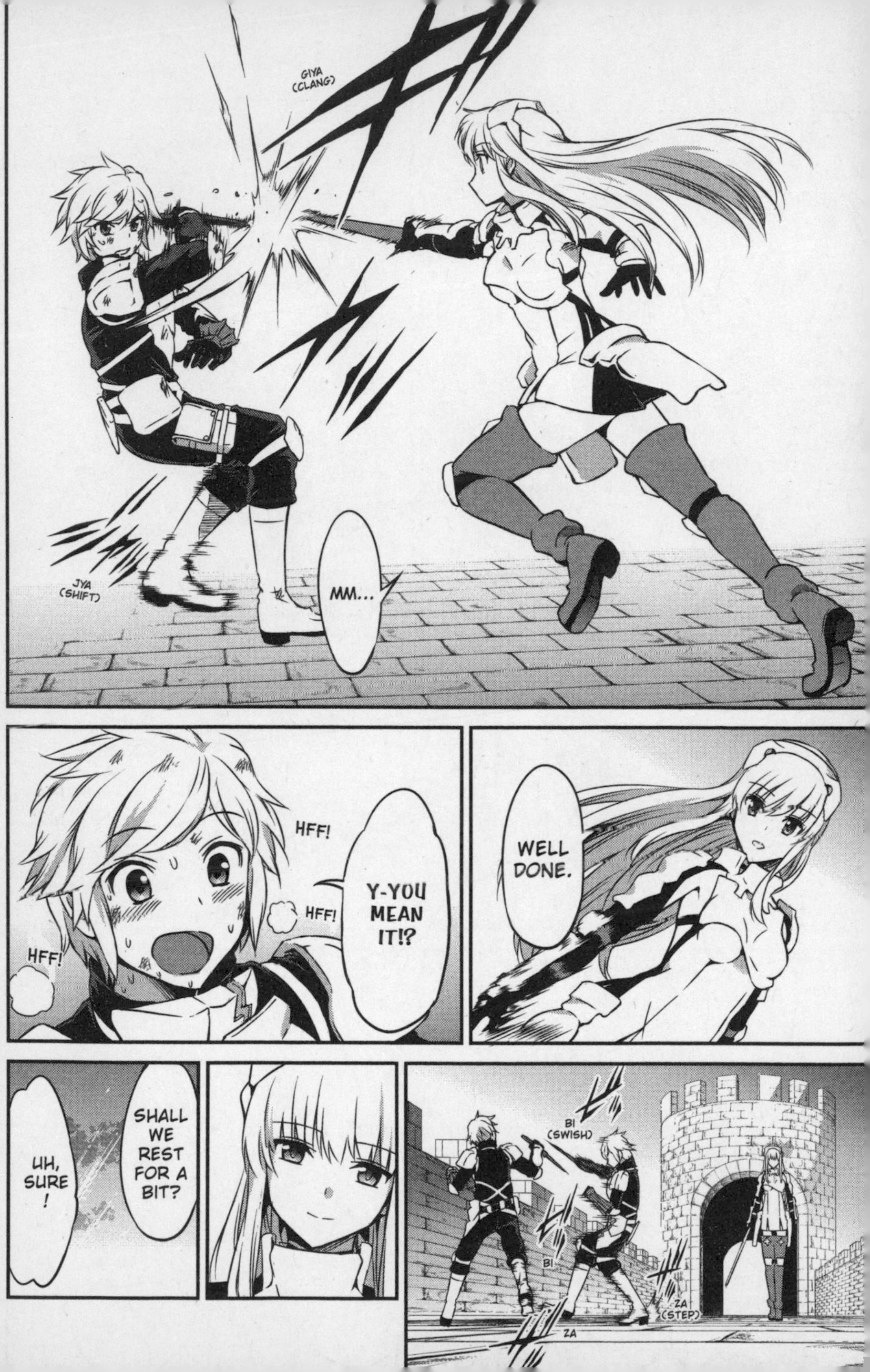
GIYA (CLANG)
MM...
JYA (SHIFT)
WELL DONE.
HFF!
Y-YOU MEAN IT!?
HFF!
HFF!
BI (SWISH)
BI
ZA (STEP)
ZA
SHALL WE REST FOR A BIT?
UH, SURE!

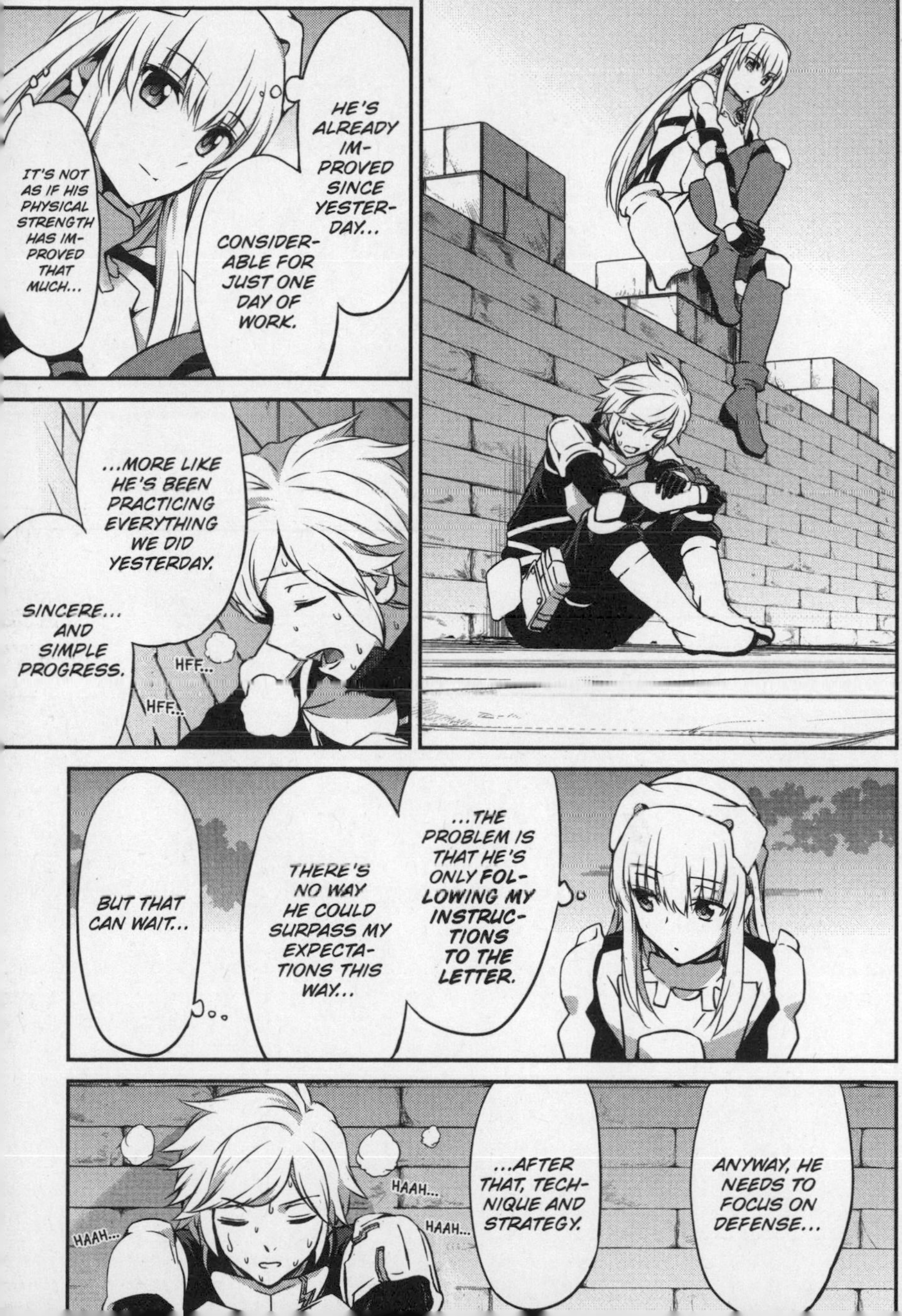
HE'S ALREADY IM-PROVED SINCE YESTER-DAY...
CONSIDER-ABLE FOR JUST ONE DAY OF WORK.
IT'S NOT AS IF HIS PHYSICAL STRENGTH HAS IM-PROVED THAT MUCH...
...MORE LIKE HE'S BEEN PRACTICING EVERYTHING WE DID YESTERDAY.
SINCERE... AND SIMPLE PROGRESS.
HFF...
HFF...
...THE PROBLEM IS THAT HE'S ONLY FOL-LOWING MY INSTRUC-TIONS TO THE LETTER.
THERE'S NO WAY HE COULD SURPASS MY EXPECTA-TIONS THIS WAY...
BUT THAT CAN WAIT...
ANYWAY, HE NEEDS TO FOCUS ON DEFENSE...
...AFTER THAT, TECH-NIQUE AND STRATEGY.
HAAH...
HAAH...
HAAH...

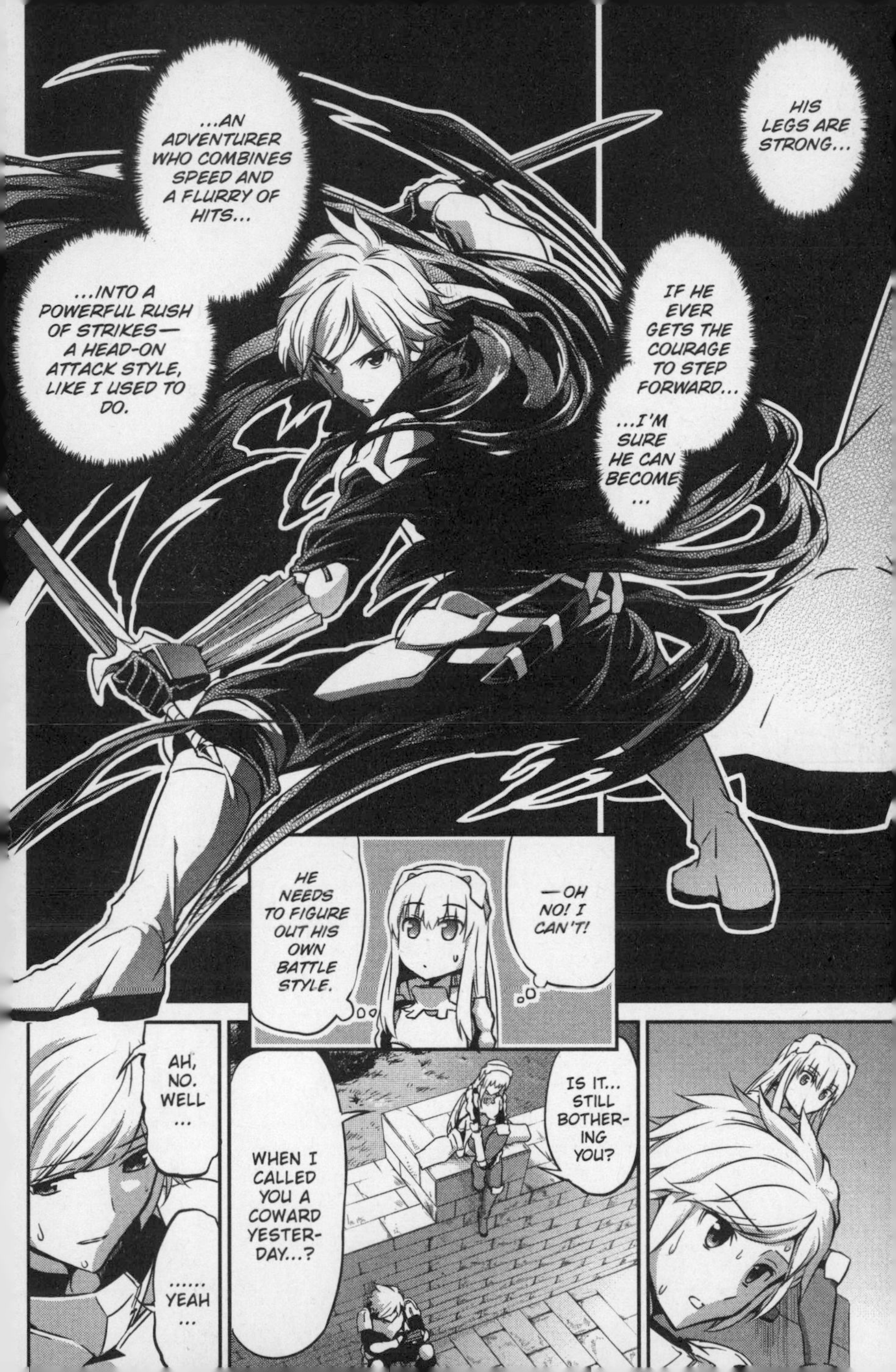
HIS LEGS ARE STRONG...
IF HE EVER GETS THE COURAGE TO STEP FORWARD...
...I'M SURE HE CAN BECOME...
...AN ADVENTURER WHO COMBINES SPEED AND A FLURRY OF HITS...
...INTO A POWERFUL RUSH OF STRIKES—A HEAD-ON ATTACK STYLE, LIKE I USED TO DO.
—OH NO! I CAN'T!
HE NEEDS TO FIGURE OUT HIS OWN BATTLE STYLE.
IS IT... STILL BOTHERING YOU?
WHEN I CALLED YOU A COWARD YESTERDAY...?
AH, NO. WELL...
......YEAH...

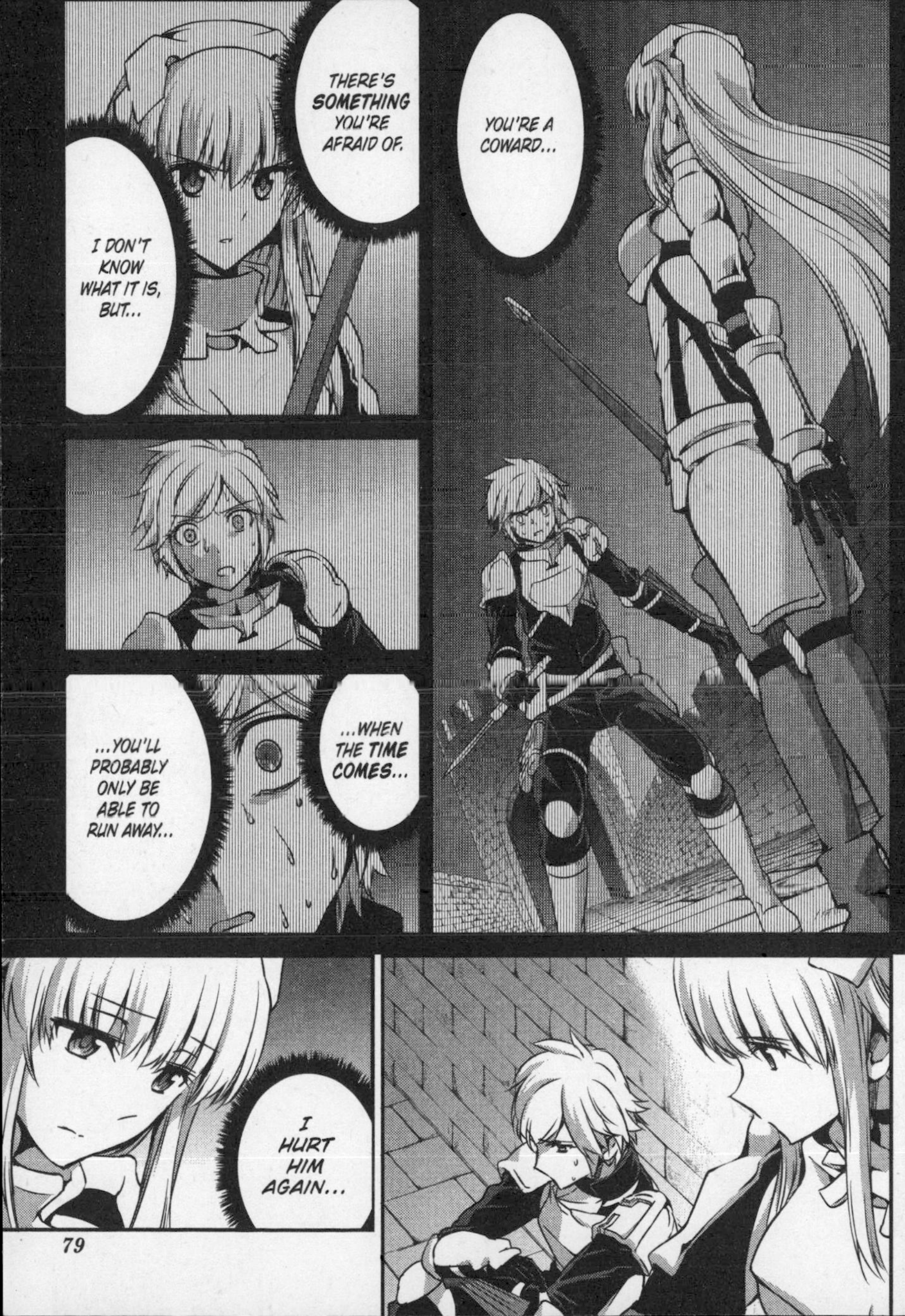
YOU'RE A COWARD...
THERE'S SOMETHING YOU'RE AFRAID OF.
I DON'T KNOW WHAT IT IS, BUT...
...WHEN THE TIME COMES...
...YOU'LL PROBABLY ONLY BE ABLE TO RUN AWAY...
I HURT HIM AGAIN...

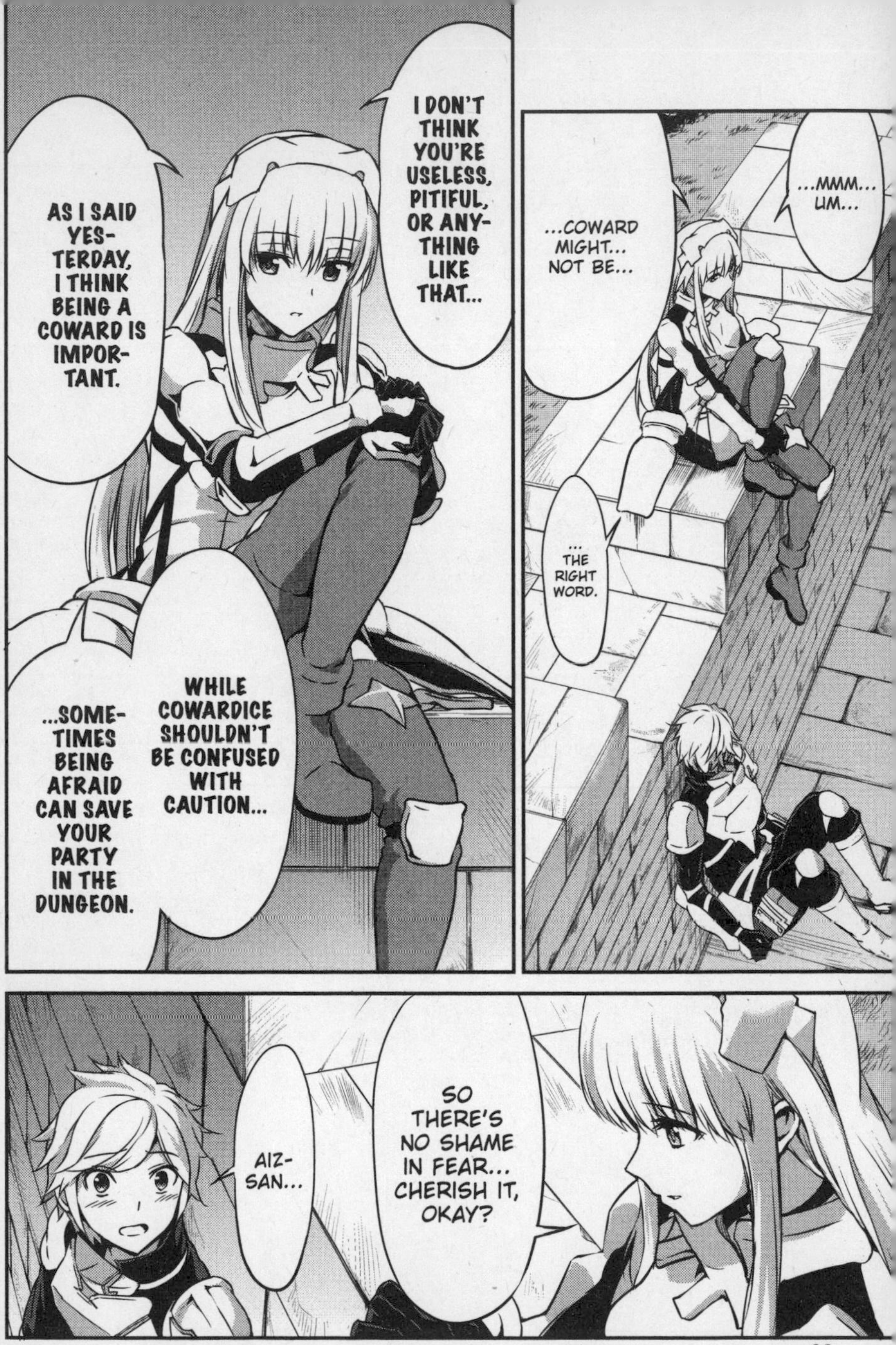
...MMM... UM...
...COWARD MIGHT... NOT BE...
... THE RIGHT WORD.
I DON'T THINK YOU'RE USELESS, PITIFUL, OR ANYTHING LIKE THAT...
AS I SAID YESTERDAY, I THINK BEING A COWARD IS IMPORTANT.
WHILE COWARDICE SHOULDN'T BE CONFUSED WITH CAUTION...
...SOMETIMES BEING AFRAID CAN SAVE YOUR PARTY IN THE DUNGEON.
SO THERE'S NO SHAME IN FEAR... CHERISH IT, OKAY?
AIZ-SAN...

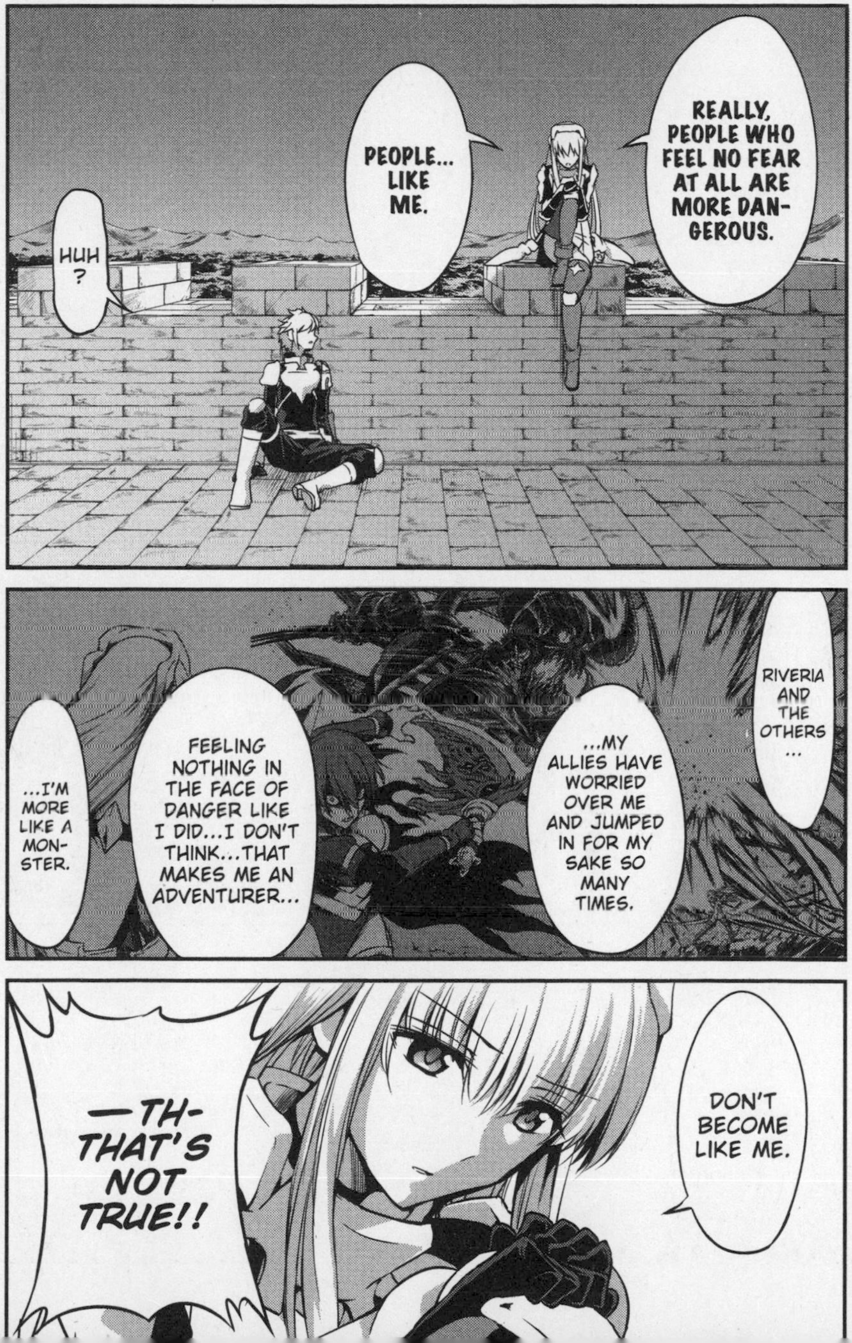
REALLY, PEOPLE WHO FEEL NO FEAR AT ALL ARE MORE DANGEROUS.
PEOPLE... LIKE ME.
HUH?
RIVERIA AND THE OTHERS...
...MY ALLIES HAVE WORRIED OVER ME AND JUMPED IN FOR MY SAKE SO MANY TIMES.
FEELING NOTHING IN THE FACE OF DANGER LIKE I DID...I DON'T THINK...THAT MAKES ME AN ADVENTURER...
...I'M MORE LIKE A MONSTER.
DON'T BECOME LIKE ME.
—TH-THAT'S NOT TRUE!!

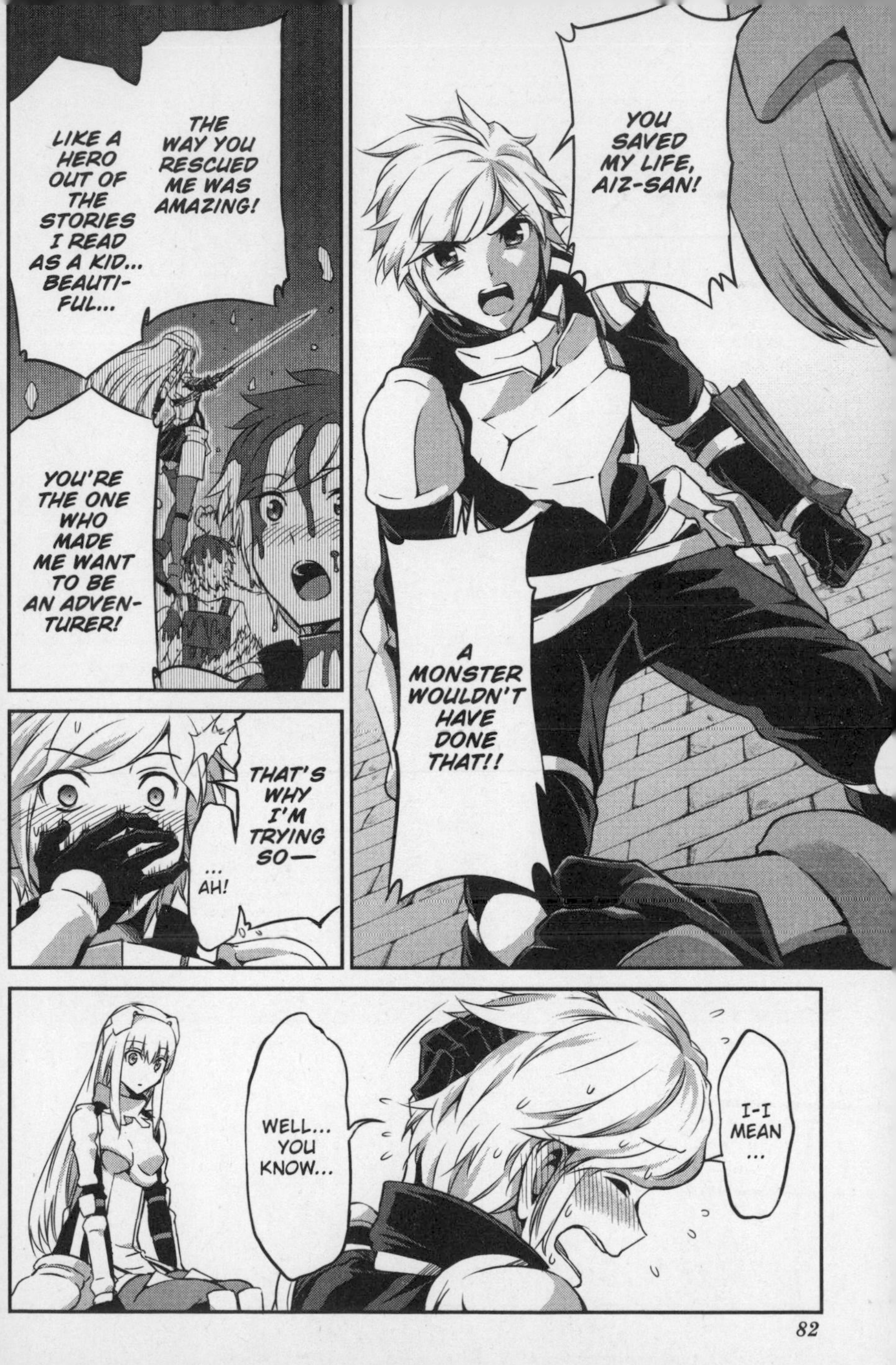
YOU SAVED MY LIFE, AIZ-SAN!
A MONSTER WOULDN'T HAVE DONE THAT!!
THE WAY YOU RESCUED ME WAS AMAZING!
LIKE A HERO OUT OF THE STORIES I READ AS A KID... BEAUTI-FUL...
YOU'RE THE ONE WHO MADE ME WANT TO BE AN ADVEN-TURER!
THAT'S WHY I'M TRYING SO—
...AH!
I-I MEAN...
WELL... YOU KNOW...

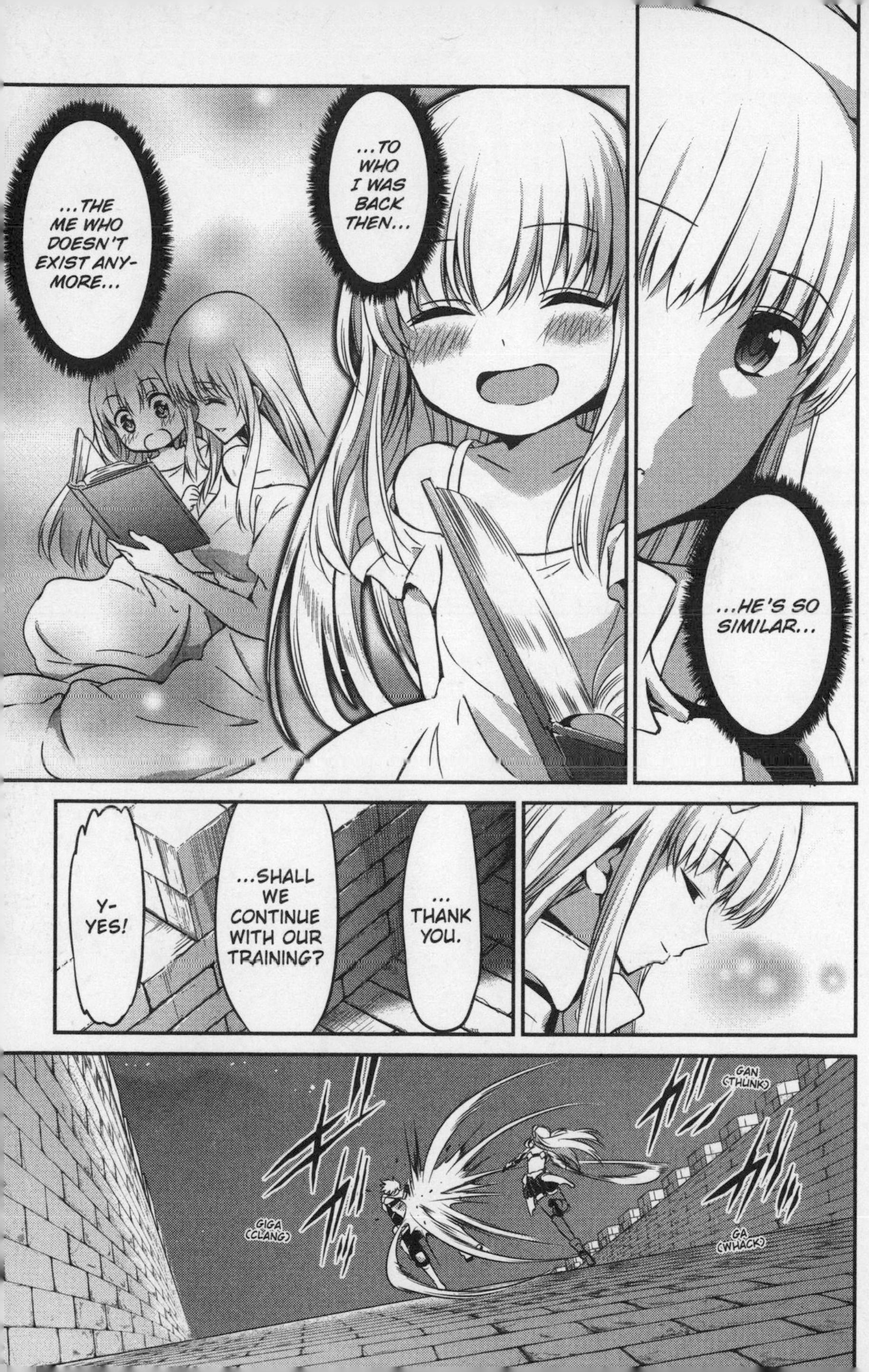
...HE'S SO SIMILAR...
...TO WHO I WAS BACK THEN...
...THE ME WHO DOESN'T EXIST ANYMORE...
...THANK YOU.
...SHALL WE CONTINUE WITH OUR TRAINING?
Y-YES!
GAN (THUNK)
GA (WHACK)
GIGA (CLANG)

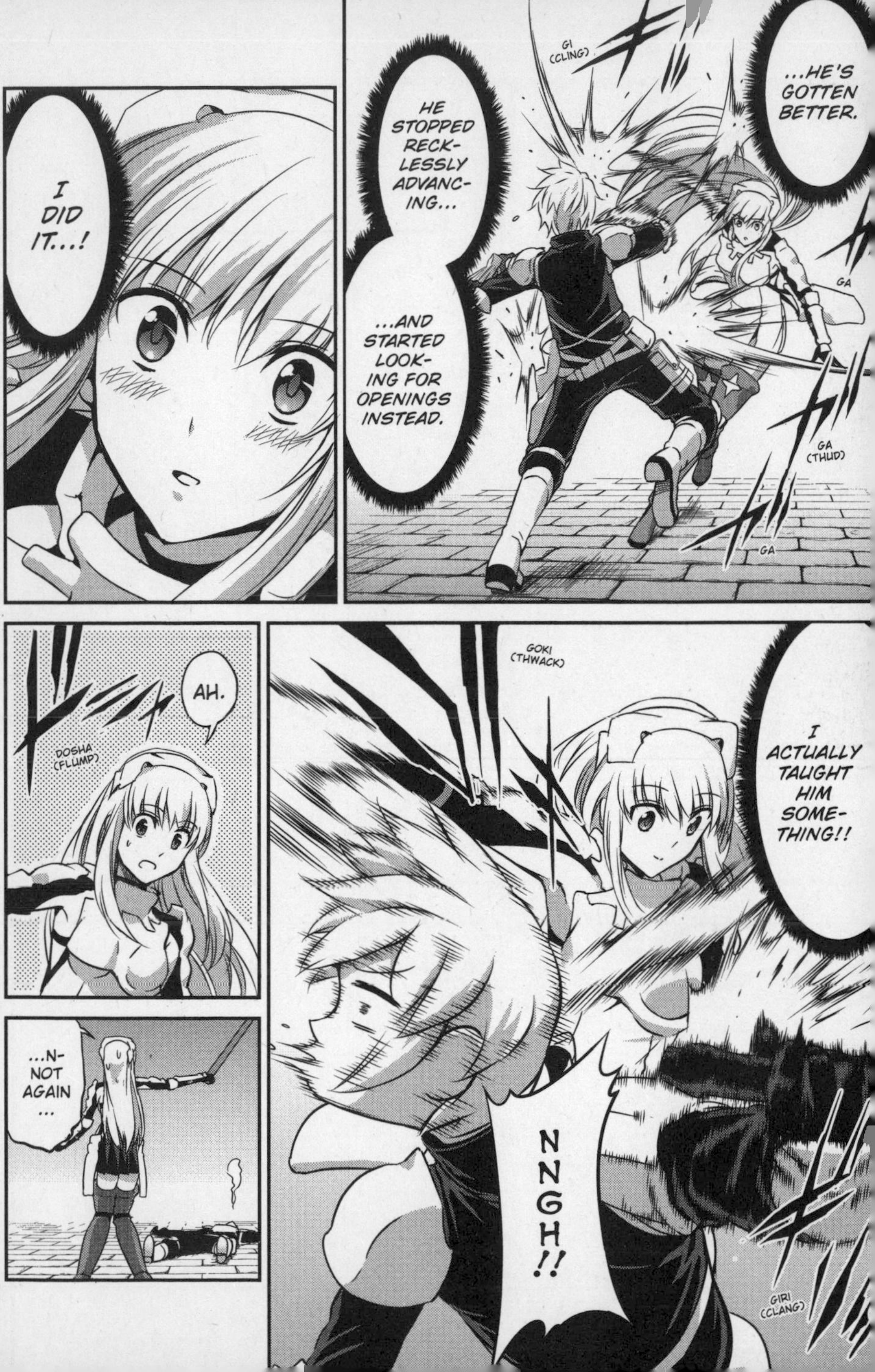
...HE'S GOTTEN BETTER.
GI (CLING)
HE STOPPED RECK-LESSLY ADVANC-ING...
...AND STARTED LOOK-ING FOR OPENINGS INSTEAD.
GA
GA (THUD)
GA
I DID IT...!
I ACTUALLY TAUGHT HIM SOME-THING!!
GOKI (THWACK)
NNGH!!
GIRI (CLANG)
AH.
DOSHA (FLUMP)
...N-NOT AGAIN ...

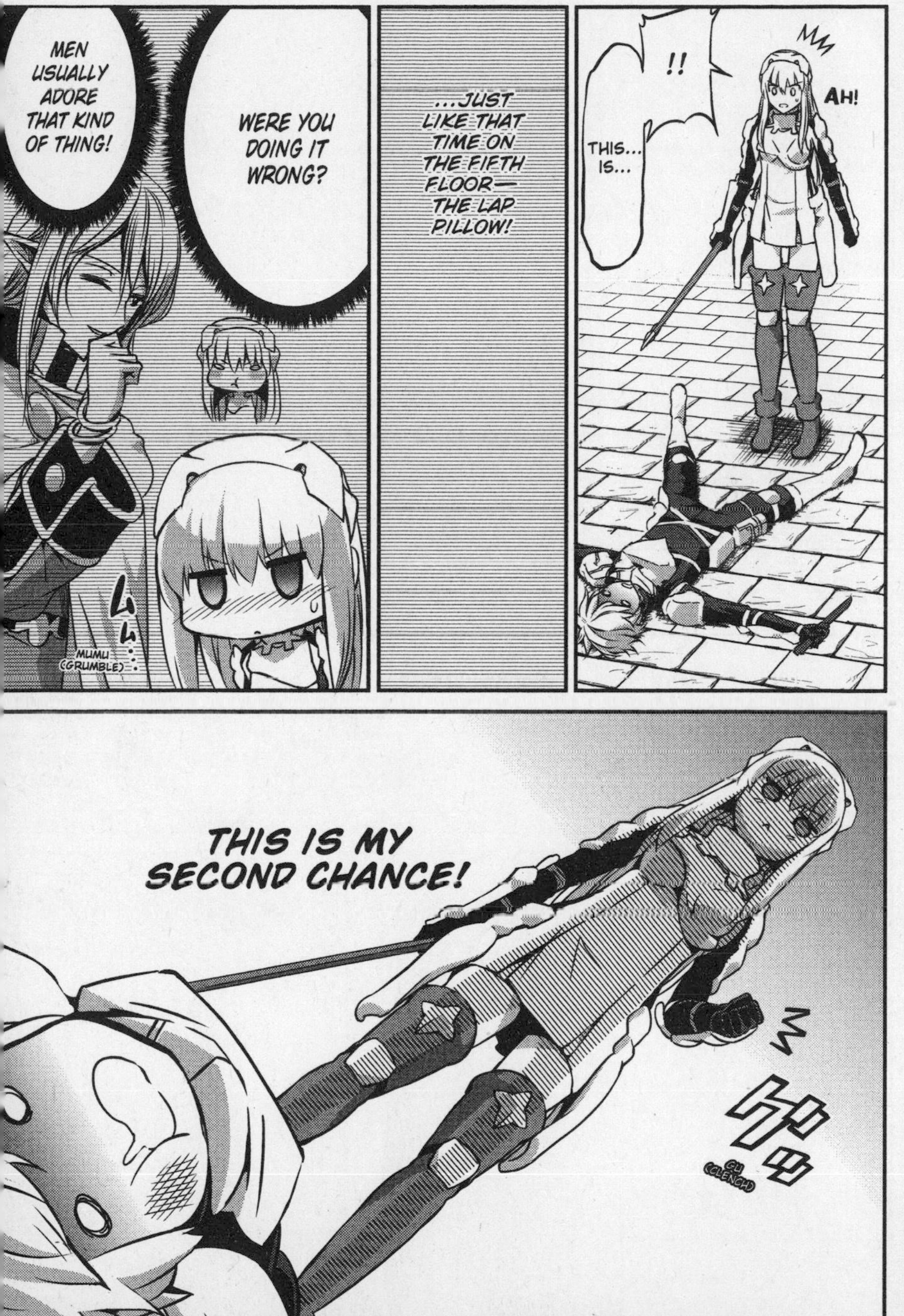
!!
AH!
THIS... IS...
...JUST LIKE THAT TIME ON THE FIFTH FLOOR—THE LAP PILLOW!
WERE YOU DOING IT WRONG?
MEN USUALLY ADORE THAT KIND OF THING!
MUMU (GRUMBLE)
THIS IS MY SECOND CHANCE!
GU (CLENCH)

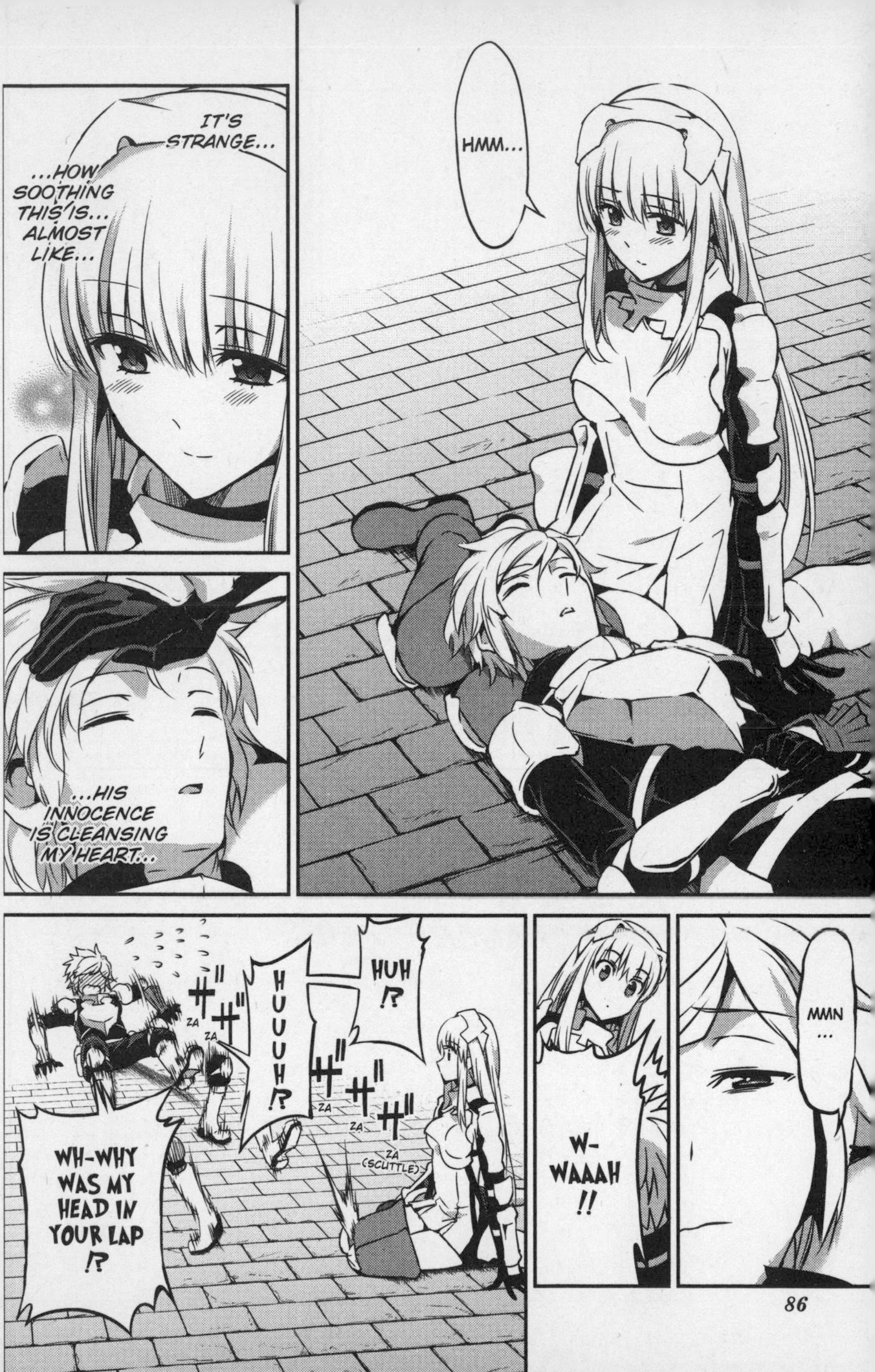
HMM...
IT'S STRANGE...
...HOW SOOTHING THIS IS... ALMOST LIKE...
...HIS INNOCENCE IS CLEANSING MY HEART...
MMN...
W-WAAAH!!
HUH!?
HUUUH!?
ザ" ZA
ザ" ZA
ザ" ZA
ザ" ZA
ザ" ZA (SCUTTLE)
WH-WHY WAS MY HEAD IN YOUR LAP!?

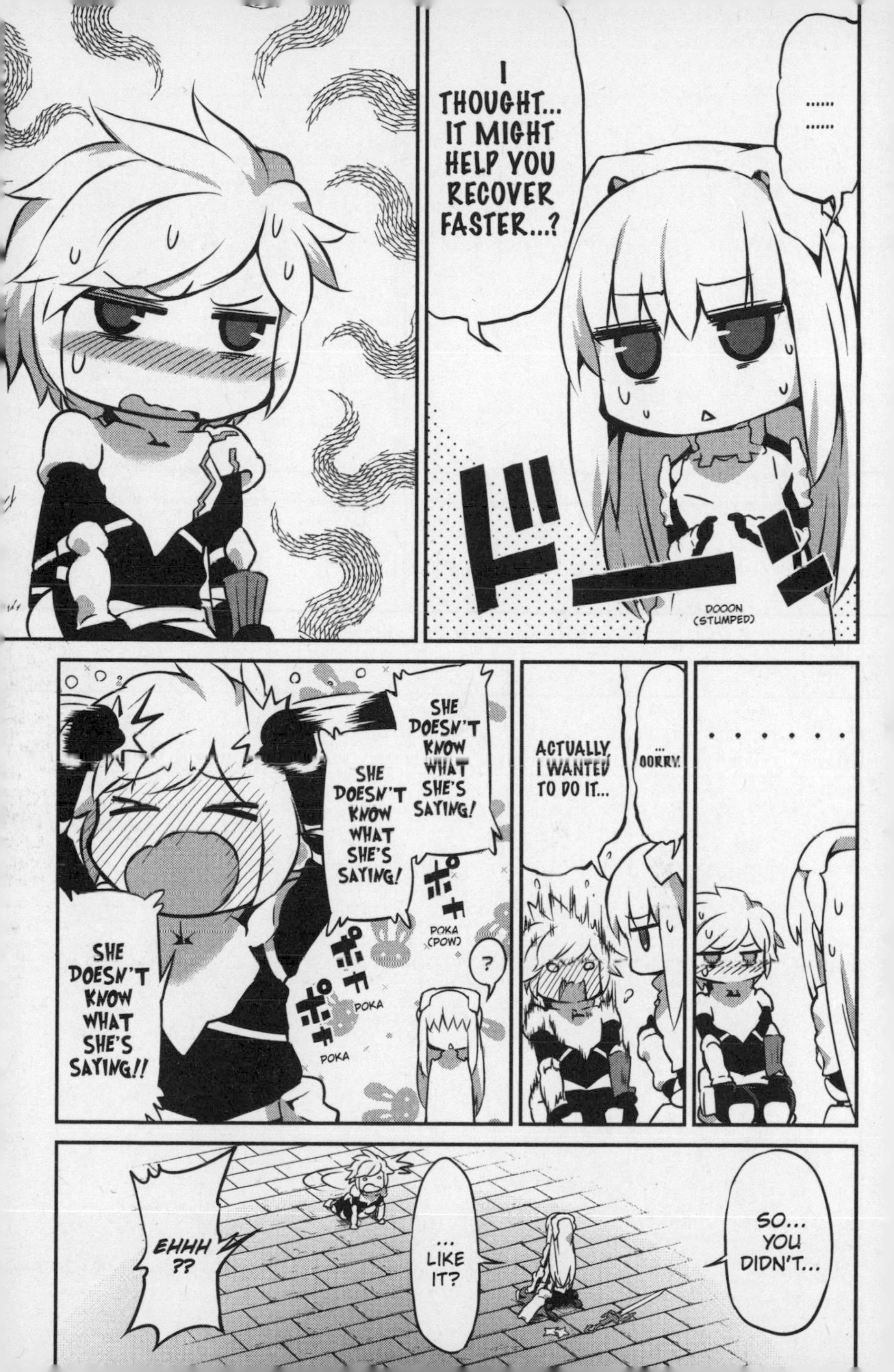
......
......
I THOUGHT... IT MIGHT HELP YOU RECOVER FASTER...?
ドーン
DOOON (STUMPED)
• • • • • •
... SORRY.
ACTUALLY, I WANTED TO DO IT...
SHE DOESN'T KNOW WHAT SHE'S SAYING!
SHE DOESN'T KNOW WHAT SHE'S SAYING!
ポカ
POKA (POW)
?
ポカ
POKA
ポカ
POKA
SHE DOESN'T KNOW WHAT SHE'S SAYING!!
SO... YOU DIDN'T...
... LIKE IT?
EHHH ??

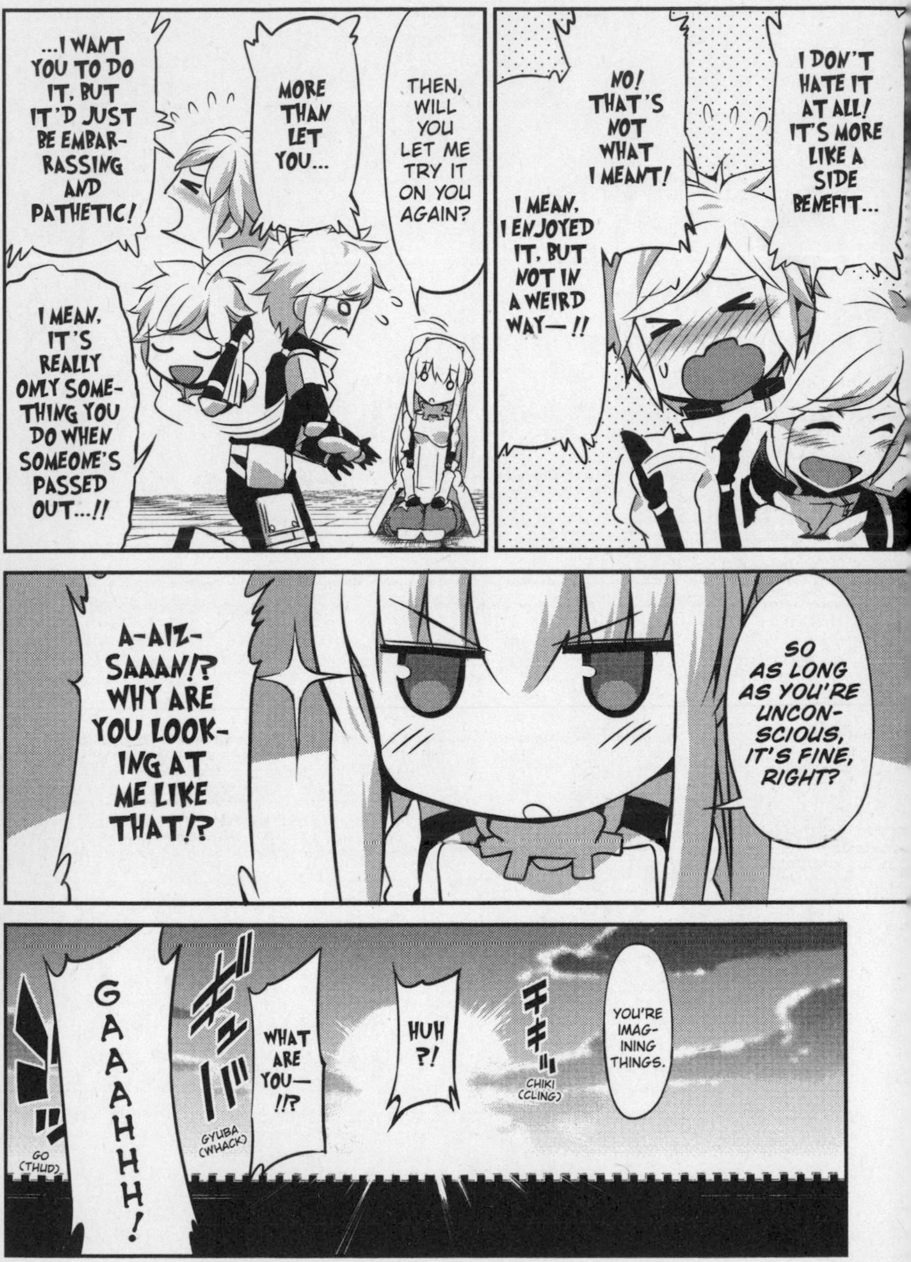
I DON'T HATE IT AT ALL! IT'S MORE LIKE A SIDE BENEFIT...
NO! THAT'S NOT WHAT I MEANT!
I MEAN, I ENJOYED IT, BUT NOT IN A WEIRD WAY—!!
THEN, WILL YOU LET ME TRY IT ON YOU AGAIN?
MORE THAN LET YOU...
...I WANT YOU TO DO IT, BUT IT'D JUST BE EMBARRASSING AND PATHETIC!
I MEAN, IT'S REALLY ONLY SOMETHING YOU DO WHEN SOMEONE'S PASSED OUT...!!
SO AS LONG AS YOU'RE UNCONSCIOUS, IT'S FINE, RIGHT?
A-AIZ-SAAAN!? WHY ARE YOU LOOKING AT ME LIKE THAT!?
YOU'RE IMAGINING THINGS.
CHIKI (CLING)
HUH?!
WHAT ARE YOU—!!?
GYUBA (WHACK)
GAAAHHH!
GO (THUD)

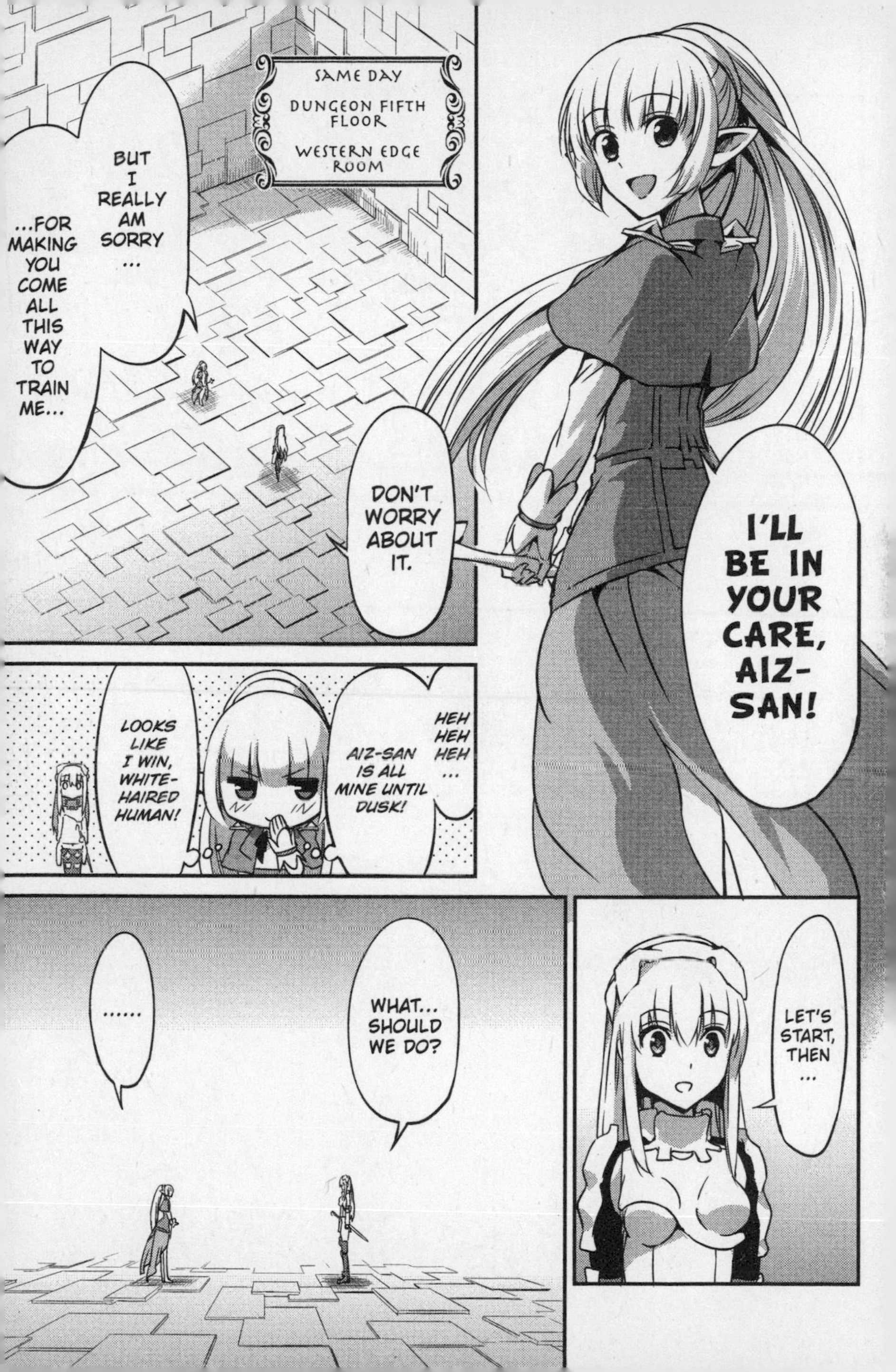
I'LL BE IN YOUR CARE, AIZ-SAN!
SAME DAY
DUNGEON FIFTH FLOOR
WESTERN EDGE ROOM
BUT I REALLY AM SORRY ...
...FOR MAKING YOU COME ALL THIS WAY TO TRAIN ME...
DON'T WORRY ABOUT IT.
HEH HEH HEH ...
AIZ-SAN IS ALL MINE UNTIL DUSK!
LOOKS LIKE I WIN, WHITE-HAIRED HUMAN!
LET'S START, THEN ...
WHAT... SHOULD WE DO?
......

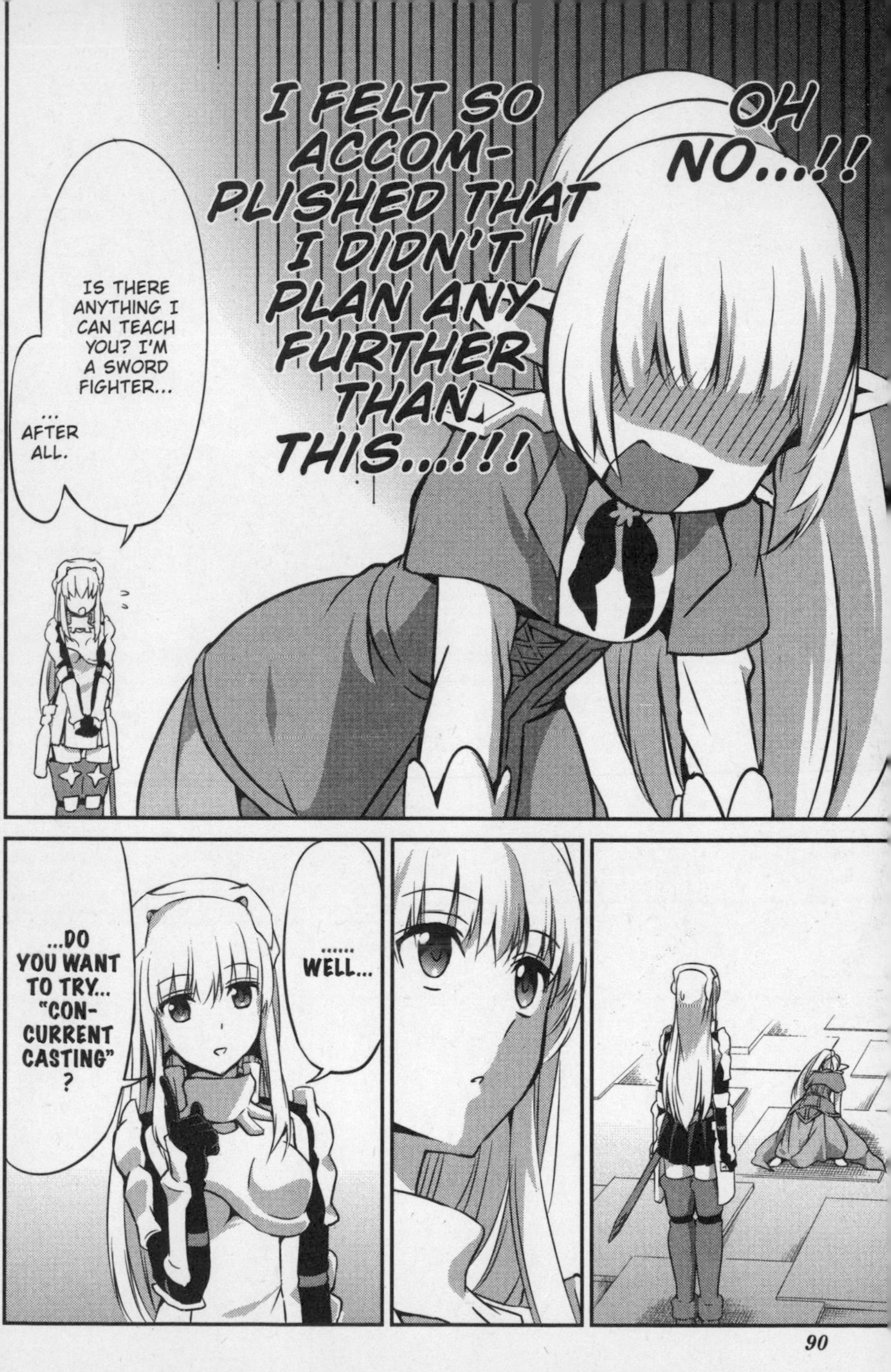
OH NO...!!
I FELT SO ACCOM-PLISHED THAT I DIDN'T PLAN ANY FURTHER THAN THIS...!!!
IS THERE ANYTHING I CAN TEACH YOU? I'M A SWORD FIGHTER...
...AFTER ALL.
......WELL...
...DO YOU WANT TO TRY... "CON-CURRENT CASTING" ?

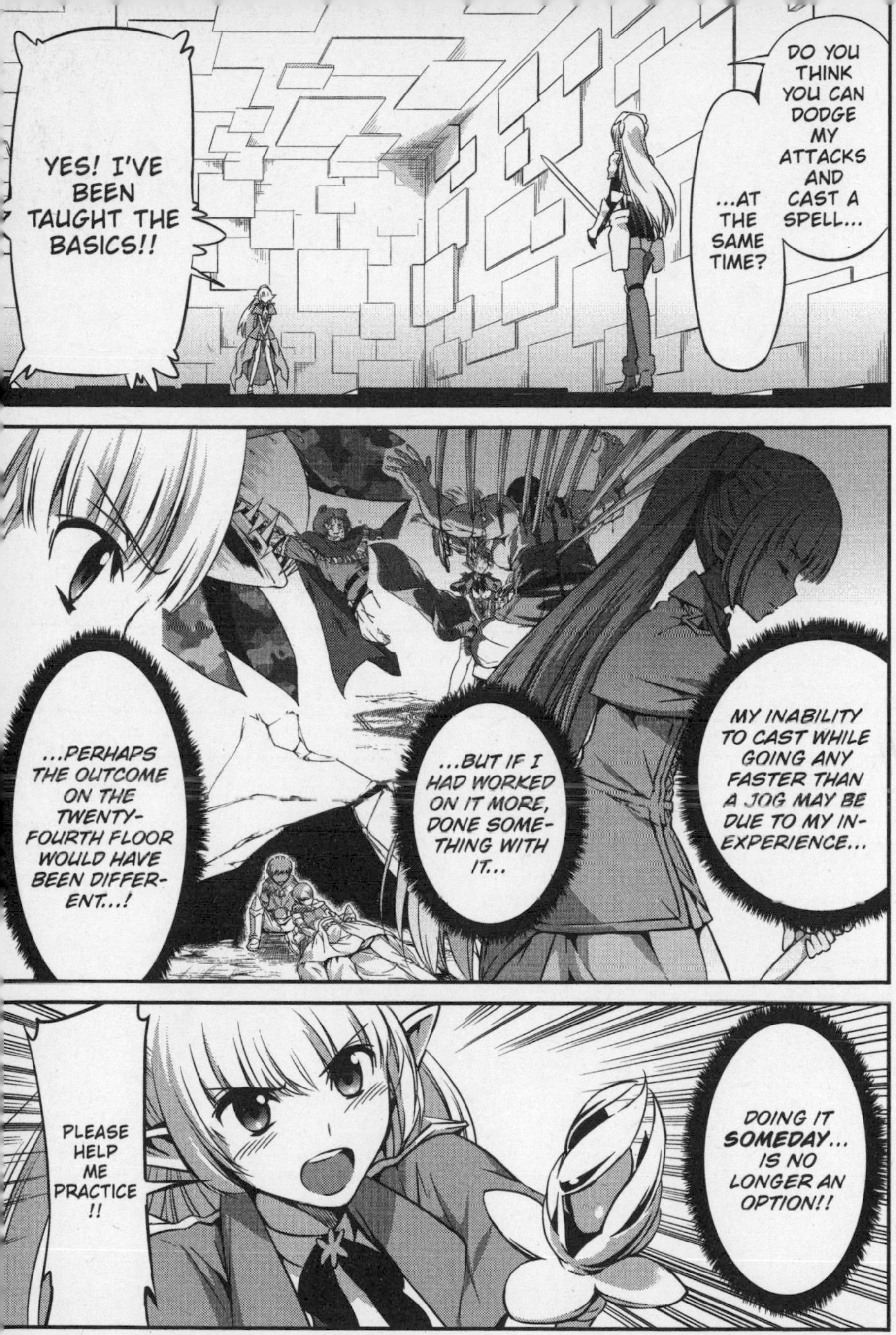
DO YOU THINK YOU CAN DODGE MY ATTACKS AND CAST A SPELL...
...AT THE SAME TIME?
YES! I'VE BEEN TAUGHT THE BASICS!!
MY INABILITY TO CAST WHILE GOING ANY FASTER THAN A JOG MAY BE DUE TO MY IN-EXPERIENCE...
...BUT IF I HAD WORKED ON IT MORE, DONE SOME-THING WITH IT...
...PERHAPS THE OUTCOME ON THE TWENTY-FOURTH FLOOR WOULD HAVE BEEN DIFFER-ENT...!
DOING IT SOMEDAY... IS NO LONGER AN OPTION!!
PLEASE HELP ME PRACTICE !!

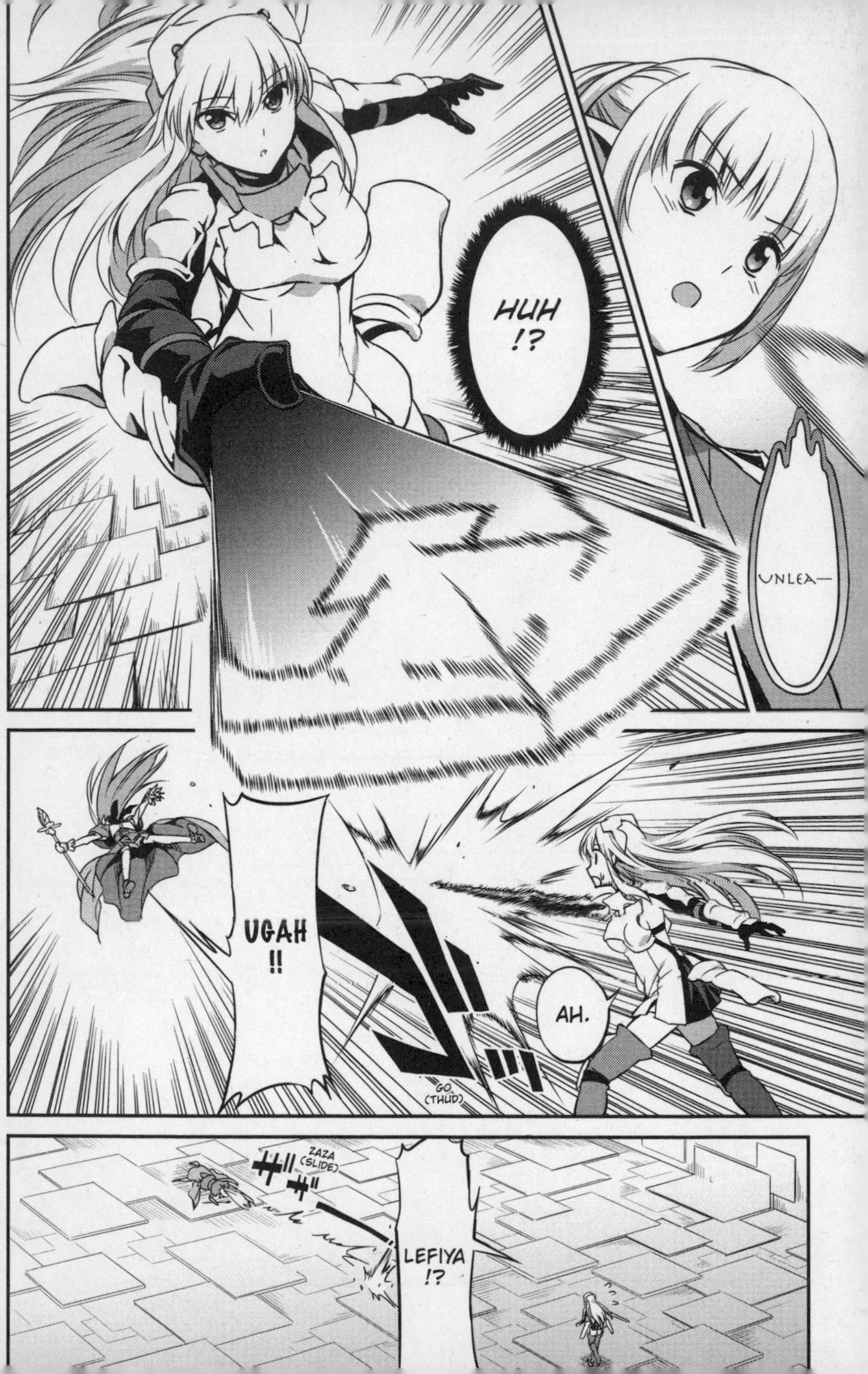
HUH !?
UNLEA—
UGAH !!
AH.
GO (THUD)
ZAZA (SLIDE)
LEFIYA !?

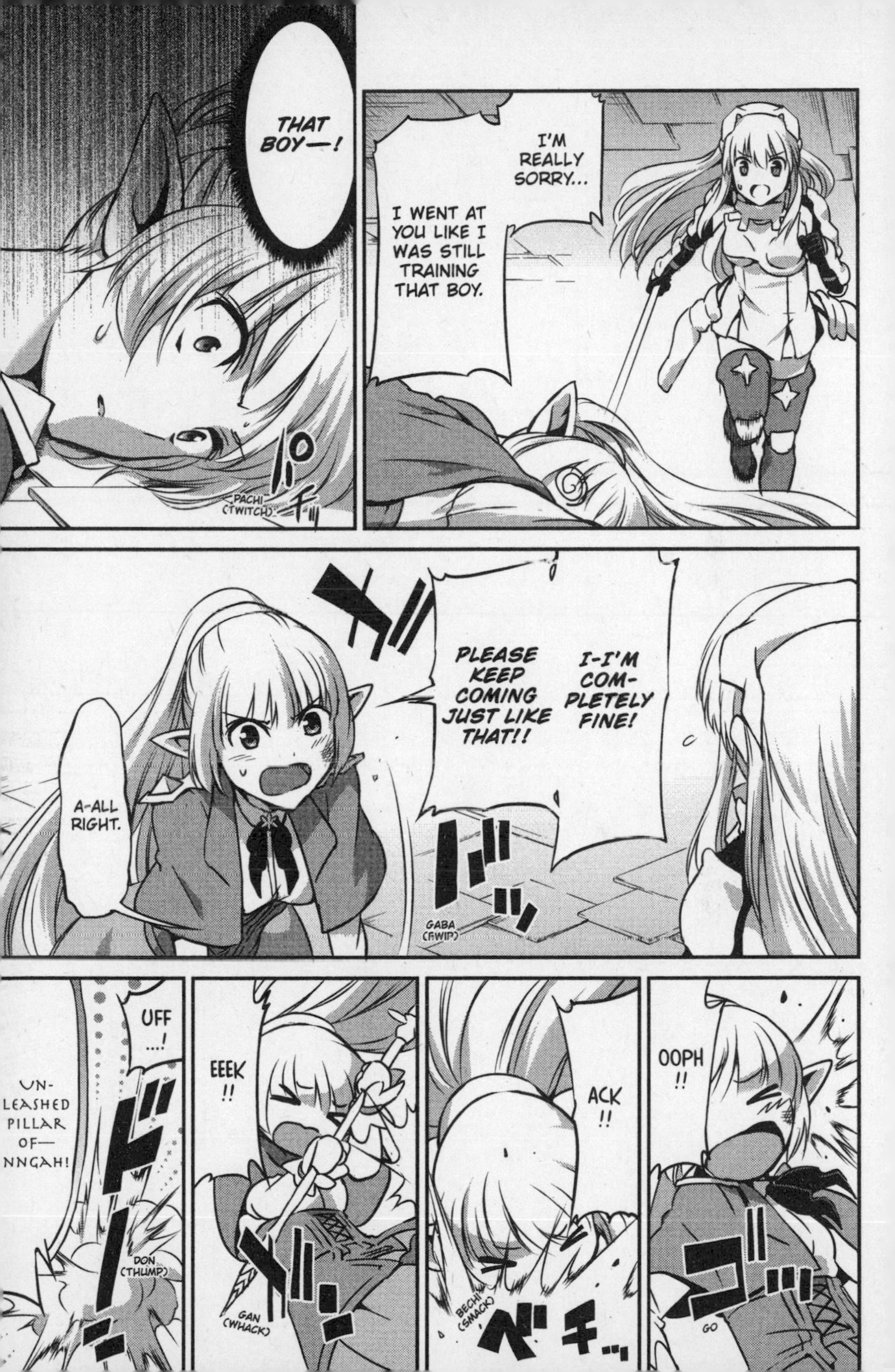

I'M REALLY SORRY...
I WENT AT YOU LIKE I WAS STILL TRAINING THAT BOY.
THAT BOY—!
PACHI (TWITCH)
I-I'M COM-PLETELY FINE!
PLEASE KEEP COMING JUST LIKE THAT!!
GABA (FWIP)
A-ALL RIGHT.
OOPH !!
GO
ACK !!
BECHI (SMACK)
EEEK !!
GAN (WHACK)
UFF ...!
UN-LEASHED PILLAR OF— NNGAH!
DON (THUMP)

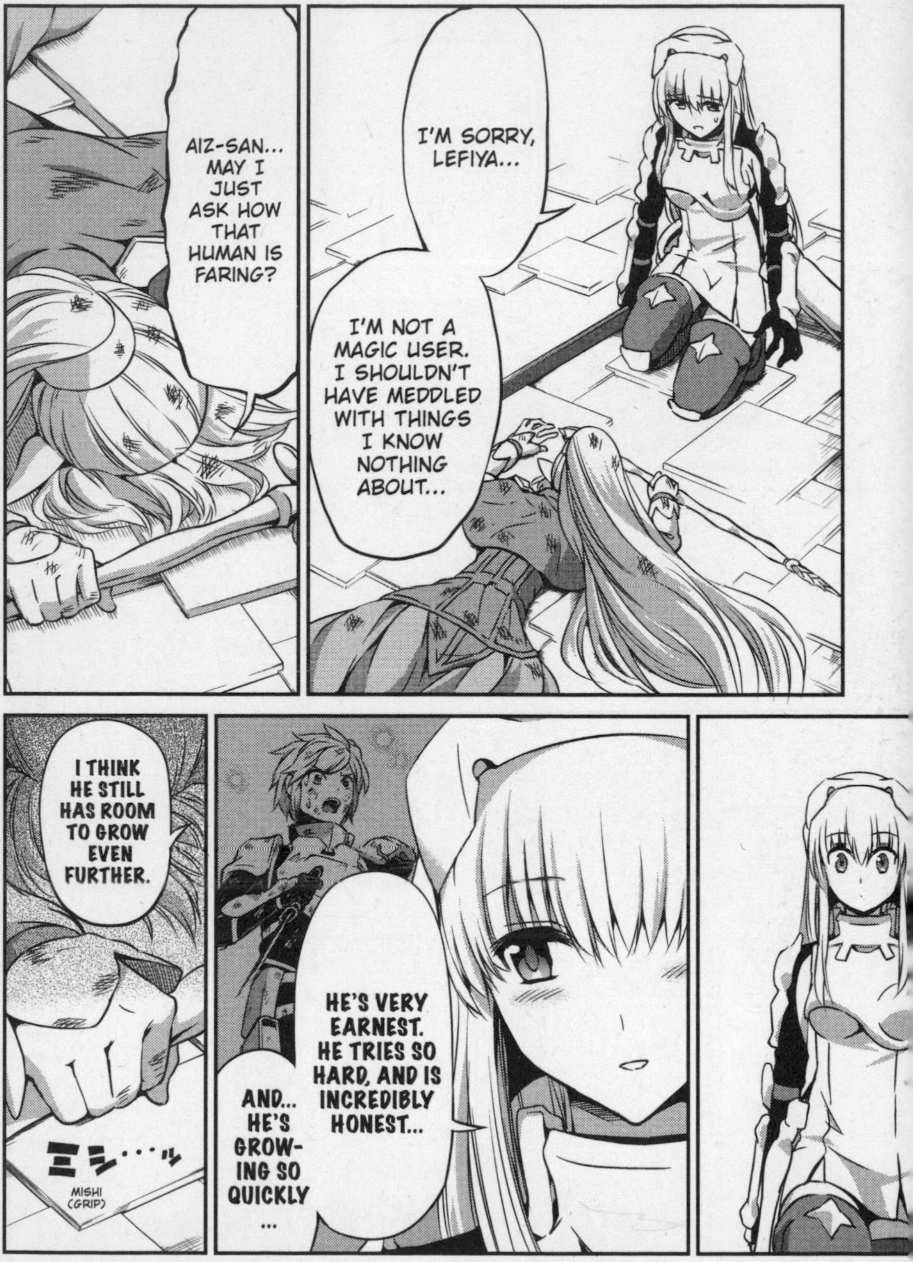
I'M SORRY, LEFIYA...
I'M NOT A MAGIC USER. I SHOULDN'T HAVE MEDDLED WITH THINGS I KNOW NOTHING ABOUT...
AIZ-SAN... MAY I JUST ASK HOW THAT HUMAN IS FARING?
HE'S VERY EARNEST. HE TRIES SO HARD, AND IS INCREDIBLY HONEST...
AND... HE'S GROWING SO QUICKLY...
I THINK HE STILL HAS ROOM TO GROW EVEN FURTHER.
ミシ…ッ
MISHI (GRIP)

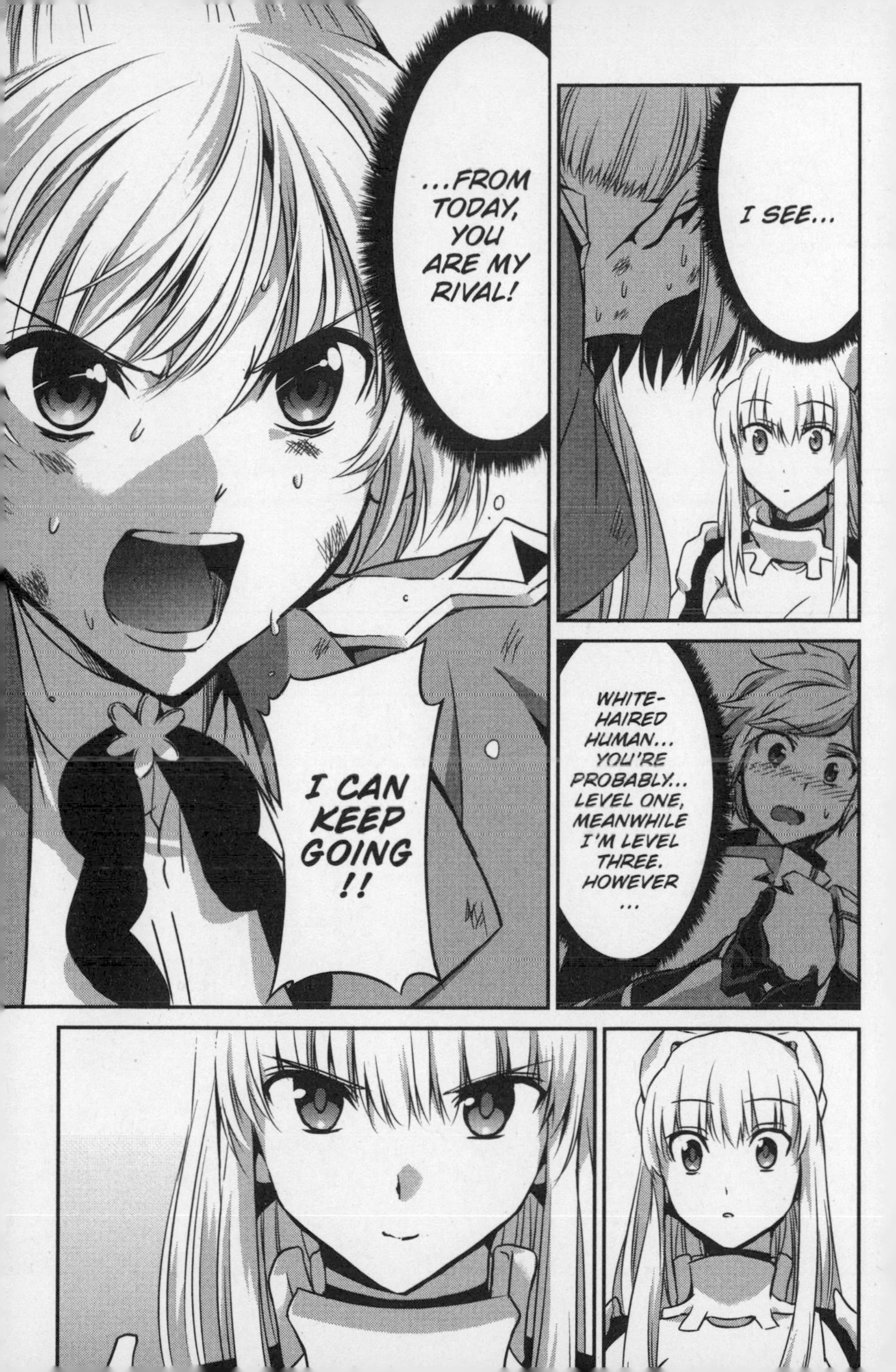

I SEE...
WHITE-HAIRED HUMAN... YOU'RE PROBABLY... LEVEL ONE, MEANWHILE I'M LEVEL THREE. HOWEVER...
...FROM TODAY, YOU ARE MY RIVAL!
I CAN KEEP GOING!!

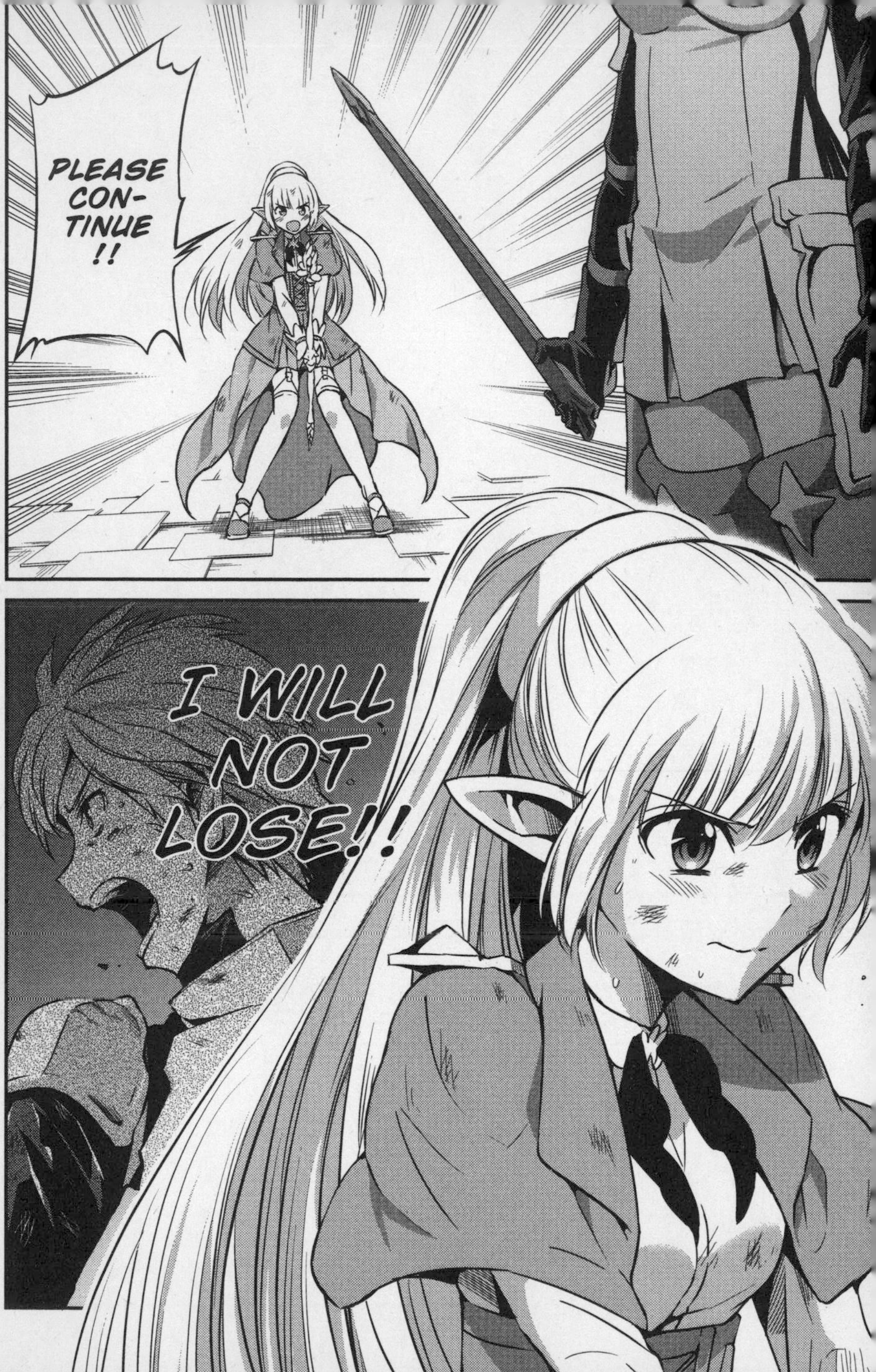
PLEASE CON-TINUE !!
I WILL NOT LOSE!!

Is it WRONG to TRY to PICK UP GIRLS in a DUNGEON? ON THE SIDE

Sword Oratoria

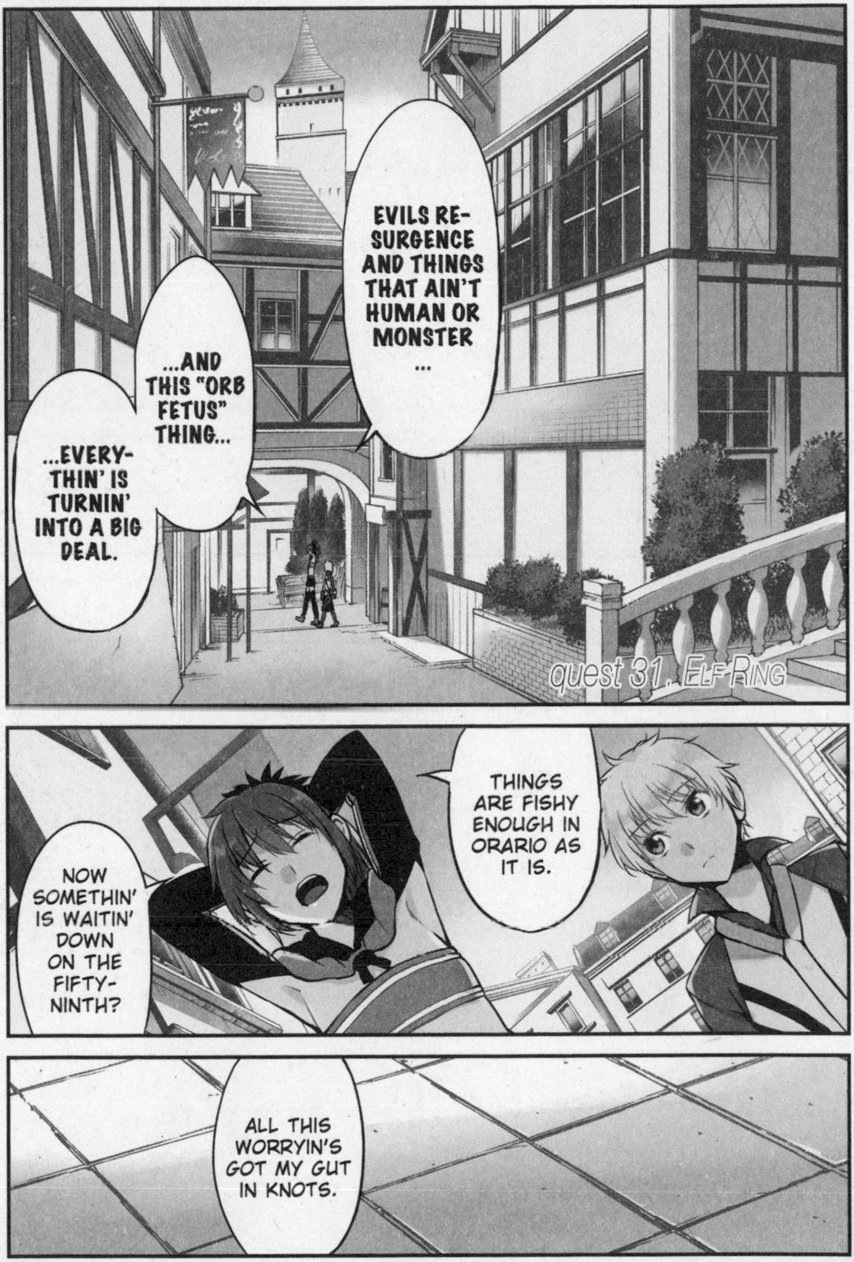
EVILS RE-SURGENCE AND THINGS THAT AIN'T HUMAN OR MONSTER ...
...AND THIS "ORB FETUS" THING...
...EVERYTHIN' IS TURNIN' INTO A BIG DEAL.
quest 31. Elf Ring
THINGS ARE FISHY ENOUGH IN ORARIO AS IT IS.
NOW SOMETHIN' IS WAITIN' DOWN ON THE FIFTY-NINTH?
ALL THIS WORRYIN'S GOT MY GUT IN KNOTS.

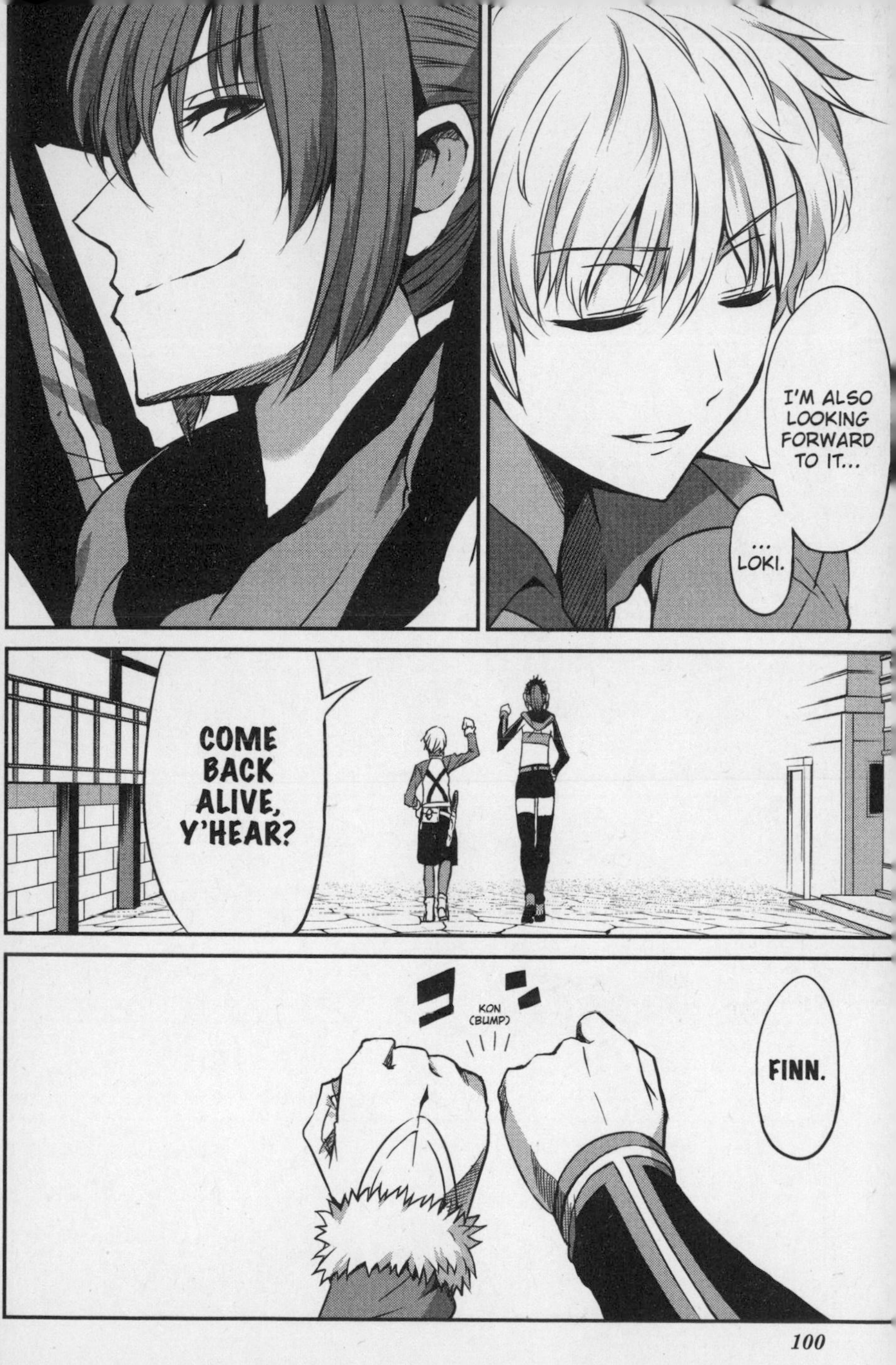
I'M ALSO LOOKING FORWARD TO IT...
... LOKI.
COME BACK ALIVE, Y'HEAR?
FINN.
KON (BUMP)

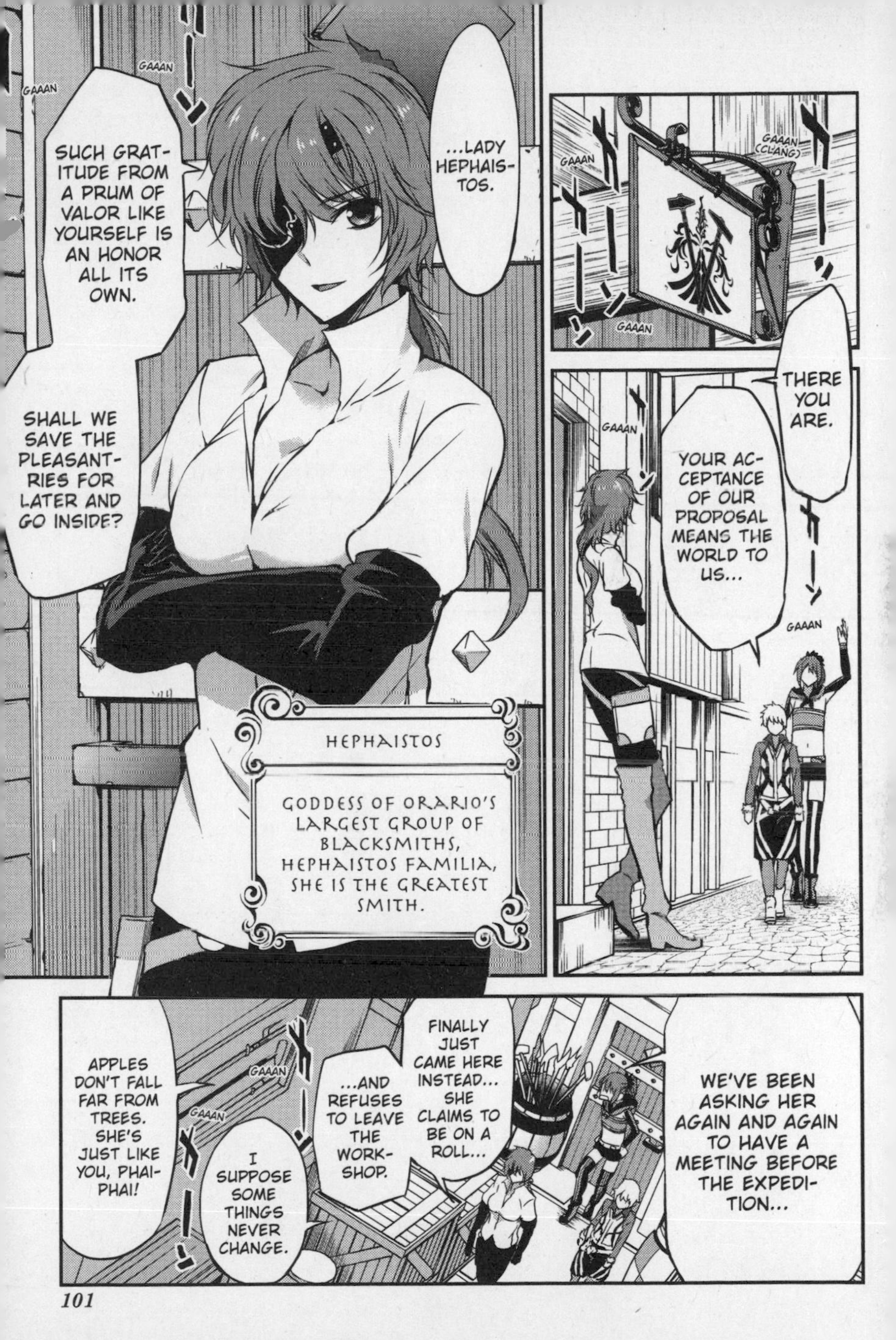
GAAAN (CLANG)
GAAAN
GAAAN
GAAAN
THERE YOU ARE.
YOUR ACCEPTANCE OF OUR PROPOSAL MEANS THE WORLD TO US...
GAAAN
...LADY HEPHAISTOS.
GAAAN
GAAAN
SUCH GRATITUDE FROM A PRUM OF VALOR LIKE YOURSELF IS AN HONOR ALL ITS OWN.
SHALL WE SAVE THE PLEASANTRIES FOR LATER AND GO INSIDE?
HEPHAISTOS
GODDESS OF ORARIO'S LARGEST GROUP OF BLACKSMITHS, HEPHAISTOS FAMILIA, SHE IS THE GREATEST SMITH.
WE'VE BEEN ASKING HER AGAIN AND AGAIN TO HAVE A MEETING BEFORE THE EXPEDITION...
FINALLY JUST CAME HERE INSTEAD... SHE CLAIMS TO BE ON A ROLL...
...AND REFUSES TO LEAVE THE WORKSHOP.
GAAAN
GAAAN
APPLES DON'T FALL FAR FROM TREES. SHE'S JUST LIKE YOU, PHAI-PHAI!
I SUPPOSE SOME THINGS NEVER CHANGE.

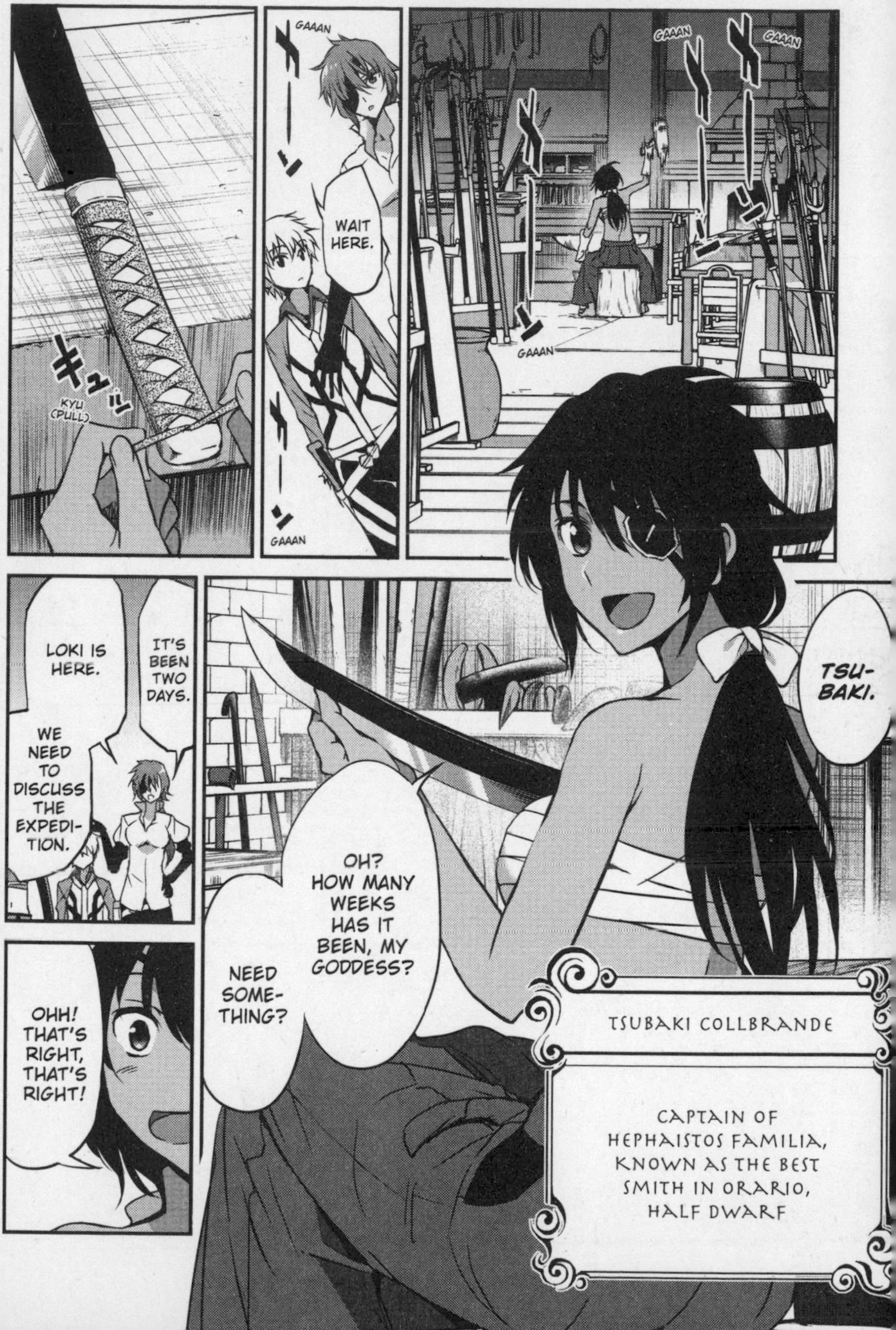
GAAAN
GAAAN
GAAAN
GAAAN
WAIT HERE.
GAAAN
KYU (PULL)
TSUBAKI.
OH? HOW MANY WEEKS HAS IT BEEN, MY GODDESS?
NEED SOMETHING?
TSUBAKI COLLBRANDE
CAPTAIN OF HEPHAISTOS FAMILIA, KNOWN AS THE BEST SMITH IN ORARIO, HALF DWARF
IT'S BEEN TWO DAYS.
LOKI IS HERE.
WE NEED TO DISCUSS THE EXPEDITION.
OHH! THAT'S RIGHT, THAT'S RIGHT!

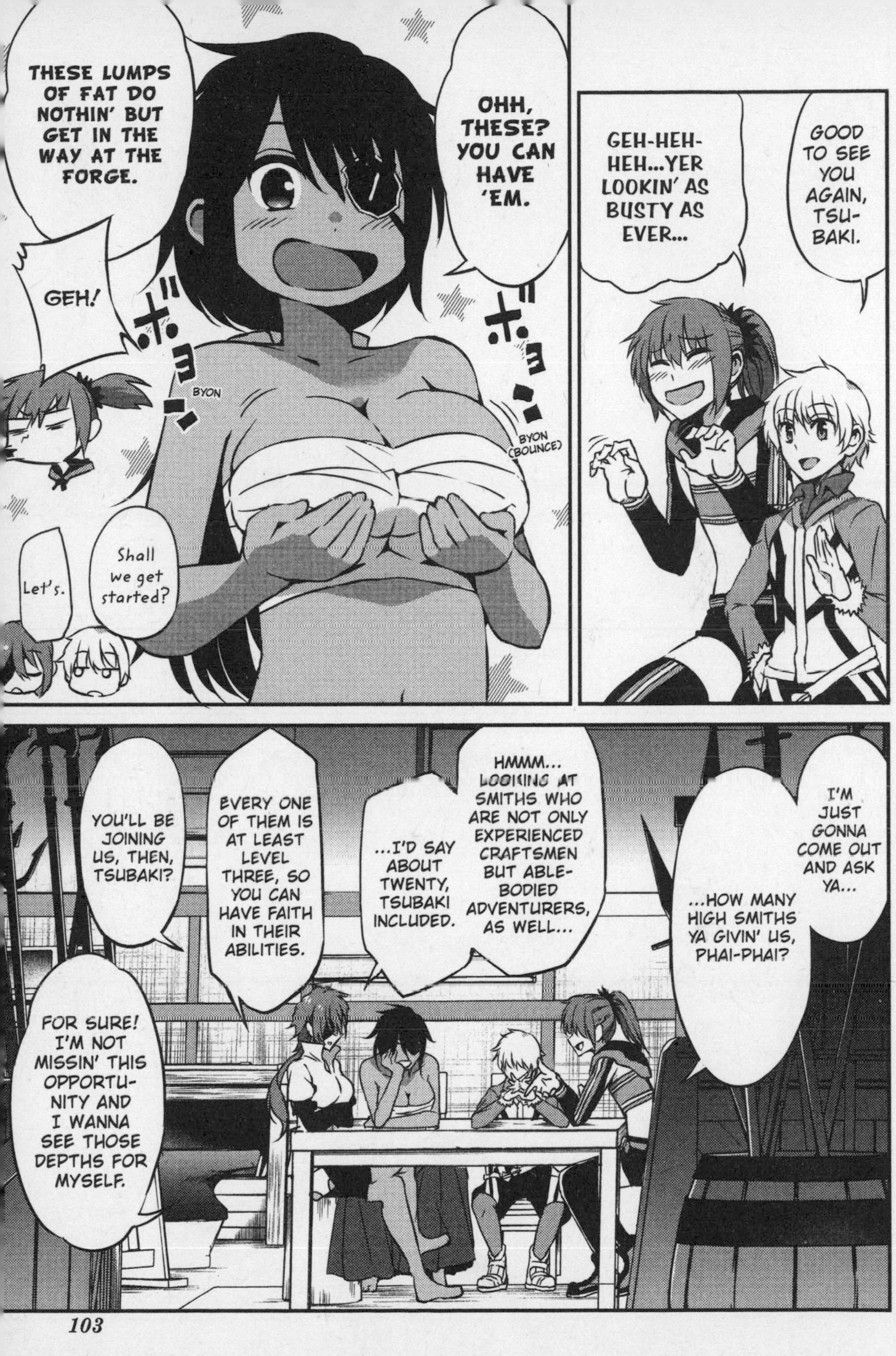
GOOD TO SEE YOU AGAIN, TSUBAKI.
GEH-HEH-HEH...YER LOOKIN' AS BUSTY AS EVER...
OHH, THESE? YOU CAN HAVE 'EM.
THESE LUMPS OF FAT DO NOTHIN' BUT GET IN THE WAY AT THE FORGE.
ボヨン
BYON (BOUNCE)
ボヨン
BYON
GEH!
Shall we get started?
Let's.
I'M JUST GONNA COME OUT AND ASK YA...
...HOW MANY HIGH SMITHS YA GIVIN' US, PHAI-PHAI?
HMMM... LOOKING AT SMITHS WHO ARE NOT ONLY EXPERIENCED CRAFTSMEN BUT ABLE-BODIED ADVENTURERS, AS WELL...
...I'D SAY ABOUT TWENTY, TSUBAKI INCLUDED.
EVERY ONE OF THEM IS AT LEAST LEVEL THREE, SO YOU CAN HAVE FAITH IN THEIR ABILITIES.
YOU'LL BE JOINING US, THEN, TSUBAKI?
FOR SURE! I'M NOT MISSIN' THIS OPPORTUNITY AND I WANNA SEE THOSE DEPTHS FOR MYSELF.

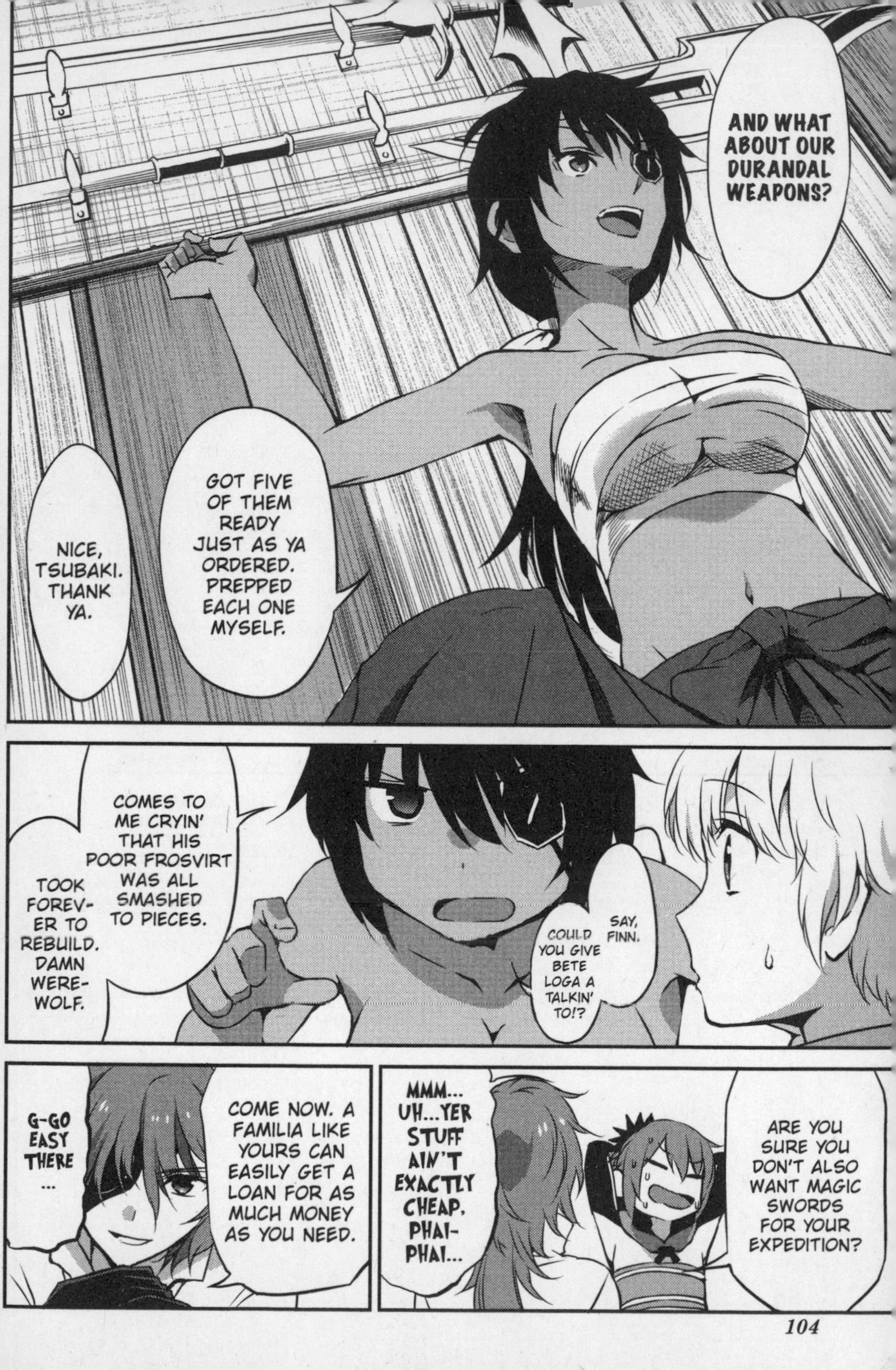
AND WHAT ABOUT OUR DURANDAL WEAPONS?
GOT FIVE OF THEM READY JUST AS YA ORDERED. PREPPED EACH ONE MYSELF.
NICE, TSUBAKI. THANK YA.
SAY, FINN.
COULD YOU GIVE BETE LOGA A TALKIN' TO!?
COMES TO ME CRYIN' THAT HIS POOR FROSVIRT WAS ALL SMASHED TO PIECES.
TOOK FOREVER TO REBUILD. DAMN WEREWOLF.
ARE YOU SURE YOU DON'T ALSO WANT MAGIC SWORDS FOR YOUR EXPEDITION?
MMM... UH...YER STUFF AIN'T EXACTLY CHEAP, PHAI-PHAI...
COME NOW. A FAMILIA LIKE YOURS CAN EASILY GET A LOAN FOR AS MUCH MONEY AS YOU NEED.
G-GO EASY THERE ...

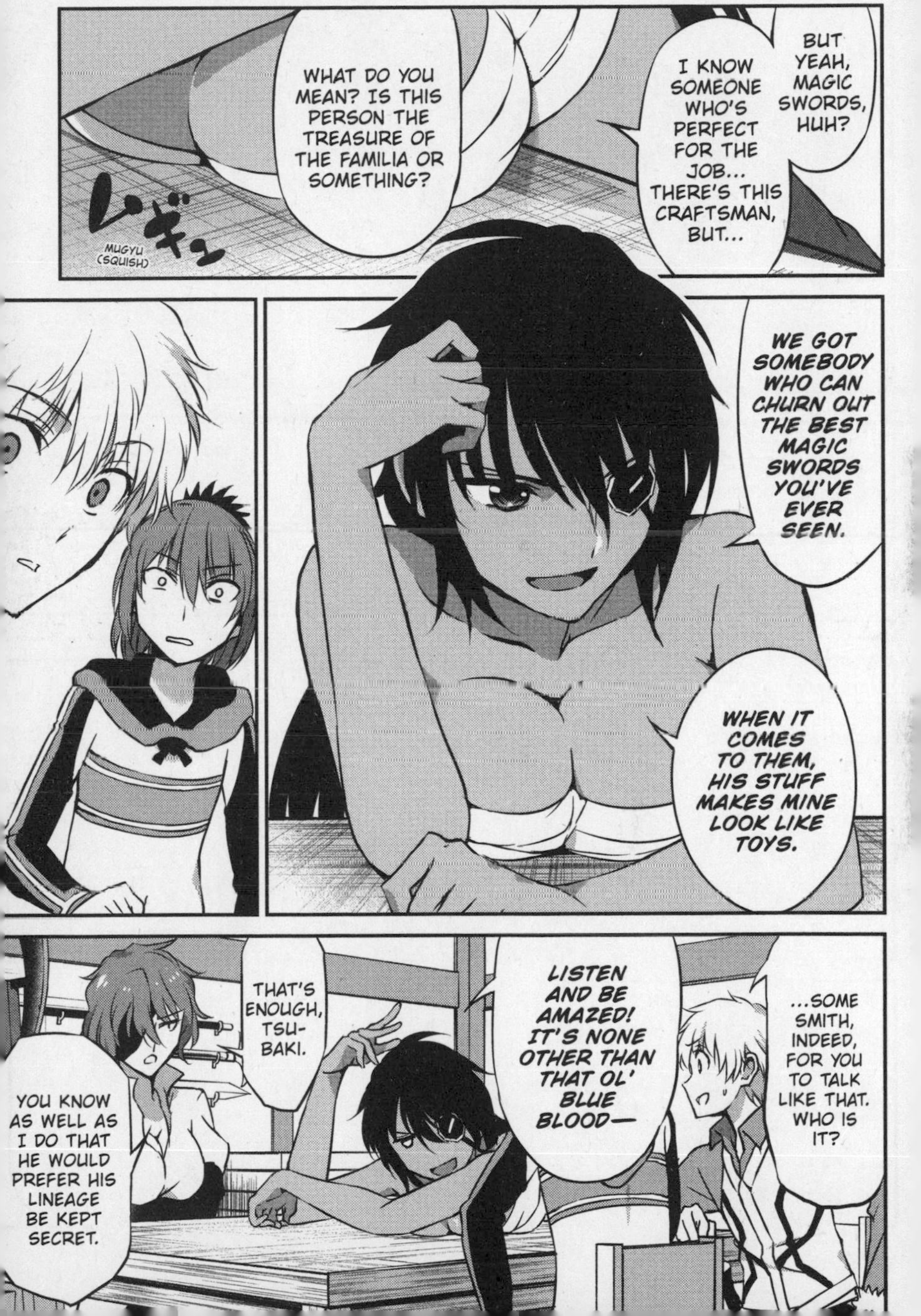
BUT YEAH, MAGIC SWORDS, HUH?
I KNOW SOMEONE WHO'S PERFECT FOR THE JOB... THERE'S THIS CRAFTSMAN, BUT...
WHAT DO YOU MEAN? IS THIS PERSON THE TREASURE OF THE FAMILIA OR SOMETHING?
ムギュ
MUGYU (SQUISH)
WE GOT SOMEBODY WHO CAN CHURN OUT THE BEST MAGIC SWORDS YOU'VE EVER SEEN.
WHEN IT COMES TO THEM, HIS STUFF MAKES MINE LOOK LIKE TOYS.
...SOME SMITH, INDEED, FOR YOU TO TALK LIKE THAT. WHO IS IT?
LISTEN AND BE AMAZED! IT'S NONE OTHER THAN THAT OL' BLUE BLOOD—
THAT'S ENOUGH, TSU-BAKI.
YOU KNOW AS WELL AS I DO THAT HE WOULD PREFER HIS LINEAGE BE KEPT SECRET.

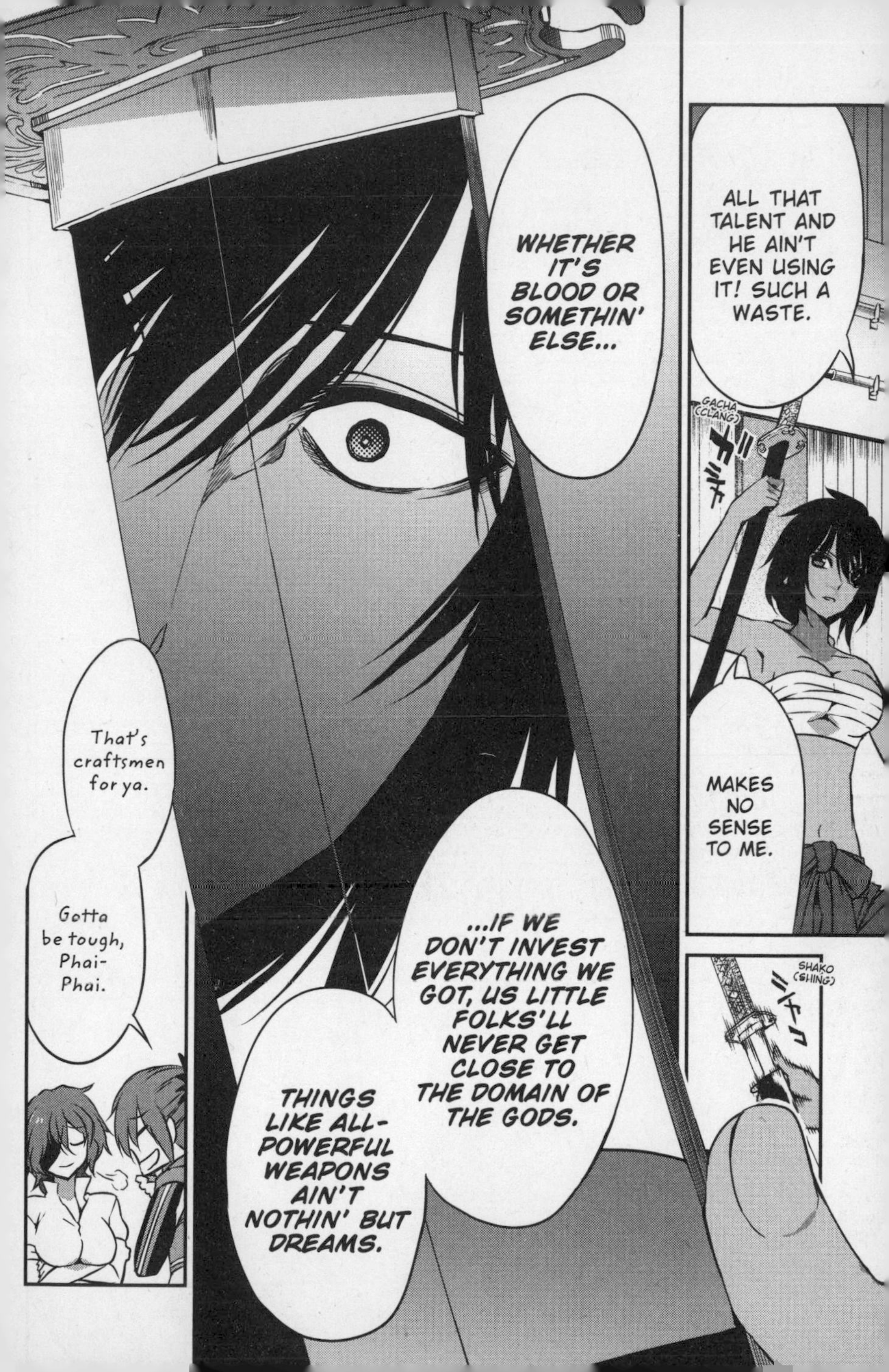
ALL THAT TALENT AND HE AIN'T EVEN USING IT! SUCH A WASTE.
GACHA (CLANG)
MAKES NO SENSE TO ME.
SHAKO (SHING)
WHETHER IT'S BLOOD OR SOMETHIN' ELSE...
...IF WE DON'T INVEST EVERYTHING WE GOT, US LITTLE FOLKS'LL NEVER GET CLOSE TO THE DOMAIN OF THE GODS.
THINGS LIKE ALL-POWERFUL WEAPONS AIN'T NOTHIN' BUT DREAMS.
That's craftsmen for ya.
Gotta be tough, Phai-Phai.

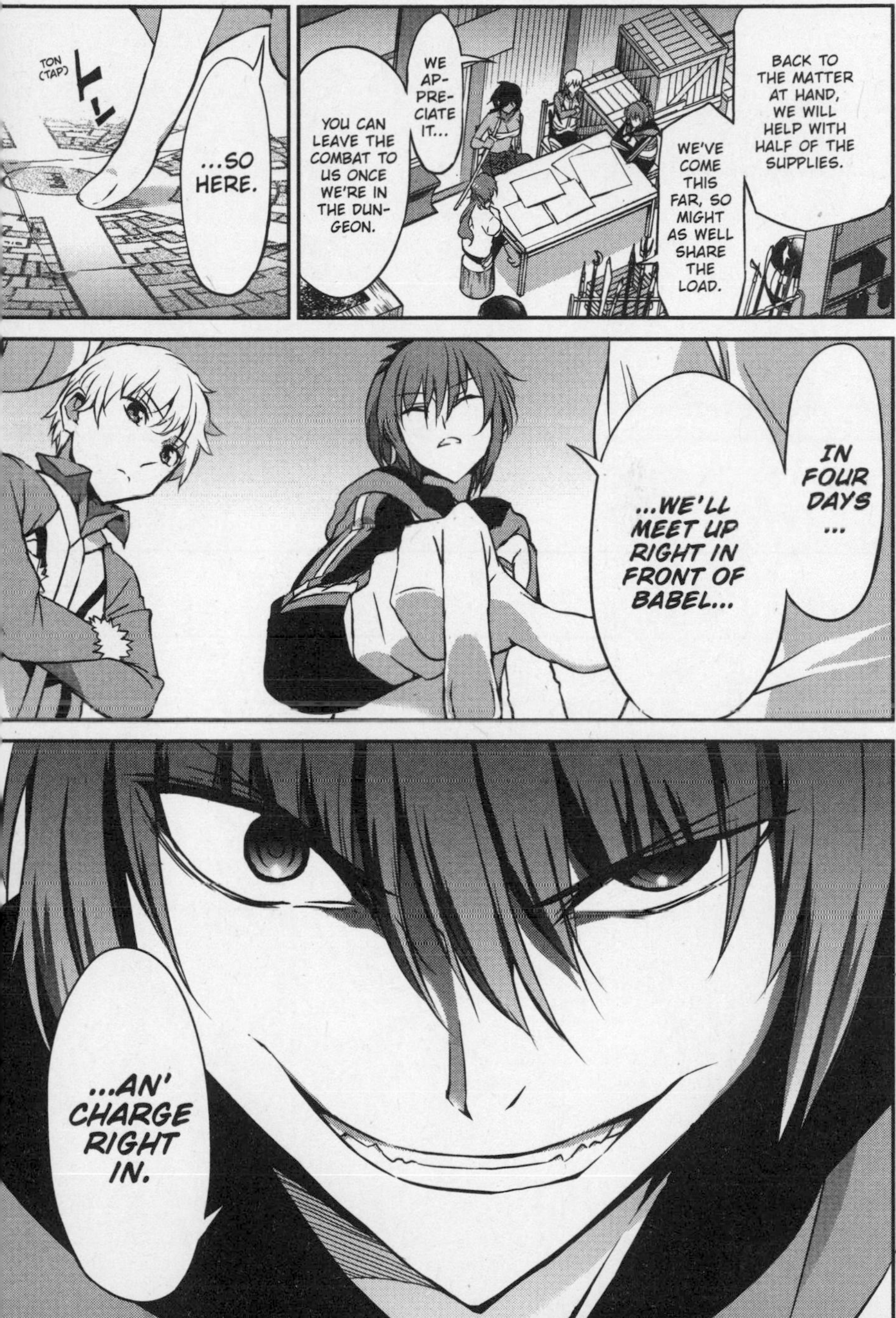
BACK TO THE MATTER AT HAND, WE WILL HELP WITH HALF OF THE SUPPLIES.
WE'VE COME THIS FAR, SO MIGHT AS WELL SHARE THE LOAD.
WE APPRECIATE IT...
YOU CAN LEAVE THE COMBAT TO US ONCE WE'RE IN THE DUNGEON.
TON (TAP)
...SO HERE.
IN FOUR DAYS ...
...WE'LL MEET UP RIGHT IN FRONT OF BABEL...
...AN' CHARGE RIGHT IN.

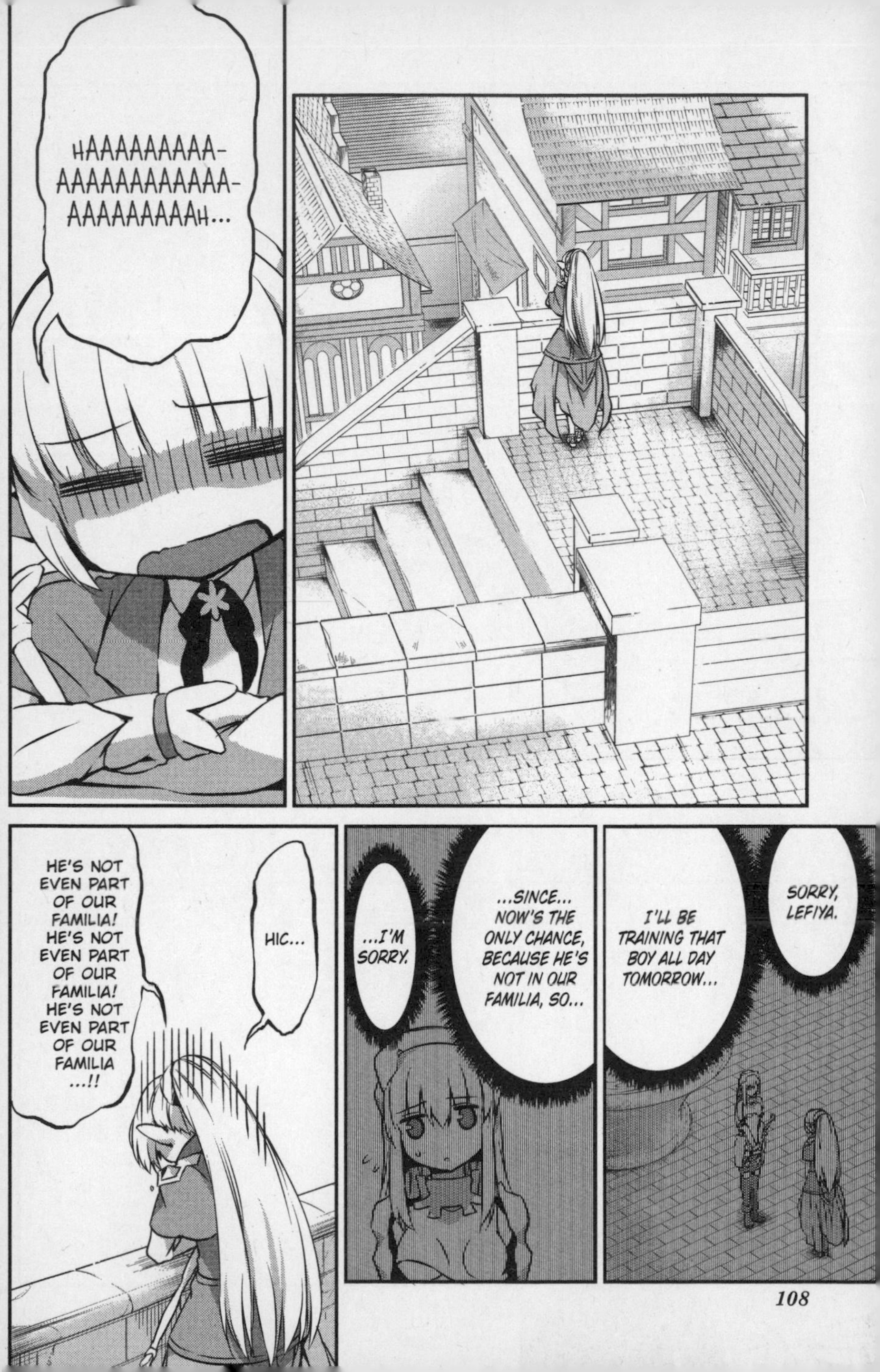
HAAAAAAAAA-AAAAAAAAAAAA-AAAAAAAAAH...
SORRY, LEFIYA.
I'LL BE TRAINING THAT BOY ALL DAY TOMORROW...
...SINCE... NOW'S THE ONLY CHANCE, BECAUSE HE'S NOT IN OUR FAMILIA, SO...
...I'M SORRY.
HIC...
HE'S NOT EVEN PART OF OUR FAMILIA! HE'S NOT EVEN PART OF OUR FAMILIA! HE'S NOT EVEN PART OF OUR FAMILIA ...!!

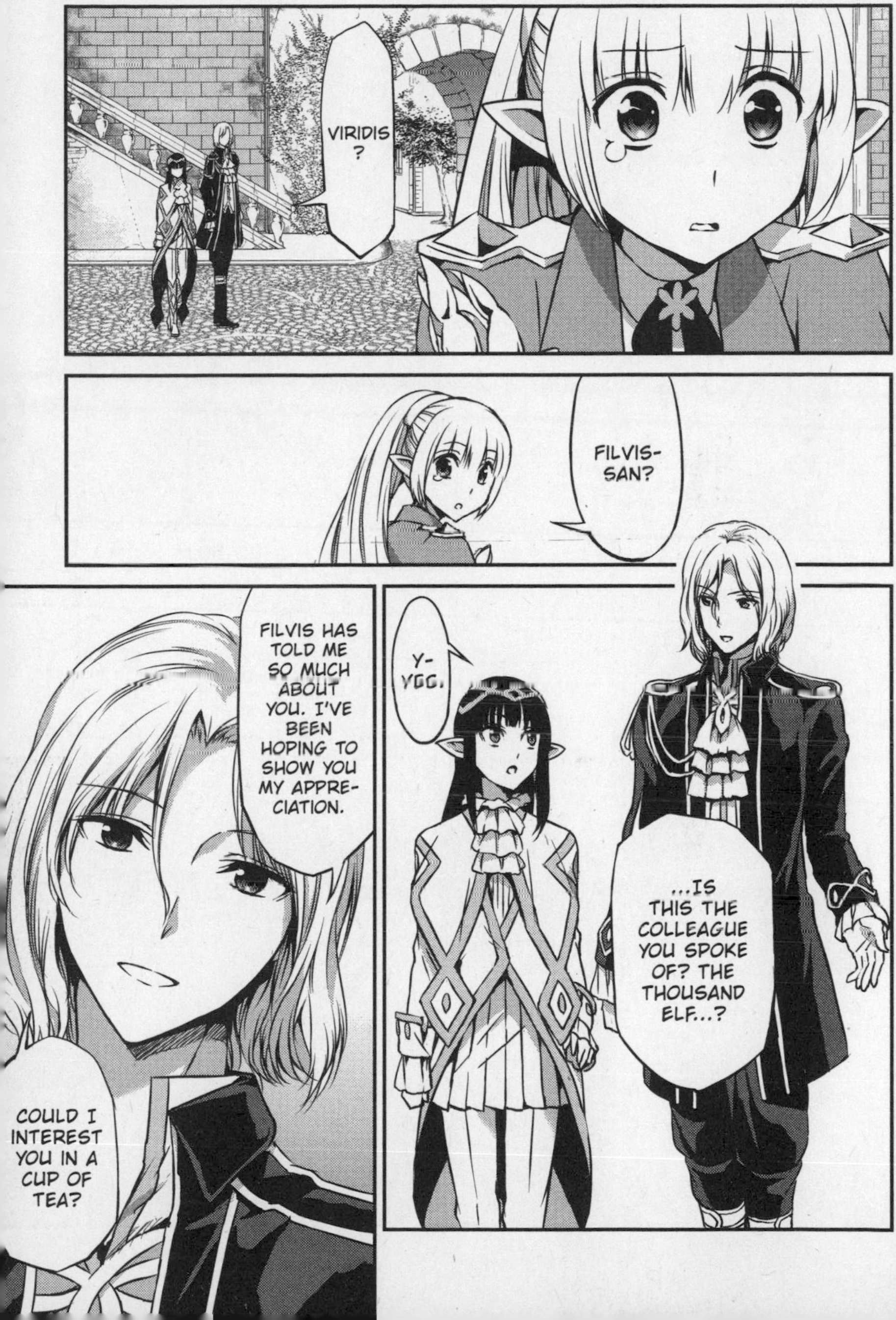
VIRIDIS?
FILVIS-SAN?
...IS THIS THE COLLEAGUE YOU SPOKE OF? THE THOUSAND ELF...?
Y-YES.
FILVIS HAS TOLD ME SO MUCH ABOUT YOU. I'VE BEEN HOPING TO SHOW YOU MY APPRECIATION.
COULD I INTEREST YOU IN A CUP OF TEA?

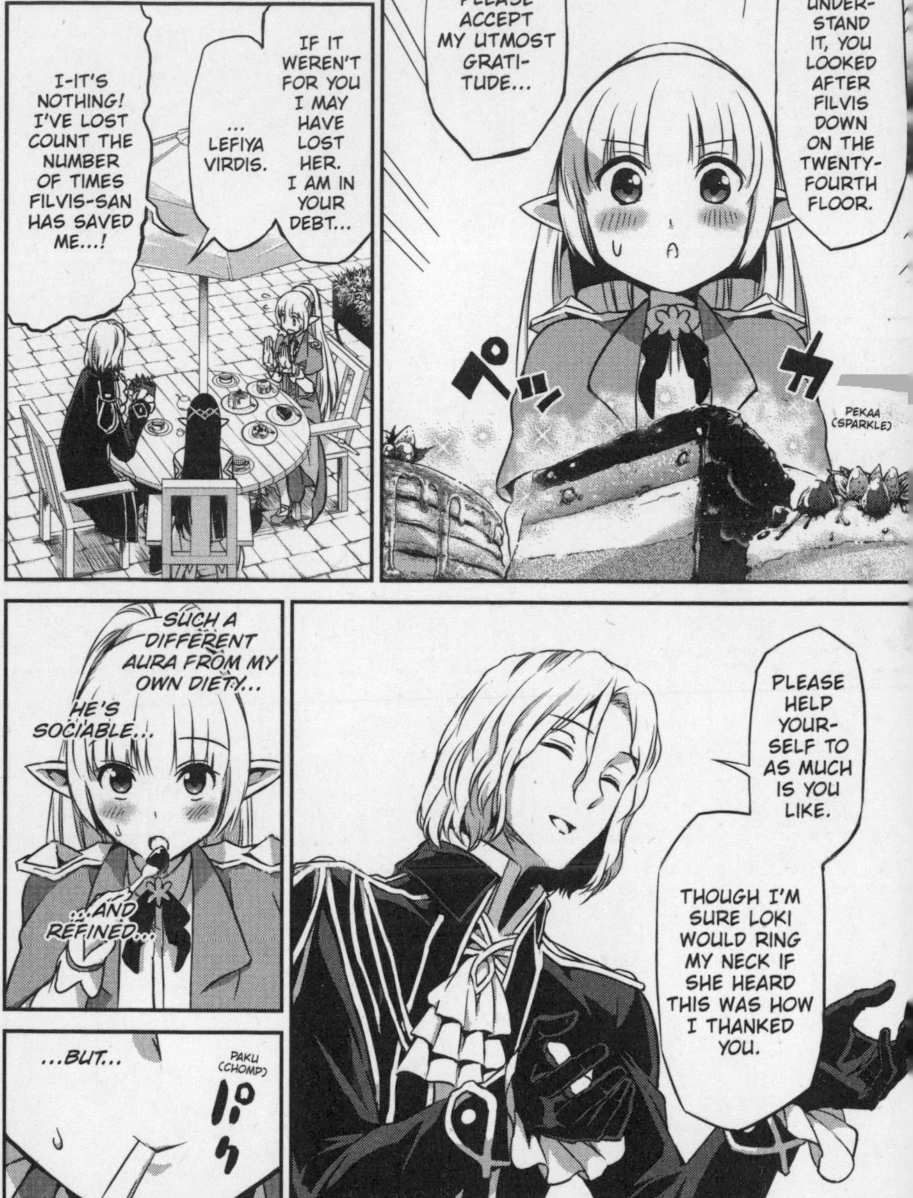
AS I UNDER-STAND IT, YOU LOOKED AFTER FILVIS DOWN ON THE TWENTY-FOURTH FLOOR.
PLEASE ACCEPT MY UTMOST GRATI-TUDE...
PEKAA (SPARKLE)
IF IT WEREN'T FOR YOU I MAY HAVE LOST HER. I AM IN YOUR DEBT...
... LEFIYA VIRDIS.
I-IT'S NOTHING! I'VE LOST COUNT THE NUMBER OF TIMES FILVIS-SAN HAS SAVED ME...!
PLEASE HELP YOUR-SELF TO AS MUCH IS YOU LIKE.
THOUGH I'M SURE LOKI WOULD RING MY NECK IF SHE HEARD THIS WAS HOW I THANKED YOU.
SUCH A DIFFERENT AURA FROM MY OWN DIETY...
HE'S SOCIABLE...
...AND REFINED...
...BUT...
PAKU (CHOMP)

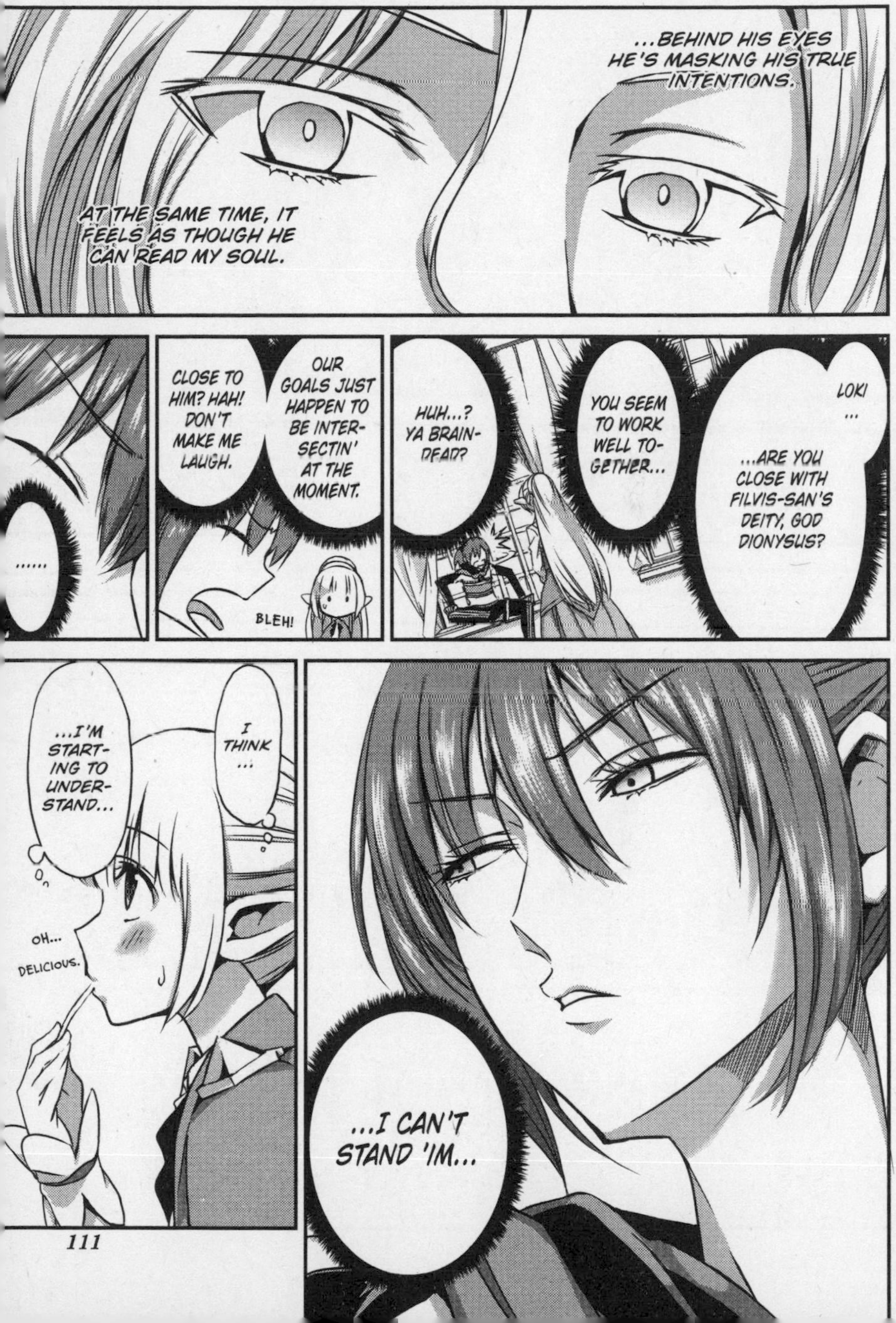

...BEHIND HIS EYES HE'S MASKING HIS TRUE INTENTIONS.
AT THE SAME TIME, IT FEELS AS THOUGH HE CAN READ MY SOUL.
LOKI...
...ARE YOU CLOSE WITH FILVIS-SAN'S DEITY, GOD DIONYSUS?
YOU SEEM TO WORK WELL TOGETHER...
HUH...? YA BRAIN-DEAD?
OUR GOALS JUST HAPPEN TO BE INTERSECTIN' AT THE MOMENT.
CLOSE TO HIM? HAH! DON'T MAKE ME LAUGH.
BLEH!
......
...I CAN'T STAND 'IM...
I THINK...
...I'M STARTING TO UNDERSTAND...
OH... DELICIOUS.

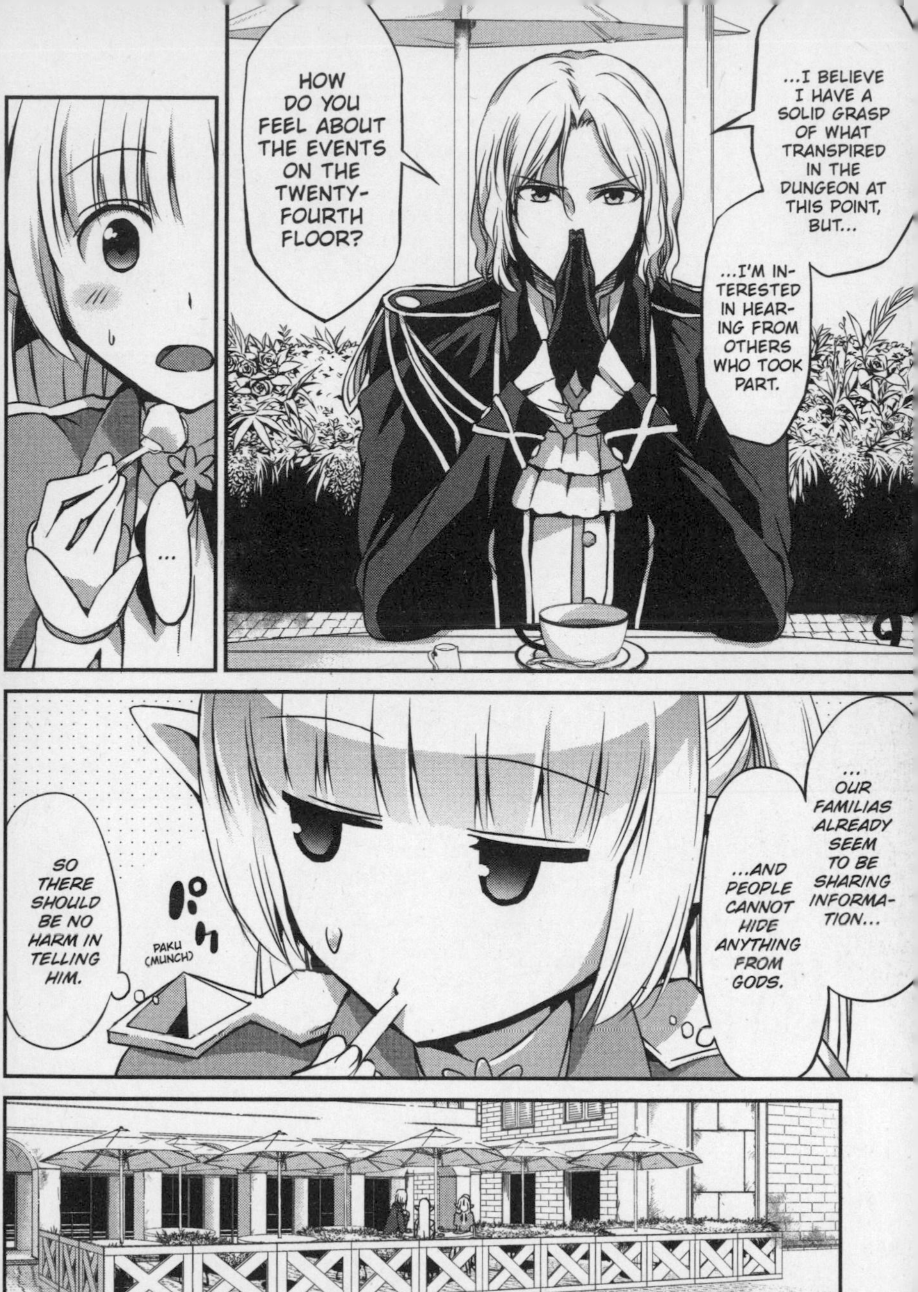
...I BELIEVE I HAVE A SOLID GRASP OF WHAT TRANSPIRED IN THE DUNGEON AT THIS POINT, BUT...
...I'M INTERESTED IN HEARING FROM OTHERS WHO TOOK PART.
HOW DO YOU FEEL ABOUT THE EVENTS ON THE TWENTY-FOURTH FLOOR?
...
...OUR FAMILIAS ALREADY SEEM TO BE SHARING INFORMATION...
...AND PEOPLE CANNOT HIDE ANYTHING FROM GODS.
ぱく
PAKU (MUNCH)
SO THERE SHOULD BE NO HARM IN TELLING HIM.

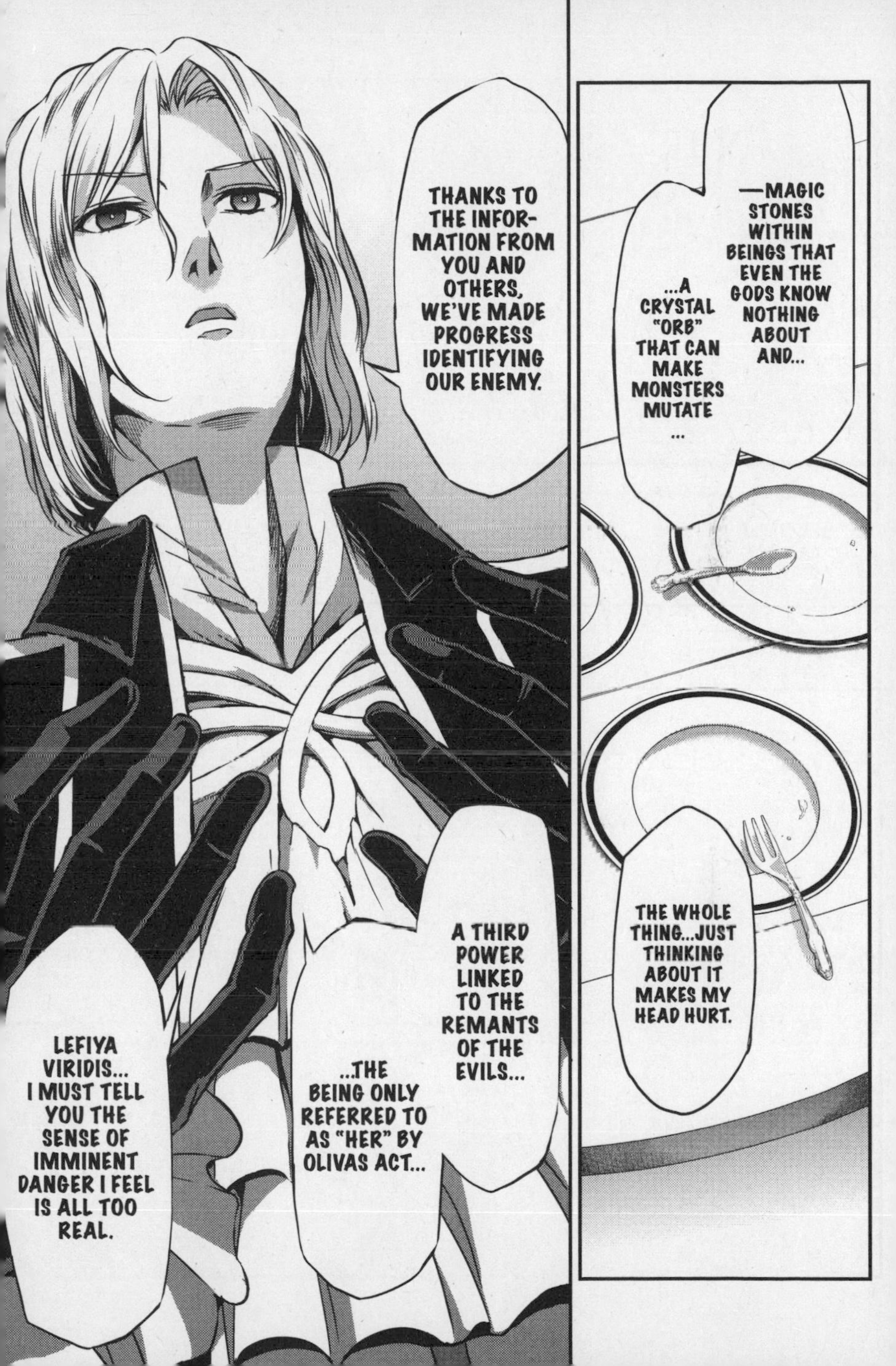
—MAGIC STONES WITHIN BEINGS THAT EVEN THE GODS KNOW NOTHING ABOUT AND...
...A CRYSTAL "ORB" THAT CAN MAKE MONSTERS MUTATE ...
THE WHOLE THING...JUST THINKING ABOUT IT MAKES MY HEAD HURT.
THANKS TO THE INFOR-MATION FROM YOU AND OTHERS, WE'VE MADE PROGRESS IDENTIFYING OUR ENEMY.
A THIRD POWER LINKED TO THE REMANTS OF THE EVILS...
...THE BEING ONLY REFERRED TO AS "HER" BY OLIVAS ACT...
LEFIYA VIRIDIS... I MUST TELL YOU THE SENSE OF IMMINENT DANGER I FEEL IS ALL TOO REAL.

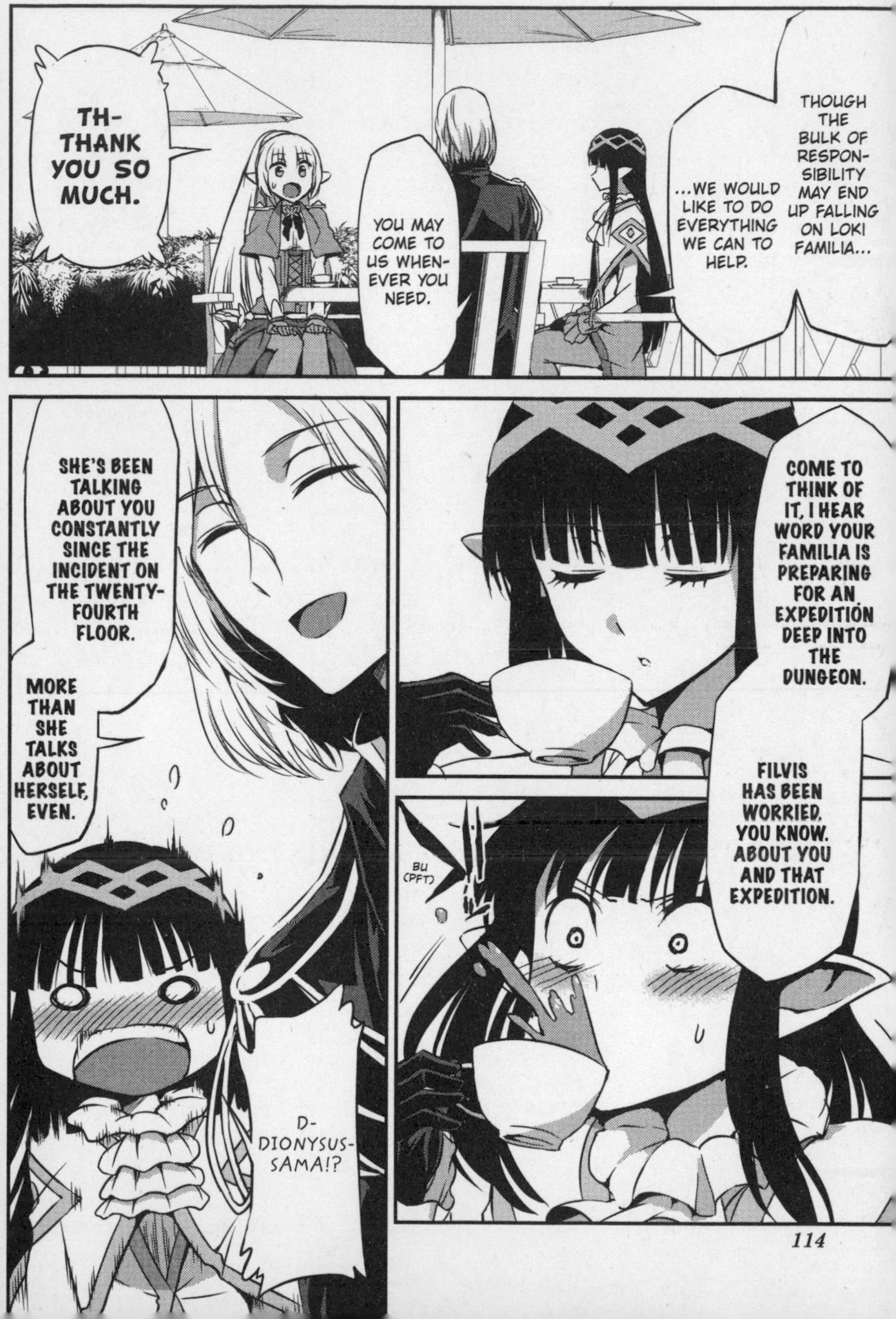
THOUGH THE BULK OF RESPON-SIBILITY MAY END UP FALLING ON LOKI FAMILIA...
...WE WOULD LIKE TO DO EVERYTHING WE CAN TO HELP.
YOU MAY COME TO US WHEN-EVER YOU NEED.
TH-THANK YOU SO MUCH.
COME TO THINK OF IT, I HEAR WORD YOUR FAMILIA IS PREPARING FOR AN EXPEDITION DEEP INTO THE DUNGEON.
FILVIS HAS BEEN WORRIED, YOU KNOW. ABOUT YOU AND THAT EXPEDITION.
BU (PFT)
SHE'S BEEN TALKING ABOUT YOU CONSTANTLY SINCE THE INCIDENT ON THE TWENTY-FOURTH FLOOR.
MORE THAN SHE TALKS ABOUT HERSELF, EVEN.
D-DIONYSUS-SAMA!?

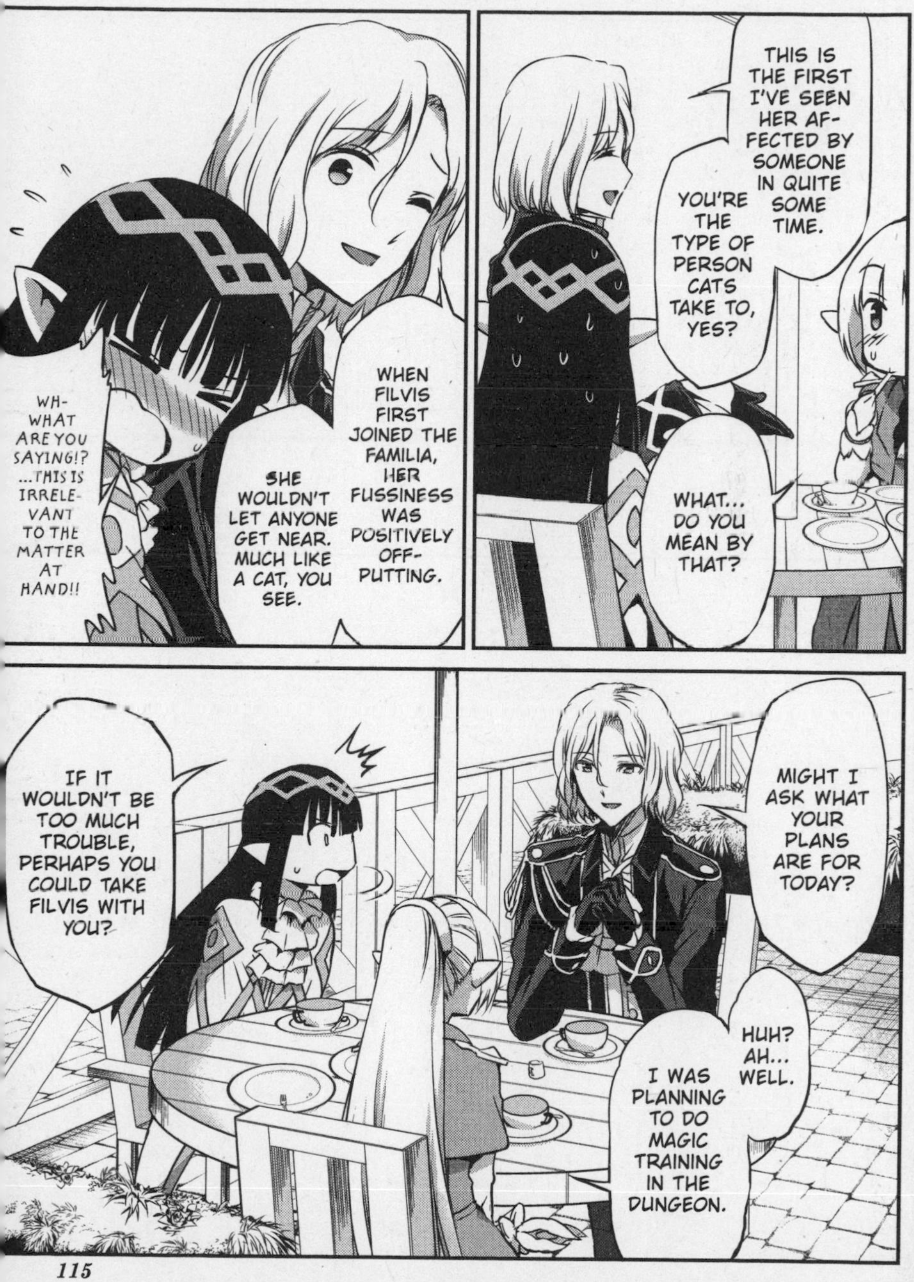
THIS IS THE FIRST I'VE SEEN HER AF-FECTED BY SOMEONE IN QUITE SOME TIME.
YOU'RE THE TYPE OF PERSON CATS TAKE TO, YES?
WHAT... DO YOU MEAN BY THAT?
WHEN FILVIS FIRST JOINED THE FAMILIA, HER FUSSINESS WAS POSITIVELY OFF-PUTTING.
SHE WOULDN'T LET ANYONE GET NEAR. MUCH LIKE A CAT, YOU SEE.
WH-WHAT ARE YOU SAYING!? ...THIS IS IRRELE-VANT TO THE MATTER AT HAND!!
MIGHT I ASK WHAT YOUR PLANS ARE FOR TODAY?
HUH? AH... WELL.
I WAS PLANNING TO DO MAGIC TRAINING IN THE DUNGEON.
IF IT WOULDN'T BE TOO MUCH TROUBLE, PERHAPS YOU COULD TAKE FILVIS WITH YOU?

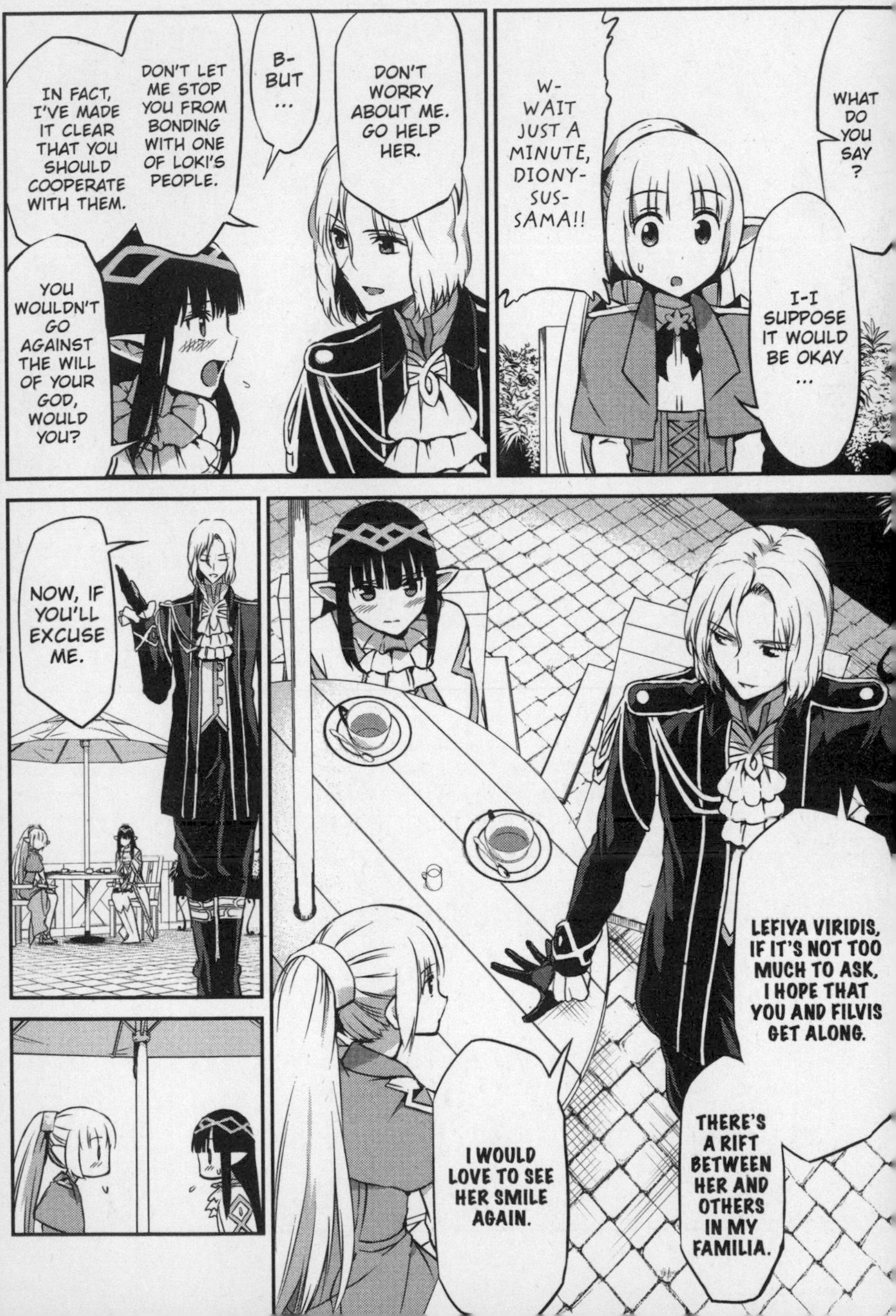
WHAT DO YOU SAY?
I-I SUPPOSE IT WOULD BE OKAY ...
W-WAIT JUST A MINUTE, DIONY-SUS-SAMA!!
DON'T WORRY ABOUT ME. GO HELP HER.
B-BUT ...
DON'T LET ME STOP YOU FROM BONDING WITH ONE OF LOKI'S PEOPLE.
IN FACT, I'VE MADE IT CLEAR THAT YOU SHOULD COOPERATE WITH THEM.
YOU WOULDN'T GO AGAINST THE WILL OF YOUR GOD, WOULD YOU?
LEFIYA VIRIDIS, IF IT'S NOT TOO MUCH TO ASK, I HOPE THAT YOU AND FILVIS GET ALONG.
THERE'S A RIFT BETWEEN HER AND OTHERS IN MY FAMILIA.
I WOULD LOVE TO SEE HER SMILE AGAIN.
NOW, IF YOU'LL EXCUSE ME.

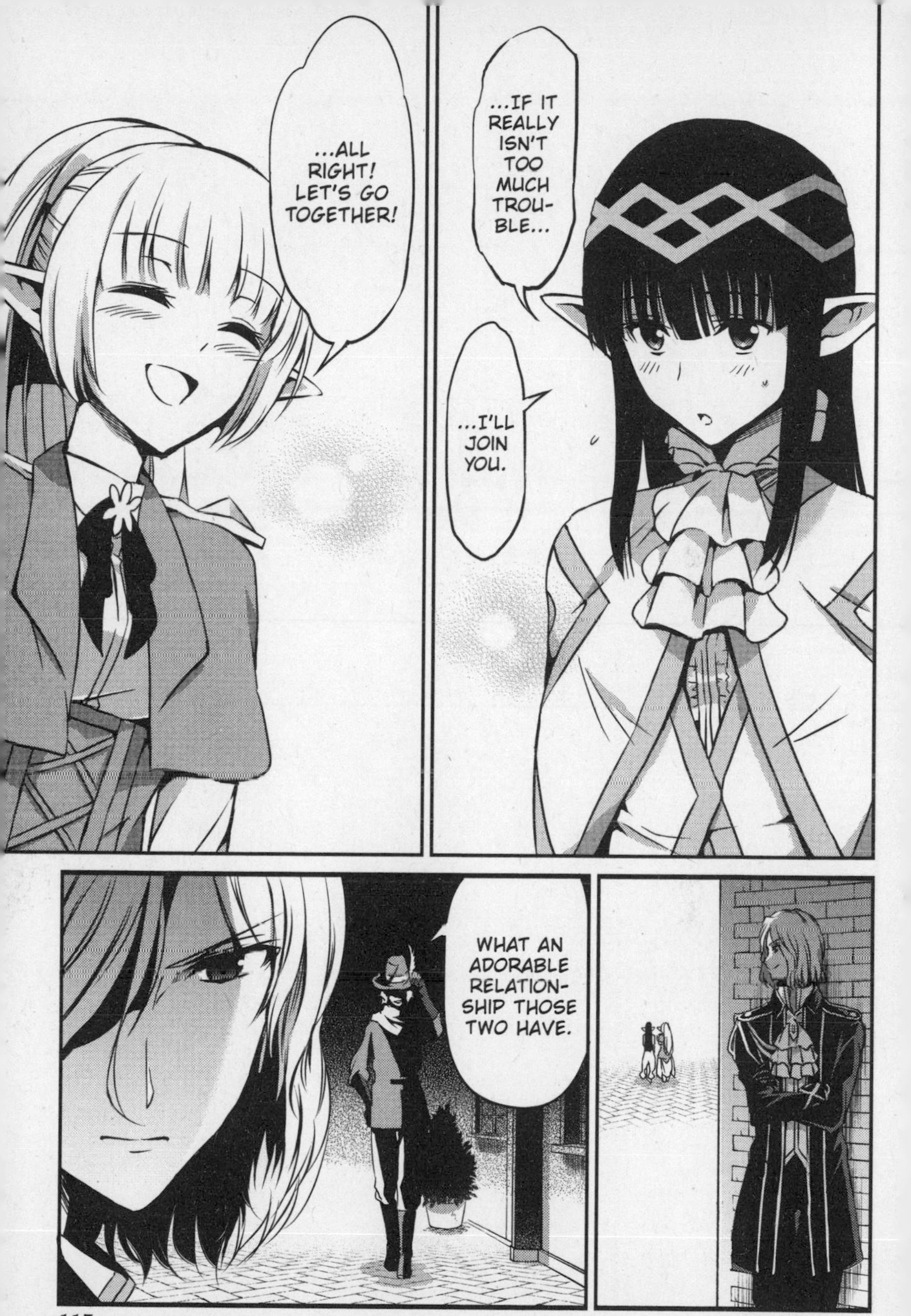
...IF IT REALLY ISN'T TOO MUCH TROUBLE...
...I'LL JOIN YOU.
...ALL RIGHT! LET'S GO TOGETHER!
WHAT AN ADORABLE RELATIONSHIP THOSE TWO HAVE.

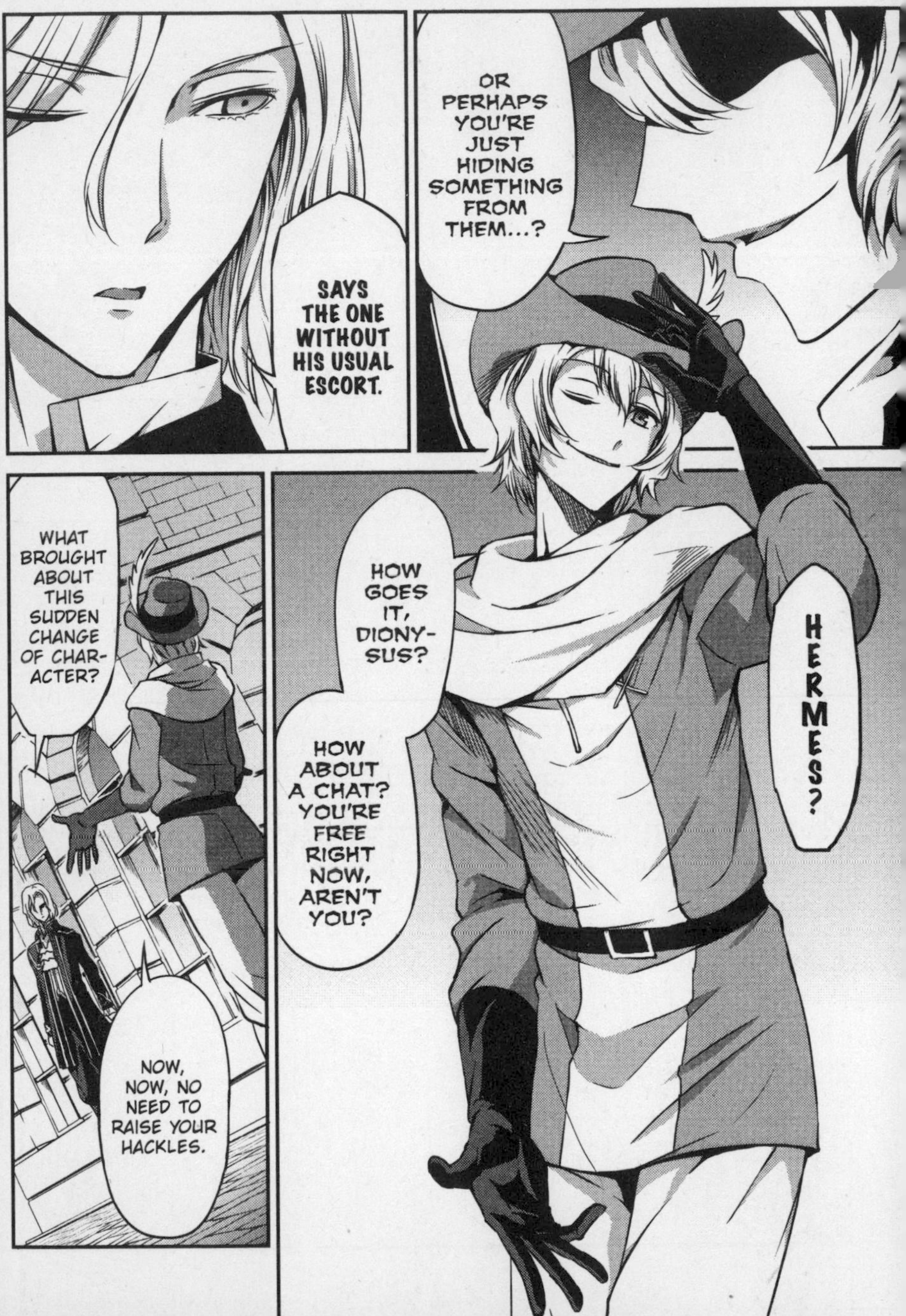
OR PERHAPS YOU'RE JUST HIDING SOMETHING FROM THEM...?
SAYS THE ONE WITHOUT HIS USUAL ESCORT.
HERMES?
HOW GOES IT, DIONYSUS?
HOW ABOUT A CHAT? YOU'RE FREE RIGHT NOW, AREN'T YOU?
WHAT BROUGHT ABOUT THIS SUDDEN CHANGE OF CHARACTER?
NOW, NOW, NO NEED TO RAISE YOUR HACKLES.

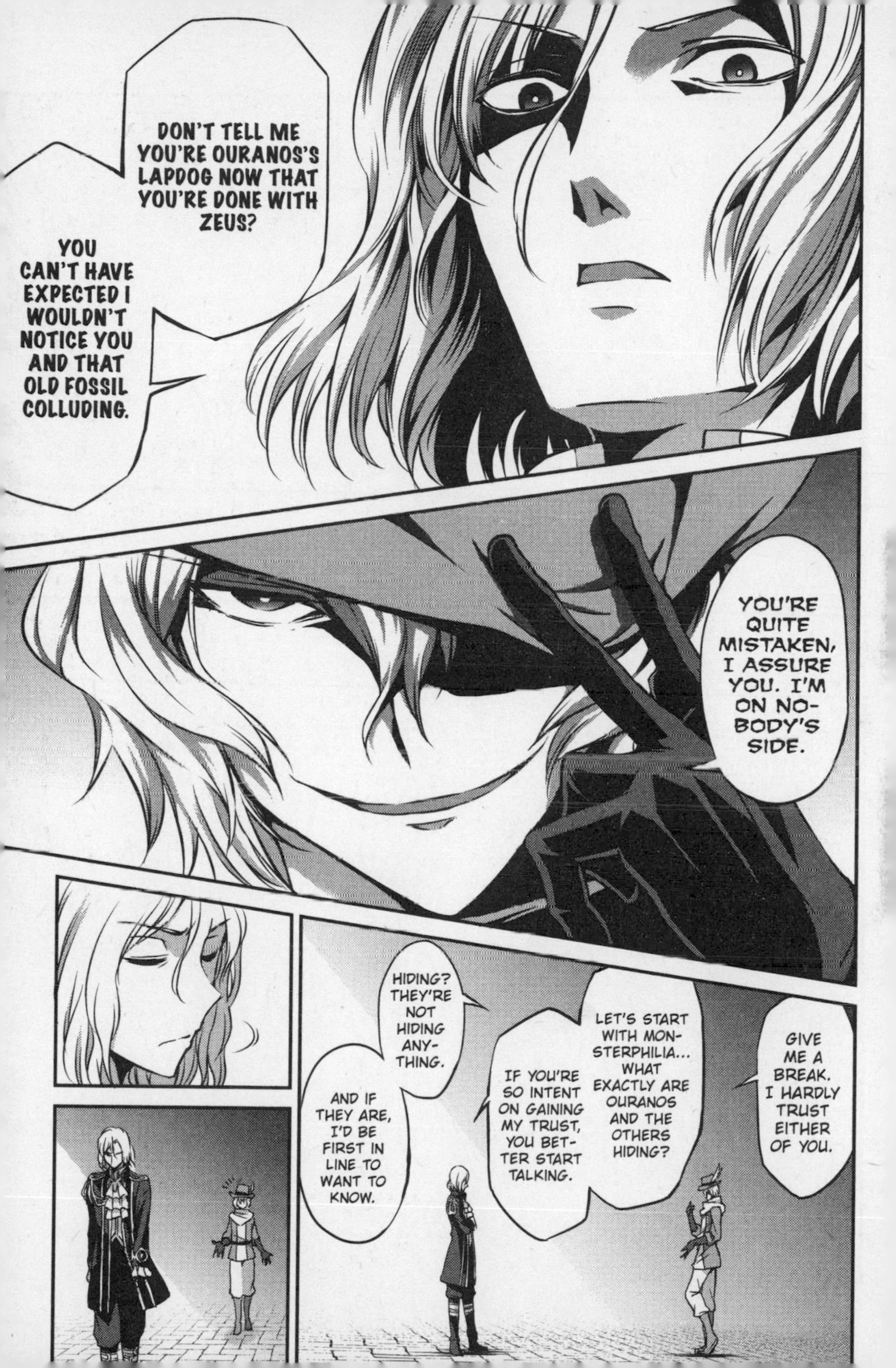
DON'T TELL ME YOU'RE OURANOS'S LAPDOG NOW THAT YOU'RE DONE WITH ZEUS?
YOU CAN'T HAVE EXPECTED I WOULDN'T NOTICE YOU AND THAT OLD FOSSIL COLLUDING.
YOU'RE QUITE MISTAKEN, I ASSURE YOU. I'M ON NO-BODY'S SIDE.
GIVE ME A BREAK. I HARDLY TRUST EITHER OF YOU.
LET'S START WITH MON-STERPHILIA... WHAT EXACTLY ARE OURANOS AND THE OTHERS HIDING?
IF YOU'RE SO INTENT ON GAINING MY TRUST, YOU BET-TER START TALKING.
HIDING? THEY'RE NOT HIDING ANY-THING.
AND IF THEY ARE, I'D BE FIRST IN LINE TO WANT TO KNOW.

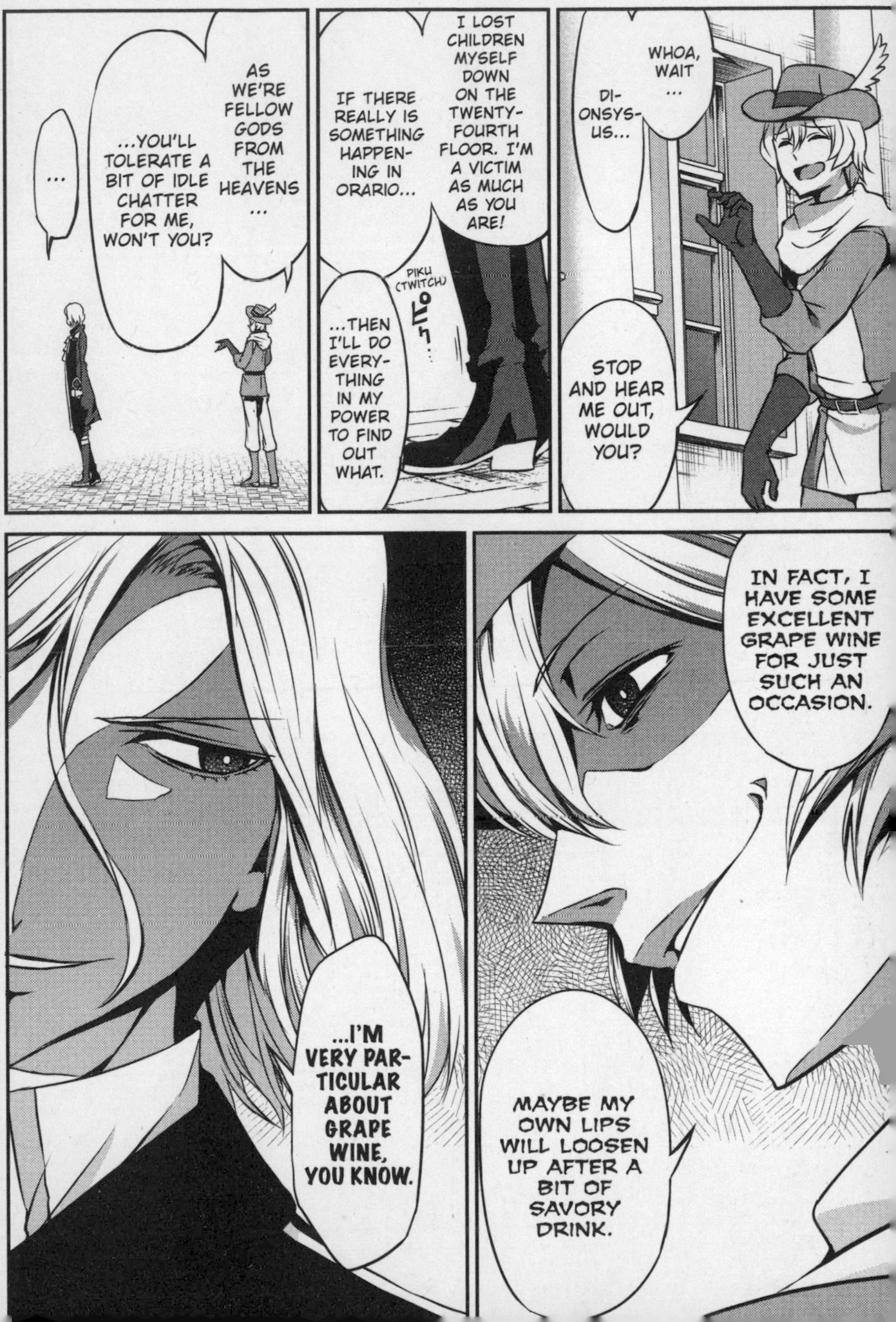
WHOA, WAIT ...
DI-ONSYS-US...
STOP AND HEAR ME OUT, WOULD YOU?
I LOST CHILDREN MYSELF DOWN ON THE TWENTY-FOURTH FLOOR. I'M A VICTIM AS MUCH AS YOU ARE!
IF THERE REALLY IS SOMETHING HAPPENING IN ORARIO...
PIKU (TWITCH)
...THEN I'LL DO EVERYTHING IN MY POWER TO FIND OUT WHAT.
AS WE'RE FELLOW GODS FROM THE HEAVENS ...
...YOU'LL TOLERATE A BIT OF IDLE CHATTER FOR ME, WON'T YOU?
...
IN FACT, I HAVE SOME EXCELLENT GRAPE WINE FOR JUST SUCH AN OCCASION.
MAYBE MY OWN LIPS WILL LOOSEN UP AFTER A BIT OF SAVORY DRINK.
...I'M VERY PARTICULAR ABOUT GRAPE WINE, YOU KNOW.

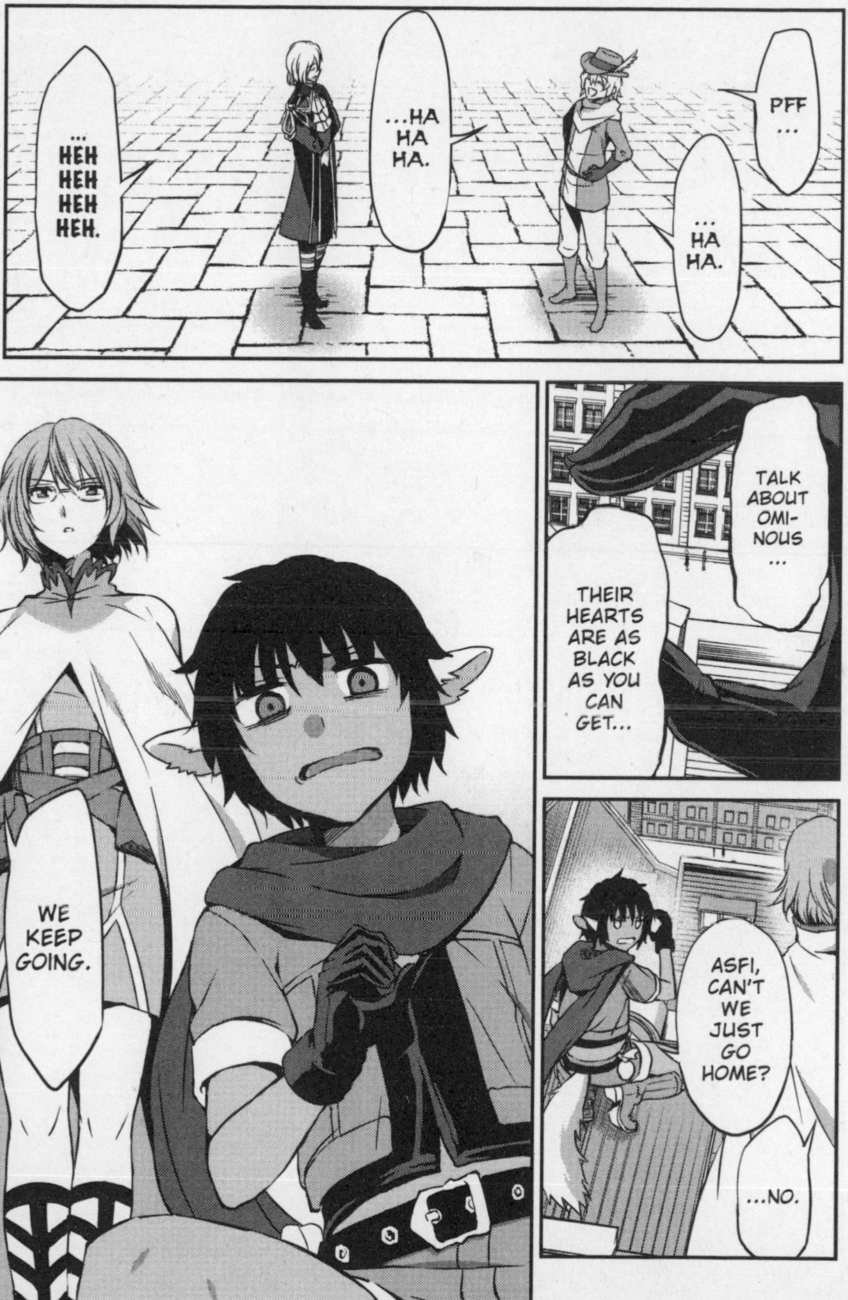
PFF...
...HA HA.
...HA HA HA.
...HEH HEH HEH HEH.
TALK ABOUT OMINOUS...
THEIR HEARTS ARE AS BLACK AS YOU CAN GET...
ASFI, CAN'T WE JUST GO HOME?
...NO.
WE KEEP GOING.

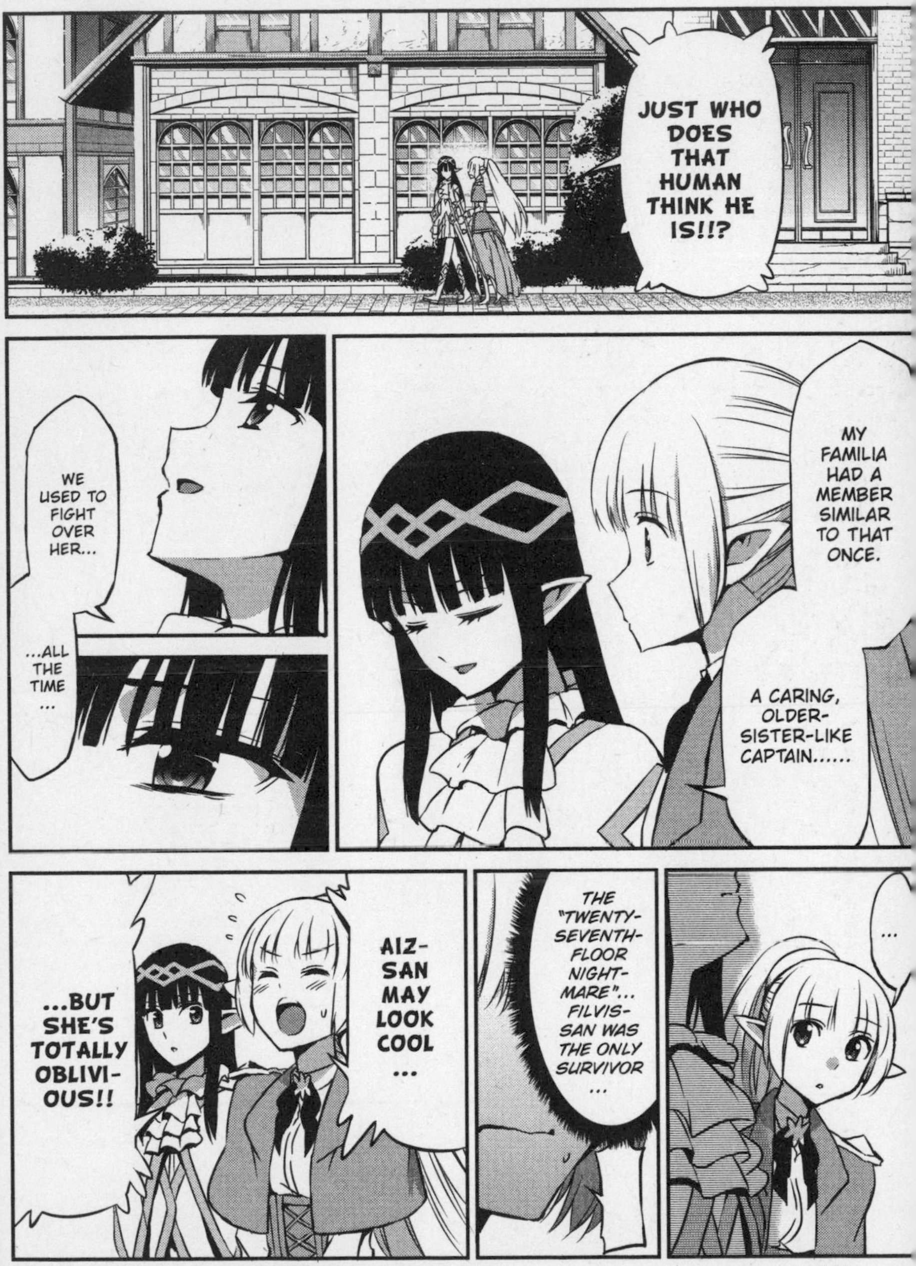
JUST WHO DOES THAT HUMAN THINK HE IS!!?
MY FAMILIA HAD A MEMBER SIMILAR TO THAT ONCE.
A CARING, OLDER-SISTER-LIKE CAPTAIN......
WE USED TO FIGHT OVER HER...
...ALL THE TIME ...
...
THE "TWENTY-SEVENTH-FLOOR NIGHTMARE"... FILVIS-SAN WAS THE ONLY SURVIVOR ...
AIZ-SAN MAY LOOK COOL ...
...BUT SHE'S TOTALLY OBLIVIOUS!!

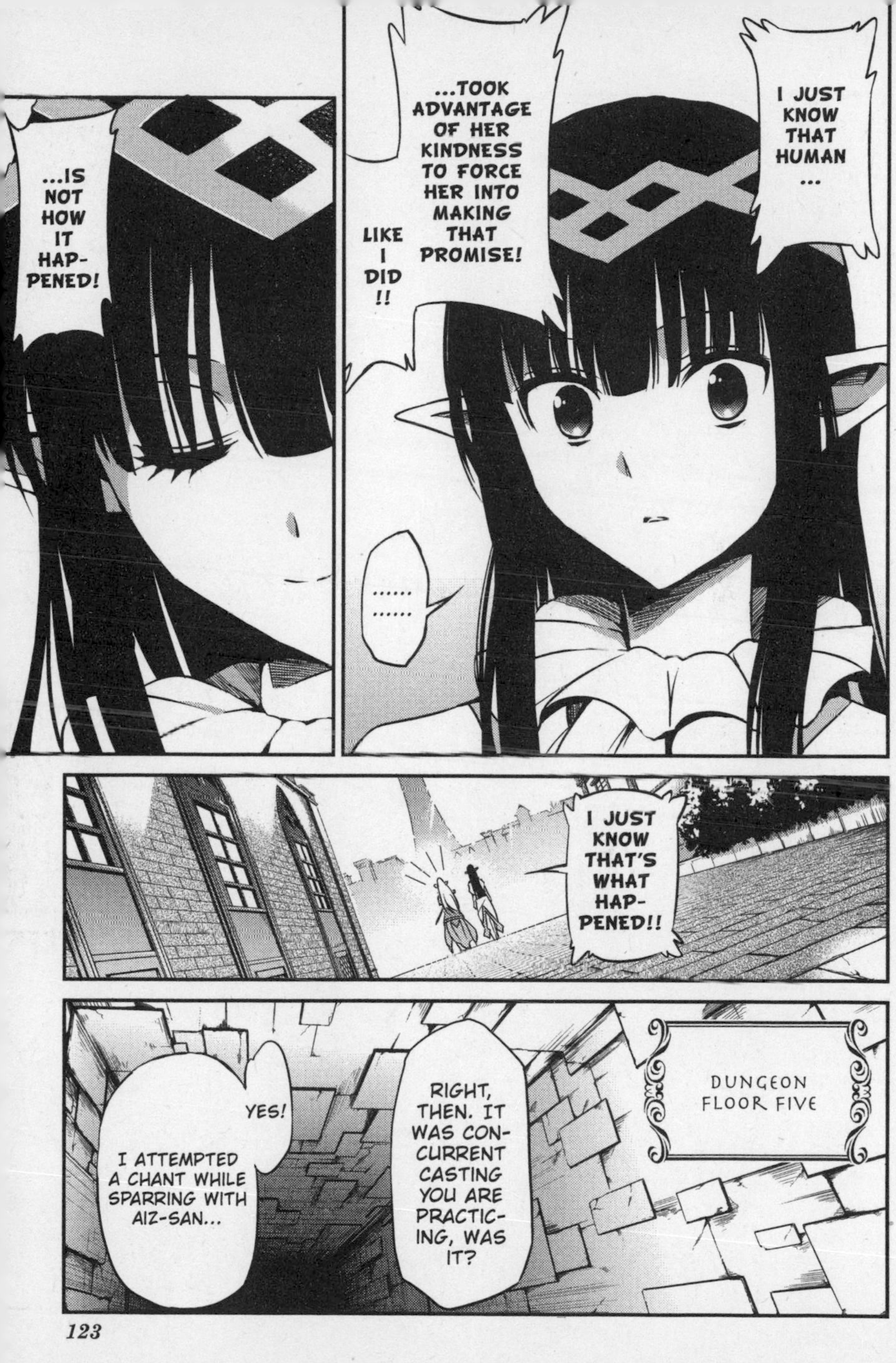
I JUST KNOW THAT HUMAN...
...TOOK ADVANTAGE OF HER KINDNESS TO FORCE HER INTO MAKING THAT PROMISE!
LIKE I DID!!
....
...IS NOT HOW IT HAPPENED!
I JUST KNOW THAT'S WHAT HAPPENED!!
DUNGEON FLOOR FIVE
RIGHT, THEN. IT WAS CONCURRENT CASTING YOU ARE PRACTICING, WAS IT?
YES!
I ATTEMPTED A CHANT WHILE SPARRING WITH AIZ-SAN...

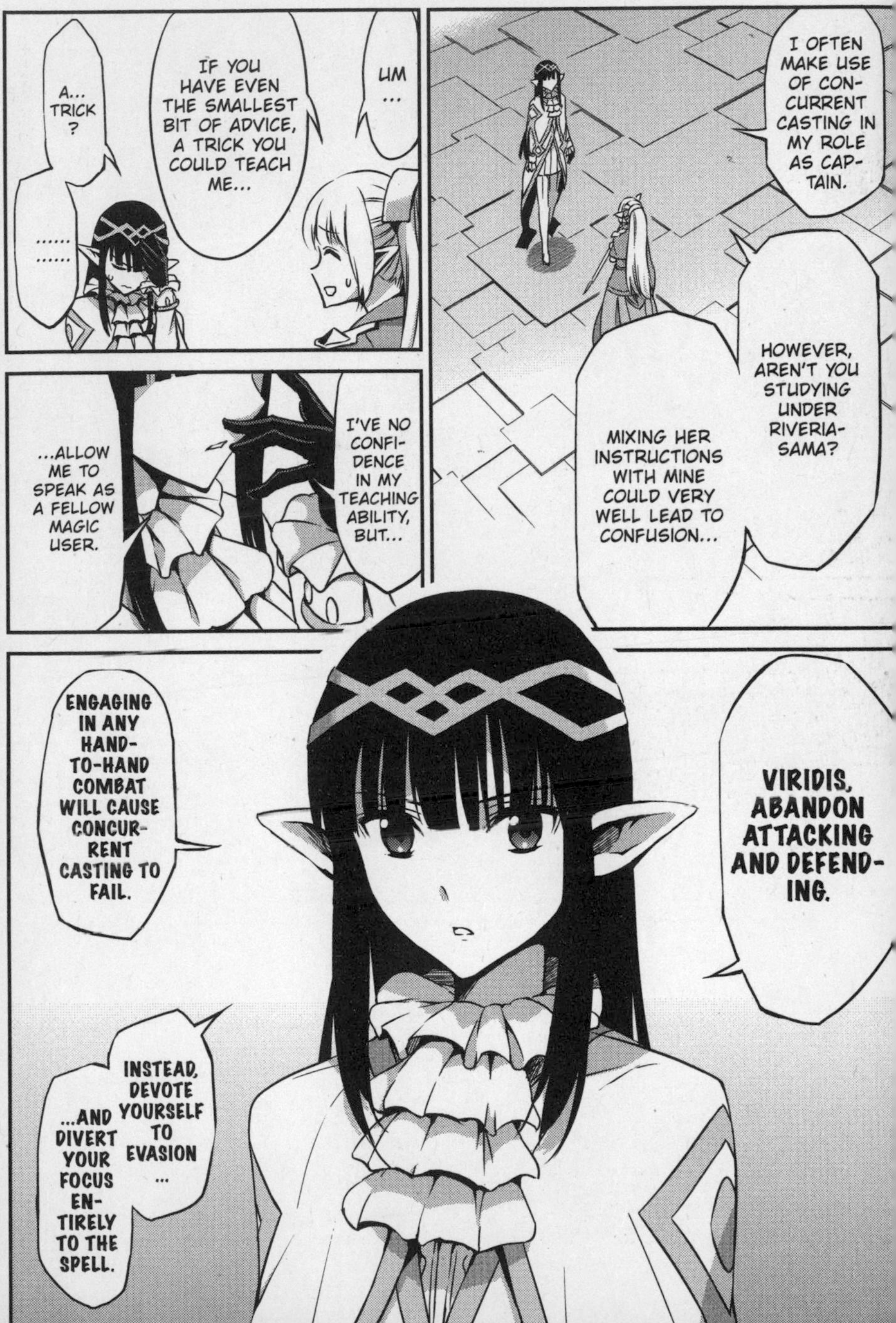

I OFTEN MAKE USE OF CONCURRENT CASTING IN MY ROLE AS CAPTAIN.
HOWEVER, AREN'T YOU STUDYING UNDER RIVERIA-SAMA?
MIXING HER INSTRUCTIONS WITH MINE COULD VERY WELL LEAD TO CONFUSION...
UM...
IF YOU HAVE EVEN THE SMALLEST BIT OF ADVICE, A TRICK YOU COULD TEACH ME...
A... TRICK?
....
I'VE NO CONFIDENCE IN MY TEACHING ABILITY, BUT...
...ALLOW ME TO SPEAK AS A FELLOW MAGIC USER.
VIRIDIS, ABANDON ATTACKING AND DEFENDING.
ENGAGING IN ANY HAND-TO-HAND COMBAT WILL CAUSE CONCURRENT CASTING TO FAIL.
INSTEAD, DEVOTE YOURSELF TO EVASION...
...AND DIVERT YOUR FOCUS ENTIRELY TO THE SPELL.

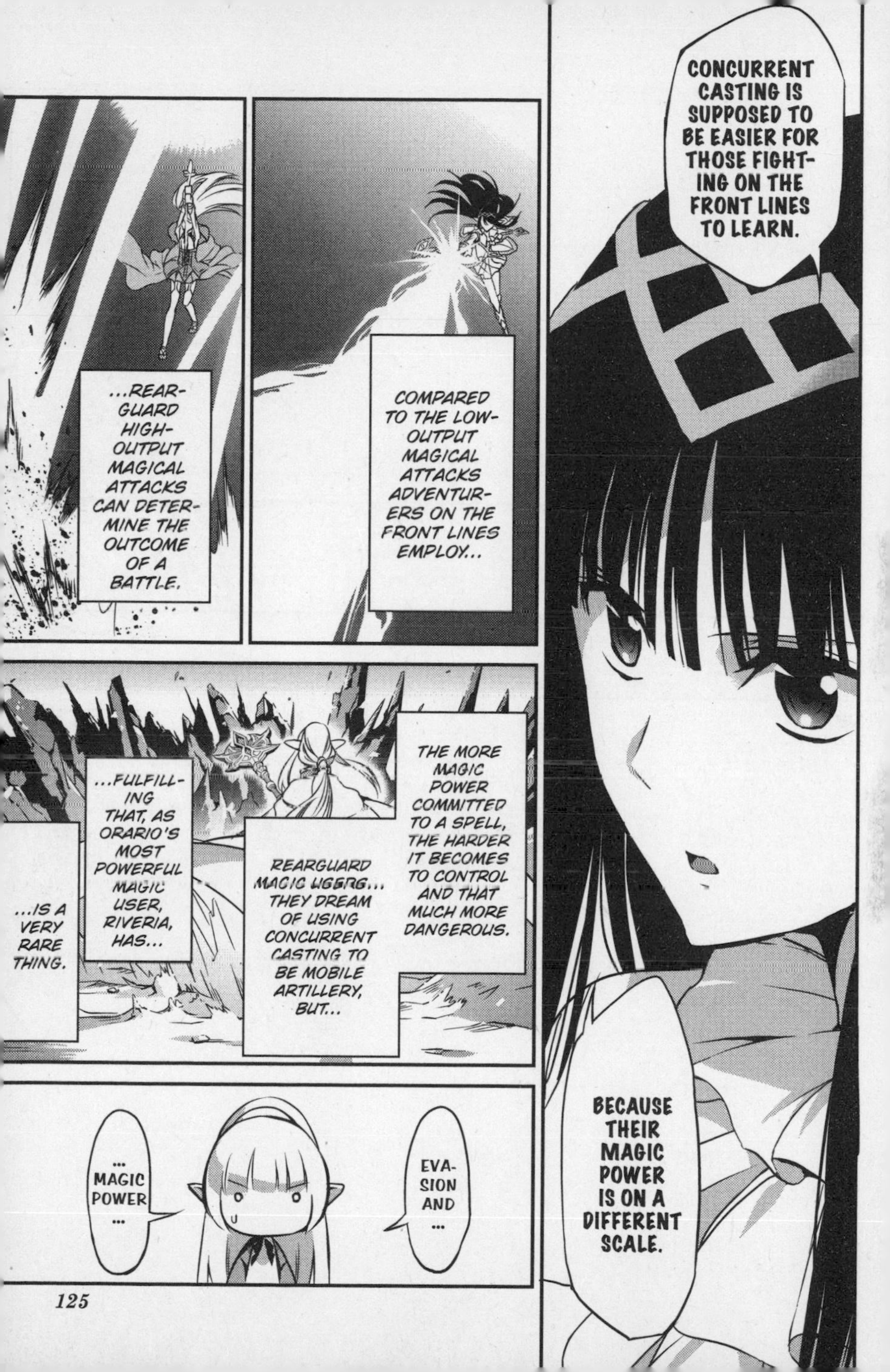

CONCURRENT CASTING IS SUPPOSED TO BE EASIER FOR THOSE FIGHTING ON THE FRONT LINES TO LEARN.
BECAUSE THEIR MAGIC POWER IS ON A DIFFERENT SCALE.
COMPARED TO THE LOW-OUTPUT MAGICAL ATTACKS ADVENTURERS ON THE FRONT LINES EMPLOY...
...REARGUARD HIGH-OUTPUT MAGICAL ATTACKS CAN DETERMINE THE OUTCOME OF A BATTLE.
THE MORE MAGIC POWER COMMITTED TO A SPELL, THE HARDER IT BECOMES TO CONTROL AND THAT MUCH MORE DANGEROUS.
REARGUARD MAGIC USERS... THEY DREAM OF USING CONCURRENT CASTING TO BE MOBILE ARTILLERY, BUT...
...FULFILLING THAT, AS ORARIO'S MOST POWERFUL MAGIC USER, RIVERIA, HAS...
...IS A VERY RARE THING.
EVASION AND ...
... MAGIC POWER ...

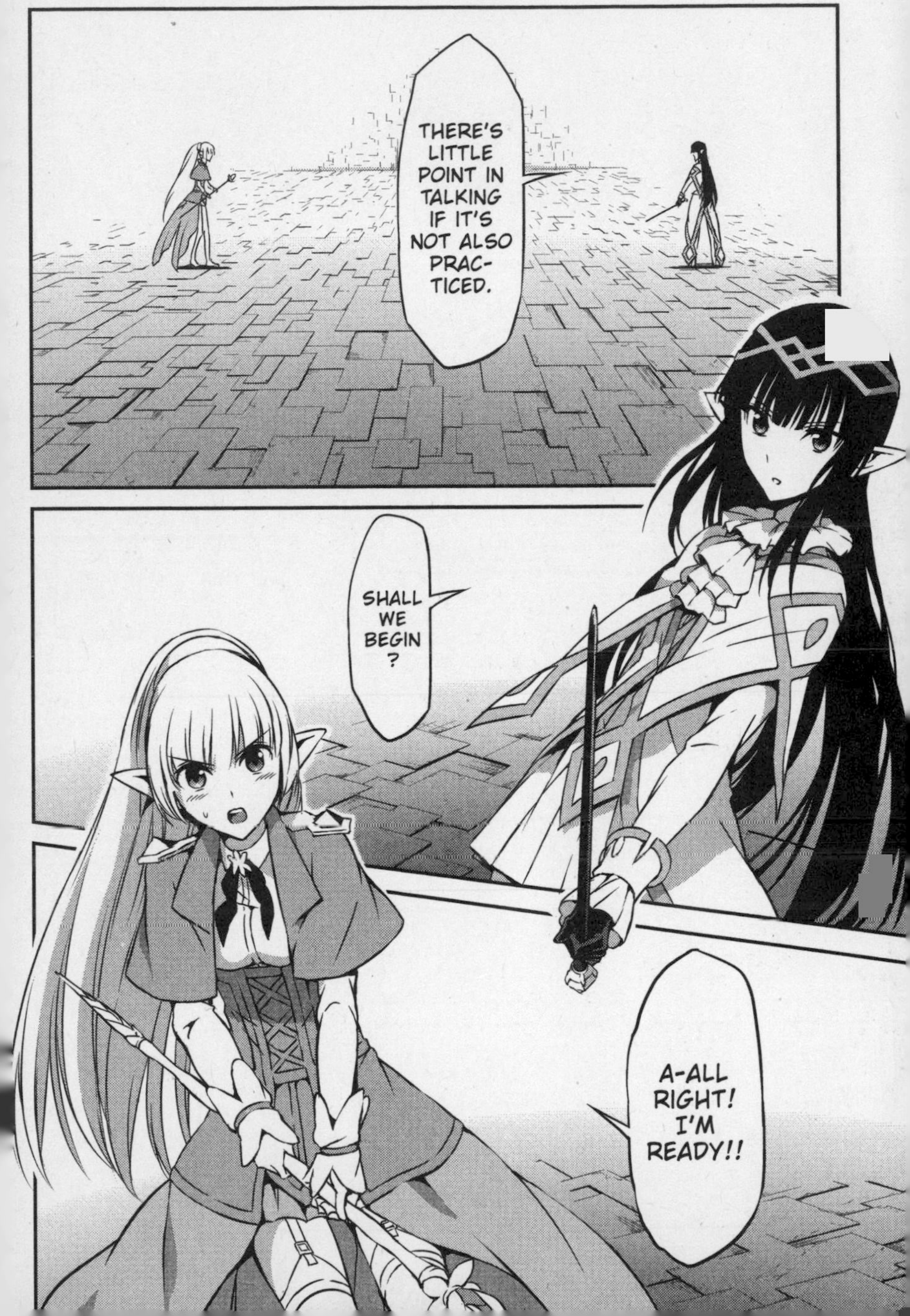
THERE'S LITTLE POINT IN TALKING IF IT'S NOT ALSO PRAC-TICED.
SHALL WE BEGIN?
A-ALL RIGHT! I'M READY!!

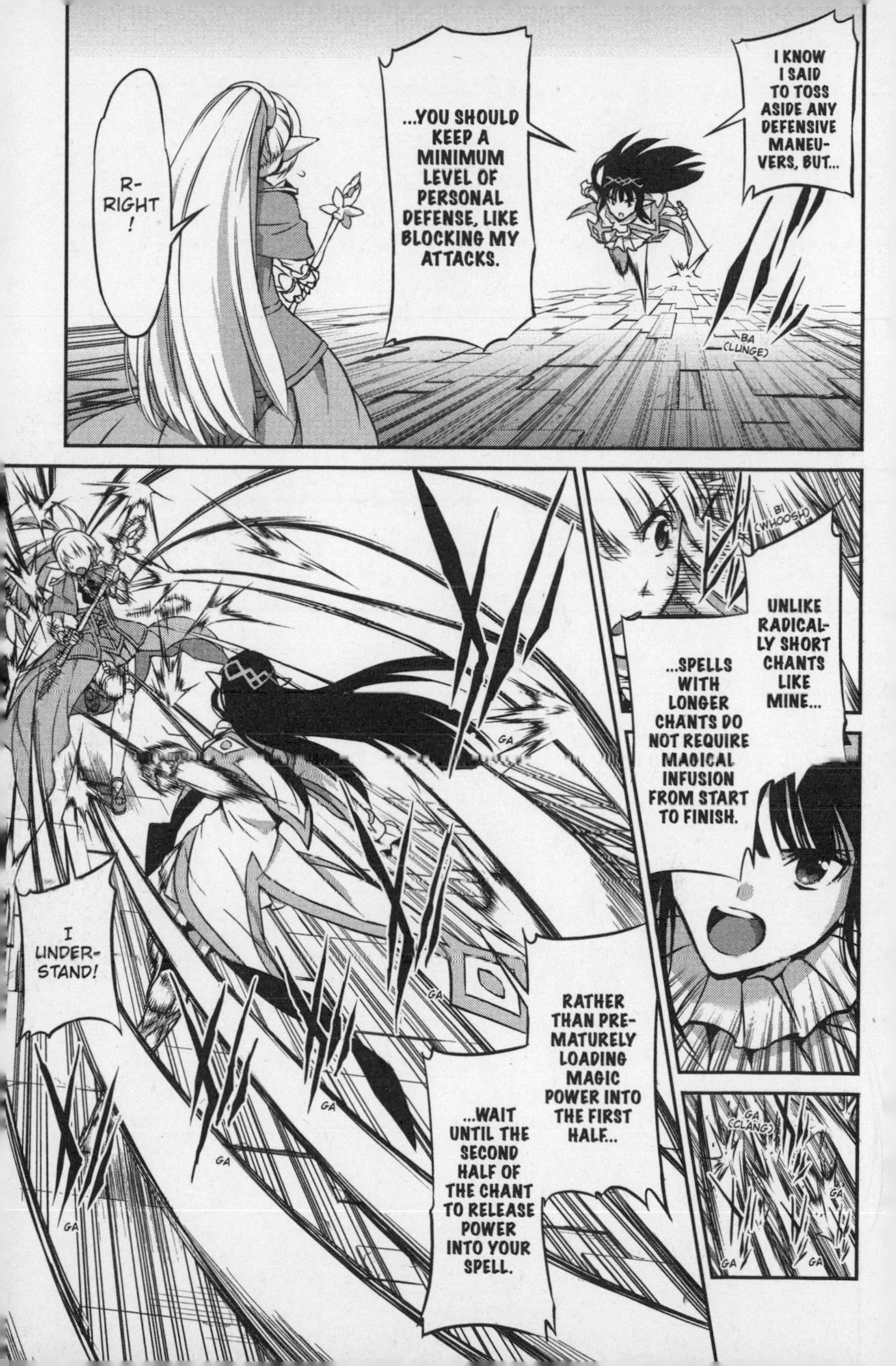
I KNOW I SAID TO TOSS ASIDE ANY DEFENSIVE MANEU-VERS, BUT...
...YOU SHOULD KEEP A MINIMUM LEVEL OF PERSONAL DEFENSE, LIKE BLOCKING MY ATTACKS.
BA (LUNGE)
R-RIGHT!
BI (WHOOSH)
UNLIKE RADICAL-LY SHORT CHANTS LIKE MINE...
...SPELLS WITH LONGER CHANTS DO NOT REQUIRE MAGICAL INFUSION FROM START TO FINISH.
RATHER THAN PRE-MATURELY LOADING MAGIC POWER INTO THE FIRST HALF...
...WAIT UNTIL THE SECOND HALF OF THE CHANT TO RELEASE POWER INTO YOUR SPELL.
GA (CLANG)
GA
GA
GA
GA
GA
GA
GA
GA
I UNDER-STAND!

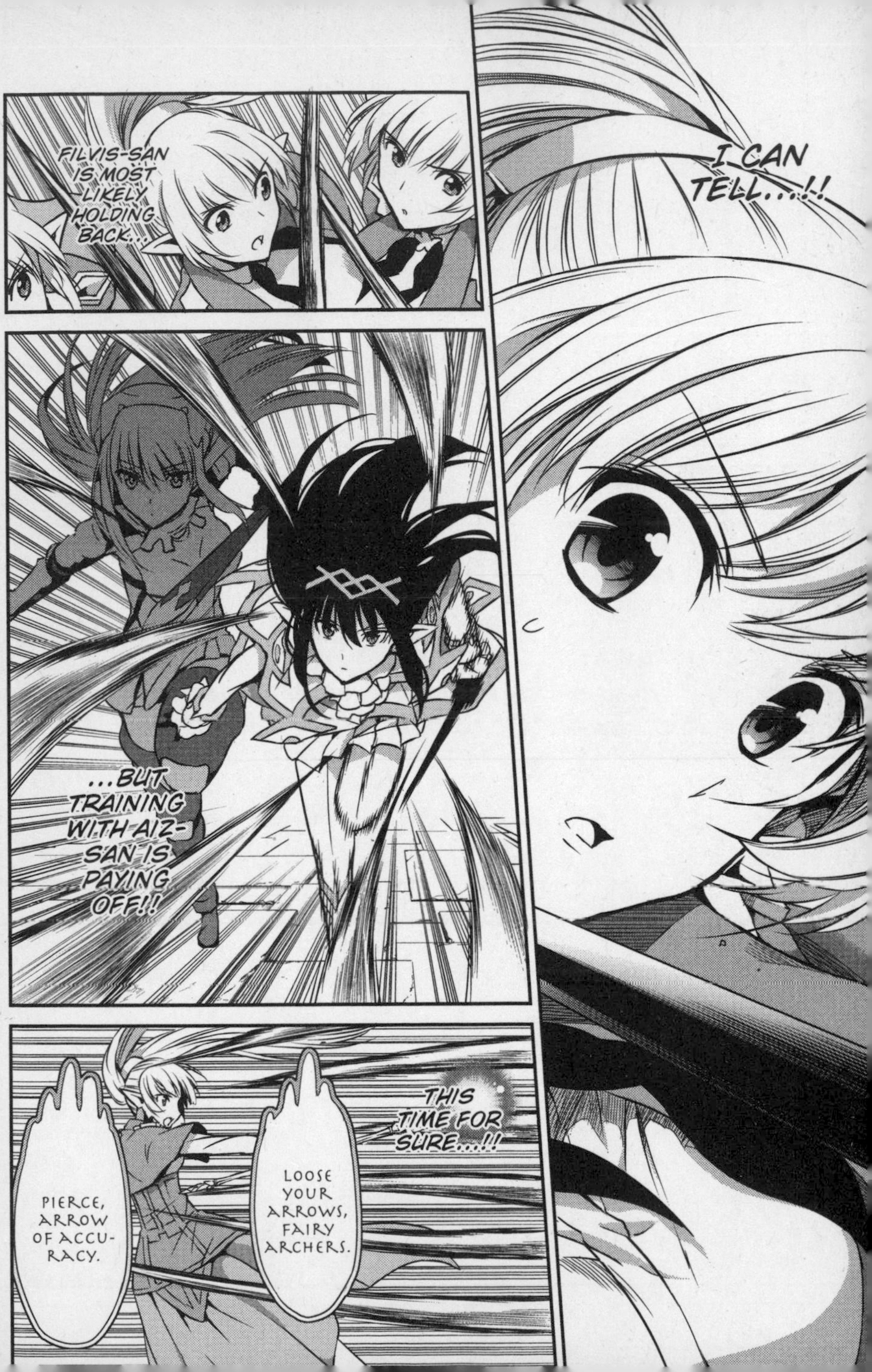
I CAN TELL...!!
FILVIS-SAN IS MOST LIKELY HOLDING BACK...
...BUT TRAINING WITH AIZ-SAN IS PAYING OFF!!
THIS TIME FOR SURE...!!
LOOSE YOUR ARROWS, FAIRY ARCHERS.
PIERCE, ARROW OF ACCU-RACY.

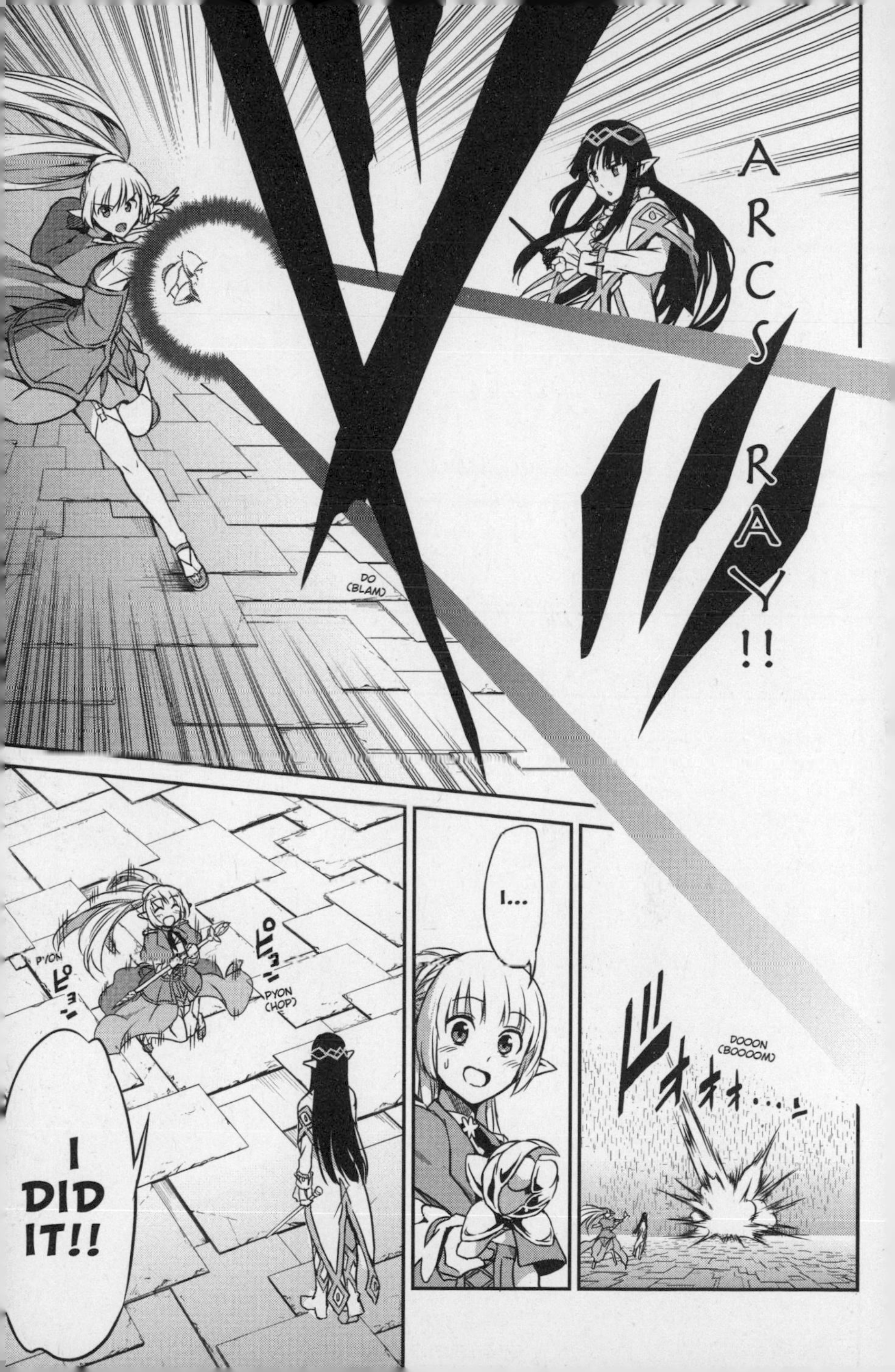
ARCSRAY!!
DO (BLAM)
DOOON (BOOOOM)
I...
PYON (HOP)
P'YON
I DID IT!!

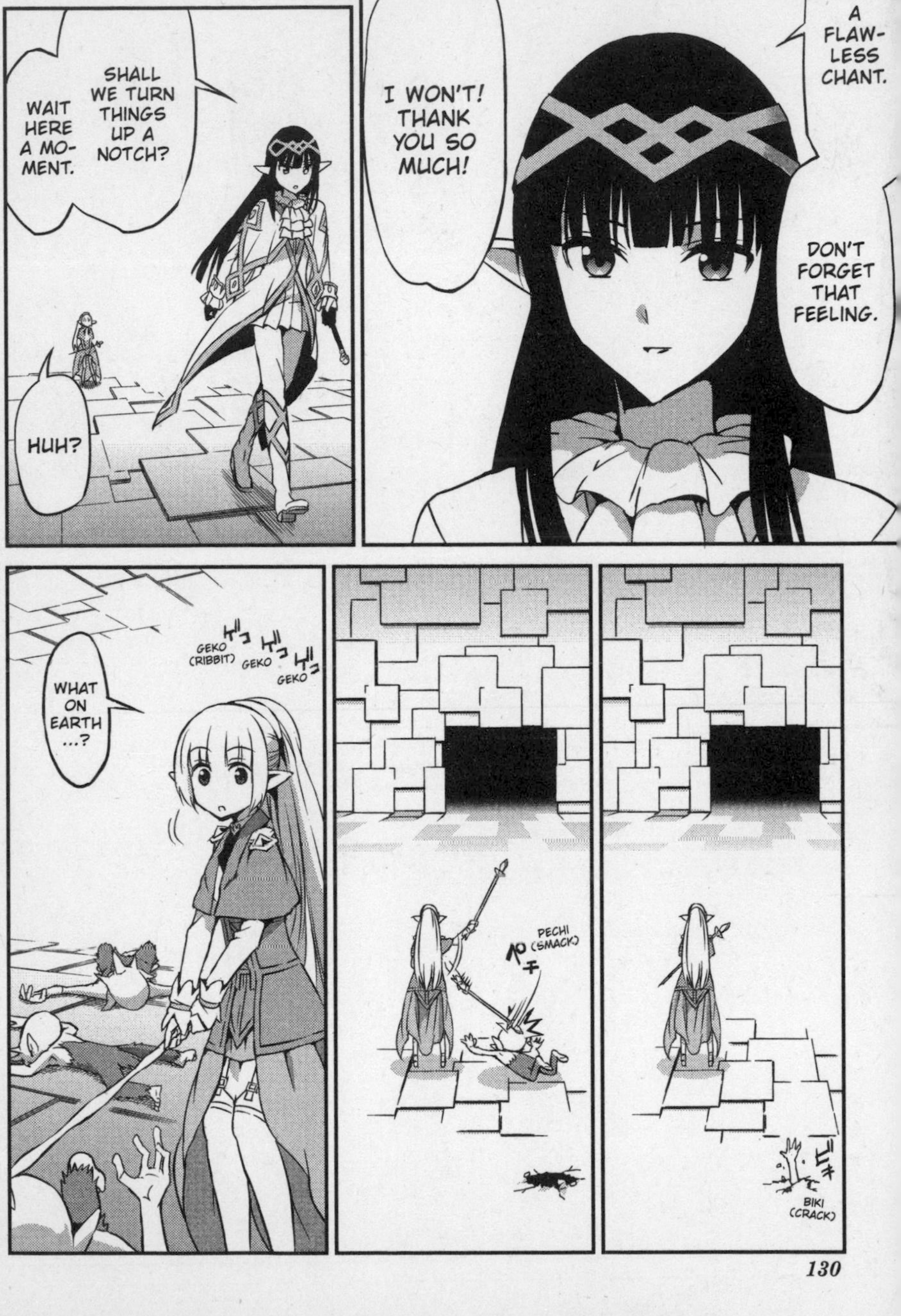
A FLAW-LESS CHANT.
DON'T FORGET THAT FEELING.
I WON'T! THANK YOU SO MUCH!
SHALL WE TURN THINGS UP A NOTCH?
WAIT HERE A MO-MENT.
HUH?
BIKI (CRACK)
PECHI (SMACK)
GEKO (RIBBIT)
GEKO
GEKO
WHAT ON EARTH ...?

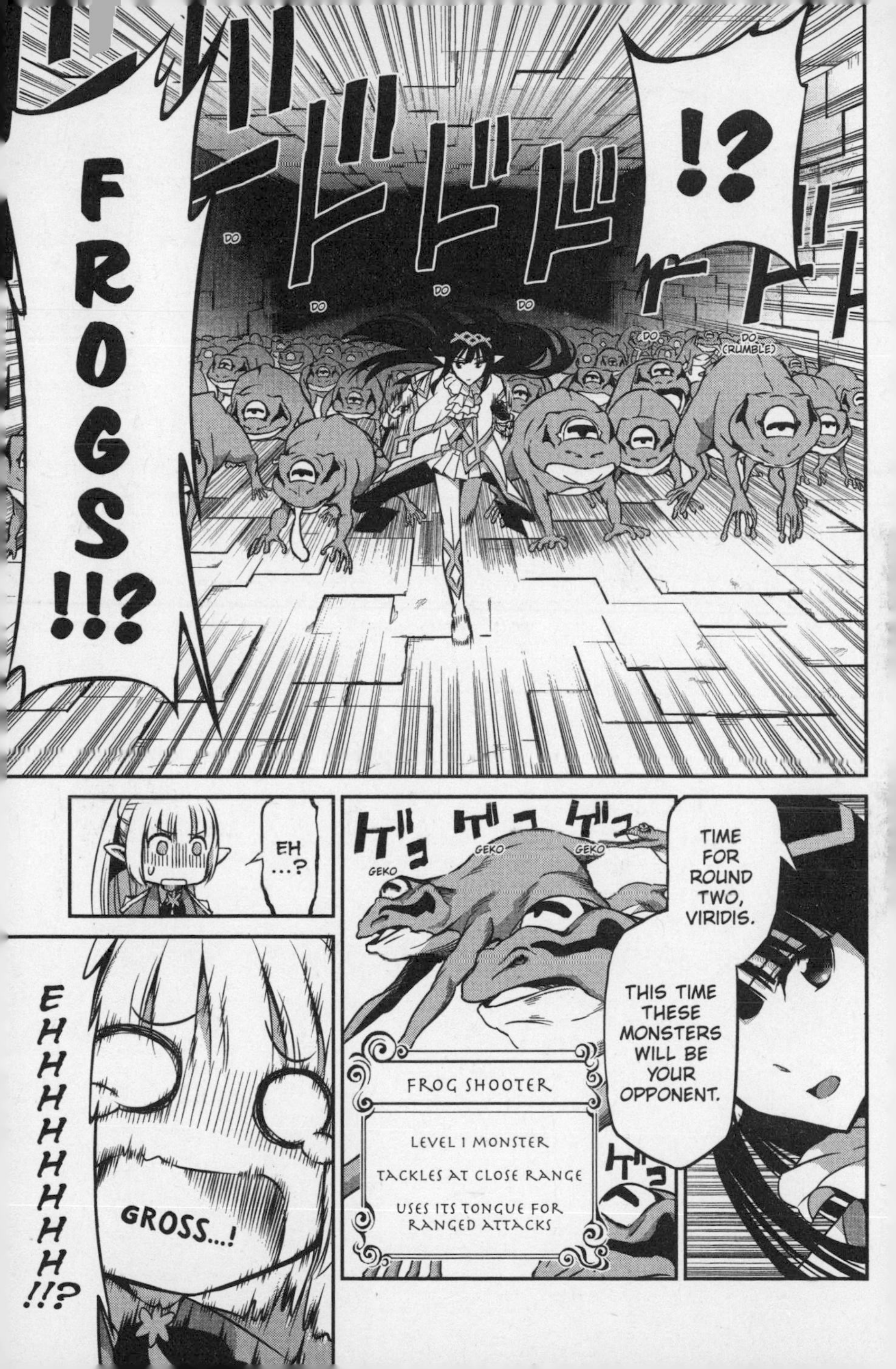
!?
DO
DO
DO
DO
DO
DO (RUMBLE)
FROGS!!?
GEKO
GEKO
GEKO
TIME FOR ROUND TWO, VIRIDIS.
THIS TIME THESE MONSTERS WILL BE YOUR OPPONENT.
FROG SHOOTER
LEVEL 1 MONSTER
TACKLES AT CLOSE RANGE
USES ITS TONGUE FOR RANGED ATTACKS
EH ...?
EHHHHHHHHHHH!!?
GROSS...!

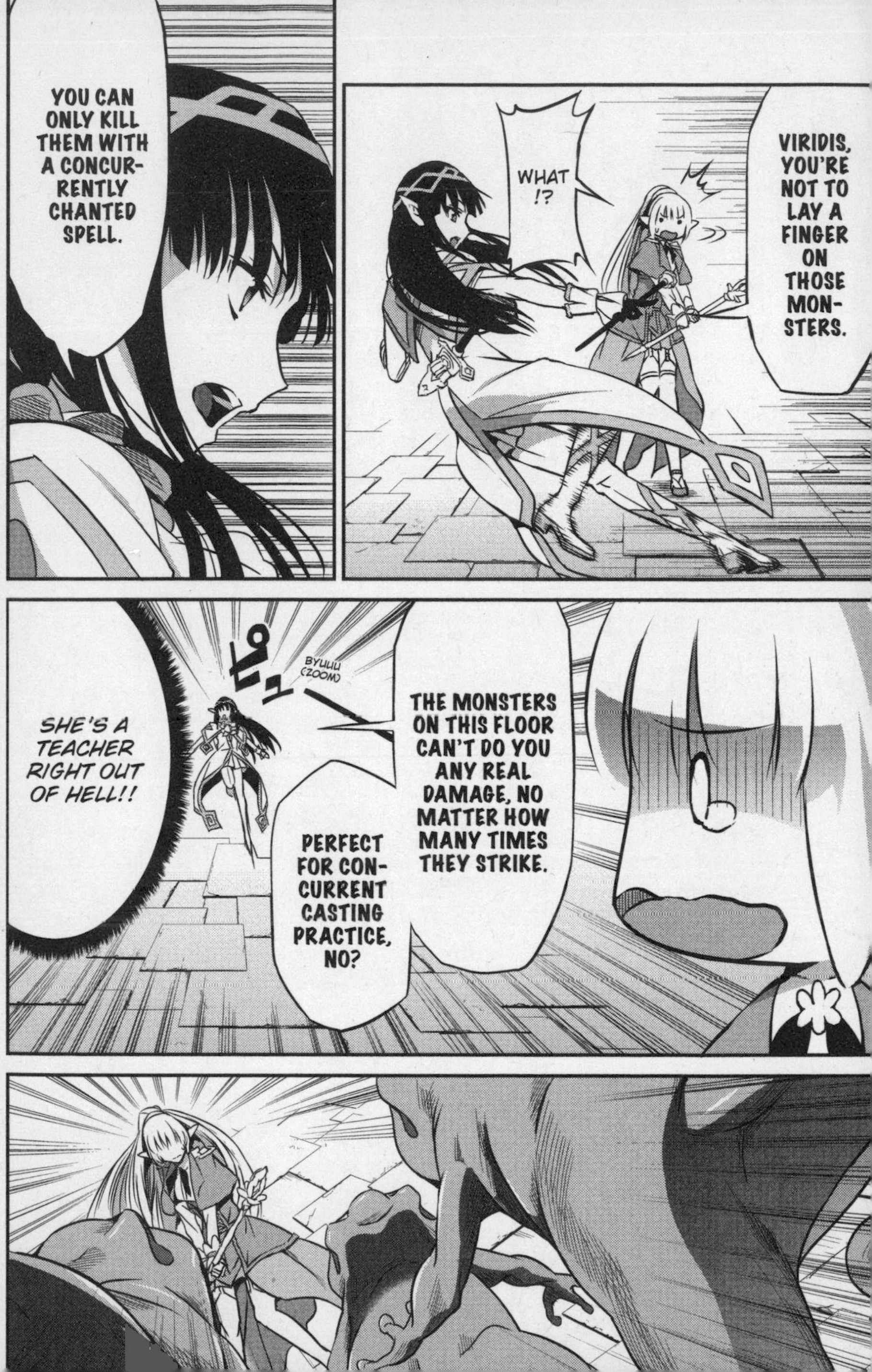
VIRIDIS, YOU'RE NOT TO LAY A FINGER ON THOSE MONSTERS.
WHAT !?
YOU CAN ONLY KILL THEM WITH A CONCUR-RENTLY CHANTED SPELL.
THE MONSTERS ON THIS FLOOR CAN'T DO YOU ANY REAL DAMAGE, NO MATTER HOW MANY TIMES THEY STRIKE.
PERFECT FOR CON-CURRENT CASTING PRACTICE, NO?
BYUUU (ZOOM)
SHE'S A TEACHER RIGHT OUT OF HELL!!

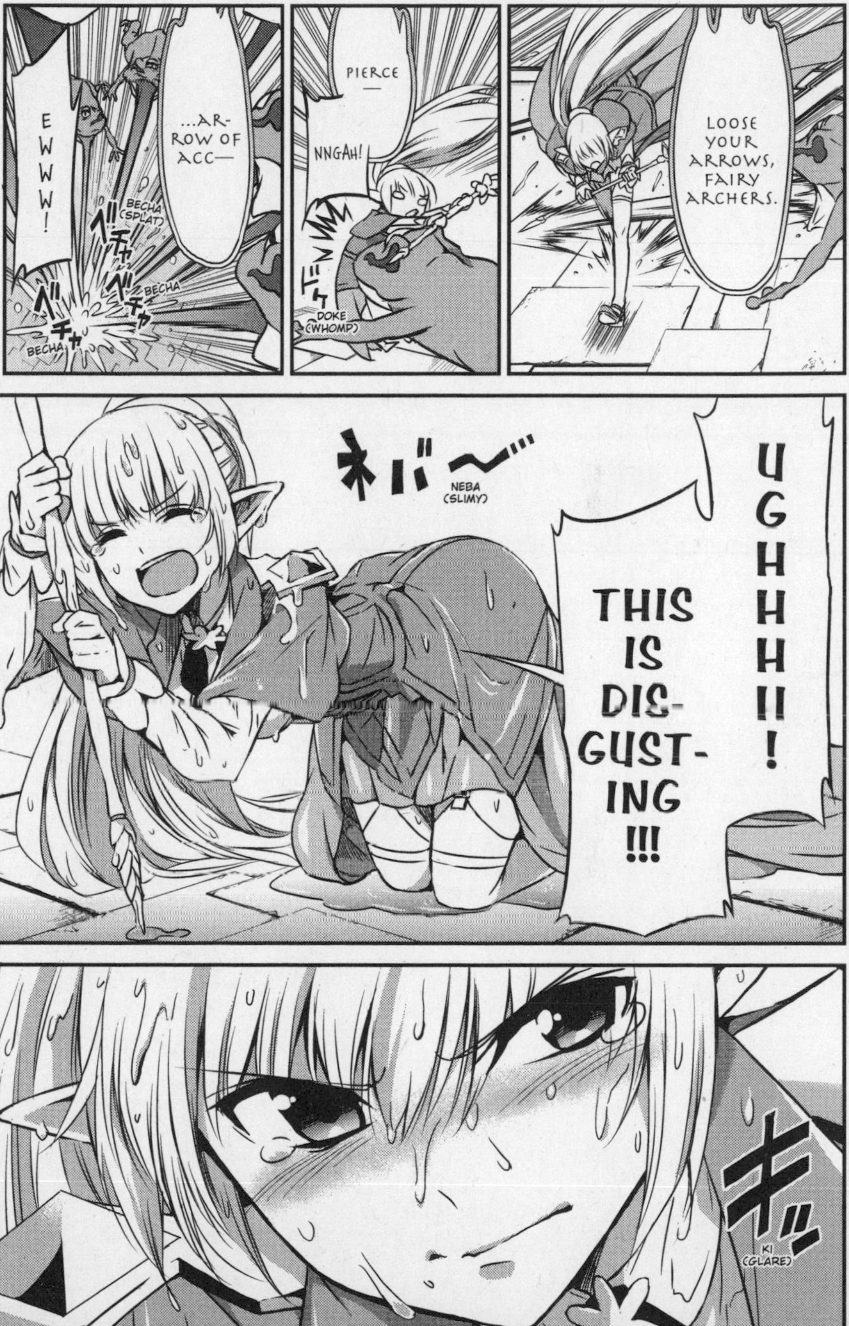
LOOSE YOUR ARROWS, FAIRY ARCHERS.
PIERCE—
NNGAH!
ドゲ
DOKE (WHOMP)
...AR-ROW OF ACC—
EWWWW!
ベチャ
BECHA (SPLAT)
ベチャ
BECHA
ベチャ
BECHA
UGHHHH!
THIS IS DIS-GUST-ING!!!
ネバ～
NEBA (SLIMY)
キッ
KI (GLARE)

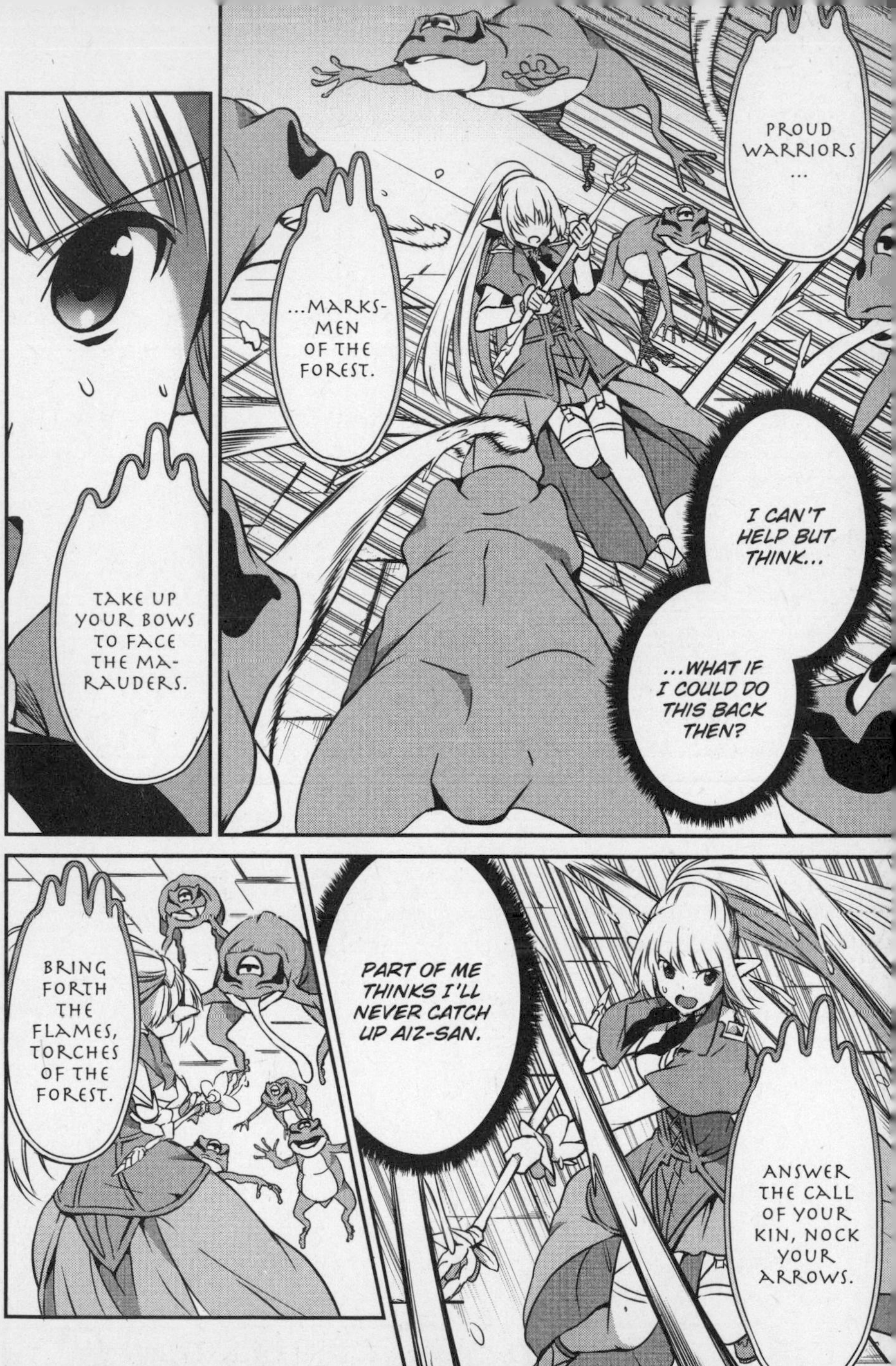
PROUD WARRIORS ...
...MARKS-MEN OF THE FOREST.
I CAN'T HELP BUT THINK...
...WHAT IF I COULD DO THIS BACK THEN?
TAKE UP YOUR BOWS TO FACE THE MA-RAUDERS.
PART OF ME THINKS I'LL NEVER CATCH UP AIZ-SAN.
ANSWER THE CALL OF YOUR KIN, NOCK YOUR ARROWS.
BRING FORTH THE FLAMES, TORCHES OF THE FOREST.

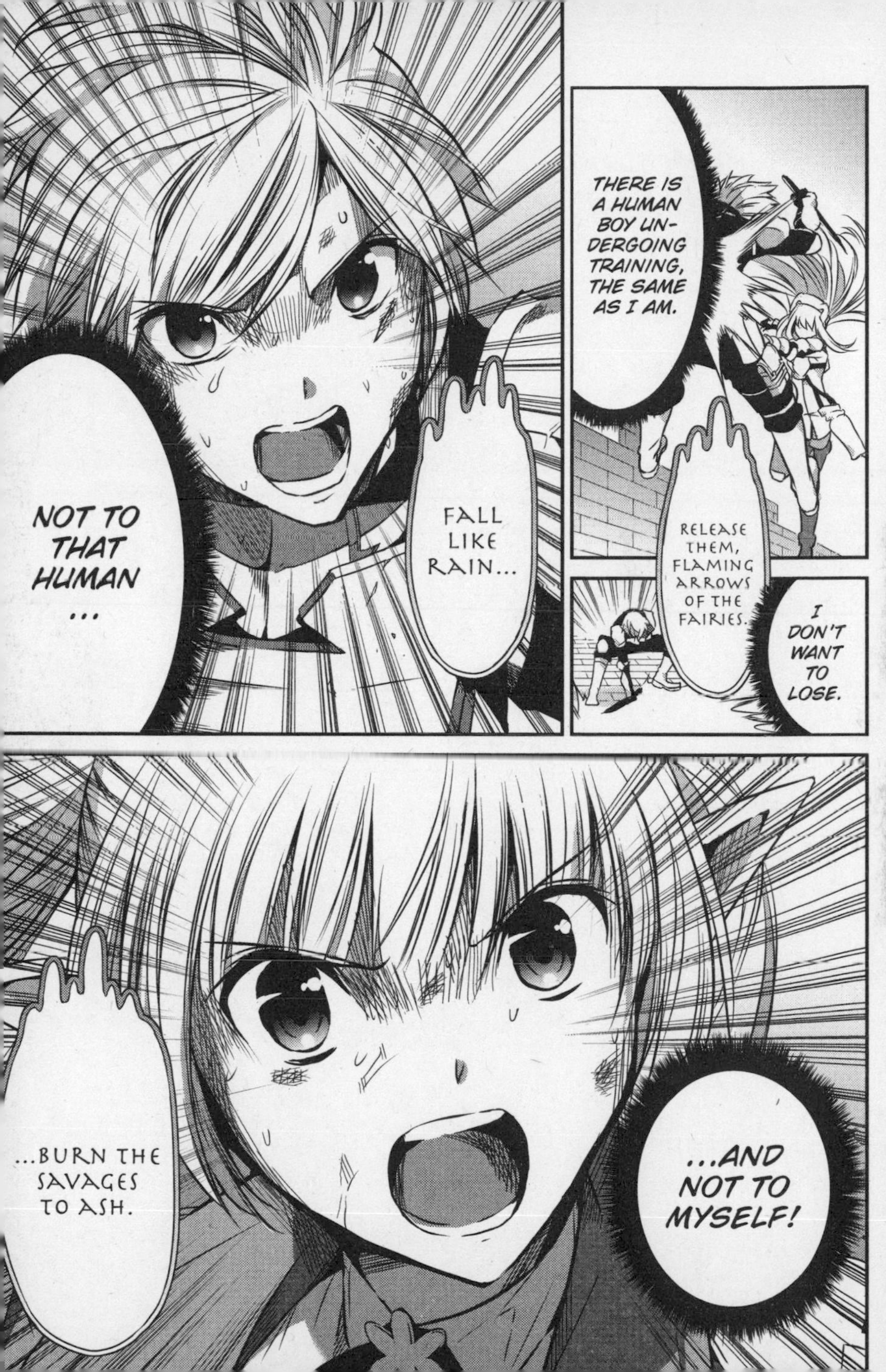
THERE IS A HUMAN BOY UN-DERGOING TRAINING, THE SAME AS I AM.
RELEASE THEM, FLAMING ARROWS OF THE FAIRIES.
I DON'T WANT TO LOSE.
FALL LIKE RAIN...
NOT TO THAT HUMAN...
...AND NOT TO MYSELF!
...BURN THE SAVAGES TO ASH.

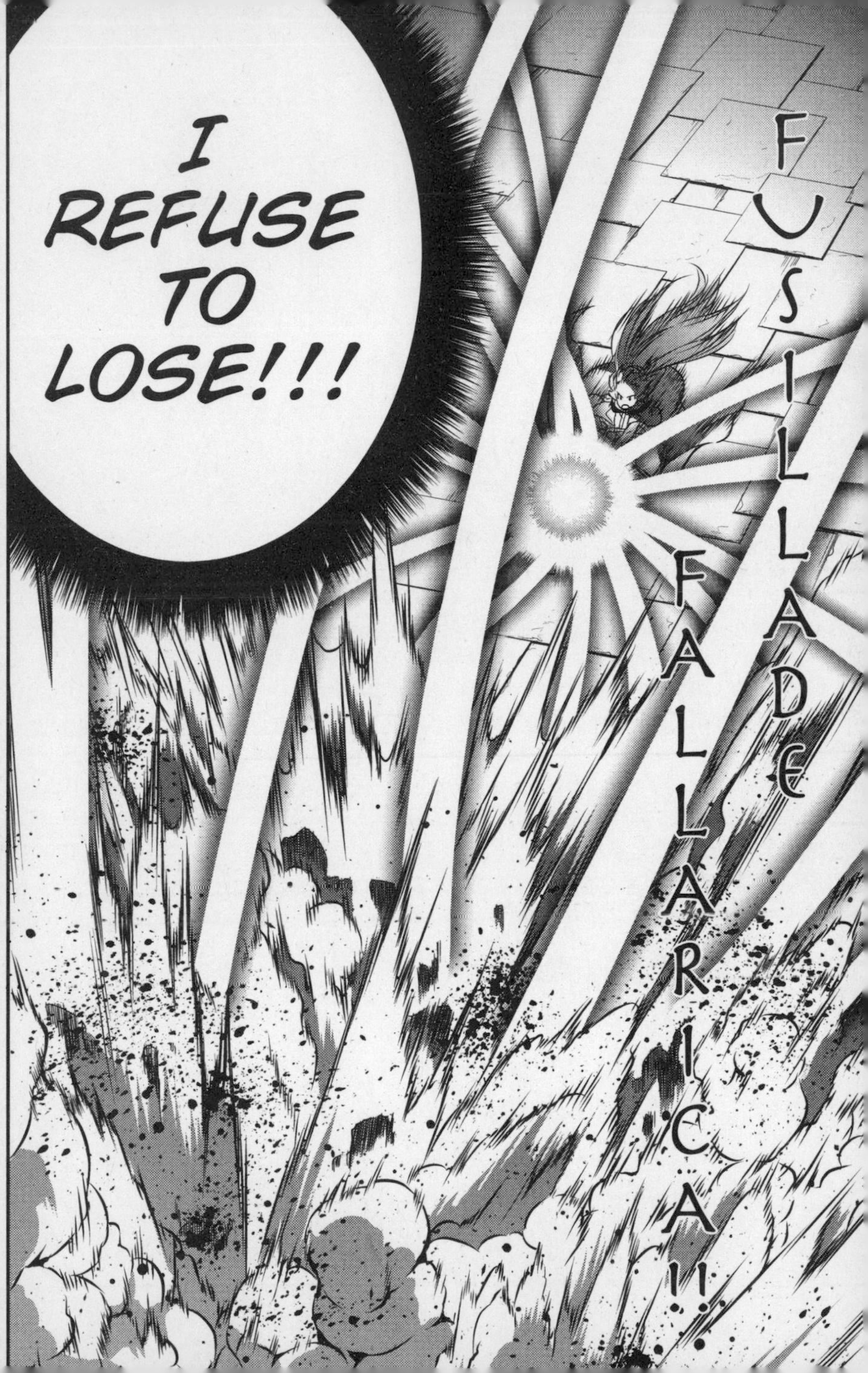
FUSILLADE
FALLARICA!!
I REFUSE TO LOSE!!!

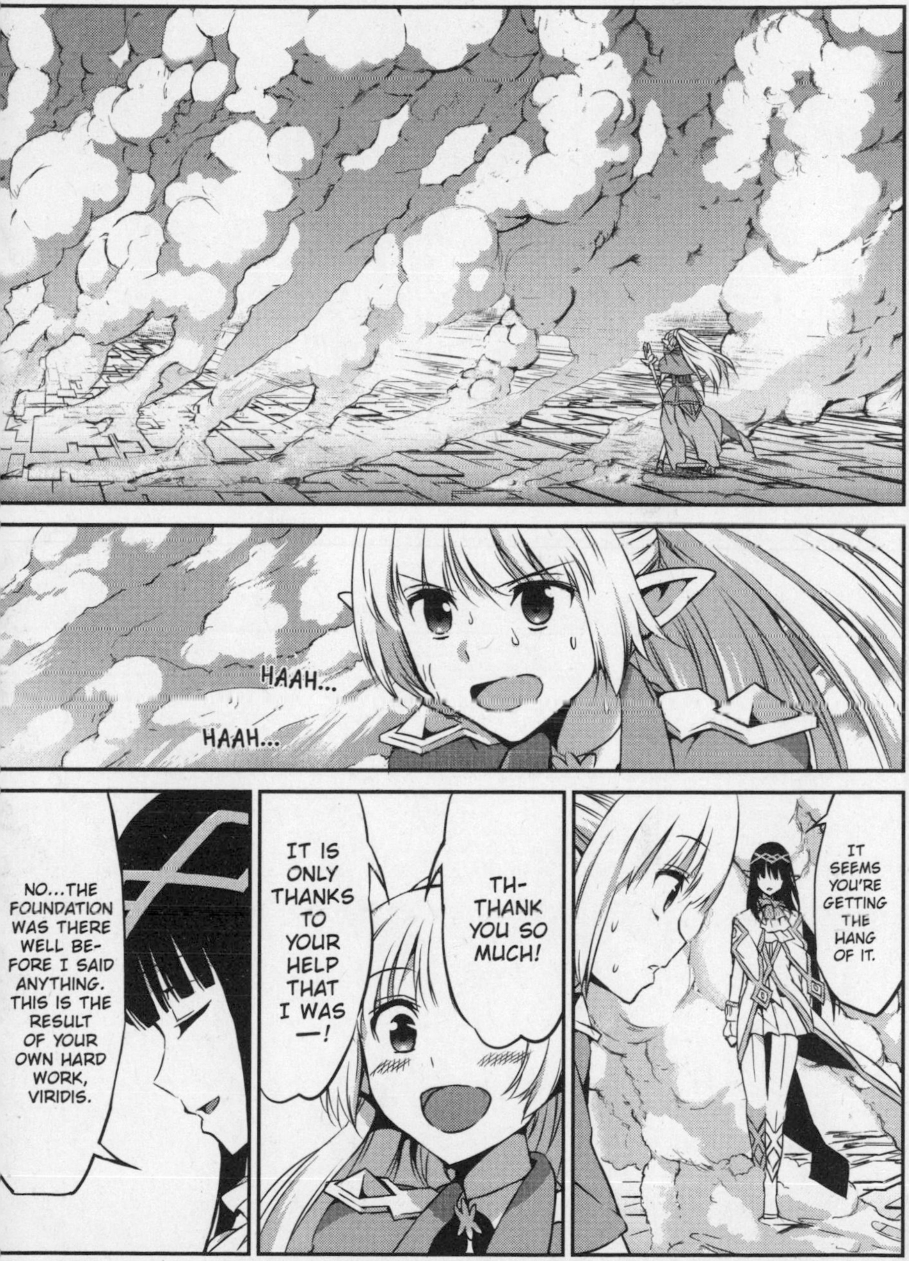
HAAH...
HAAH...
IT SEEMS YOU'RE GETTING THE HANG OF IT.
TH-THANK YOU SO MUCH!
IT IS ONLY THANKS TO YOUR HELP THAT I WAS—!
NO...THE FOUNDATION WAS THERE WELL BEFORE I SAID ANYTHING. THIS IS THE RESULT OF YOUR OWN HARD WORK, VIRIDIS.

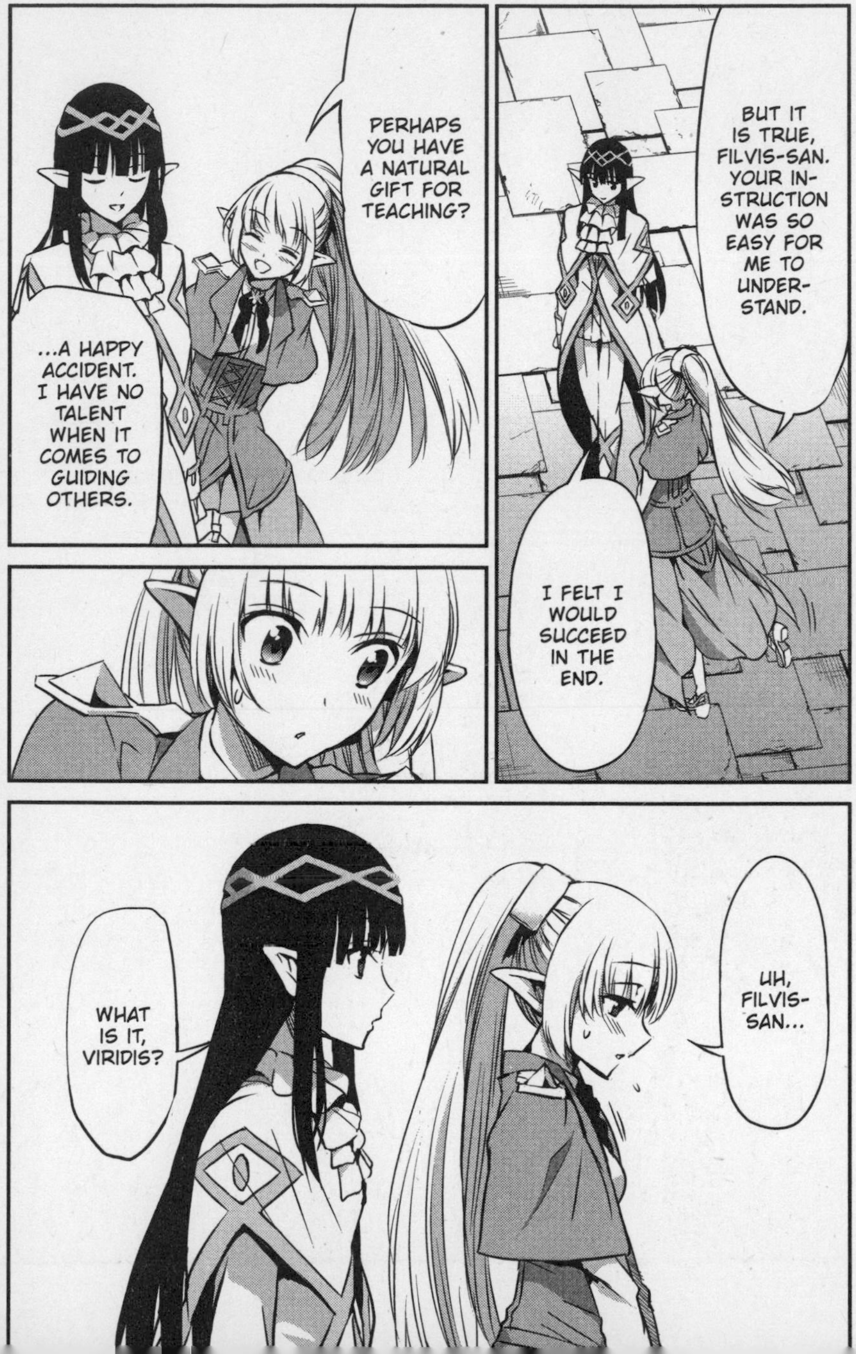
BUT IT IS TRUE, FILVIS-SAN. YOUR INSTRUCTION WAS SO EASY FOR ME TO UNDERSTAND.
I FELT I WOULD SUCCEED IN THE END.
PERHAPS YOU HAVE A NATURAL GIFT FOR TEACHING?
...A HAPPY ACCIDENT. I HAVE NO TALENT WHEN IT COMES TO GUIDING OTHERS.
UH, FILVIS-SAN...
WHAT IS IT, VIRIDIS?

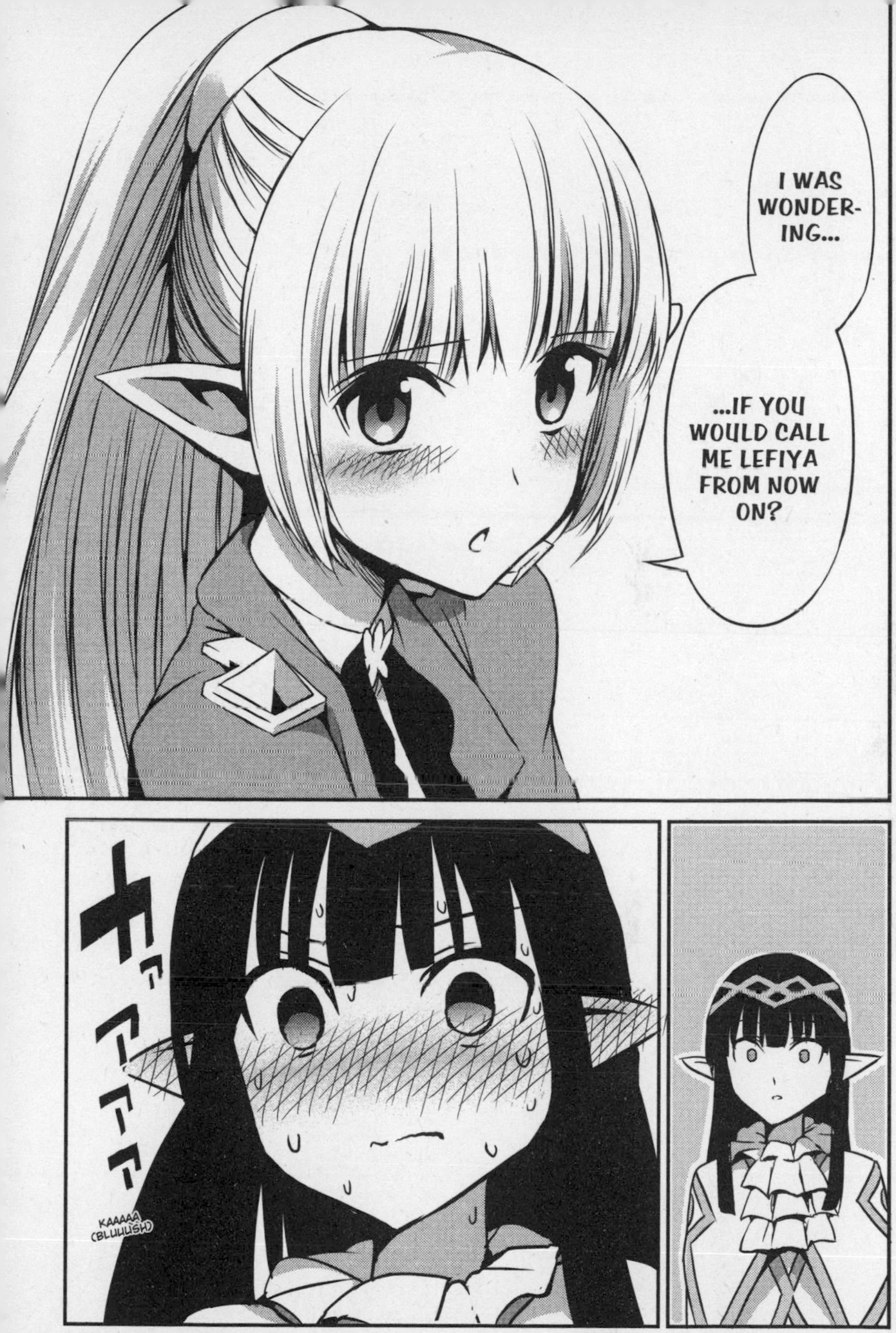
I WAS WONDER-ING...
...IF YOU WOULD CALL ME LEFIYA FROM NOW ON?
カァアァァ
KAAAAA (BLUUUSH)

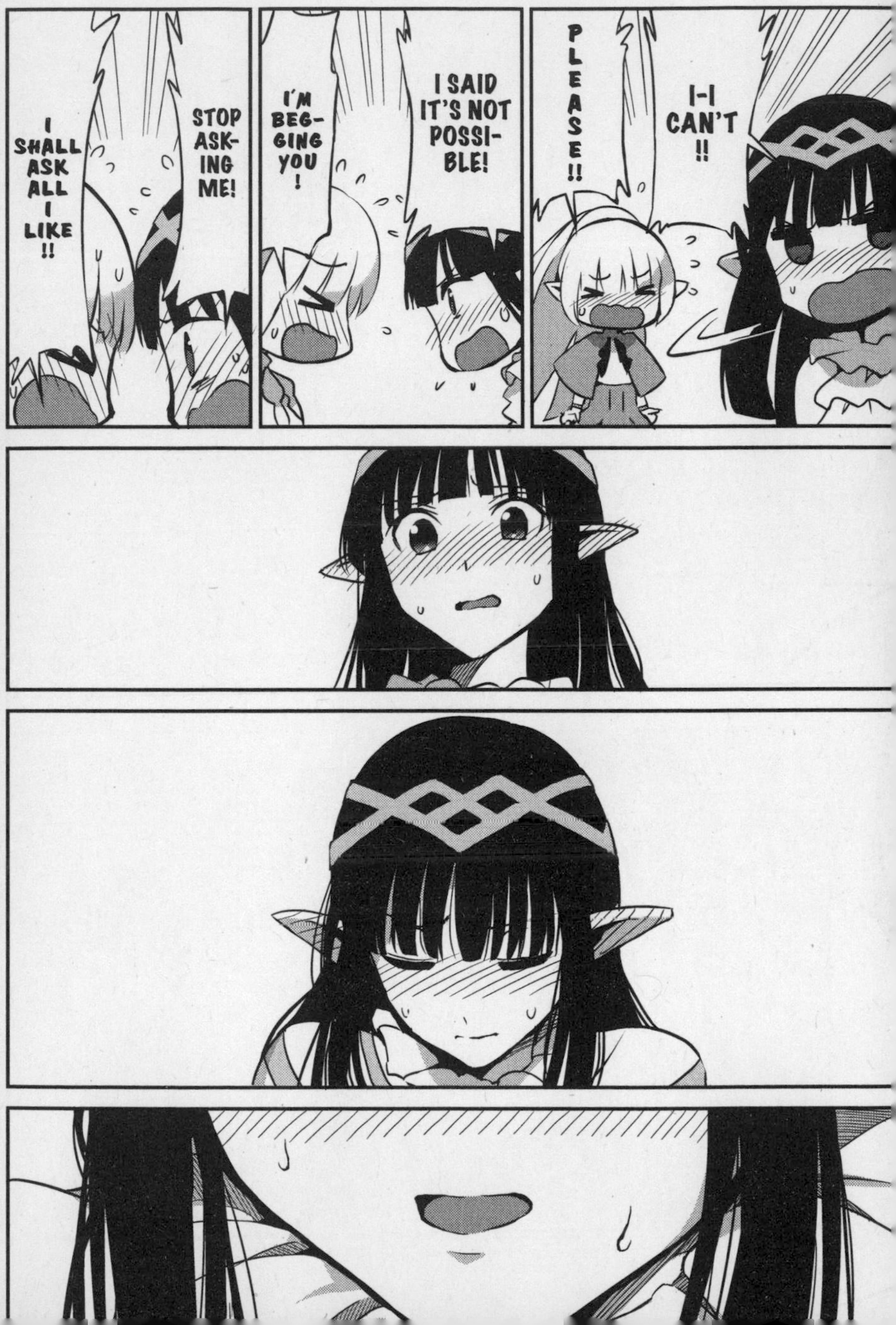
I-I CAN'T!!
PLEASE!!
I SAID IT'S NOT POSSI-BLE!
I'M BEG-GING YOU!
STOP ASK-ING ME!
I SHALL ASK ALL I LIKE!!

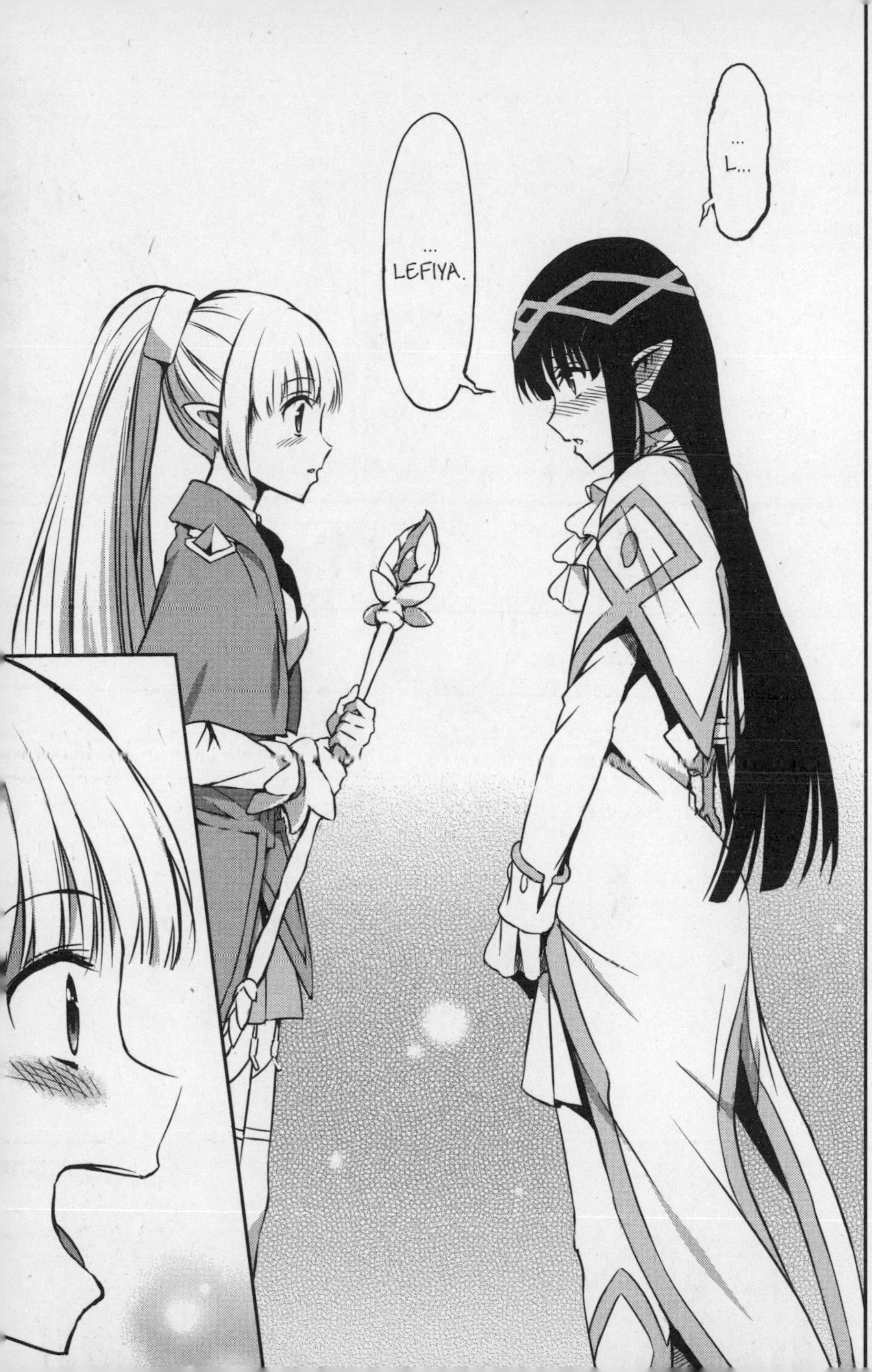
... L...
... LEFIYA.

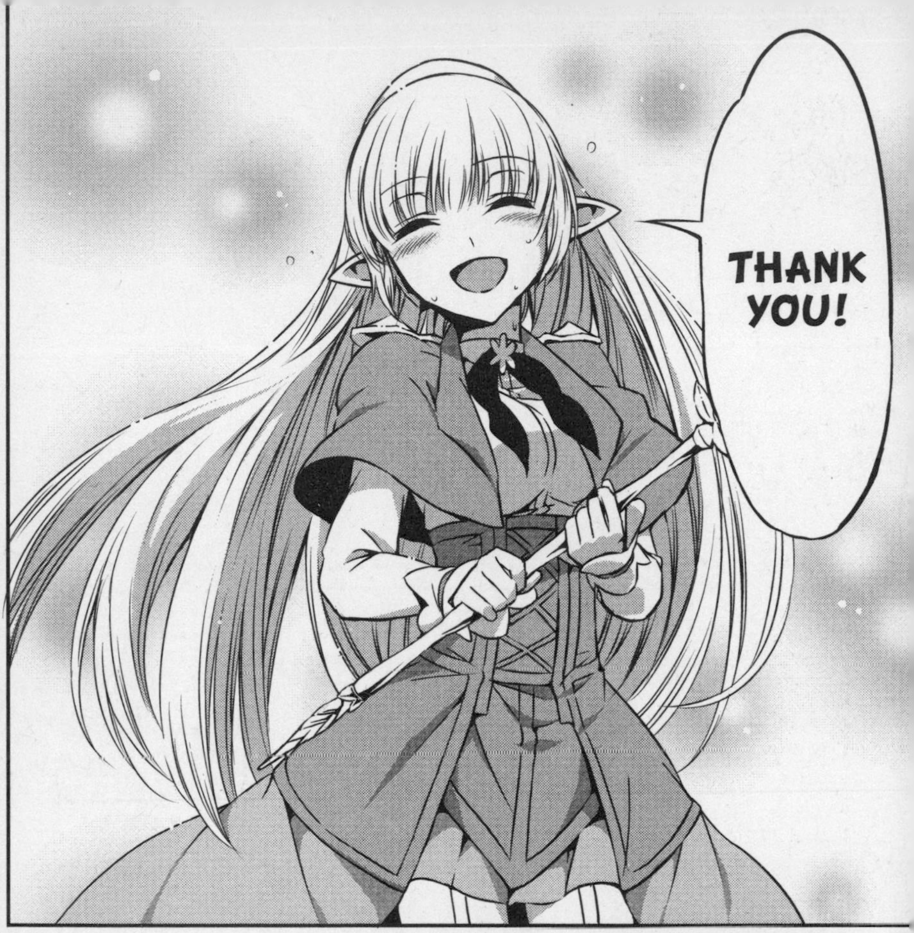
THANK YOU!

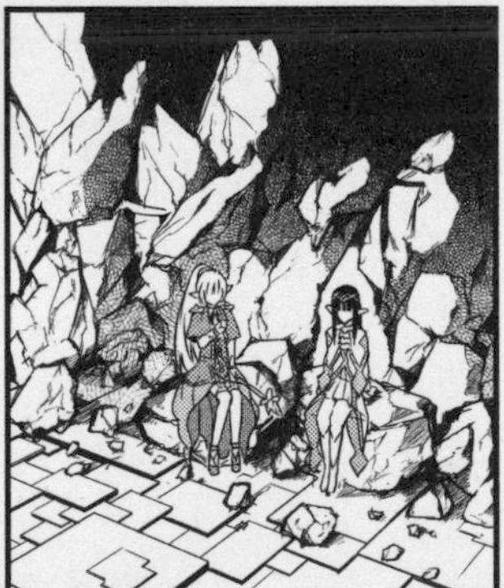

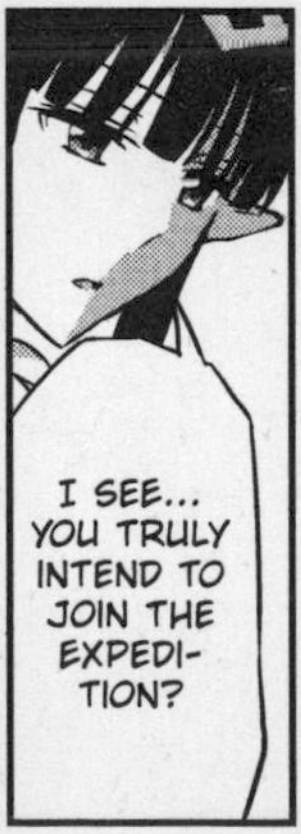
I SEE... YOU TRULY INTEND TO JOIN THE EXPEDITION?

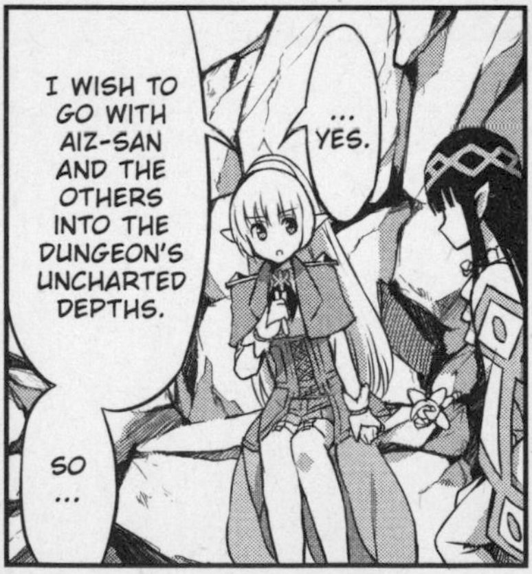
...YES.
I WISH TO GO WITH AIZ-SAN AND THE OTHERS INTO THE DUNGEON'S UNCHARTED DEPTHS.
SO ...

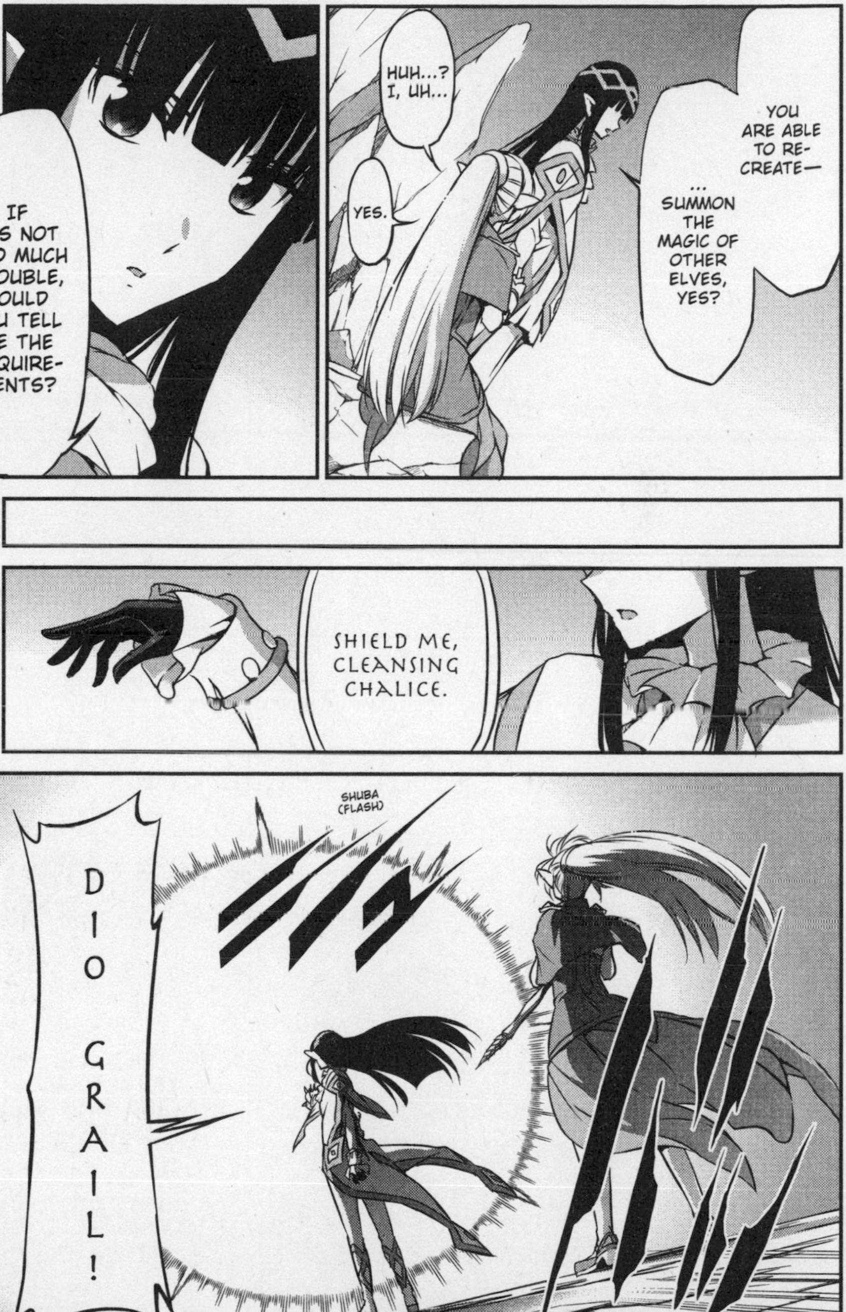

YOU ARE ABLE TO RE-CREATE—
... SUMMON THE MAGIC OF OTHER ELVES, YES?
HUH...? I, UH...
YES.
IF IT'S NOT TOO MUCH TROUBLE, COULD YOU TELL ME THE REQUIREMENTS?
SHIELD ME, CLEANSING CHALICE.
SHUBA (FLASH)
DIO GRAIL!

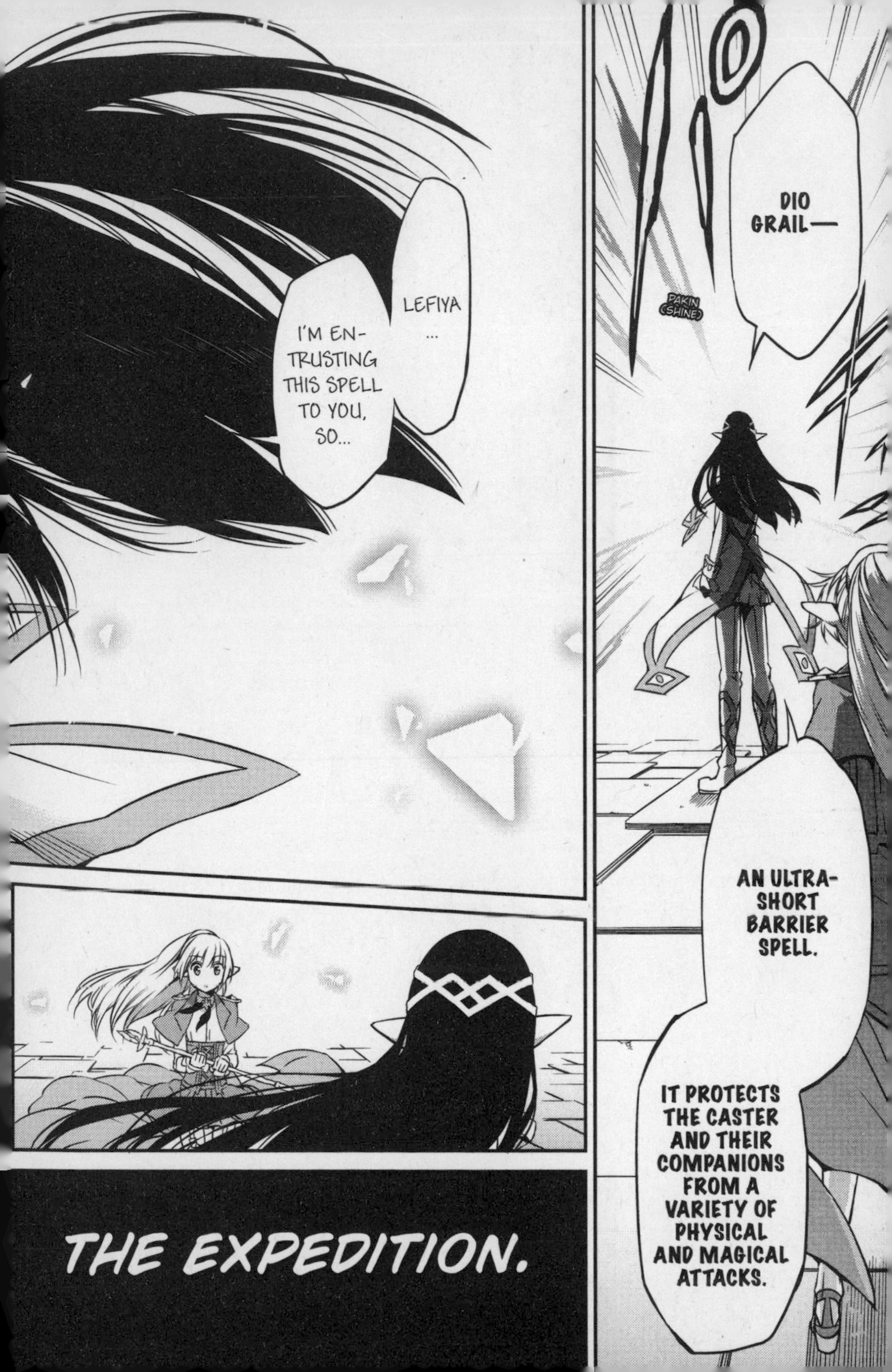
DIO GRAIL—
PAKIN (SHINE)
AN ULTRA-SHORT BARRIER SPELL.
IT PROTECTS THE CASTER AND THEIR COMPANIONS FROM A VARIETY OF PHYSICAL AND MAGICAL ATTACKS.
LEFIYA…
I'M EN-TRUSTING THIS SPELL TO YOU, SO…
THE EXPEDITION.

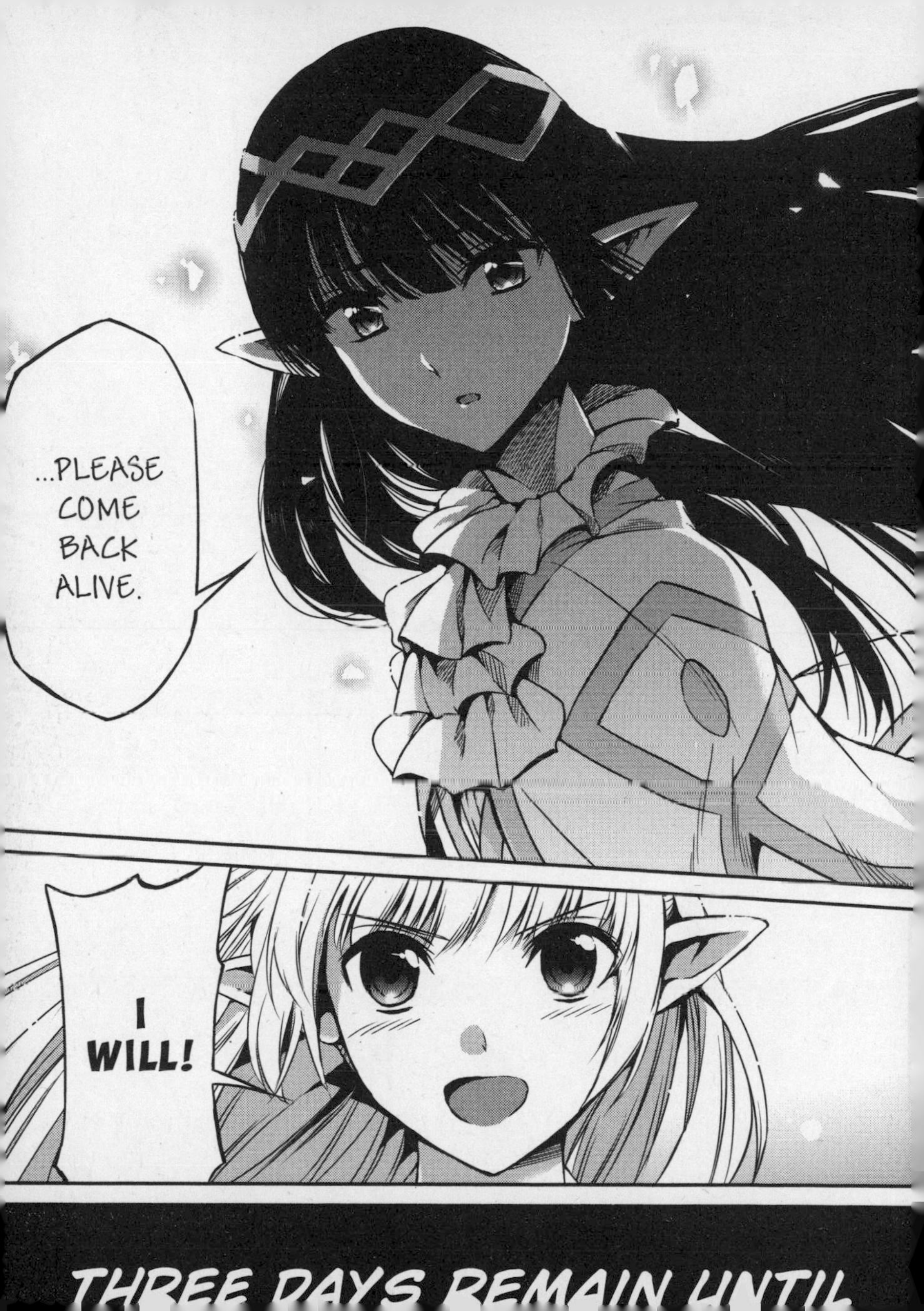
...PLEASE COME BACK ALIVE.
I WILL!
THREE DAYS REMAIN UNTIL

Is It Wrong to Try to Pick Up Girls in a Dungeon? On the Side

Sword Oratoria

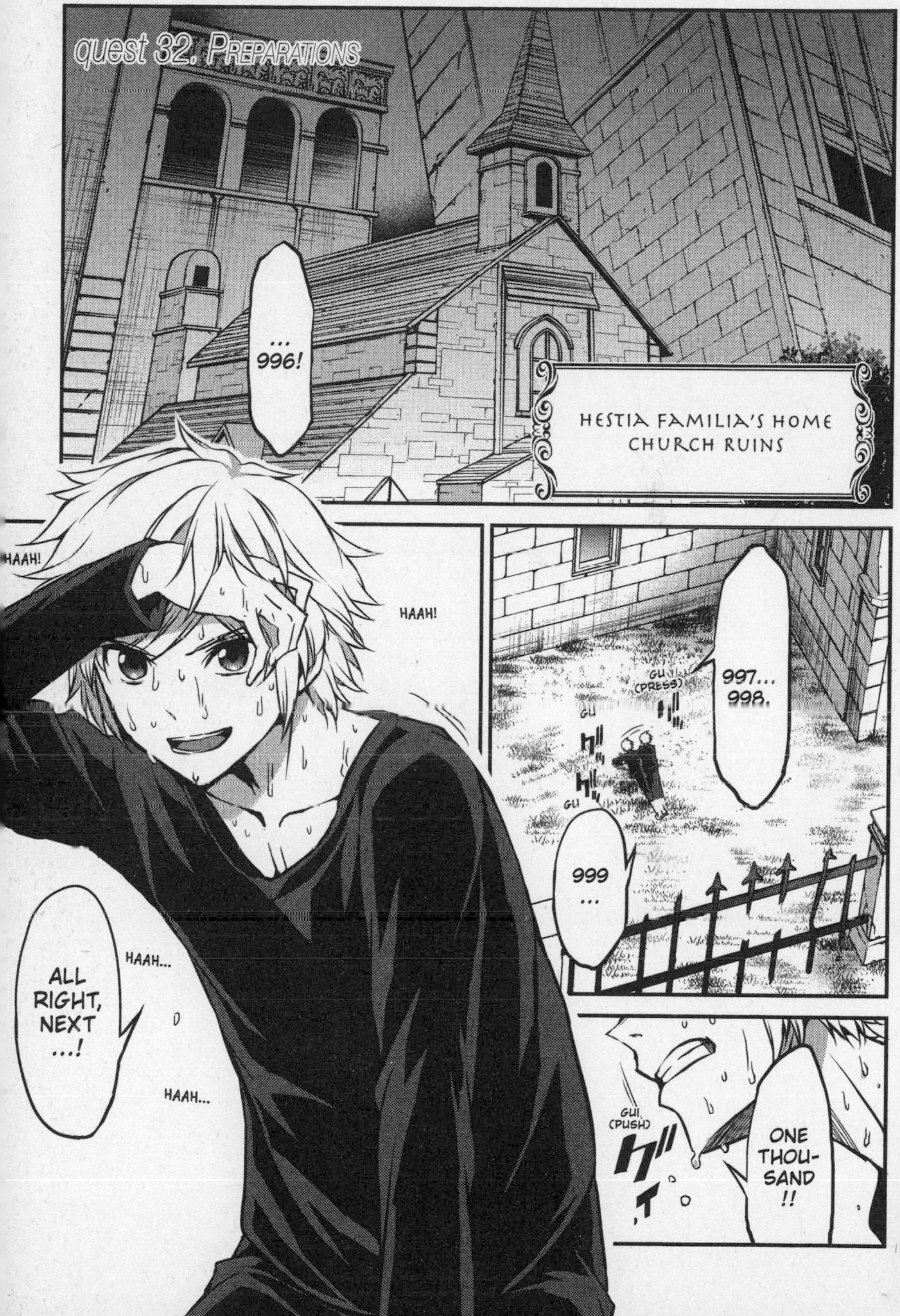
quest 32. Preparations
... 996!
Hestia Familia's Home
Church Ruins
GU (PRESS)
997... 998.
GU
GU
999 ...
GUI (PUSH)
ONE THOUSAND!!
HAAH!
HAAH!
HAAH...
ALL RIGHT, NEXT ...!
HAAH...

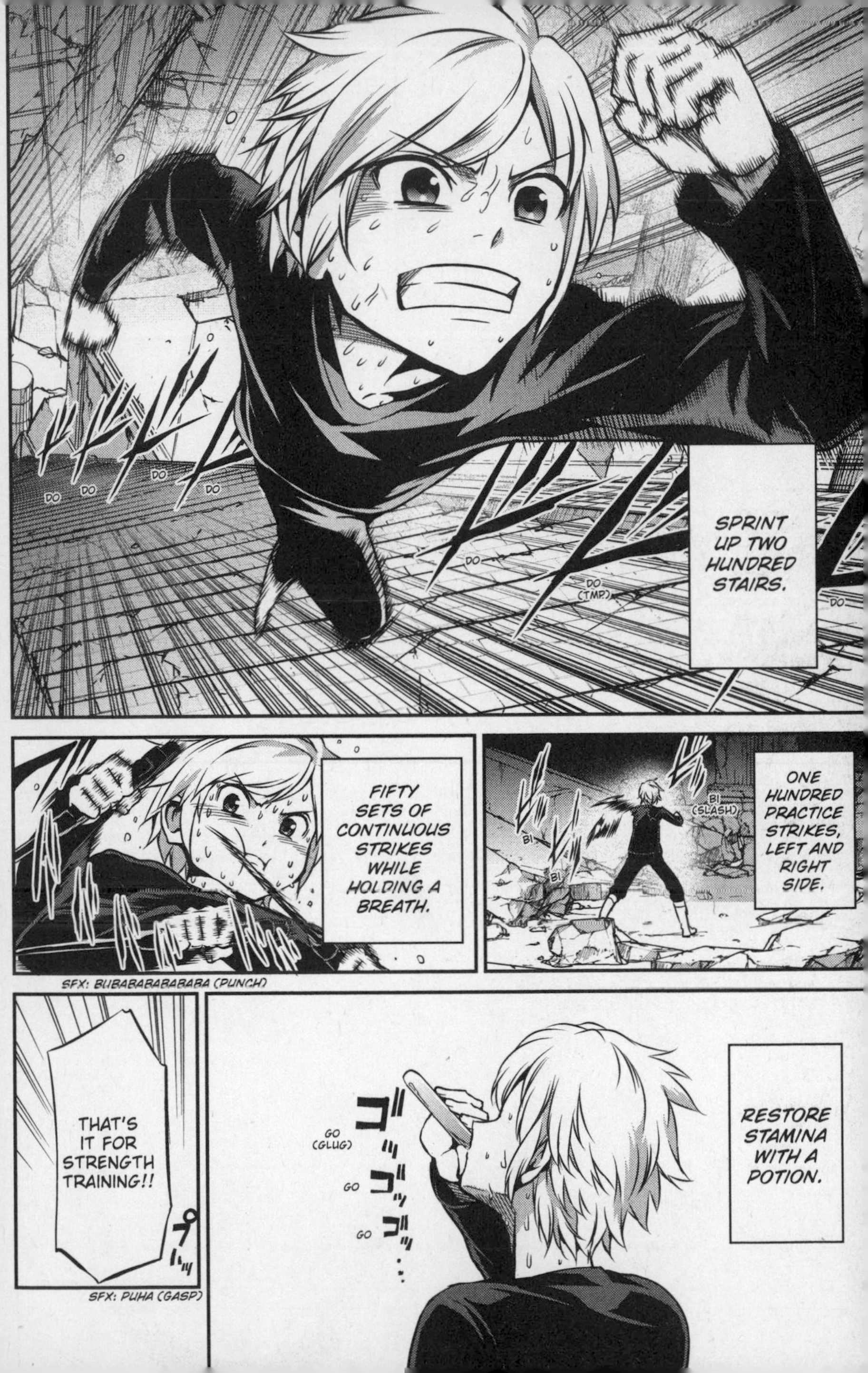
SPRINT UP TWO HUNDRED STAIRS.
DO
DO (TMP)
DO
DO
DO
DO
DO
ONE HUNDRED PRACTICE STRIKES, LEFT AND RIGHT SIDE.
BI (SLASH)
BI
BI
FIFTY SETS OF CONTINUOUS STRIKES WHILE HOLDING A BREATH.
SFX: BUBABABABABABA (PUNCH)
RESTORE STAMINA WITH A POTION.
GO (GLUG)
GO
GO
THAT'S IT FOR STRENGTH TRAINING!!
SFX: PUHA (GASP)

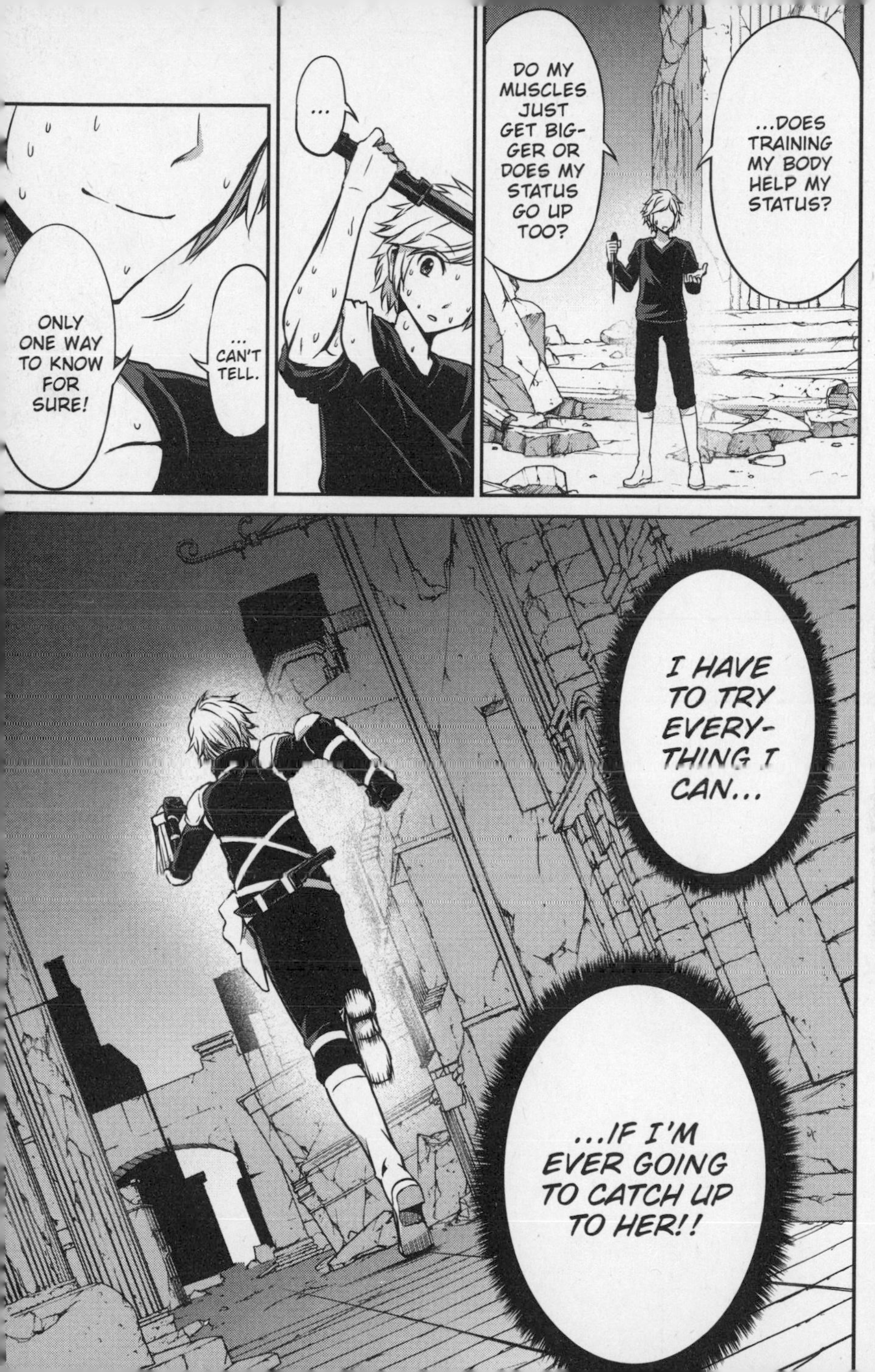
...DOES TRAINING MY BODY HELP MY STATUS?
DO MY MUSCLES JUST GET BIG-GER OR DOES MY STATUS GO UP TOO?
...
...CAN'T TELL.
ONLY ONE WAY TO KNOW FOR SURE!
I HAVE TO TRY EVERY-THING I CAN...
...IF I'M EVER GOING TO CATCH UP TO HER!!

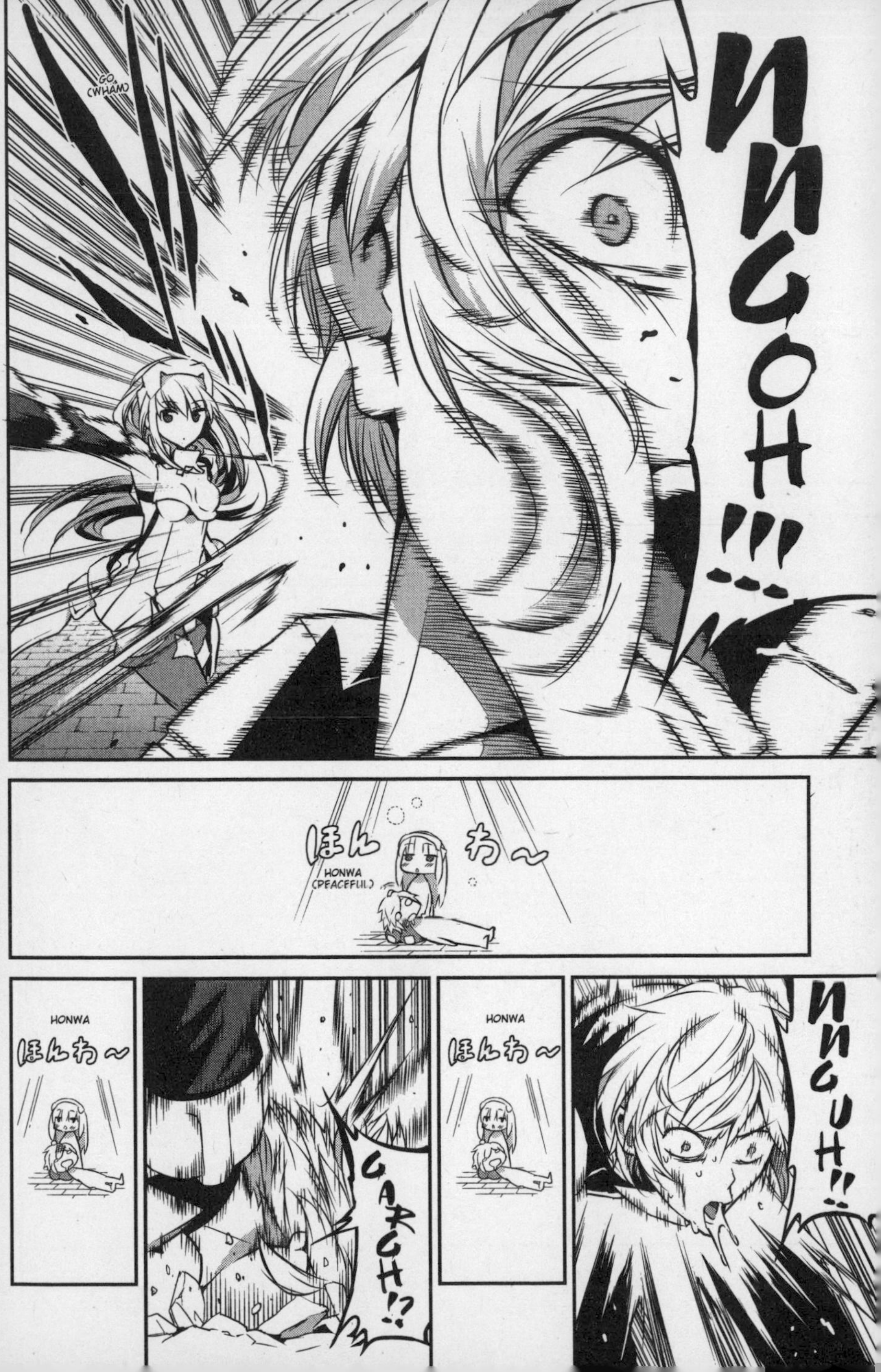
NNGOH!!!
GO (WHAM)
ほんわ～
HONWA (PEACEFUL)
NNGUH!!
HONWA
ほんわ～
GARGH!?
HONWA
ほんわ～

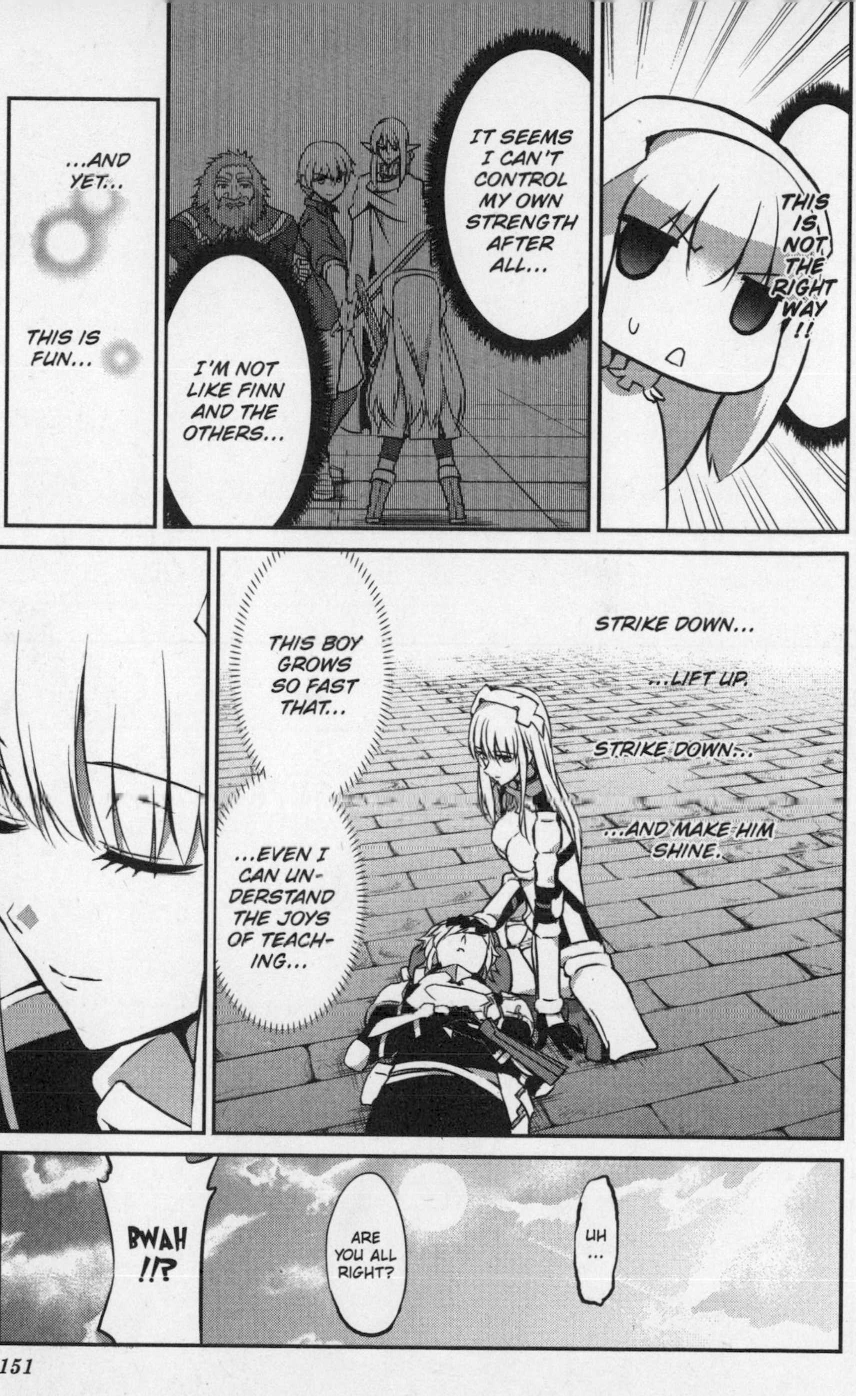
THIS IS NOT THE RIGHT WAY!!
IT SEEMS I CAN'T CONTROL MY OWN STRENGTH AFTER ALL...
I'M NOT LIKE FINN AND THE OTHERS...
...AND YET...
THIS IS FUN...
STRIKE DOWN...
...LIFT UP.
STRIKE DOWN...
...AND MAKE HIM SHINE.
THIS BOY GROWS SO FAST THAT...
...EVEN I CAN UNDERSTAND THE JOYS OF TEACHING...
UH ...
ARE YOU ALL RIGHT?
BWAH !!?

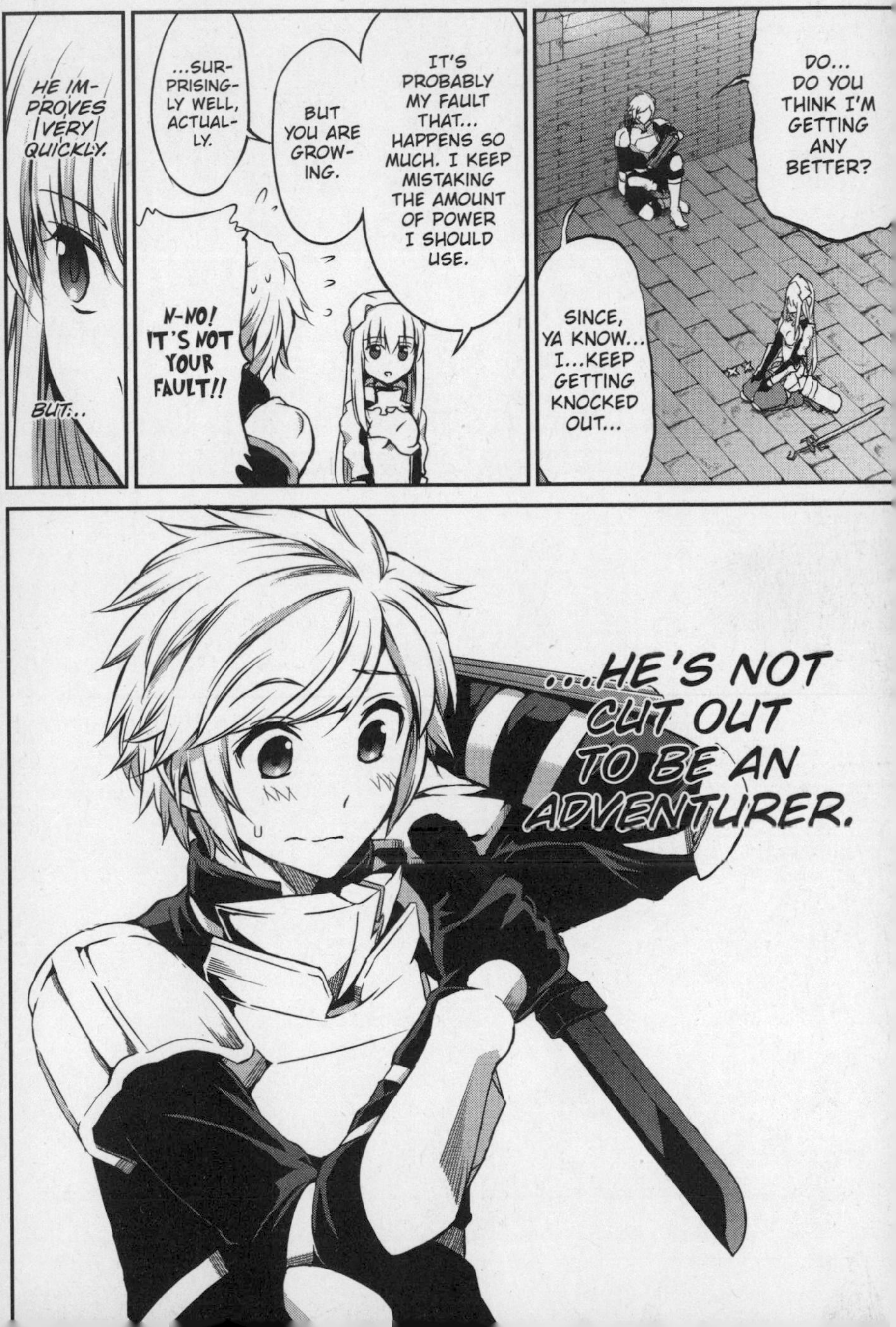
DO... DO YOU THINK I'M GETTING ANY BETTER?
SINCE, YA KNOW... I...KEEP GETTING KNOCKED OUT...
IT'S PROBABLY MY FAULT THAT... HAPPENS SO MUCH. I KEEP MISTAKING THE AMOUNT OF POWER I SHOULD USE.
BUT YOU ARE GROWING.
...SUR-PRISING-LY WELL, ACTUAL-LY.
N-NO! IT'S NOT YOUR FAULT!!
HE IM-PROVES VERY QUICKLY.
BUT...
...HE'S NOT CUT OUT TO BE AN ADVENTURER.

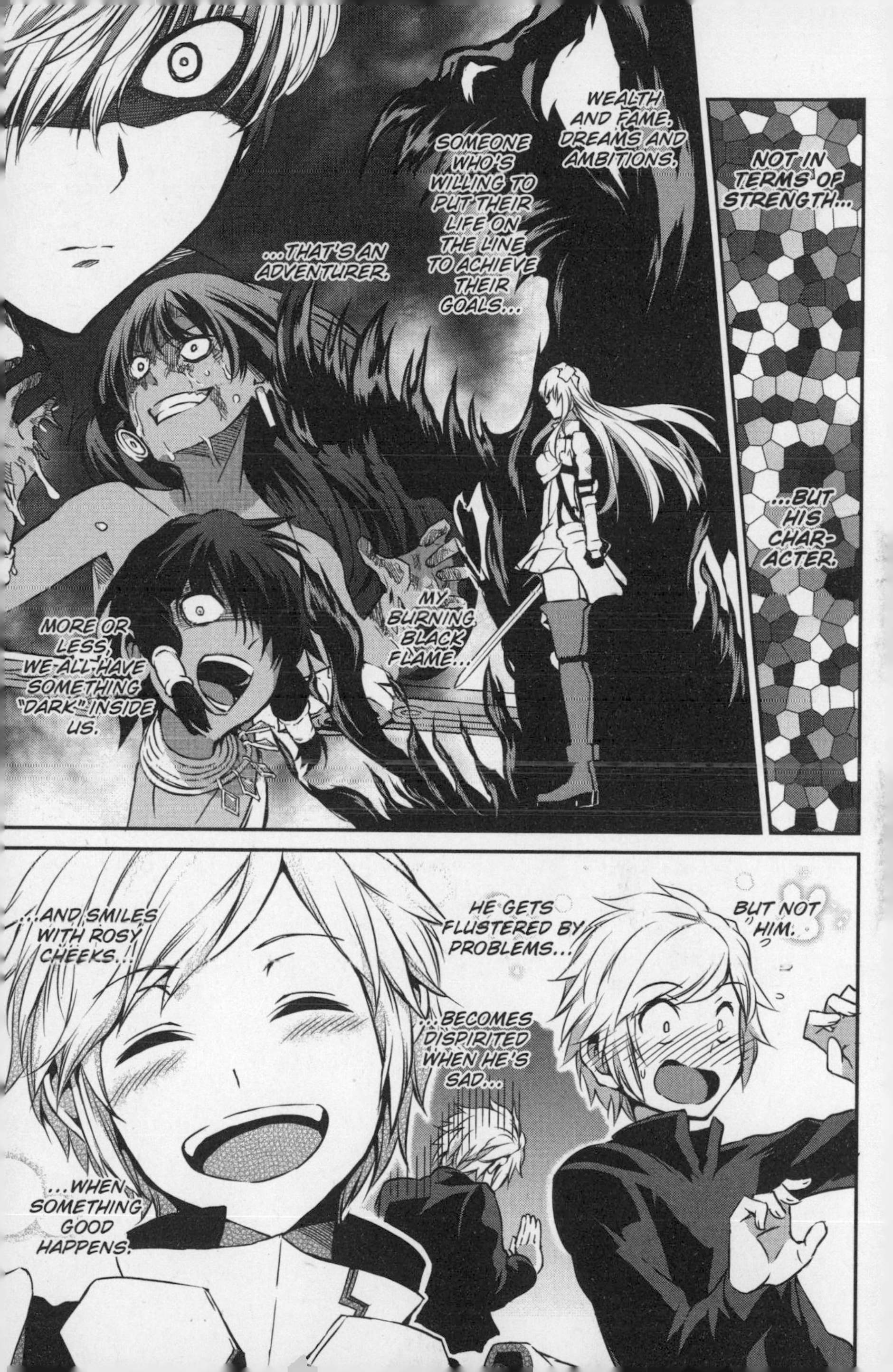
NOT IN TERMS OF STRENGTH...
...BUT HIS CHARACTER.
WEALTH AND FAME, DREAMS AND AMBITIONS.
SOMEONE WHO'S WILLING TO PUT THEIR LIFE ON THE LINE TO ACHIEVE THEIR GOALS...
...THAT'S AN ADVENTURER.
MY BURNING BLACK FLAME...
MORE OR LESS, WE ALL HAVE SOMETHING "DARK" INSIDE US.
BUT NOT HIM.
HE GETS FLUSTERED BY PROBLEMS...
...BECOMES DISPIRITED WHEN HE'S SAD...
...AND SMILES WITH ROSY CHEEKS...
...WHEN SOMETHING GOOD HAPPENS.

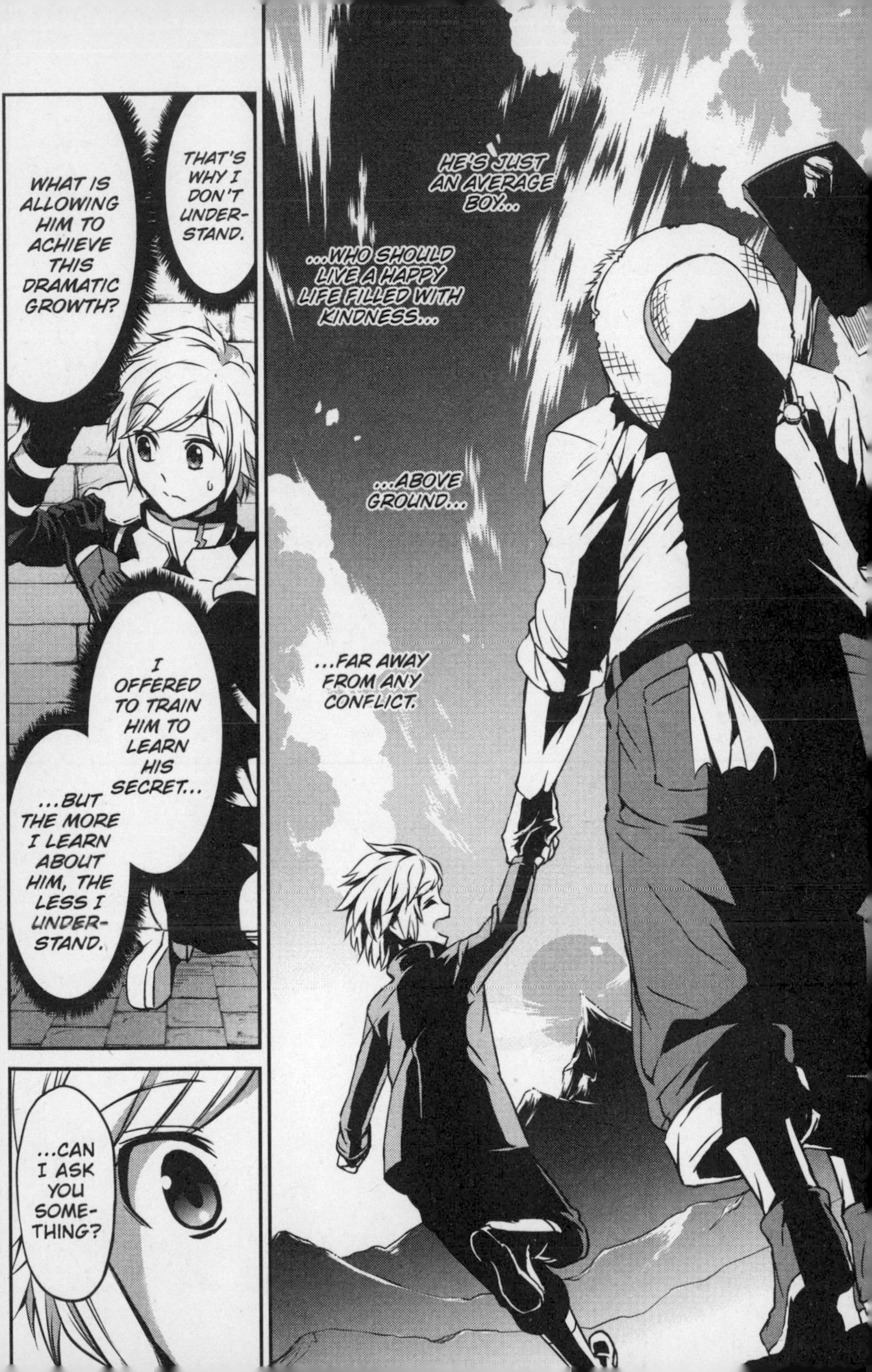
HE'S JUST AN AVERAGE BOY...
...WHO SHOULD LIVE A HAPPY LIFE FILLED WITH KINDNESS...
...ABOVE GROUND...
...FAR AWAY FROM ANY CONFLICT.
THAT'S WHY I DON'T UNDER-STAND.
WHAT IS ALLOWING HIM TO ACHIEVE THIS DRAMATIC GROWTH?
I OFFERED TO TRAIN HIM TO LEARN HIS SECRET...
...BUT THE MORE I LEARN ABOUT HIM, THE LESS I UNDER-STAND.
...CAN I ASK YOU SOMETHING?

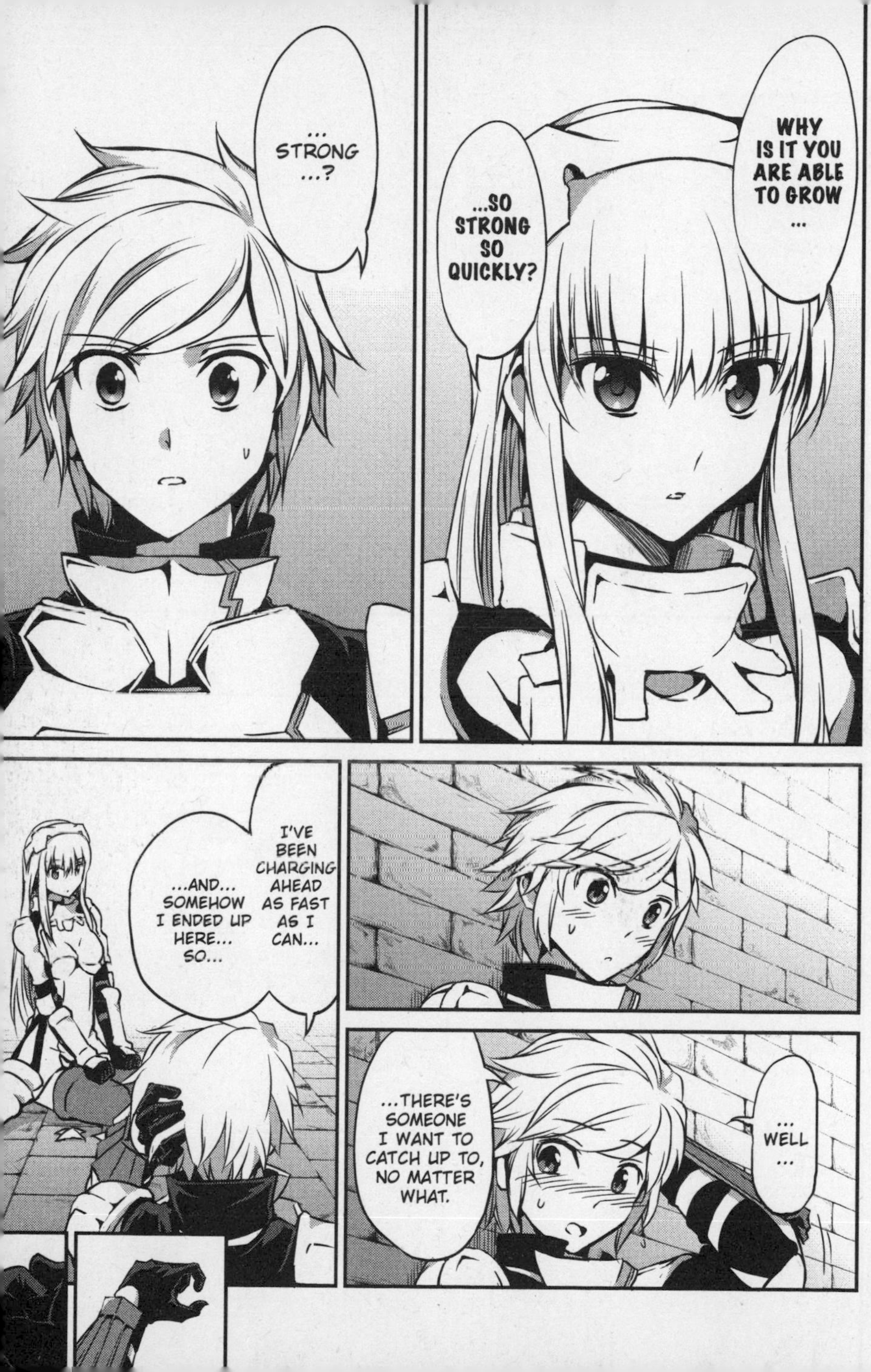
WHY IS IT YOU ARE ABLE TO GROW ...
...SO STRONG SO QUICKLY?
... STRONG ...?
... WELL ...
...THERE'S SOMEONE I WANT TO CATCH UP TO, NO MATTER WHAT.
I'VE BEEN CHARGING AHEAD AS FAST AS I CAN...
...AND... SOMEHOW I ENDED UP HERE... SO...

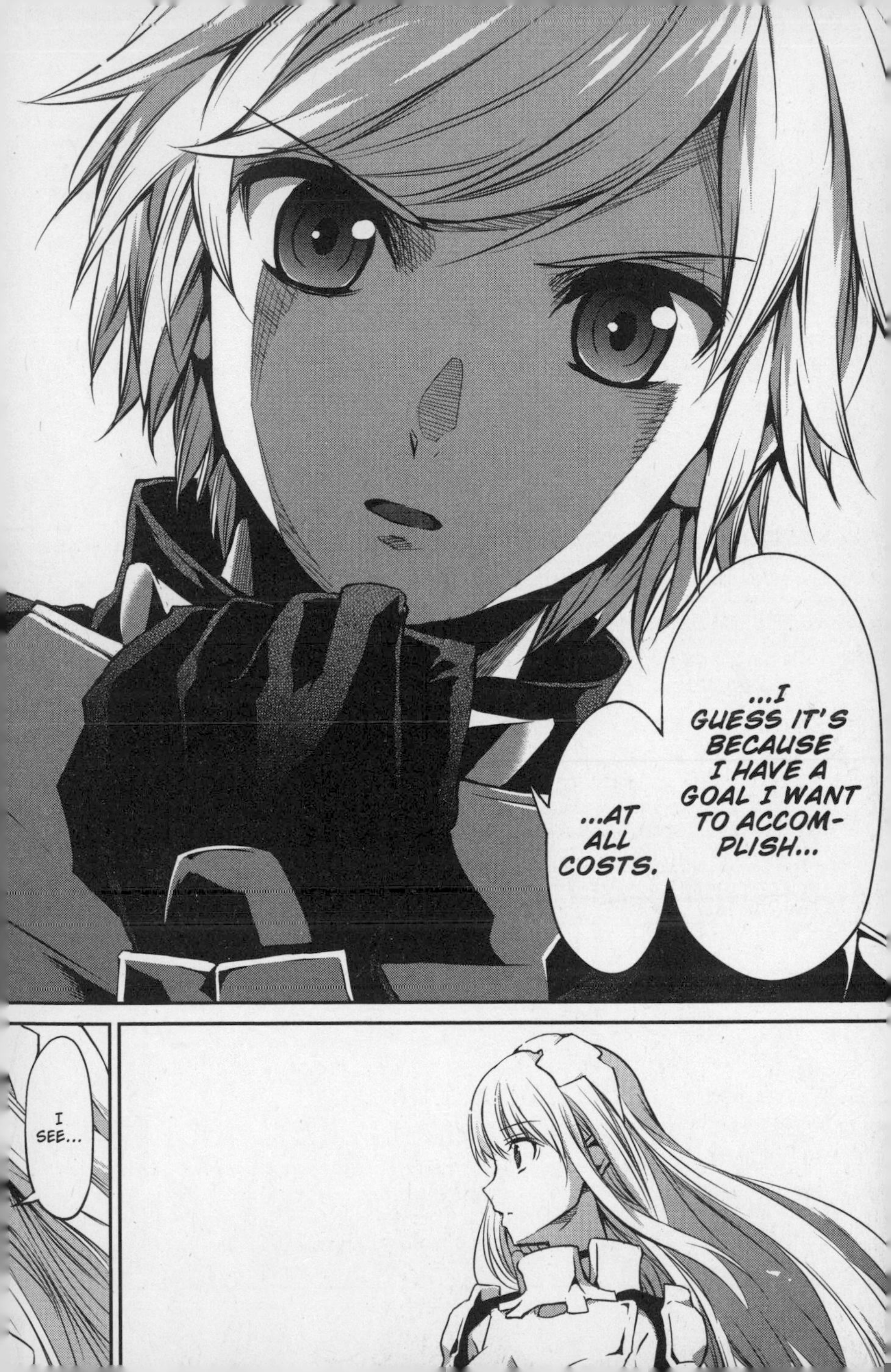
...I GUESS IT'S BECAUSE I HAVE A GOAL I WANT TO ACCOMPLISH...
...AT ALL COSTS.
I SEE...

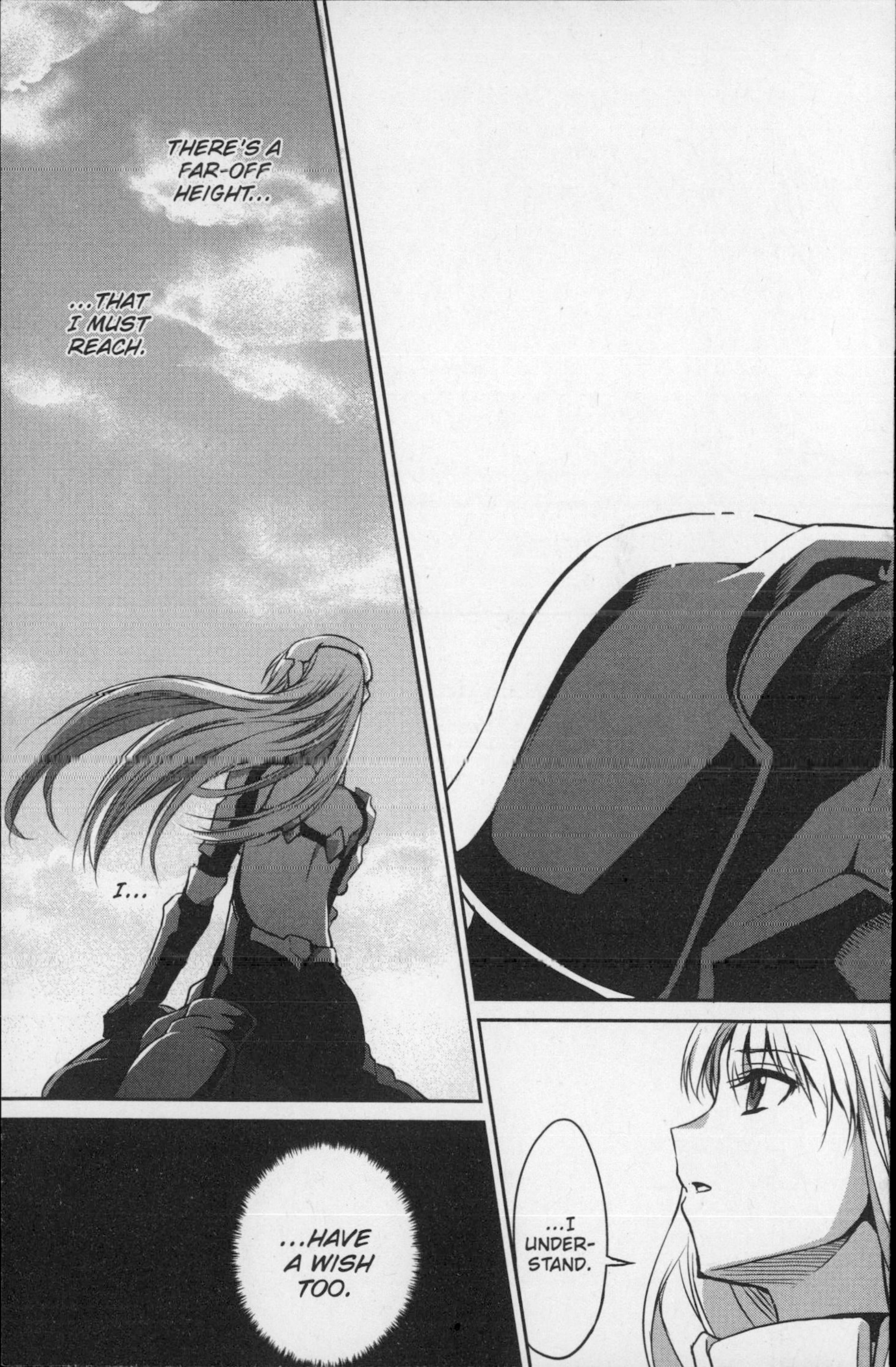
THERE'S A FAR-OFF HEIGHT...
...THAT I MUST REACH.
I...
...I UNDERSTAND.
...HAVE A WISH TOO.

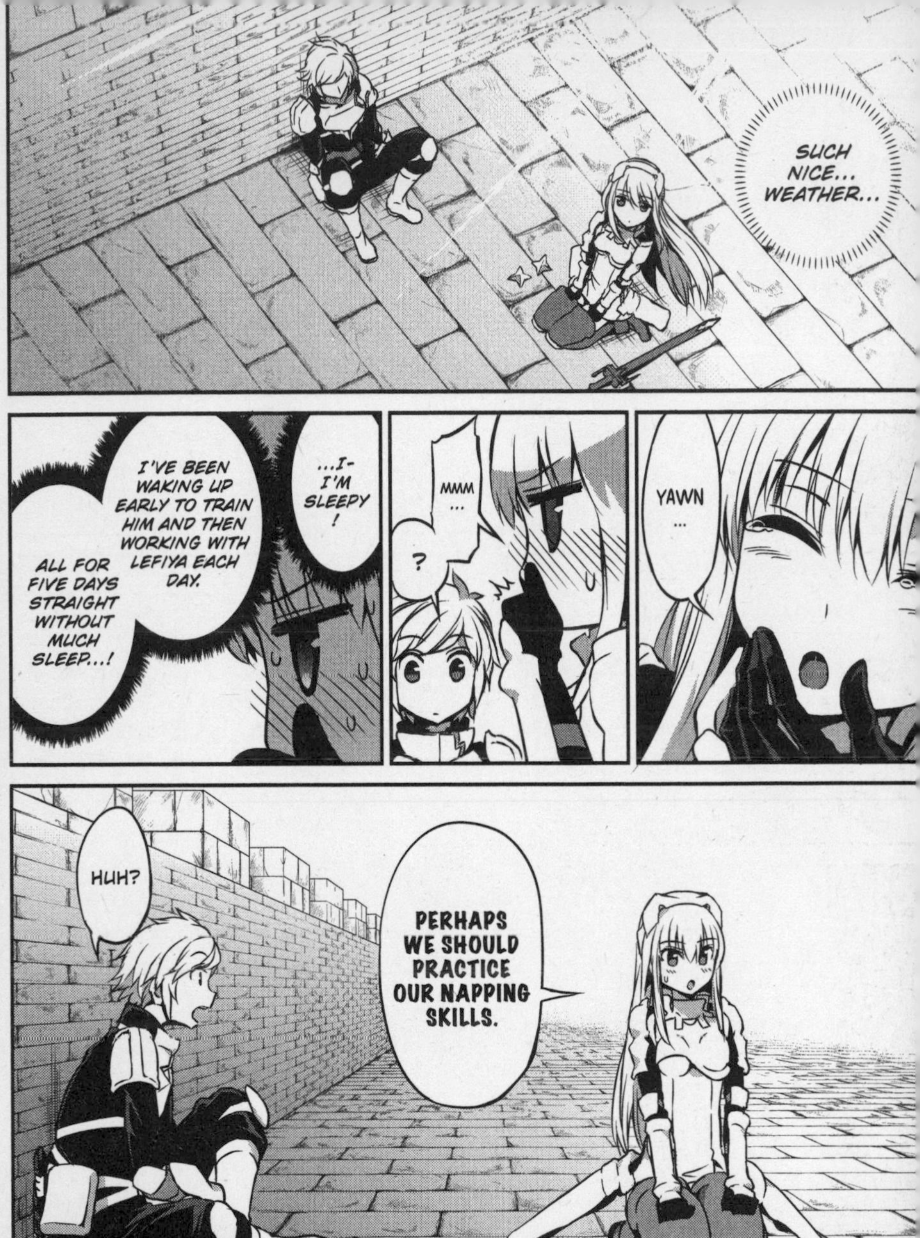
SUCH NICE... WEATHER...
YAWN ...
MMM ...
?
...I- I'M SLEEPY!
I'VE BEEN WAKING UP EARLY TO TRAIN HIM AND THEN WORKING WITH LEFIYA EACH DAY.
ALL FOR FIVE DAYS STRAIGHT WITHOUT MUCH SLEEP...!
PERHAPS WE SHOULD PRACTICE OUR NAPPING SKILLS.
HUH?

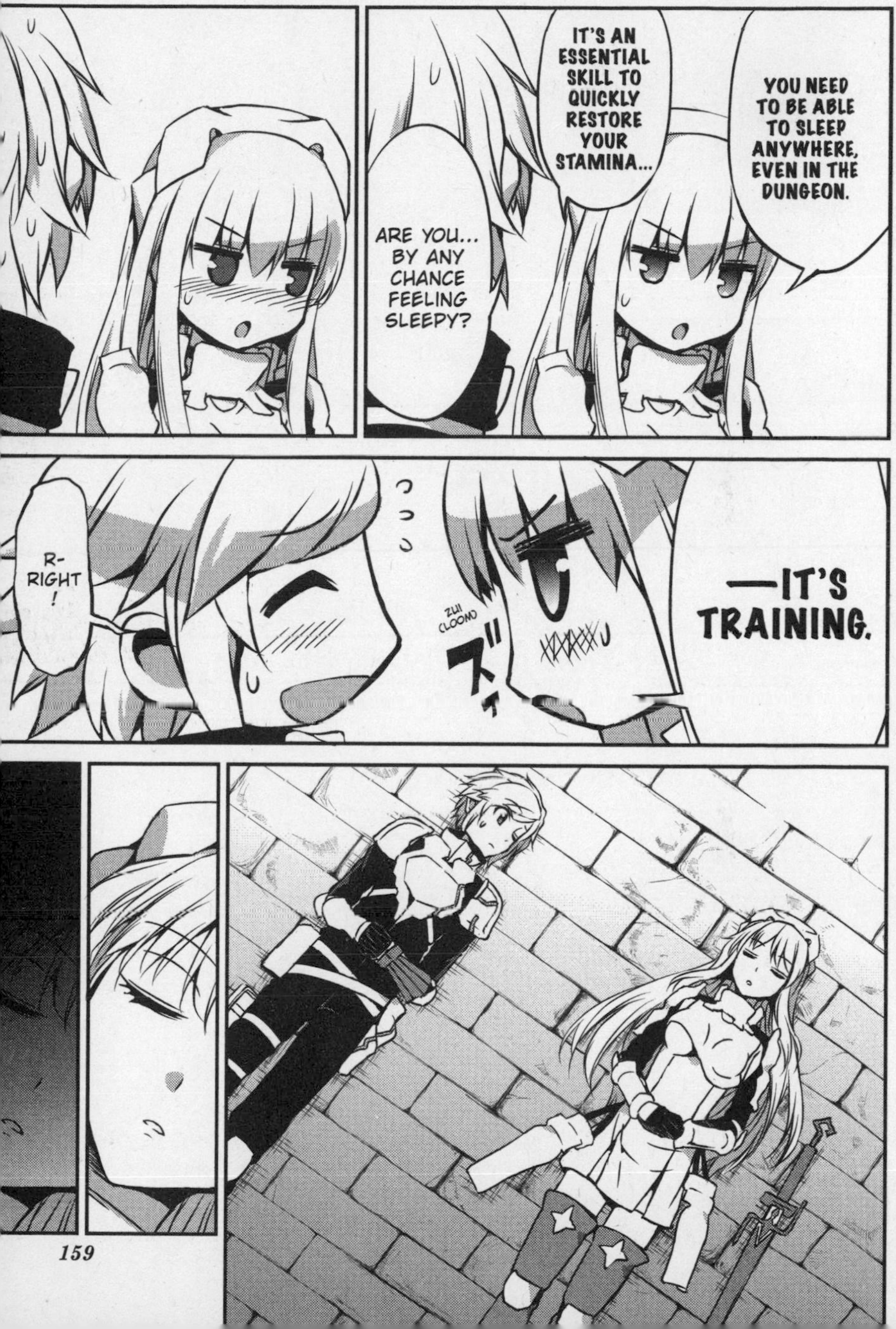
YOU NEED TO BE ABLE TO SLEEP ANYWHERE, EVEN IN THE DUNGEON.
IT'S AN ESSENTIAL SKILL TO QUICKLY RESTORE YOUR STAMINA...
ARE YOU... BY ANY CHANCE FEELING SLEEPY?
—IT'S TRAINING.
ZUI (LOOM)
R-RIGHT!

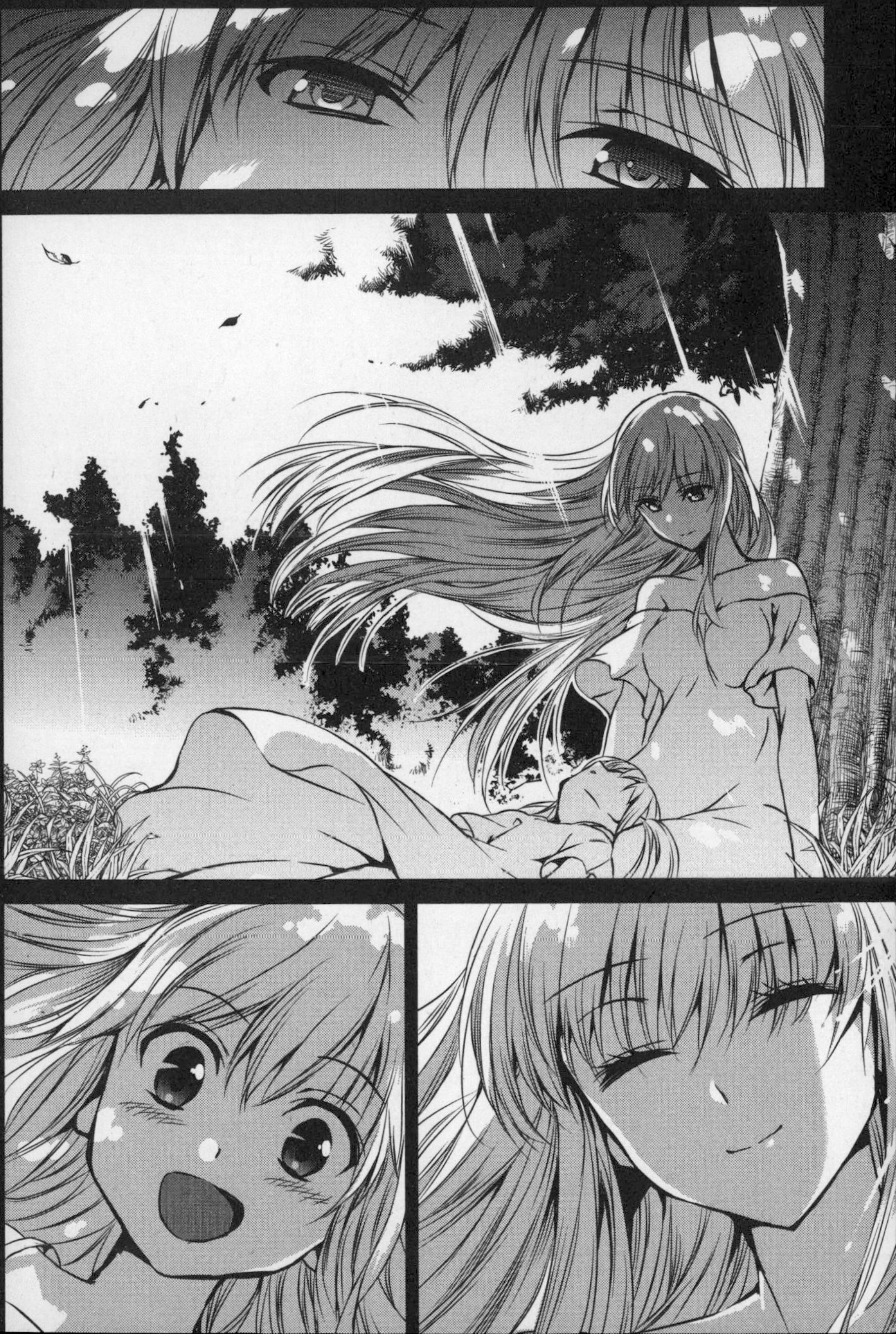

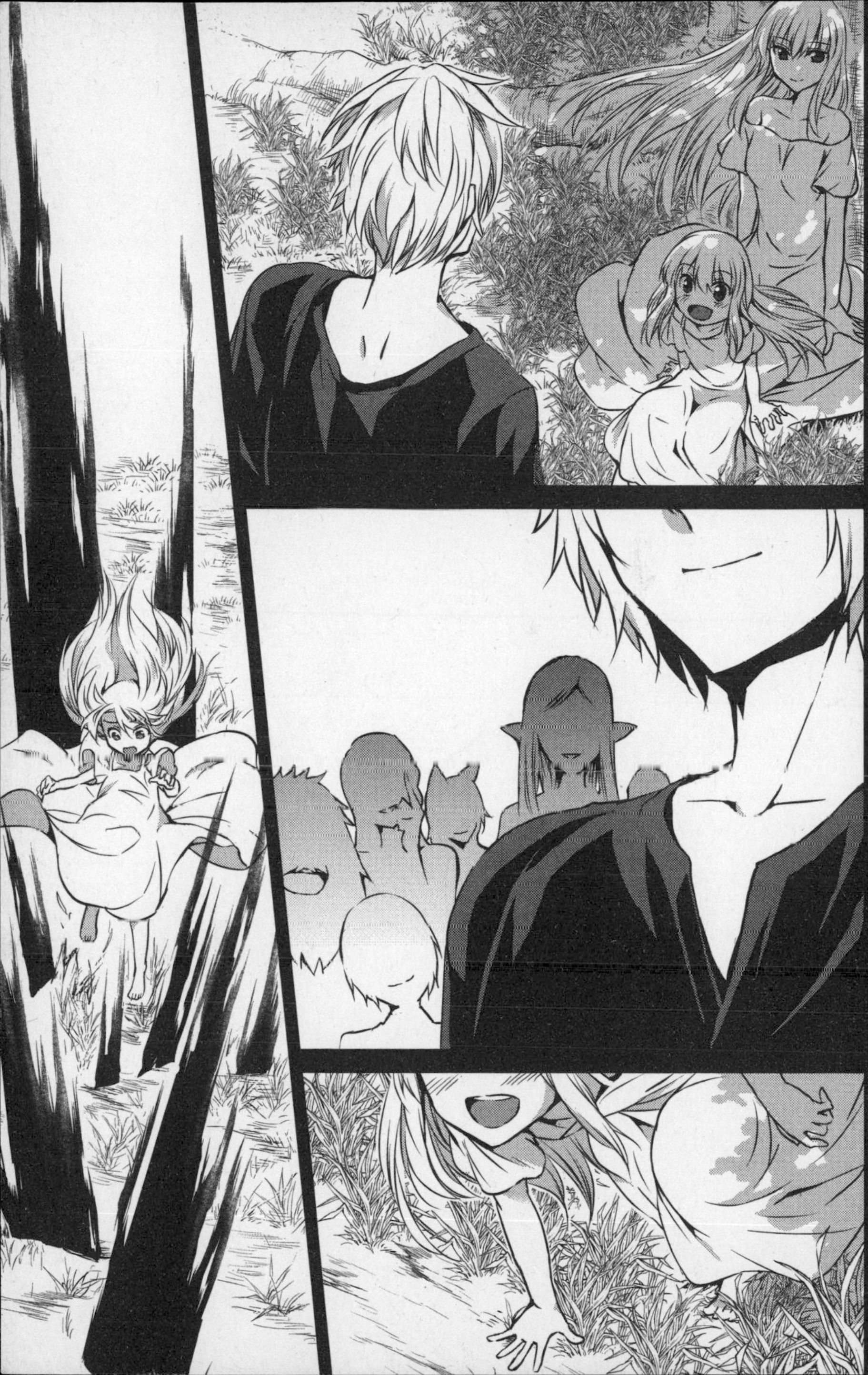

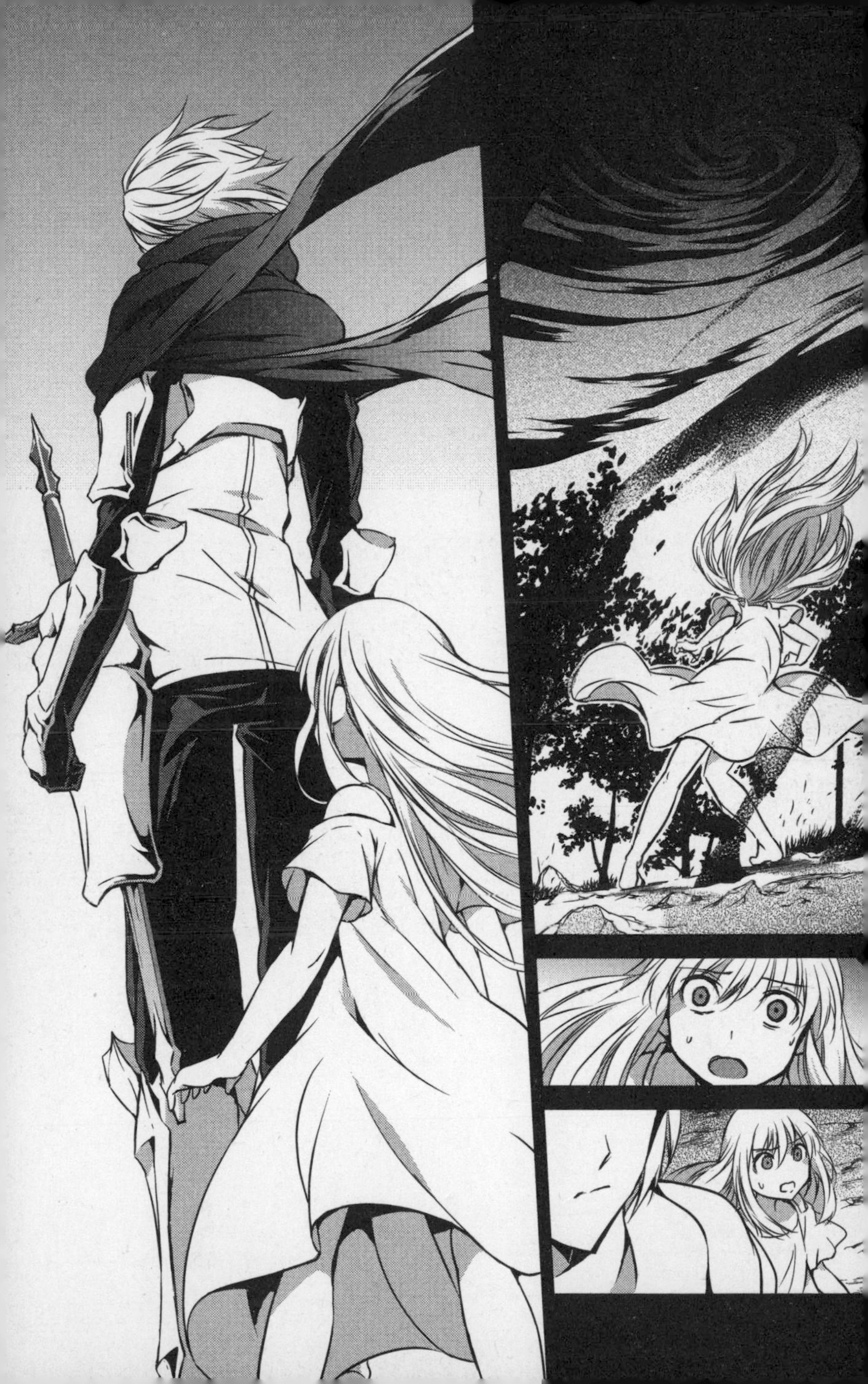

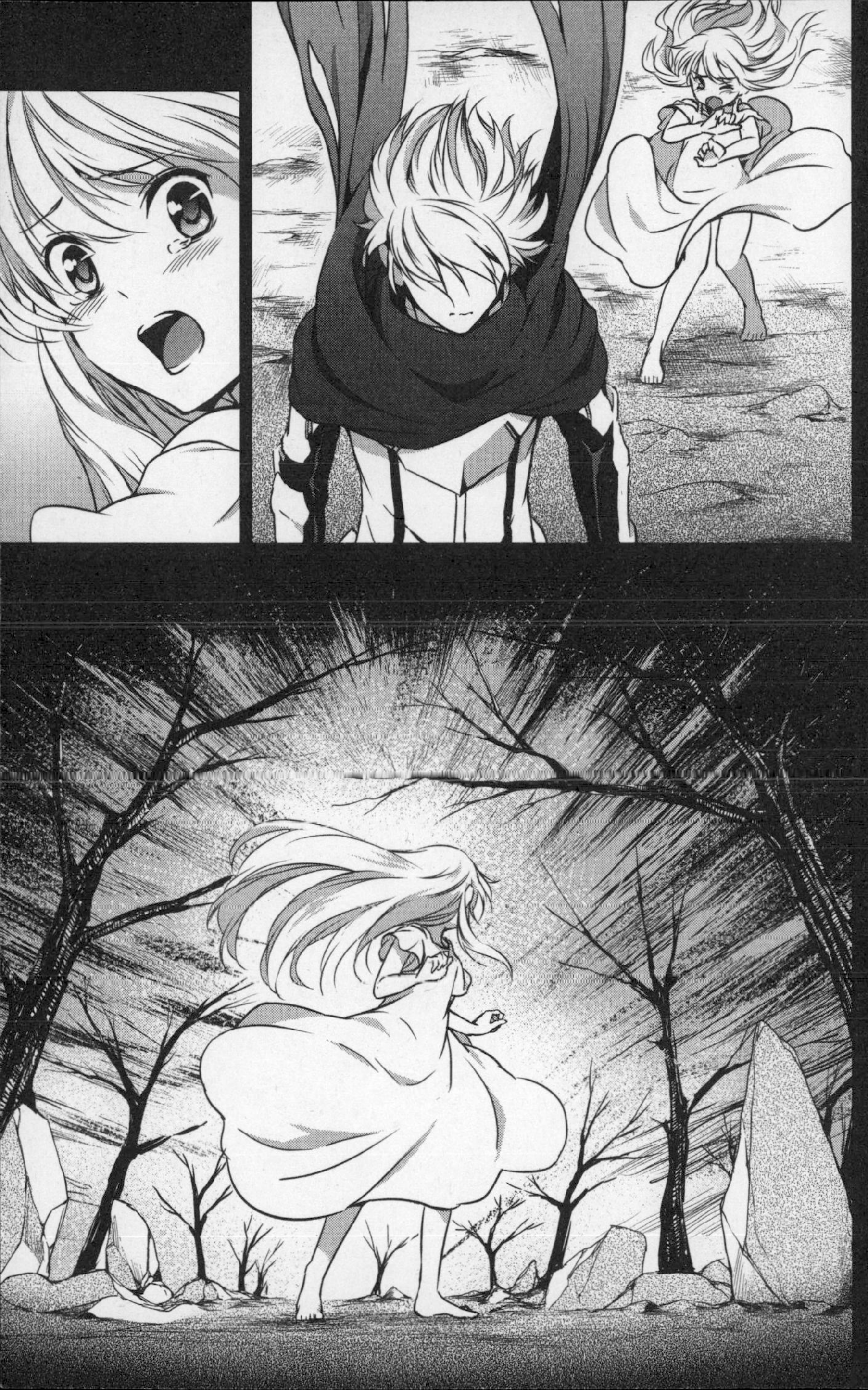

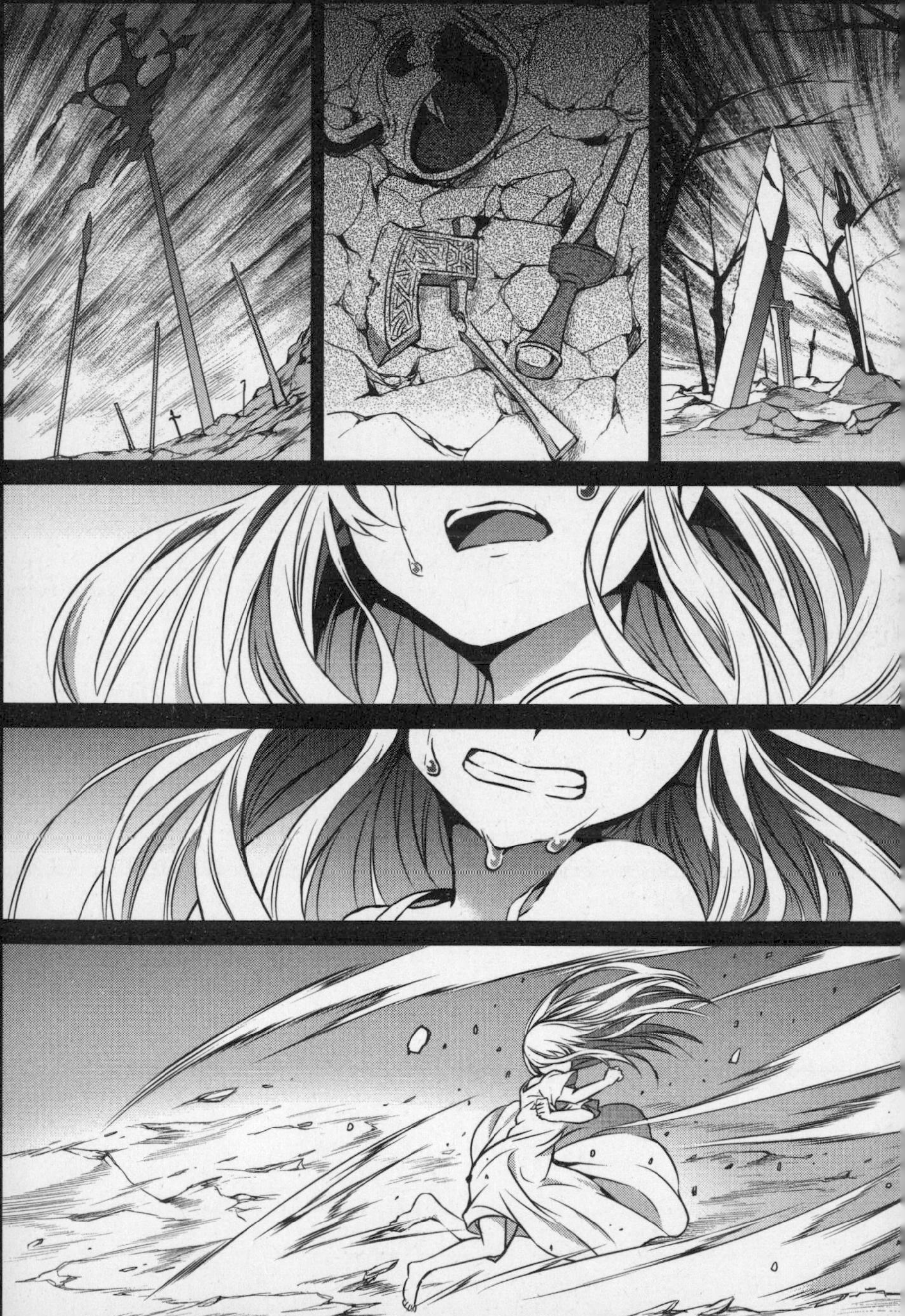

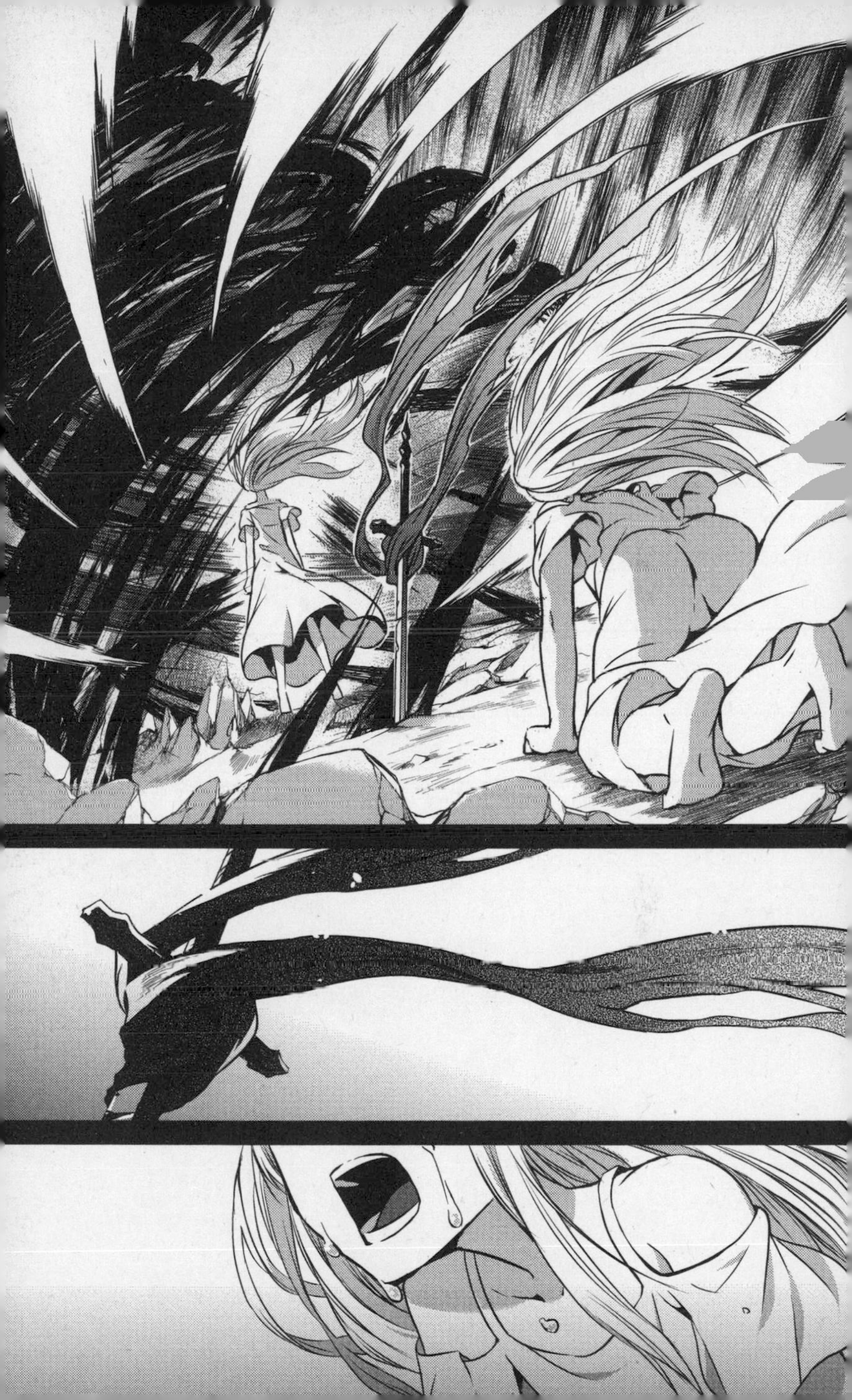

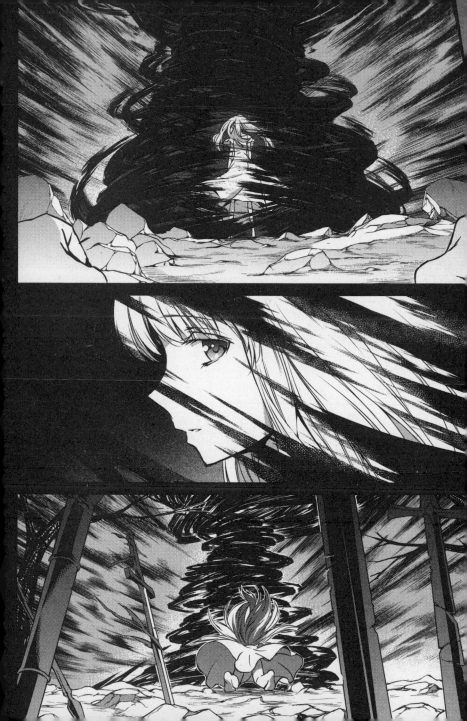

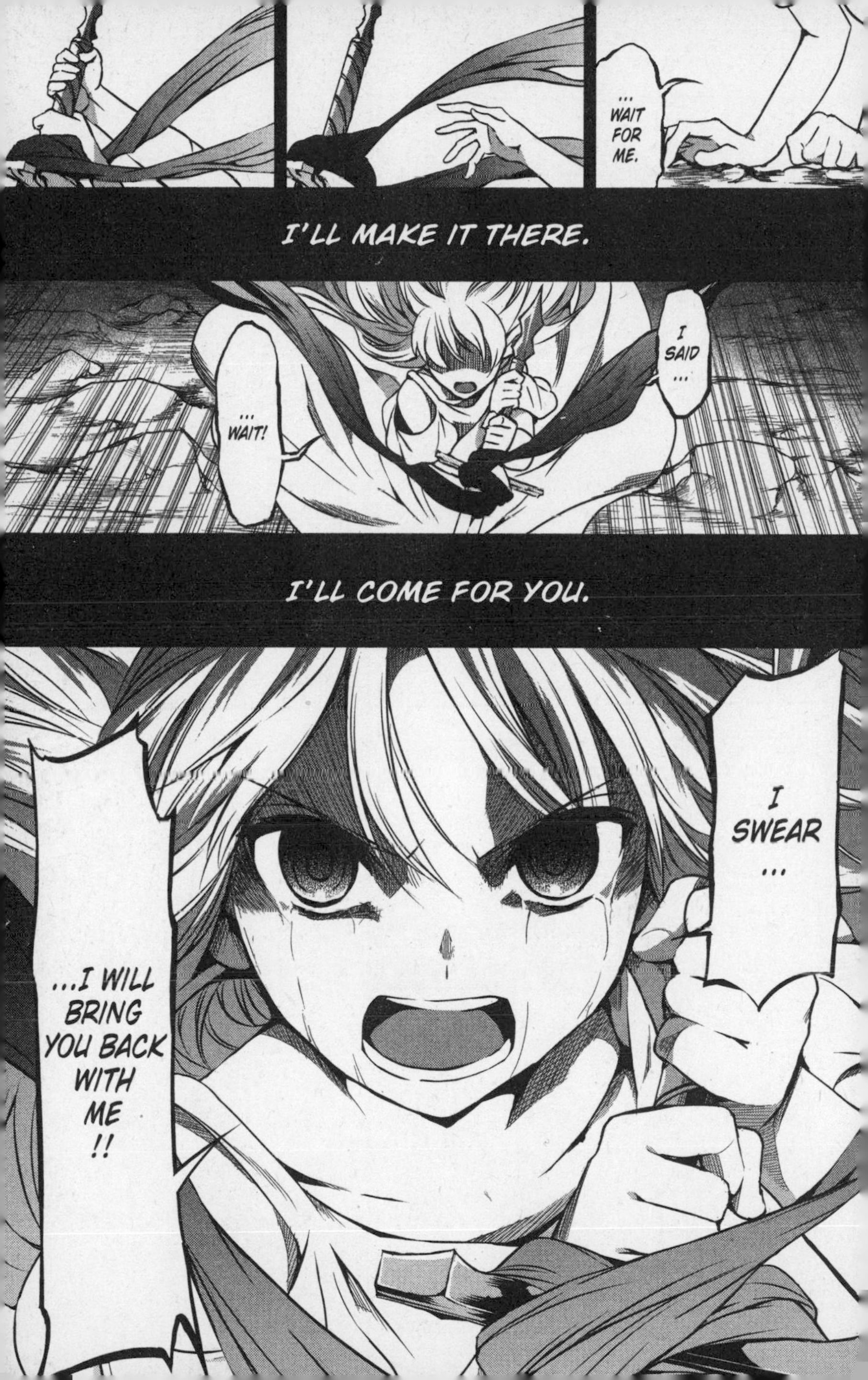

... WAIT FOR ME.
I'LL MAKE IT THERE.
I SAID ...
... WAIT!
I'LL COME FOR YOU.
I SWEAR ...
...I WILL BRING YOU BACK WITH ME !!

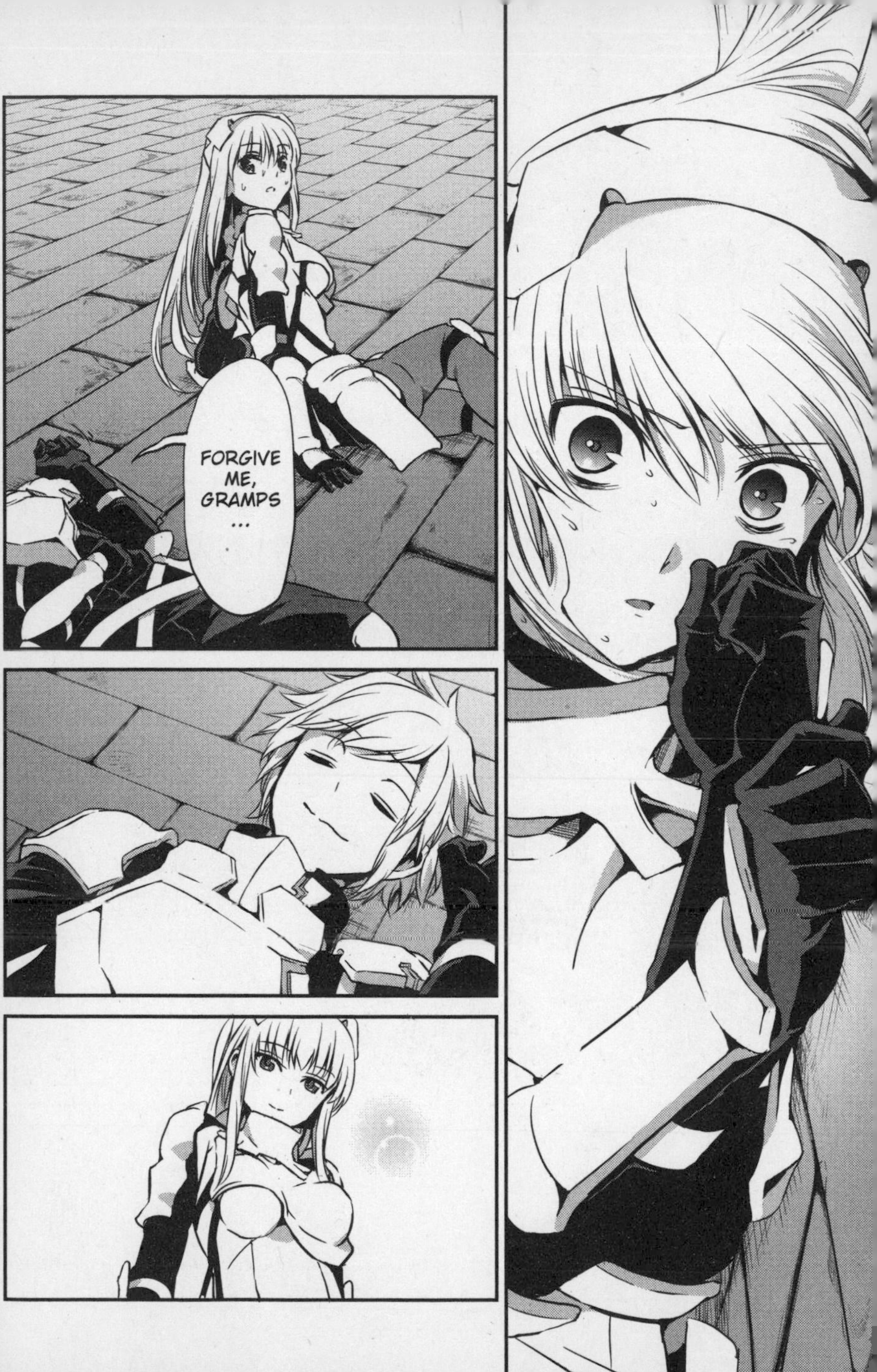
FORGIVE ME, GRAMPS ...

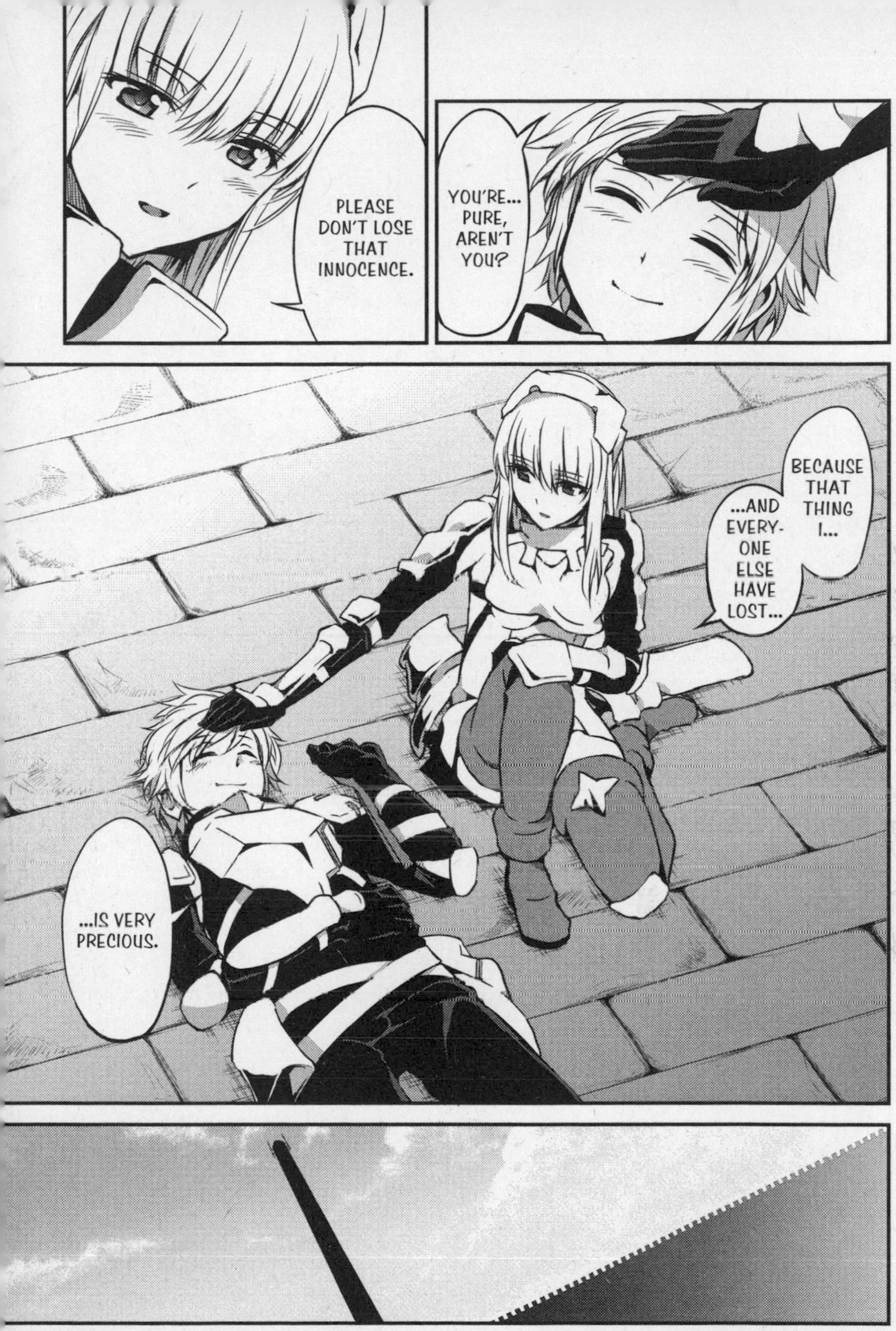
YOU'RE... PURE, AREN'T YOU?
PLEASE DON'T LOSE THAT INNOCENCE.
BECAUSE THAT THING I...
...AND EVERY-ONE ELSE HAVE LOST...
...IS VERY PRECIOUS.

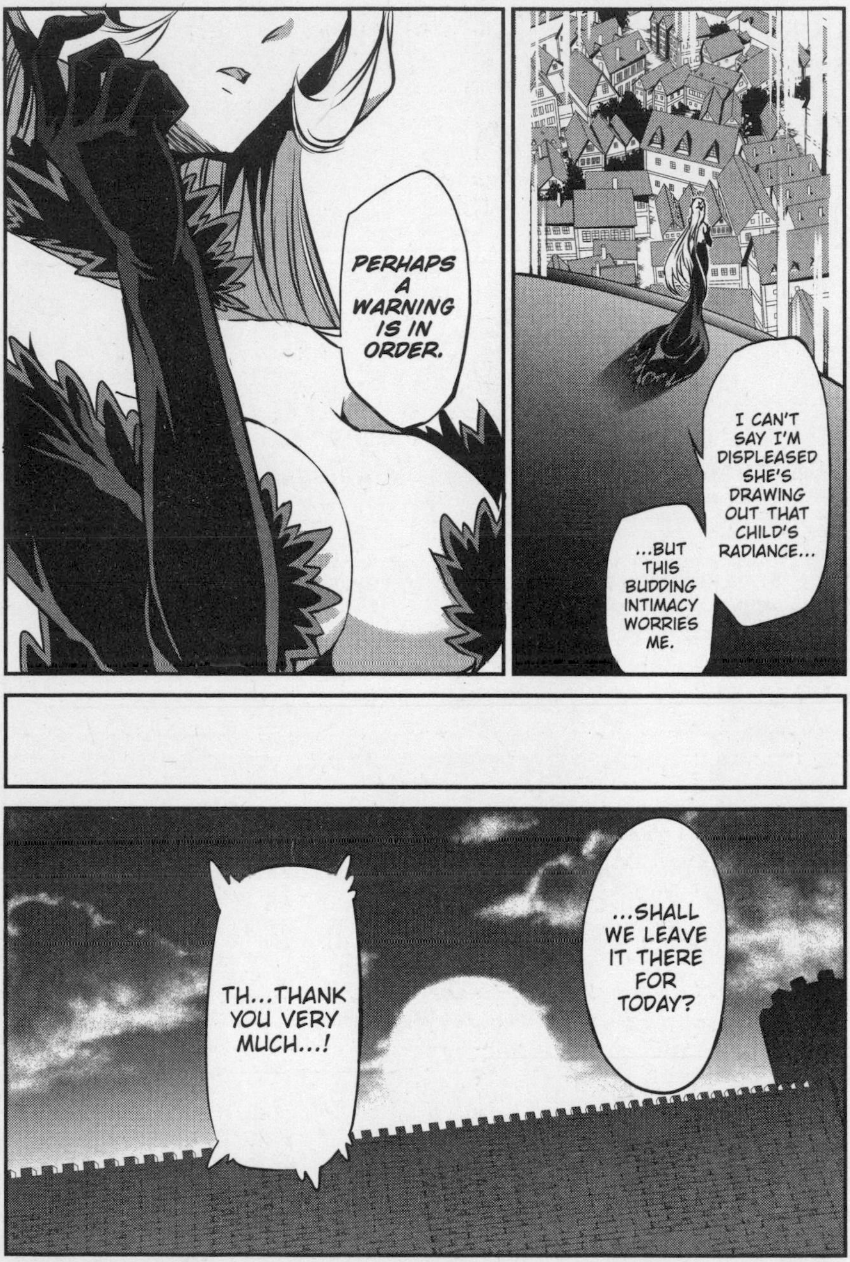
I CAN'T SAY I'M DISPLEASED SHE'S DRAWING OUT THAT CHILD'S RADIANCE...
...BUT THIS BUDDING INTIMACY WORRIES ME.
PERHAPS A WARNING IS IN ORDER.
...SHALL WE LEAVE IT THERE FOR TODAY?
TH...THANK YOU VERY MUCH...!

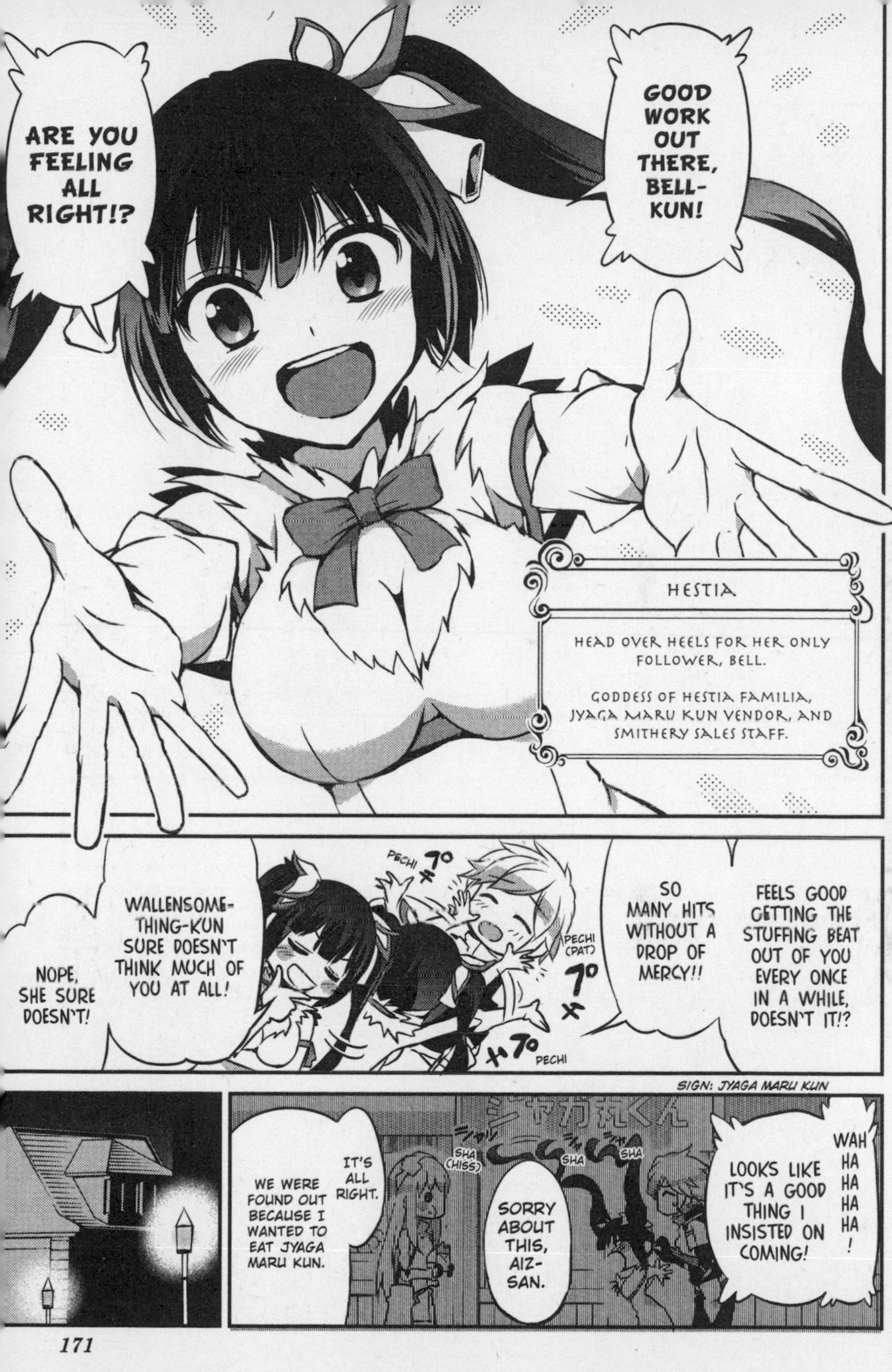
GOOD WORK OUT THERE, BELL-KUN!
ARE YOU FEELING ALL RIGHT!?
HESTIA
HEAD OVER HEELS FOR HER ONLY FOLLOWER, BELL.
GODDESS OF HESTIA FAMILIA, JYAGA MARU KUN VENDOR, AND SMITHERY SALES STAFF.
FEELS GOOD GETTING THE STUFFING BEAT OUT OF YOU EVERY ONCE IN A WHILE, DOESN'T IT!?
SO MANY HITS WITHOUT A DROP OF MERCY!!
PECHI (PAT)
PECHI
PECHI
WALLENSOMETHING-KUN SURE DOESN'T THINK MUCH OF YOU AT ALL!
NOPE, SHE SURE DOESN'T!
SIGN: JYAGA MARU KUN
WAH HA HA HA HA!
LOOKS LIKE IT'S A GOOD THING I INSISTED ON COMING!
SHA
SHA
SHA (CHISS)
SORRY ABOUT THIS, AIZ-SAN.
IT'S ALL RIGHT.
WE WERE FOUND OUT BECAUSE I WANTED TO EAT JYAGA MARU KUN.

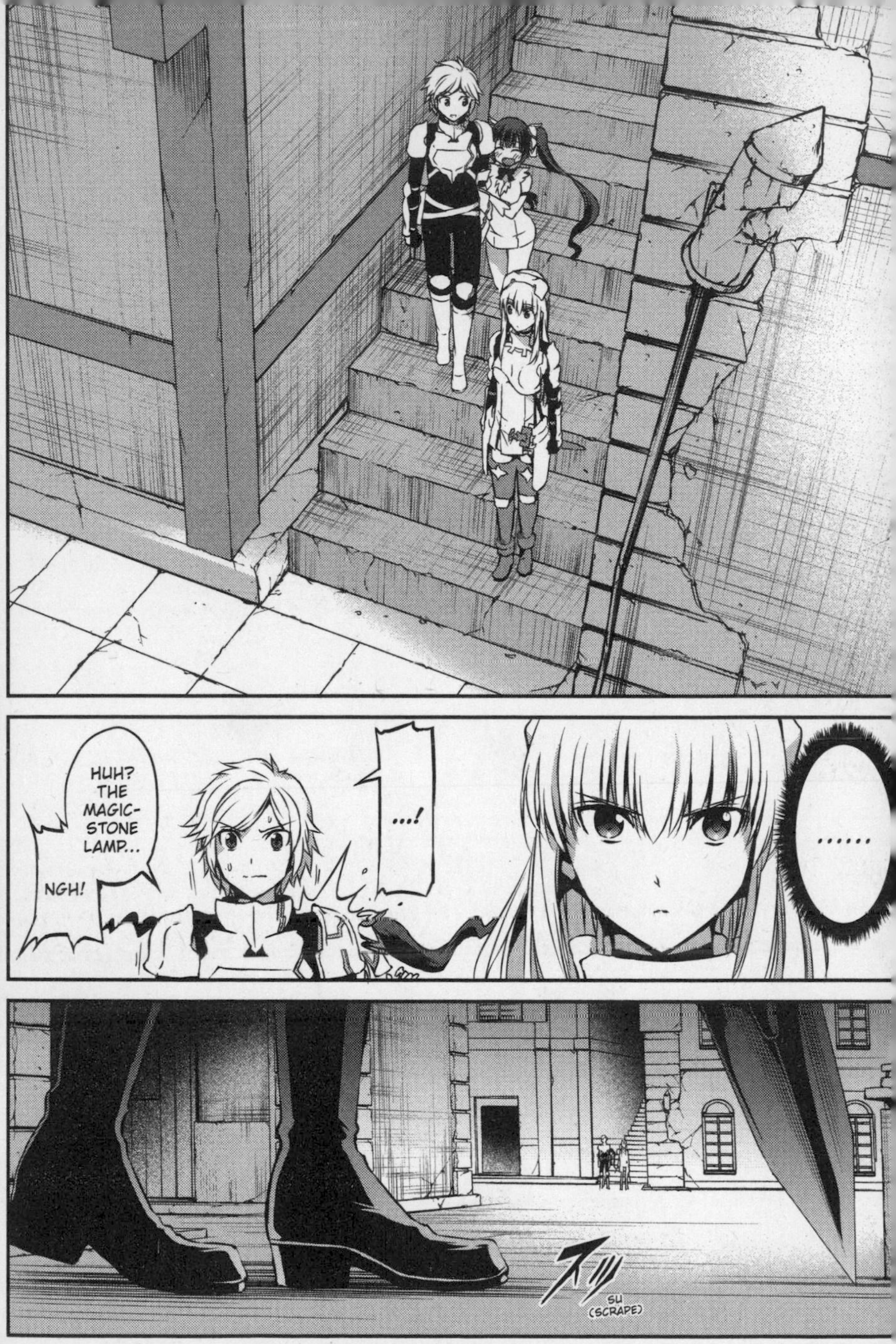
......
...!
HUH? THE MAGIC-STONE LAMP...
NGH!
SU (SCRAPE)

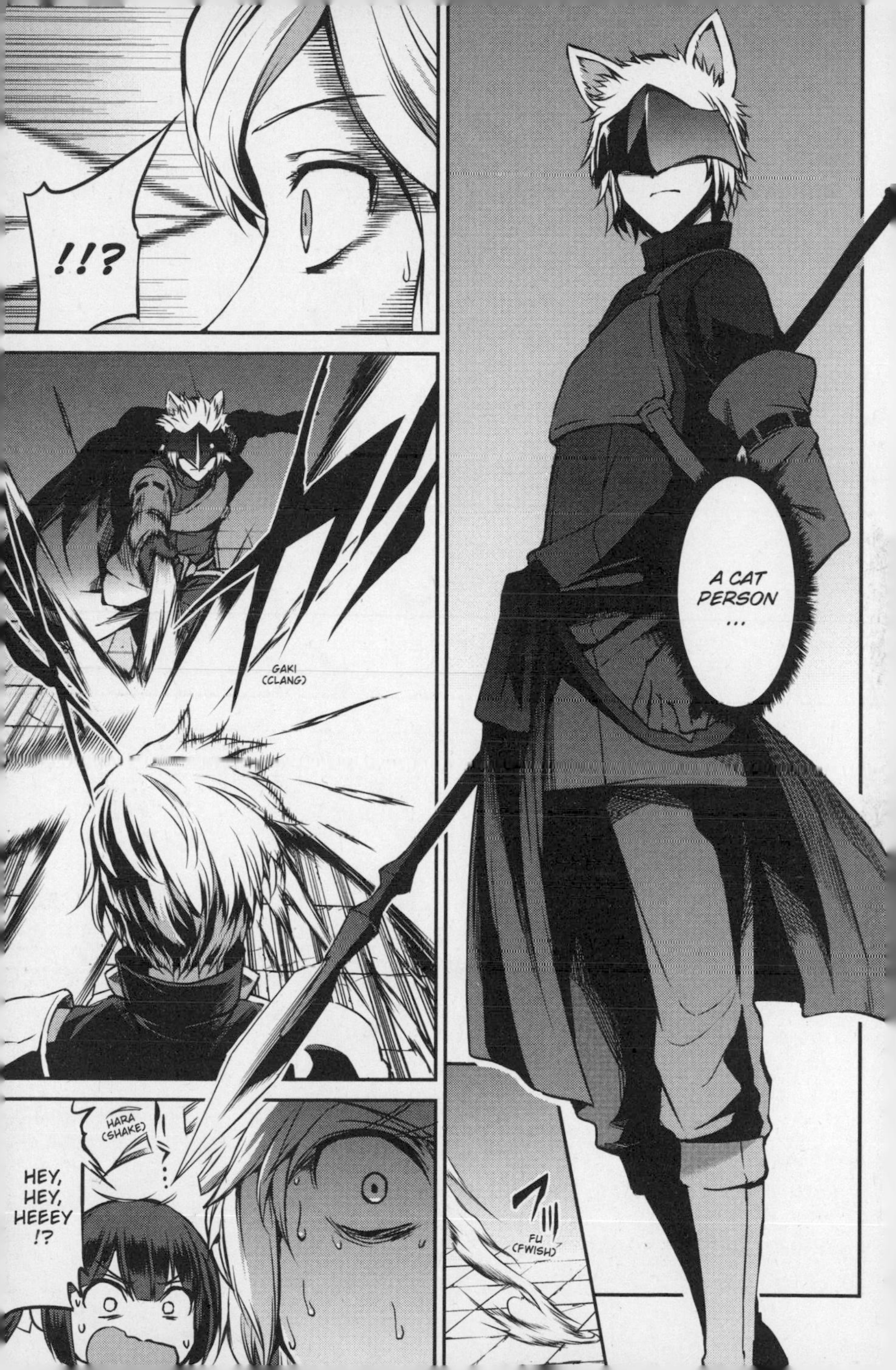

A CAT PERSON ...
FU (FWISH)
!!?
GAKI (CLANG)
HARA (SHAKE)
HEY, HEY, HEEEY !?

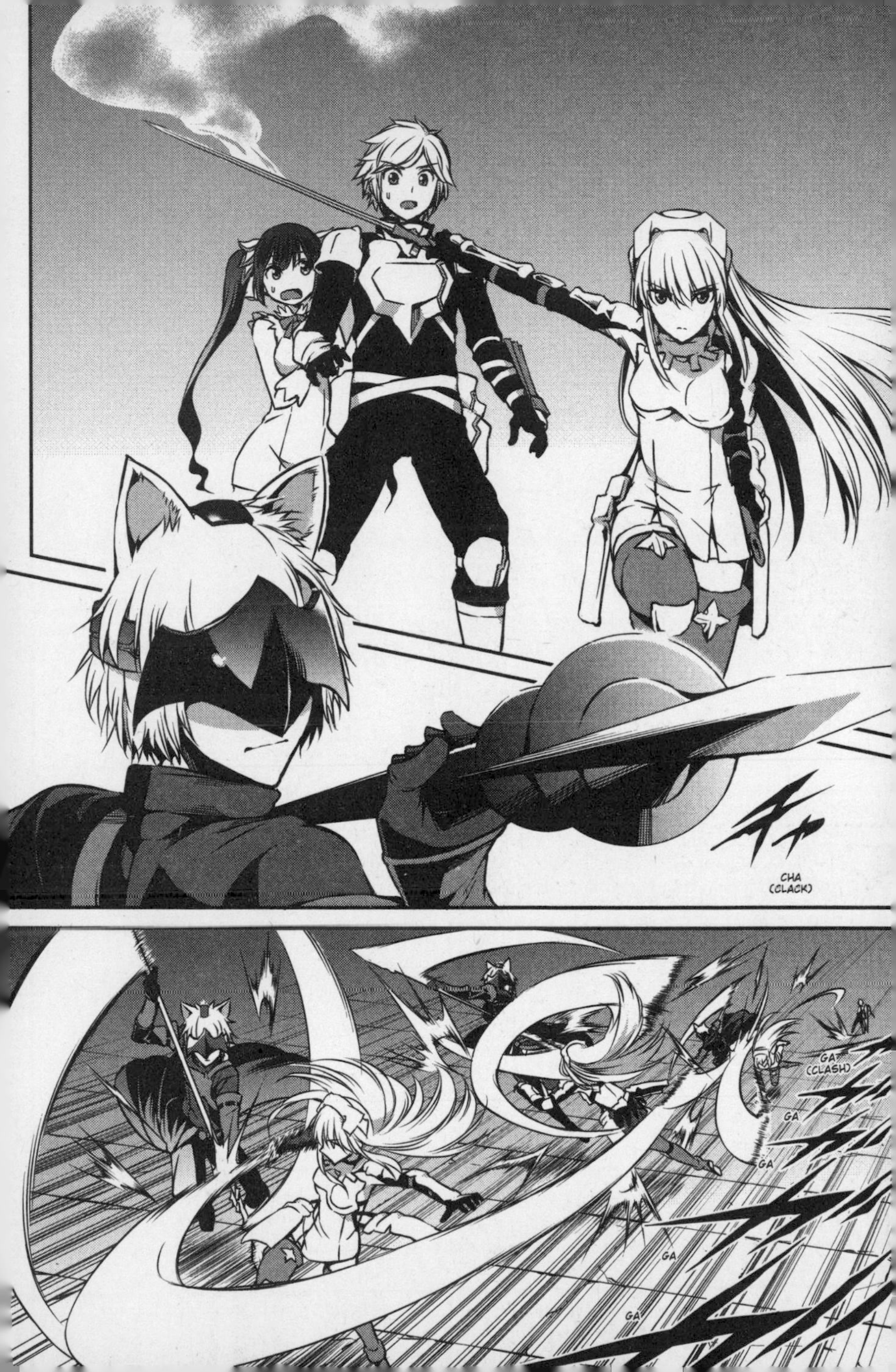
CHA
(CLACK)
GA
(CLASH)
GA
GA
GA
GA

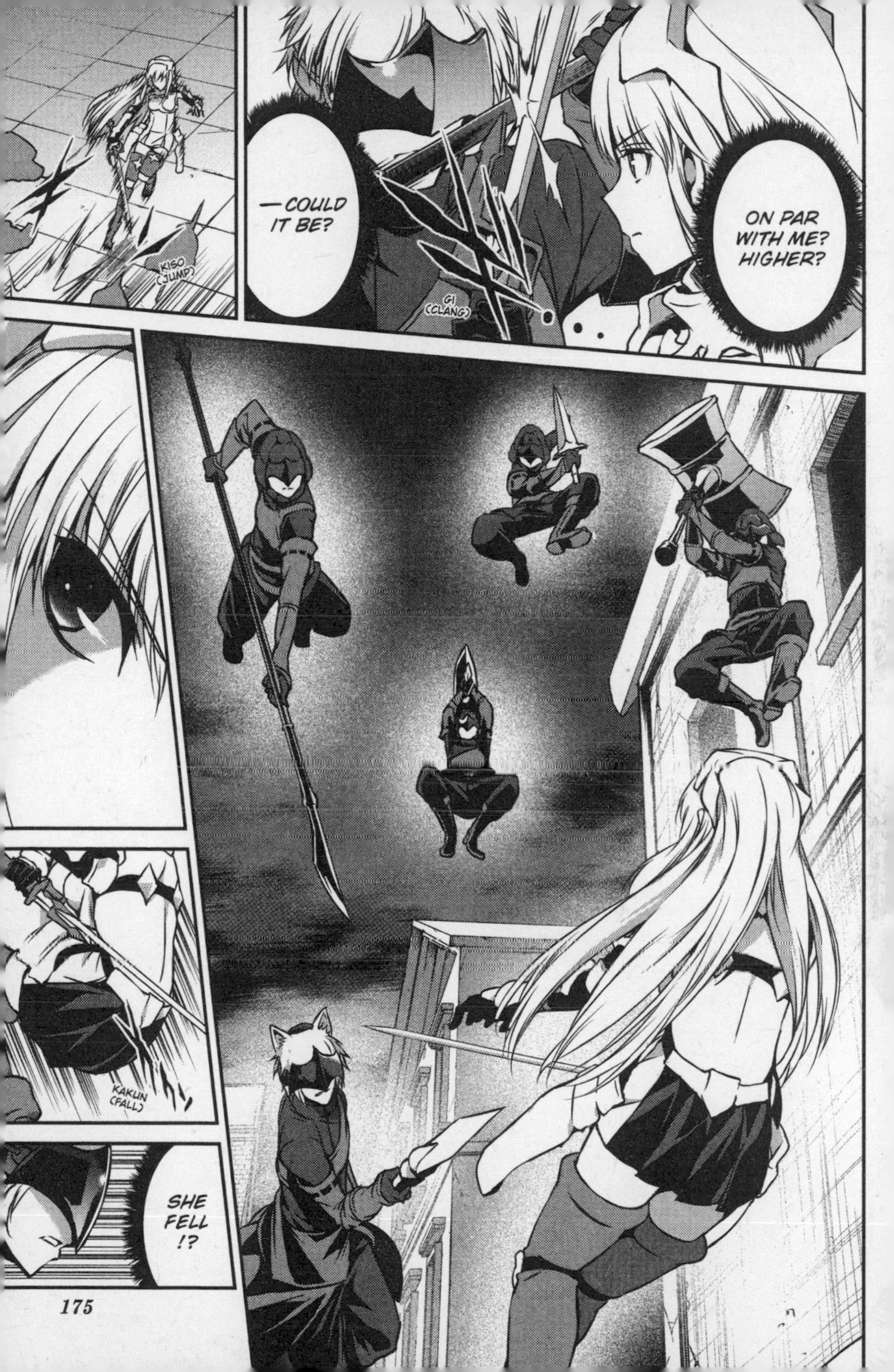
ON PAR WITH ME? HIGHER?
—COULD IT BE?
GI (CLANG)
KISO (JUMP)
KAKUN (FALL)
SHE FELL !?

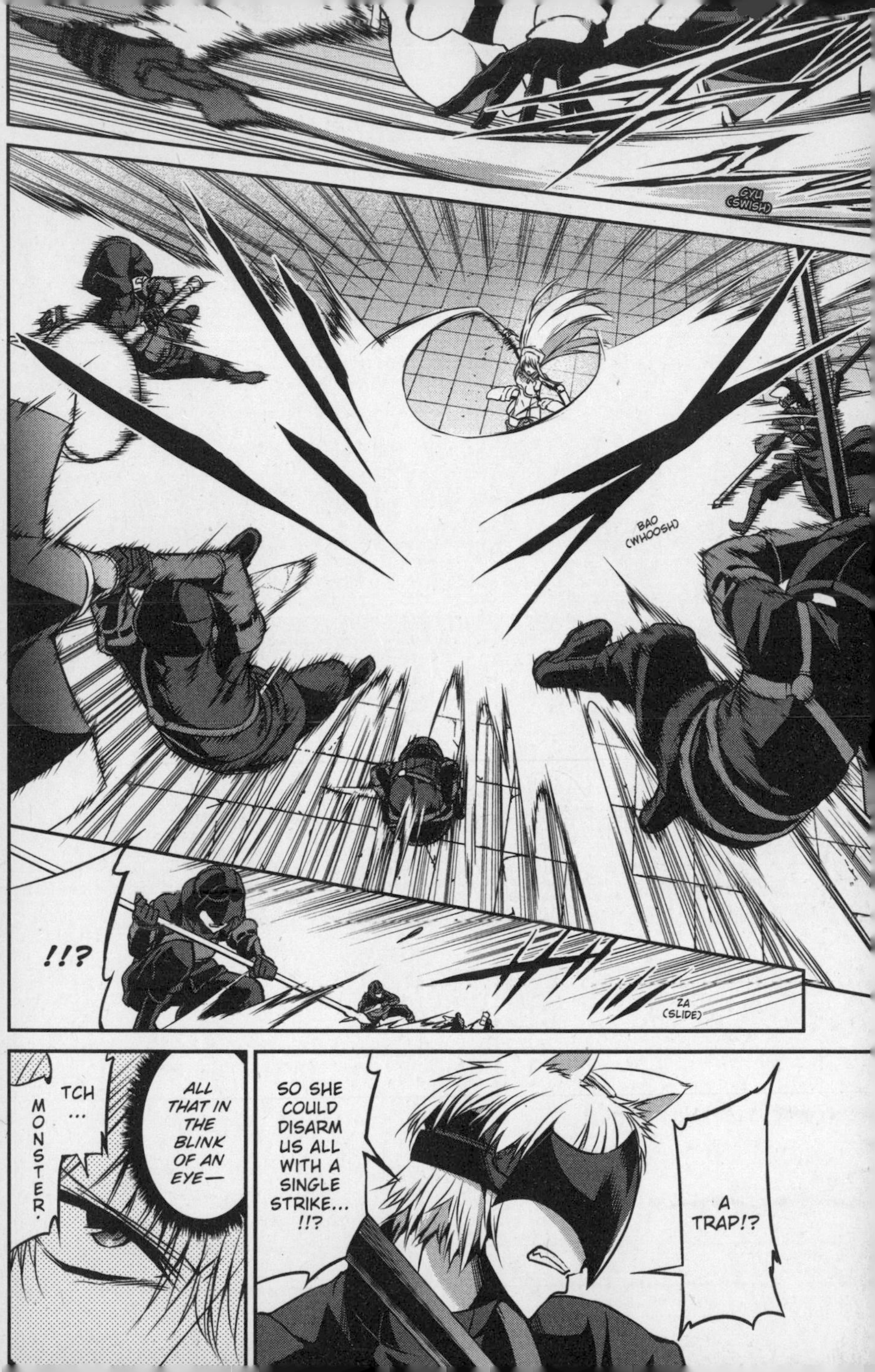
GYU (SWISH)
BAO (WHOOSH)
ZA (SLIDE)
!!?
A TRAP!?
SO SHE COULD DISARM US ALL WITH A SINGLE STRIKE...!!?
ALL THAT IN THE BLINK OF AN EYE—
TCH...
MONSTER.

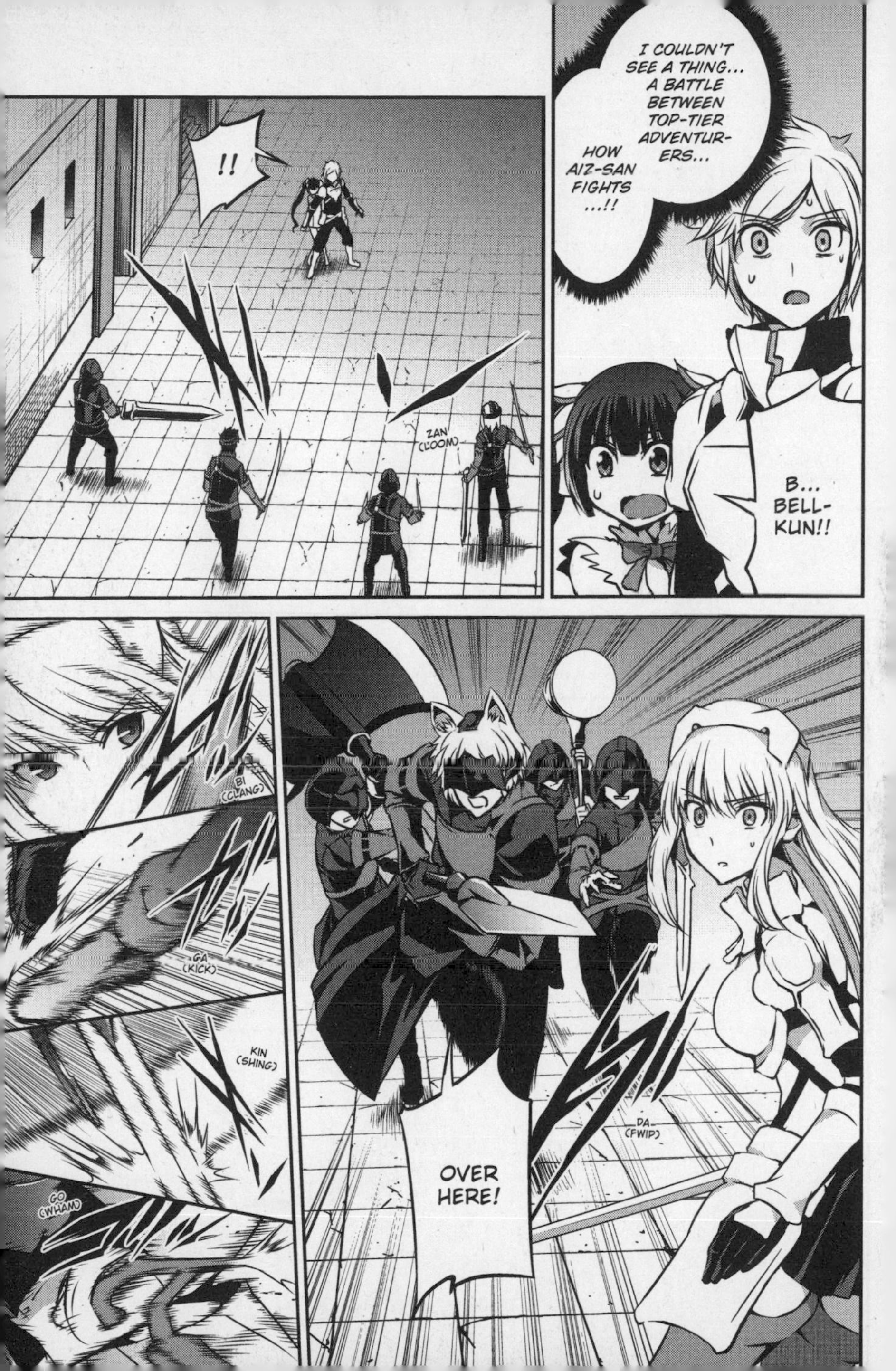
I COULDN'T SEE A THING... A BATTLE BETWEEN TOP-TIER ADVENTURERS...
HOW AIZ-SAN FIGHTS ...!!
B... BELL-KUN!!
!!
ZAN (LOOM)
DA (FWIP)
OVER HERE!
BI (CLANG)
GA (KICK)
KIN (SHING)
GO (WHAM)

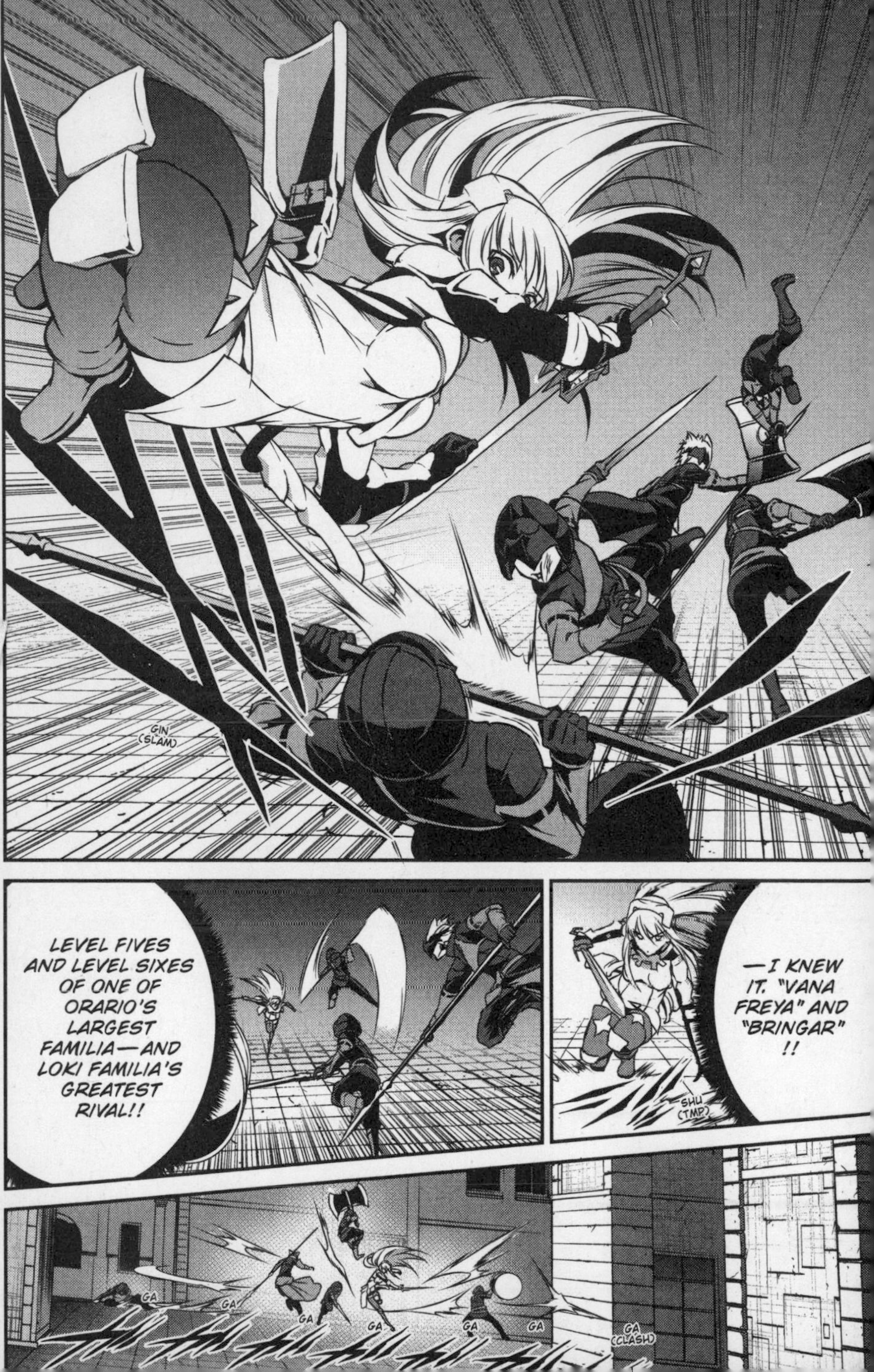
GIN (SLAM)
—I KNEW IT. "VANA FREYA" AND "BRINGAR" !!
SHU (TMP)
LEVEL FIVES AND LEVEL SIXES OF ONE OF ORARIO'S LARGEST FAMILIA—AND LOKI FAMILIA'S GREATEST RIVAL!!
GA
GA
GA
GA
GA
GA
GA (CLASH)

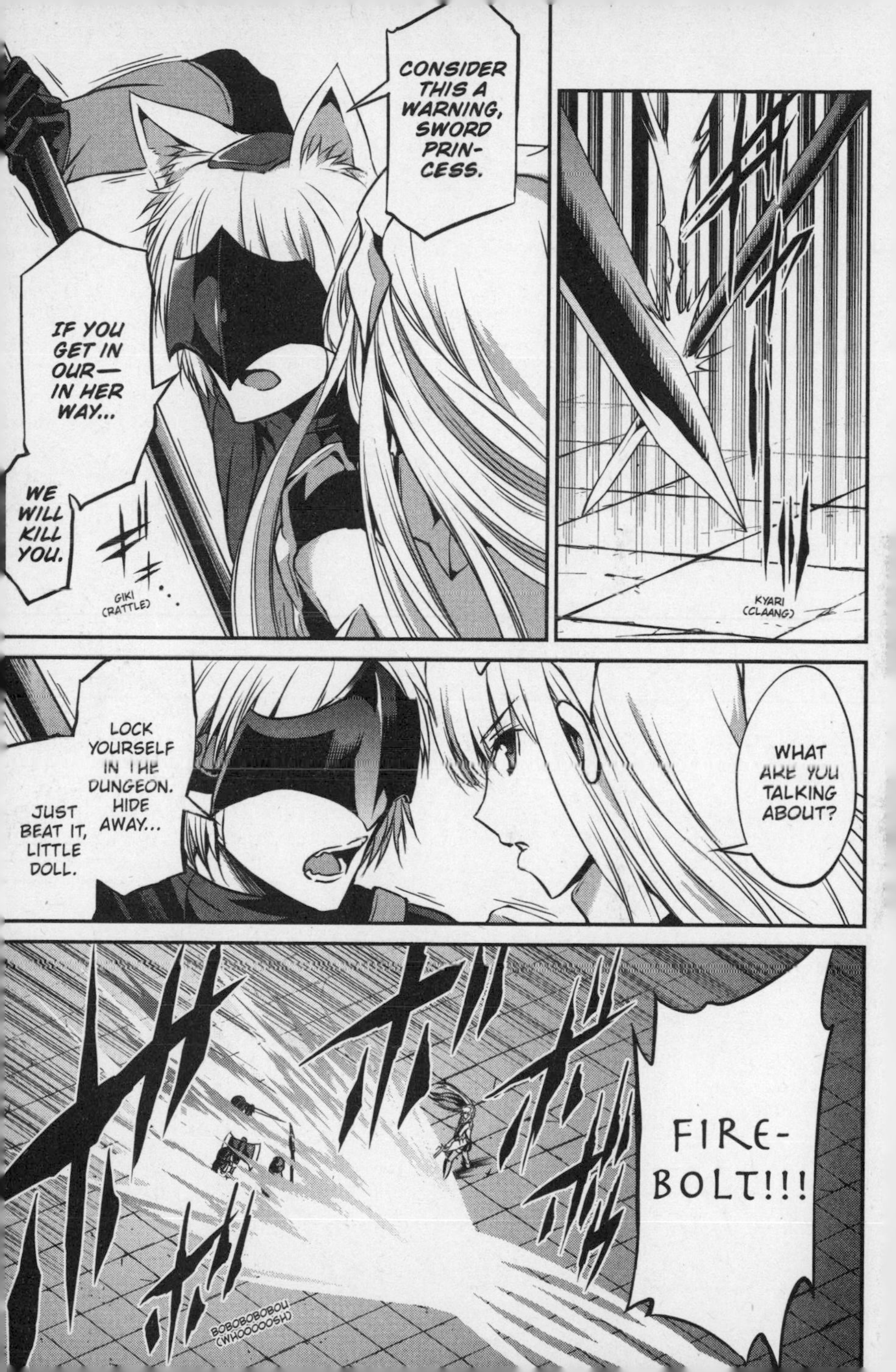
KYARI (CLAANG)
CONSIDER THIS A WARNING, SWORD PRIN-CESS.
IF YOU GET IN OUR— IN HER WAY...
WE WILL KILL YOU.
GIKI (RATTLE)
WHAT ARE YOU TALKING ABOUT?
LOCK YOURSELF IN THE DUNGEON. HIDE AWAY...
JUST BEAT IT, LITTLE DOLL.
FIRE-BOLT!!!
BOBOBOBOBOU (WHOOOOOSH)

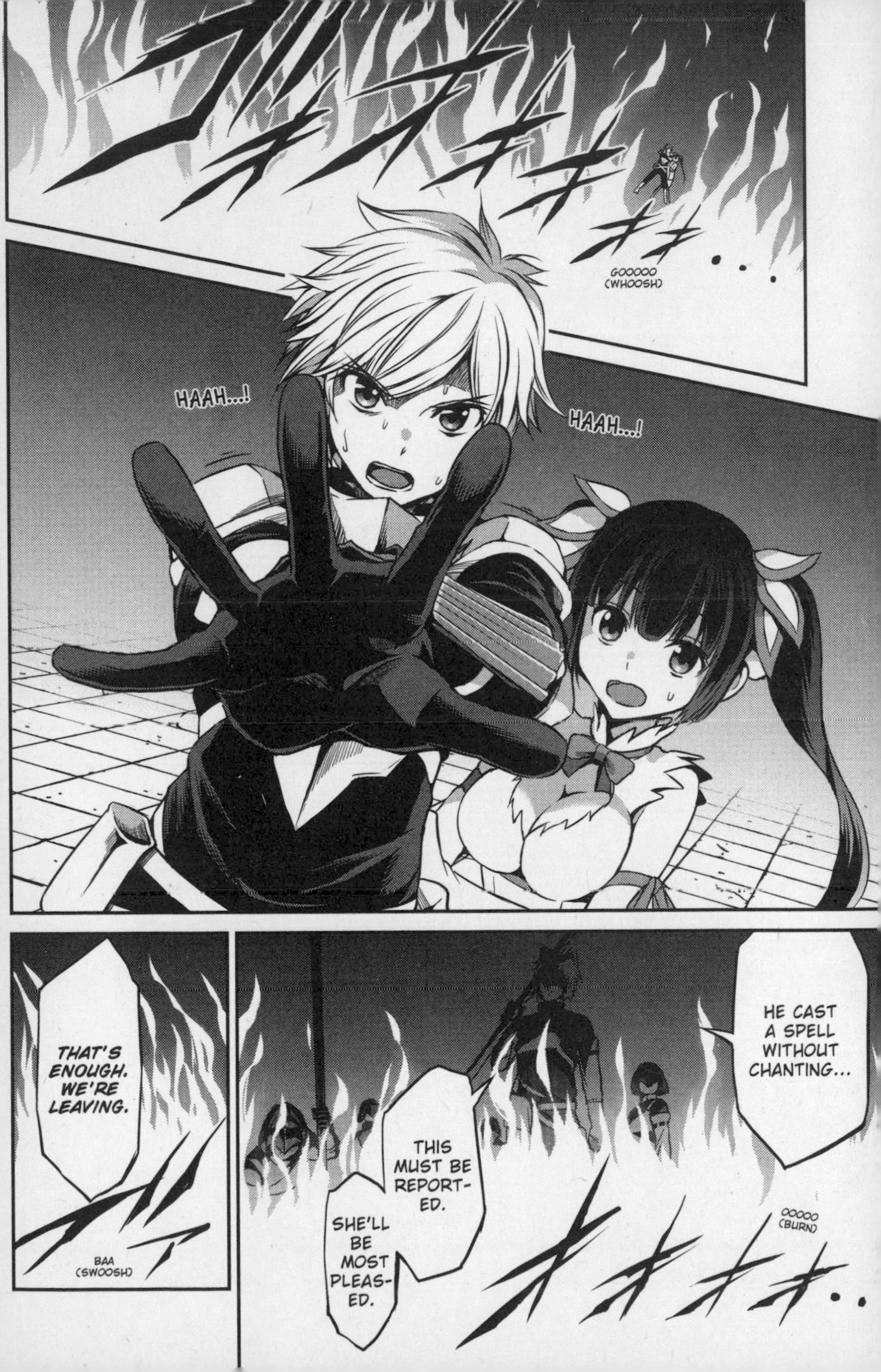
GOOOOO (WHOOSH)
HAAH...!
HAAH...!
HE CAST A SPELL WITHOUT CHANTING...
OOOOO (BURN)
THIS MUST BE REPORT-ED.
SHE'LL BE MOST PLEAS-ED.
THAT'S ENOUGH. WE'RE LEAVING.
BAA (SWOOSH)

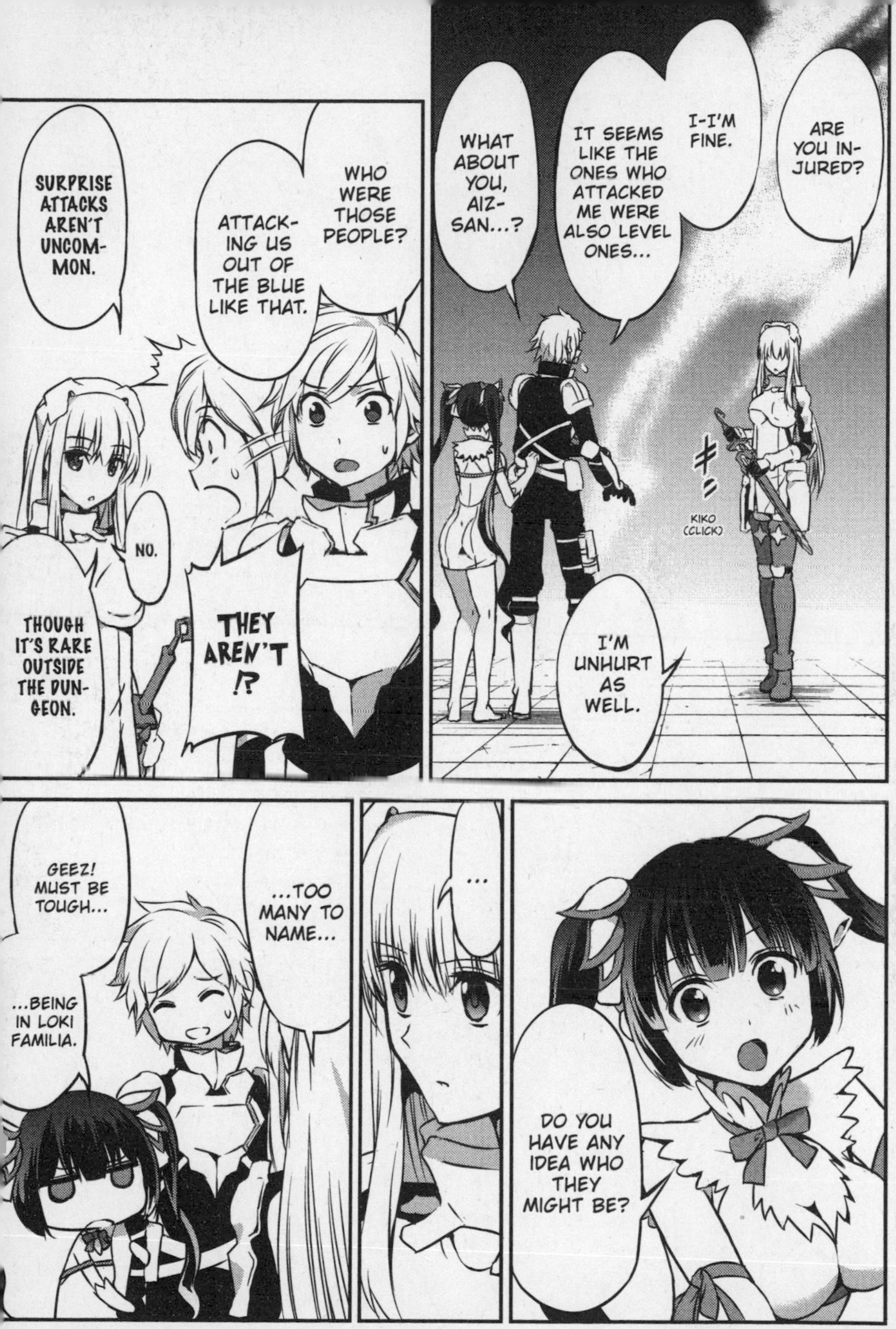
ARE YOU IN-JURED?
I-I'M FINE.
IT SEEMS LIKE THE ONES WHO ATTACKED ME WERE ALSO LEVEL ONES...
WHAT ABOUT YOU, AIZ-SAN...?
KIKO (CLICK)
I'M UNHURT AS WELL.
WHO WERE THOSE PEOPLE?
ATTACKING US OUT OF THE BLUE LIKE THAT.
SURPRISE ATTACKS AREN'T UNCOMMON.
THEY AREN'T !?
NO.
THOUGH IT'S RARE OUTSIDE THE DUNGEON.
DO YOU HAVE ANY IDEA WHO THEY MIGHT BE?
...
...TOO MANY TO NAME...
GEEZ! MUST BE TOUGH...
...BEING IN LOKI FAMILIA.

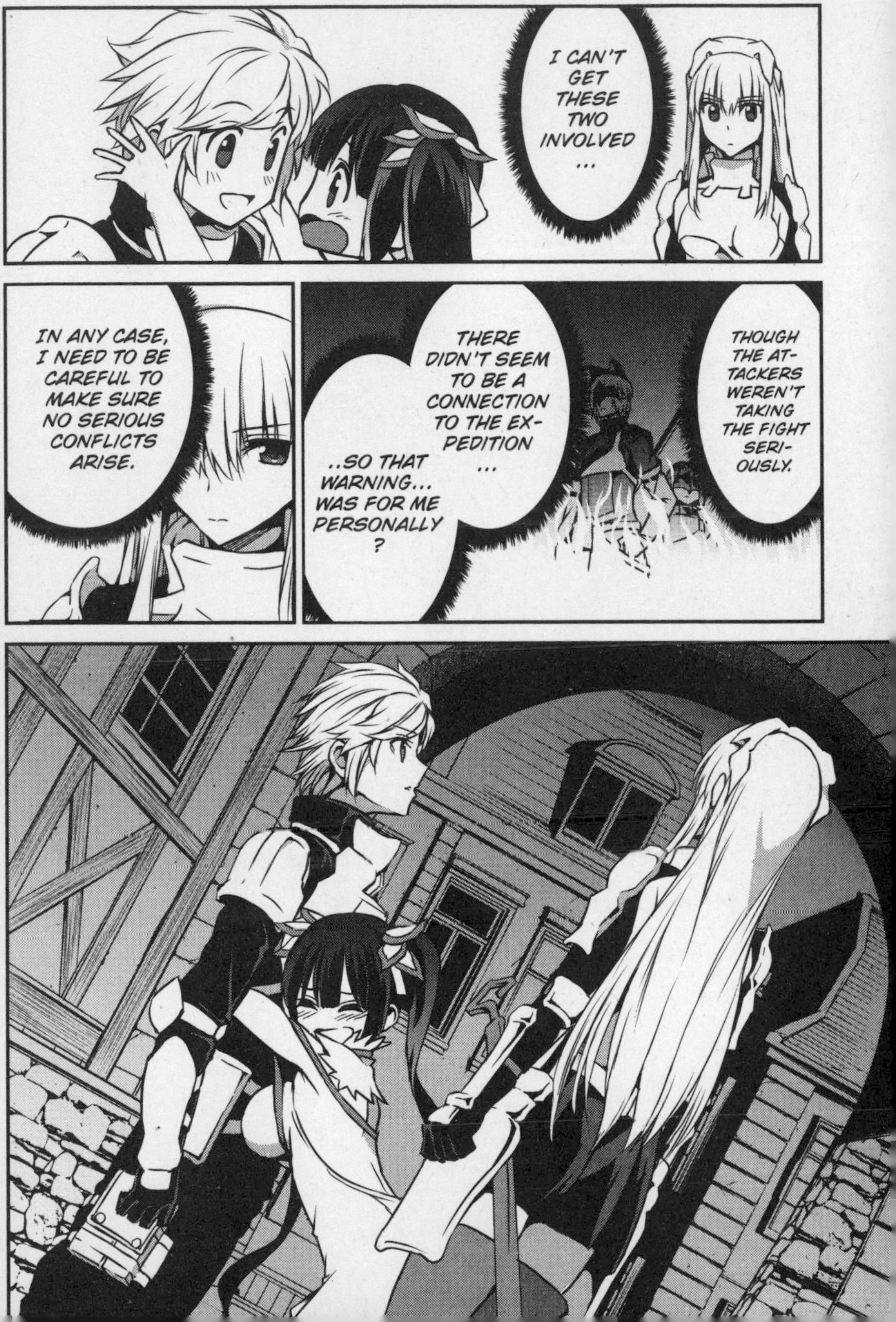
I CAN'T GET THESE TWO INVOLVED...
THOUGH THE ATTACKERS WEREN'T TAKING THE FIGHT SERIOUSLY.
THERE DIDN'T SEEM TO BE A CONNECTION TO THE EXPEDITION...
...SO THAT WARNING... WAS FOR ME PERSONALLY?
IN ANY CASE, I NEED TO BE CAREFUL TO MAKE SURE NO SERIOUS CONFLICTS ARISE.

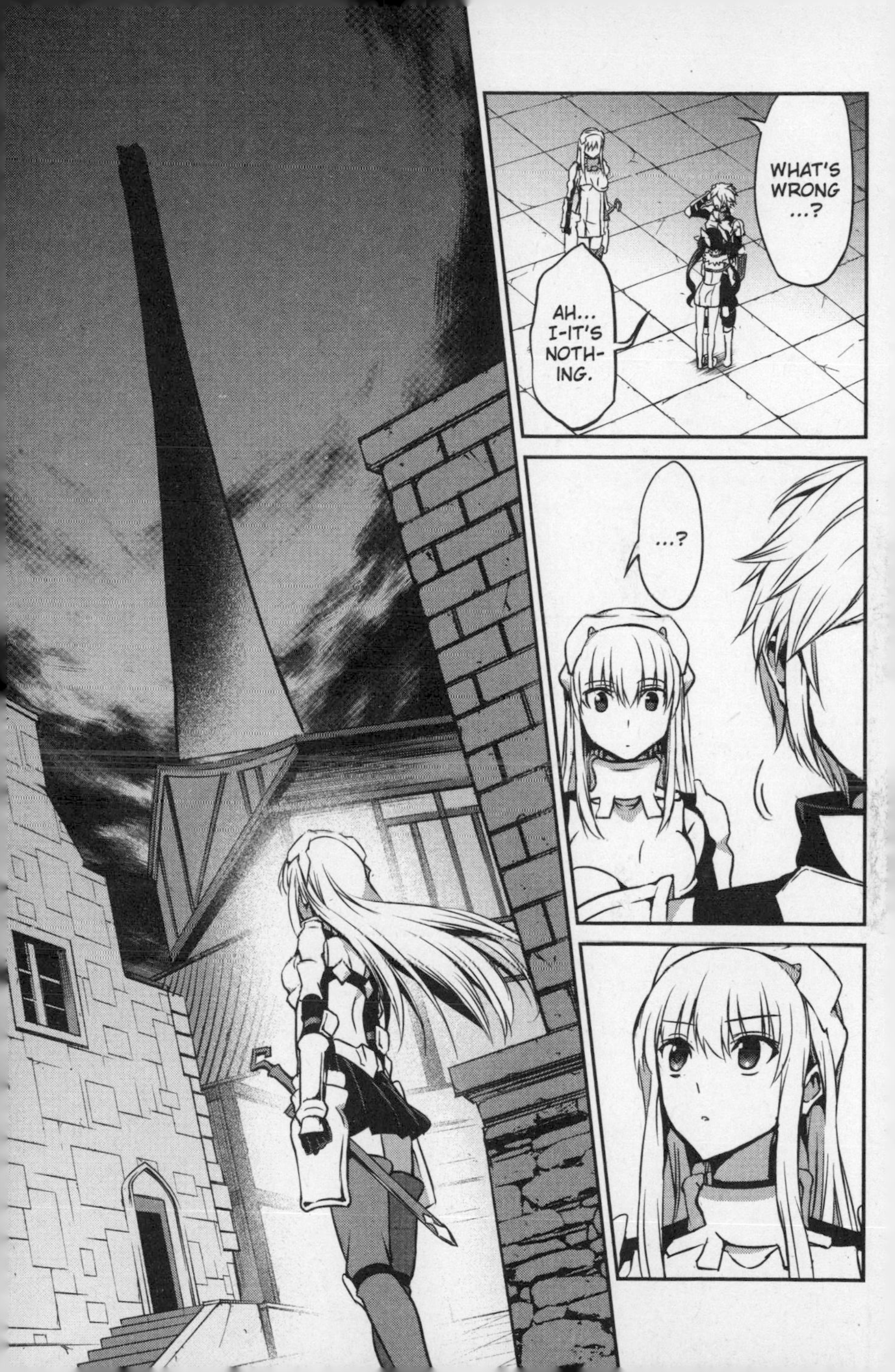
WHAT'S WRONG ...?
AH... I-IT'S NOTHING.
...?

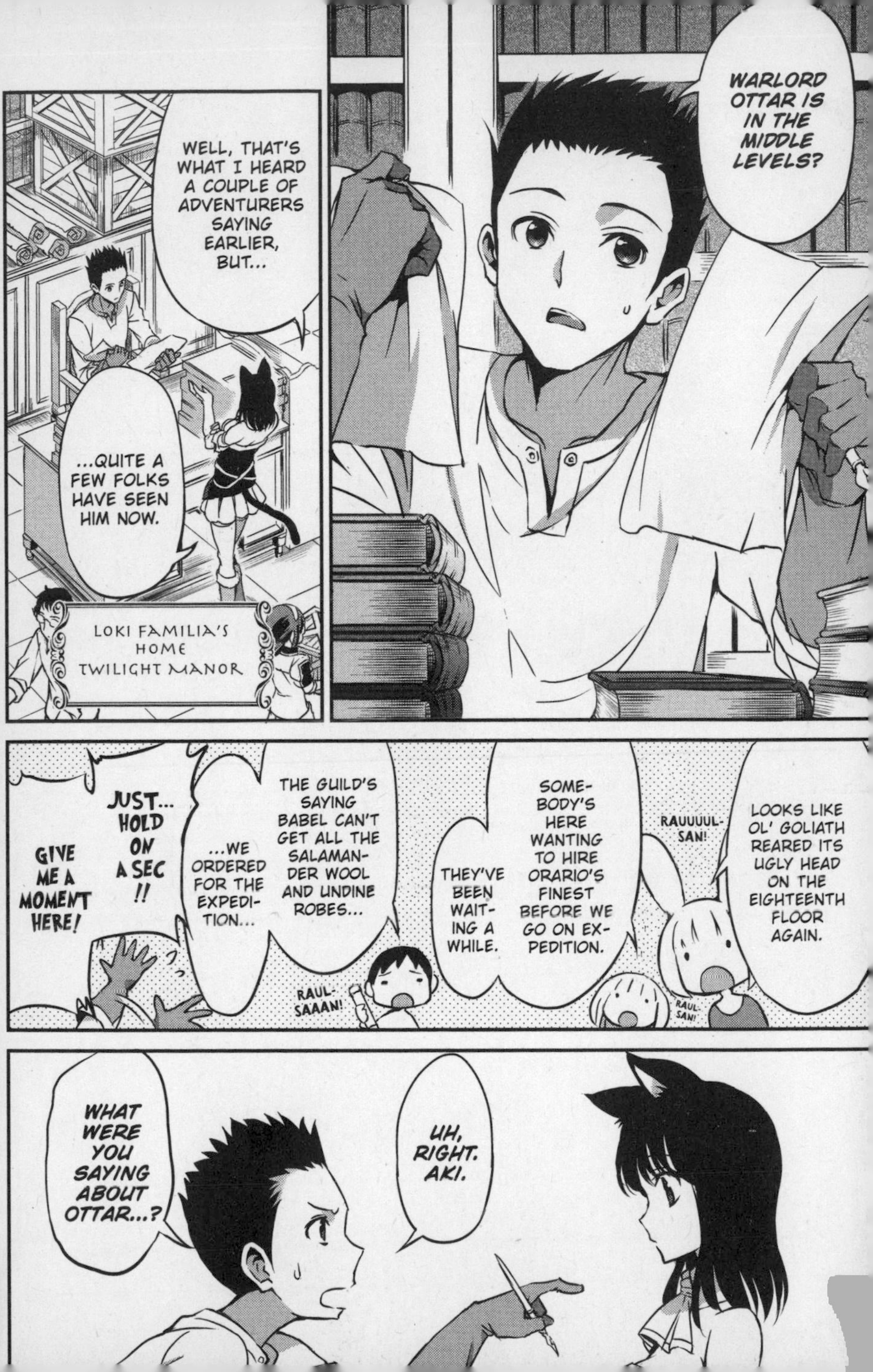
WARLORD OTTAR IS IN THE MIDDLE LEVELS?
WELL, THAT'S WHAT I HEARD A COUPLE OF ADVENTURERS SAYING EARLIER, BUT...
...QUITE A FEW FOLKS HAVE SEEN HIM NOW.
LOKI FAMILIA'S HOME TWILIGHT MANOR
LOOKS LIKE OL' GOLIATH REARED ITS UGLY HEAD ON THE EIGHTEENTH FLOOR AGAIN.
RAUUUUL-SAN!
RAUL-SAN!
SOMEBODY'S HERE WANTING TO HIRE ORARIO'S FINEST BEFORE WE GO ON EXPEDITION.
THEY'VE BEEN WAITING A WHILE.
RAUL-SAAAN!
THE GUILD'S SAYING BABEL CAN'T GET ALL THE SALAMANDER WOOL AND UNDINE ROBES...
...WE ORDERED FOR THE EXPEDITION...
JUST... HOLD ON A SEC !!
GIVE ME A MOMENT HERE!
UH, RIGHT. AKI.
WHAT WERE YOU SAYING ABOUT OTTAR...?

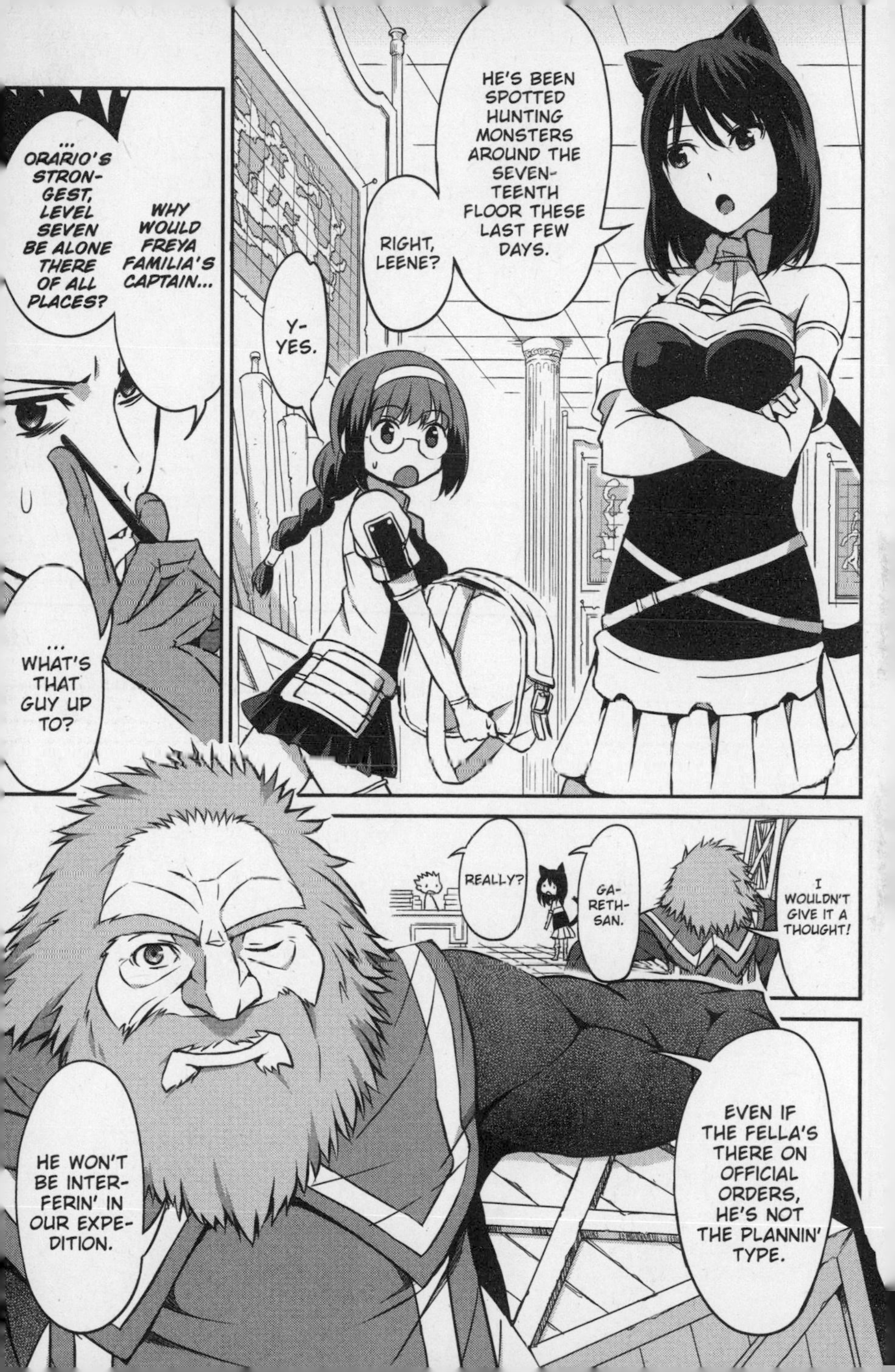
HE'S BEEN SPOTTED HUNTING MONSTERS AROUND THE SEVENTEENTH FLOOR THESE LAST FEW DAYS.
RIGHT, LEENE?
Y-YES.
WHY WOULD FREYA FAMILIA'S CAPTAIN...
...ORARIO'S STRONGEST, LEVEL SEVEN BE ALONE THERE OF ALL PLACES?
...WHAT'S THAT GUY UP TO?
I WOULDN'T GIVE IT A THOUGHT!
GARETH-SAN.
REALLY?
EVEN IF THE FELLA'S THERE ON OFFICIAL ORDERS, HE'S NOT THE PLANNIN' TYPE.
HE WON'T BE INTERFERIN' IN OUR EXPEDITION.

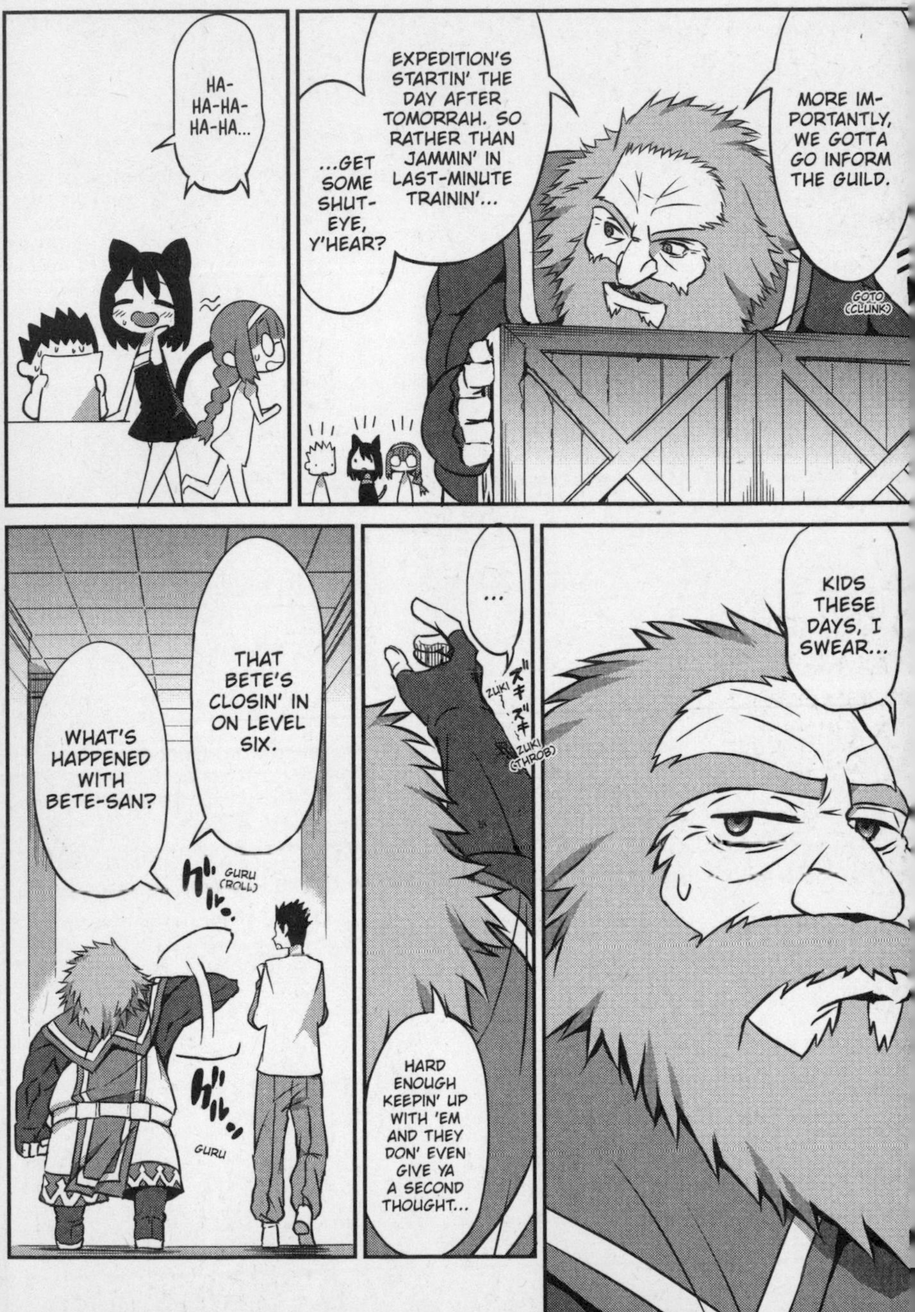
MORE IMPORTANTLY, WE GOTTA GO INFORM THE GUILD.
EXPEDITION'S STARTIN' THE DAY AFTER TOMORRAH. SO RATHER THAN JAMMIN' IN LAST-MINUTE TRAININ'...
...GET SOME SHUT-EYE, Y'HEAR?
GOTO (CLUNK)
HA-HA-HA-HA-HA...
KIDS THESE DAYS, I SWEAR...
...
ZUKI ZUKI (THROB)
HARD ENOUGH KEEPIN' UP WITH 'EM AND THEY DON' EVEN GIVE YA A SECOND THOUGHT...
THAT BETE'S CLOSIN' IN ON LEVEL SIX.
WHAT'S HAPPENED WITH BETE-SAN?
GURU (ROLL)
GURU

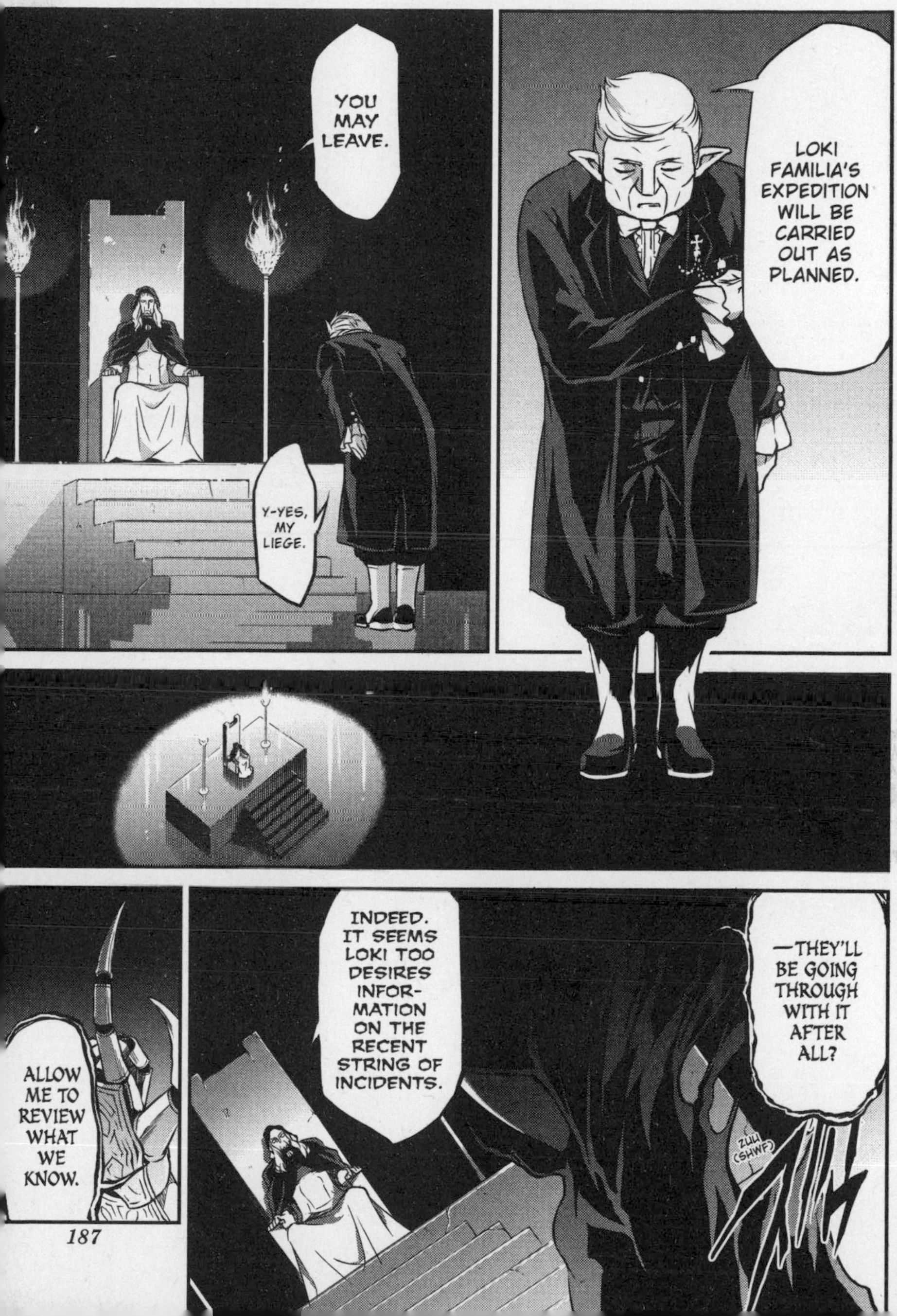
LOKI FAMILIA'S EXPEDITION WILL BE CARRIED OUT AS PLANNED.
YOU MAY LEAVE.
Y-YES, MY LIEGE.
—THEY'LL BE GOING THROUGH WITH IT AFTER ALL?
ZUU (SHWF)
INDEED. IT SEEMS LOKI TOO DESIRES INFOR-MATION ON THE RECENT STRING OF INCIDENTS.
ALLOW ME TO REVIEW WHAT WE KNOW.

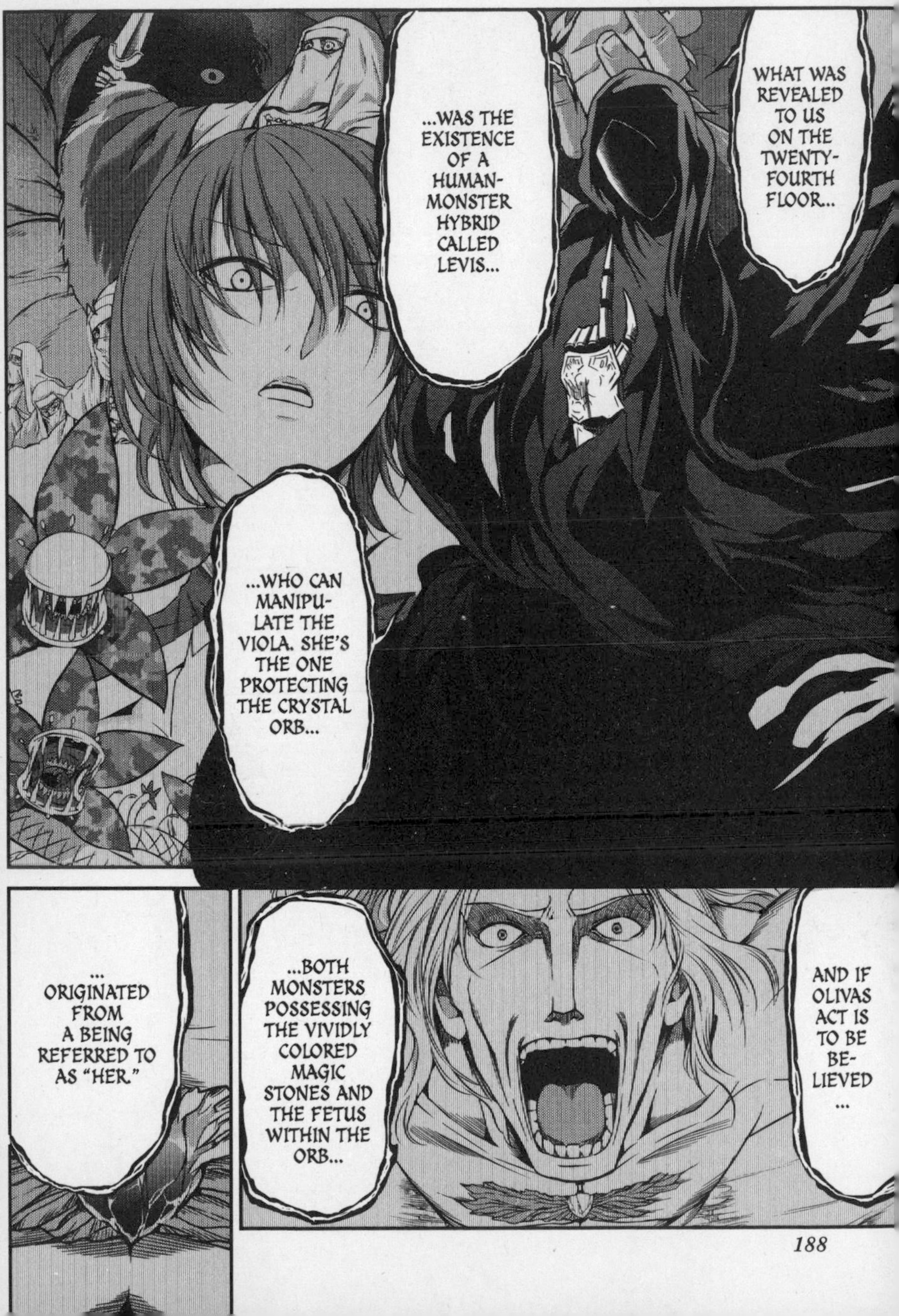
WHAT WAS REVEALED TO US ON THE TWENTY-FOURTH FLOOR...
...WAS THE EXISTENCE OF A HUMAN-MONSTER HYBRID CALLED LEVIS...
...WHO CAN MANIPULATE THE VIOLA. SHE'S THE ONE PROTECTING THE CRYSTAL ORB...
AND IF OLIVAS ACT IS TO BE BELIEVED...
...BOTH MONSTERS POSSESSING THE VIVIDLY COLORED MAGIC STONES AND THE FETUS WITHIN THE ORB...
...ORIGINATED FROM A BEING REFERRED TO AS "HER."

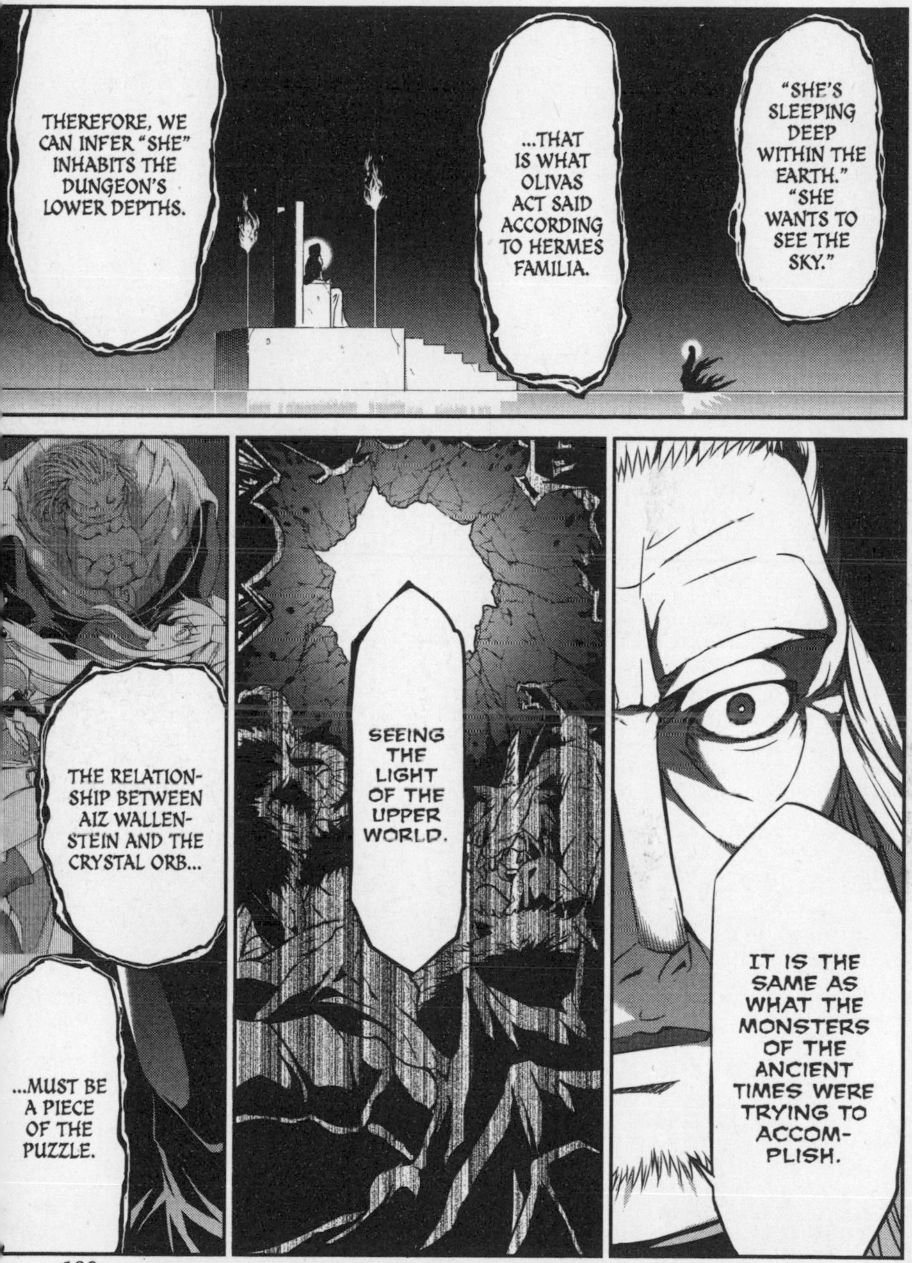
"SHE'S SLEEPING DEEP WITHIN THE EARTH." "SHE WANTS TO SEE THE SKY."
...THAT IS WHAT OLIVAS ACT SAID ACCORDING TO HERMES FAMILIA.
THEREFORE, WE CAN INFER "SHE" INHABITS THE DUNGEON'S LOWER DEPTHS.
IT IS THE SAME AS WHAT THE MONSTERS OF THE ANCIENT TIMES WERE TRYING TO ACCOM-PLISH.
SEEING THE LIGHT OF THE UPPER WORLD.
THE RELATION-SHIP BETWEEN AIZ WALLEN-STEIN AND THE CRYSTAL ORB...
...MUST BE A PIECE OF THE PUZZLE.

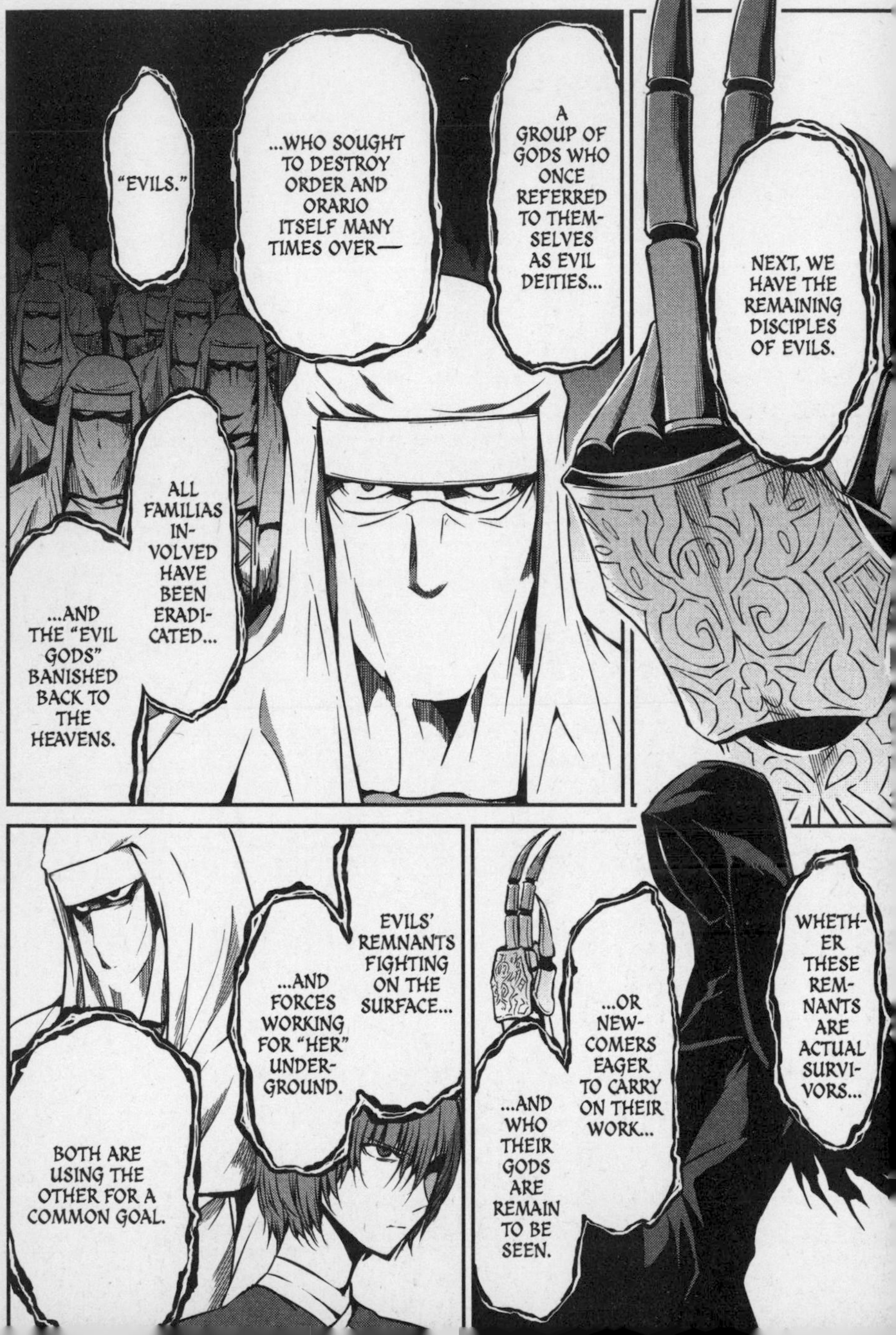
NEXT, WE HAVE THE REMAINING DISCIPLES OF EVILS.
A GROUP OF GODS WHO ONCE REFERRED TO THEMSELVES AS EVIL DEITIES...
...WHO SOUGHT TO DESTROY ORDER AND ORARIO ITSELF MANY TIMES OVER—
"EVILS."
ALL FAMILIAS INVOLVED HAVE BEEN ERADICATED...
...AND THE "EVIL GODS" BANISHED BACK TO THE HEAVENS.
WHETHER THESE REMNANTS ARE ACTUAL SURVIVORS...
...OR NEWCOMERS EAGER TO CARRY ON THEIR WORK...
...AND WHO THEIR GODS ARE REMAIN TO BE SEEN.
EVILS' REMNANTS FIGHTING ON THE SURFACE...
...AND FORCES WORKING FOR "HER" UNDERGROUND.
BOTH ARE USING THE OTHER FOR A COMMON GOAL.

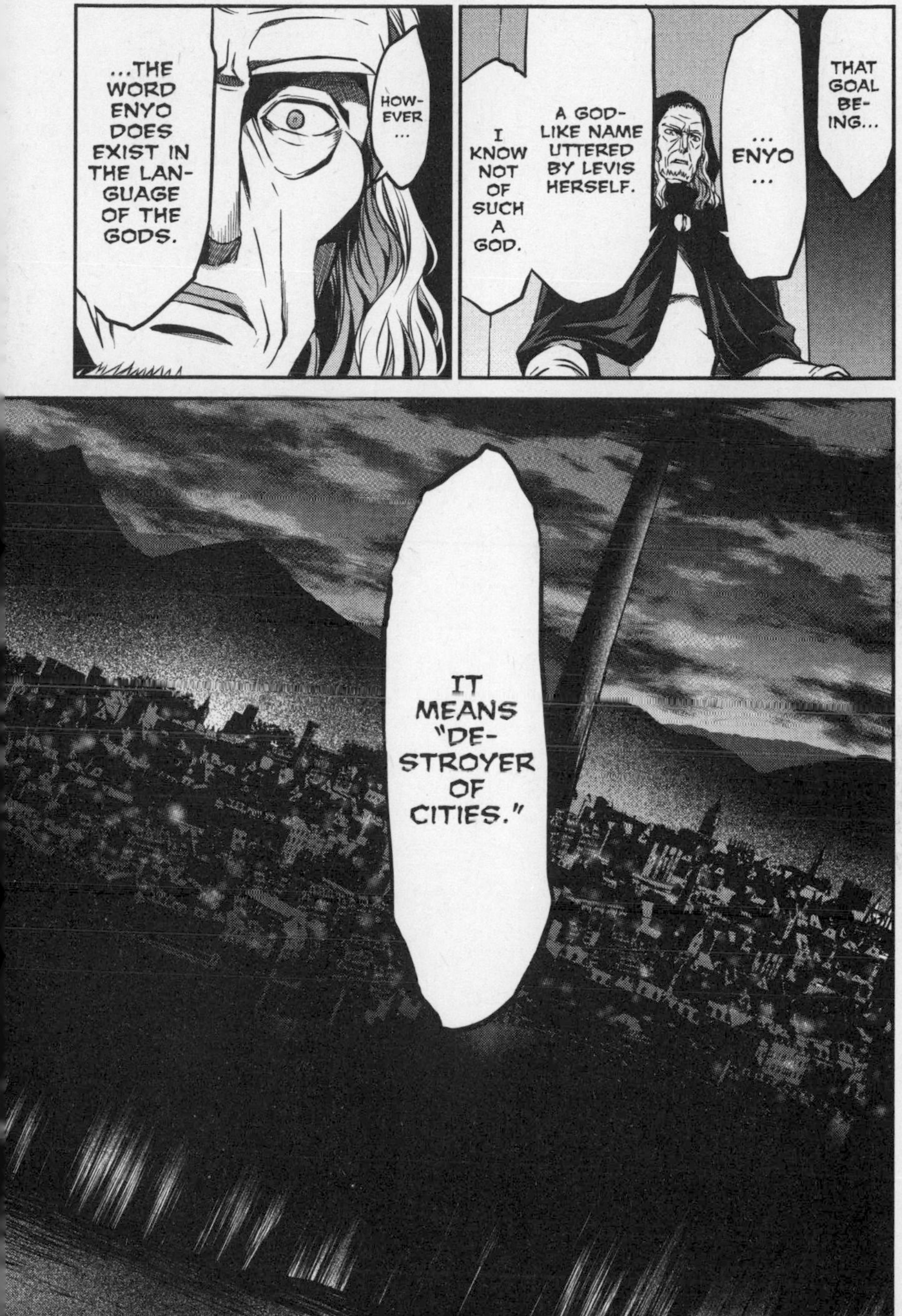
THAT GOAL BEING...
...ENYO...
A GOD-LIKE NAME UTTERED BY LEVIS HERSELF.
I KNOW NOT OF SUCH A GOD.
HOWEVER...
...THE WORD ENYO DOES EXIST IN THE LANGUAGE OF THE GODS.
IT MEANS "DESTROYER OF CITIES."

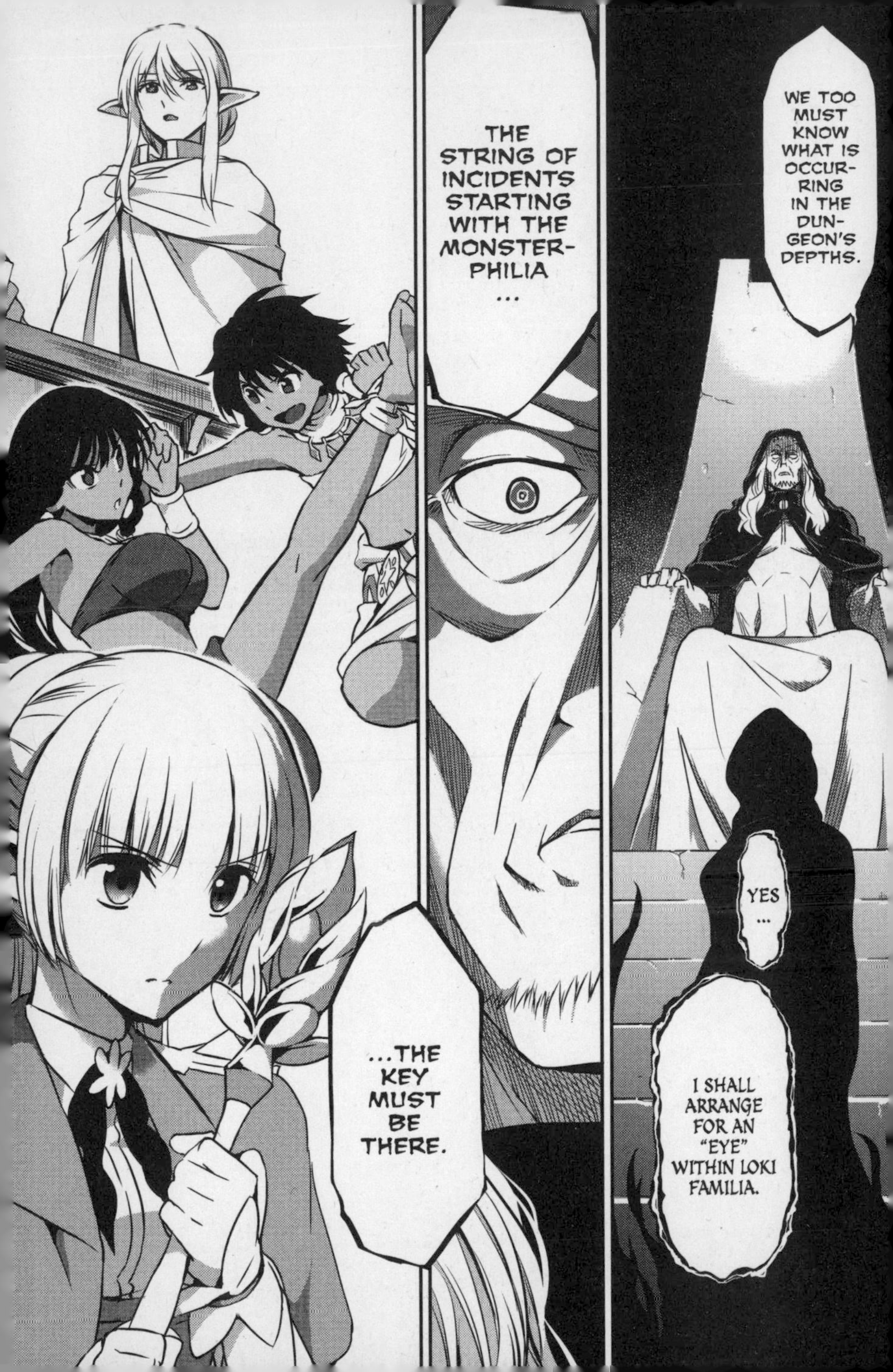
WE TOO MUST KNOW WHAT IS OCCUR-RING IN THE DUN-GEON'S DEPTHS.
YES ...
I SHALL ARRANGE FOR AN "EYE" WITHIN LOKI FAMILIA.
THE STRING OF INCIDENTS STARTING WITH THE MONSTER-PHILIA ...
...THE KEY MUST BE THERE.

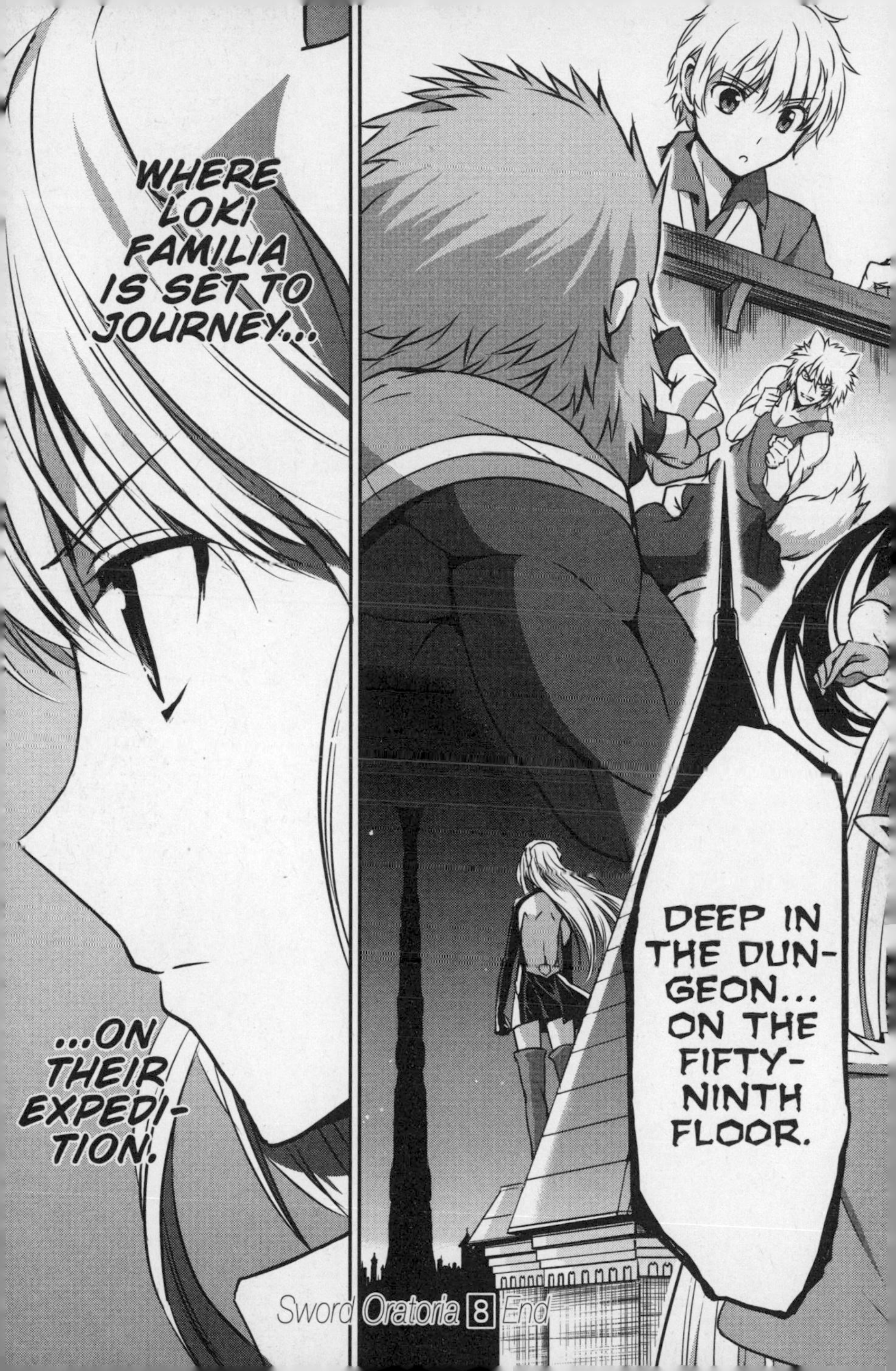
DEEP IN THE DUN-GEON... ON THE FIFTY-NINTH FLOOR.
WHERE LOKI FAMILIA IS SET TO JOURNEY...
...ON THEIR EXPEDI-TION.
Sword Oratoria 8 End

Is it WRONG to try to PICK UP GIRLS IN A DUNGEON? ON THE SIDE

Sword Oratoria

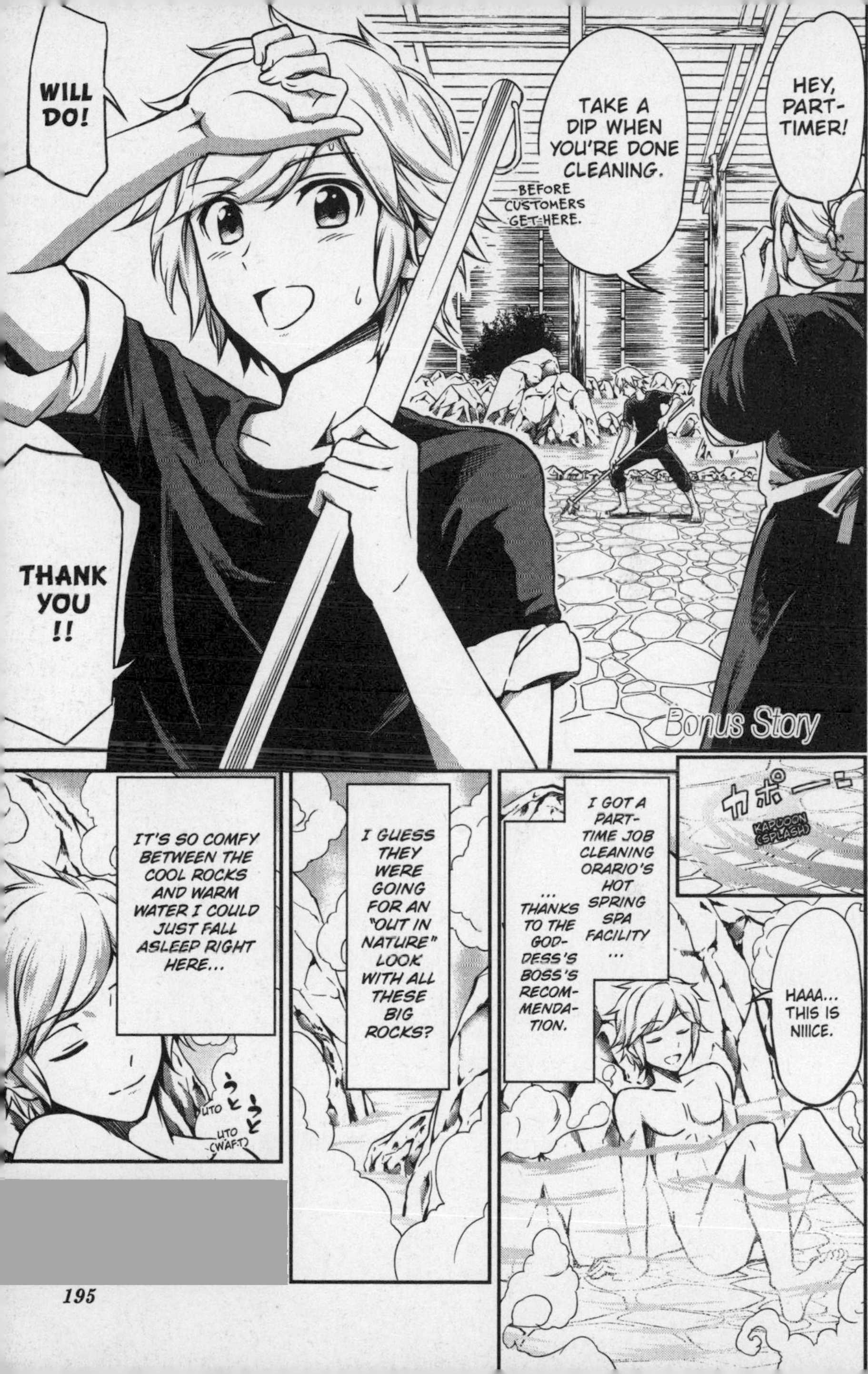
HEY, PART-TIMER!
TAKE A DIP WHEN YOU'RE DONE CLEANING.
—BEFORE CUSTOMERS GET HERE.
WILL DO!
THANK YOU !!
Bonus Story
カポーン
KAPOOON (SPLASH)
HAAA... THIS IS NIIICE.
I GOT A PART-TIME JOB CLEANING ORARIO'S HOT SPRING SPA FACILITY ...
... THANKS TO THE GOD-DESS'S BOSS'S RECOM-MENDA-TION.
I GUESS THEY WERE GOING FOR AN "OUT IN NATURE" LOOK WITH ALL THESE BIG ROCKS?
IT'S SO COMFY BETWEEN THE COOL ROCKS AND WARM WATER I COULD JUST FALL ASLEEP RIGHT HERE...
うとうと
UTO UTO (WAFT)

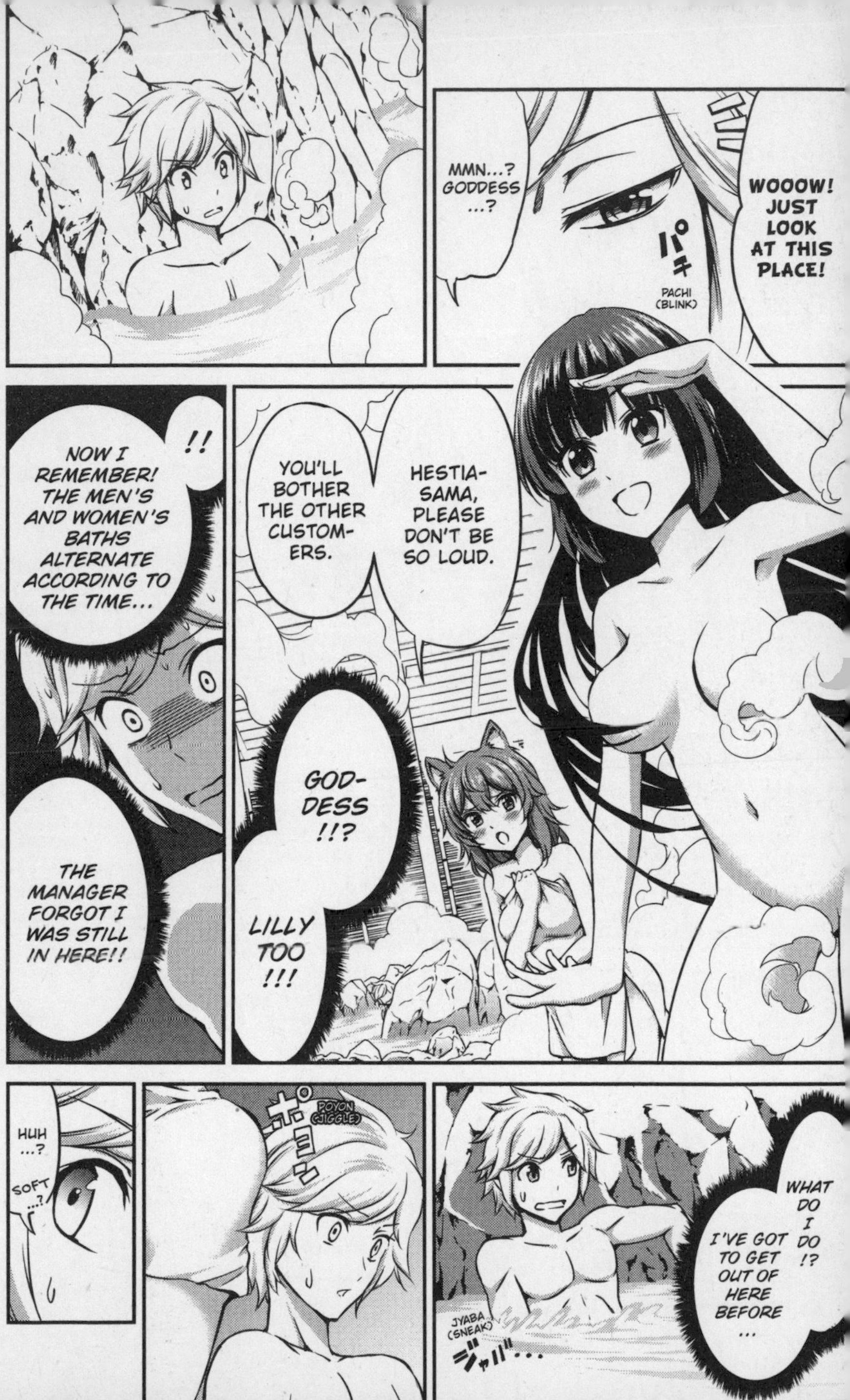
WOOOW! JUST LOOK AT THIS PLACE!
MMN...? GODDESS ...?
パチ
PACHI (BLINK)
HESTIA-SAMA, PLEASE DON'T BE SO LOUD.
YOU'LL BOTHER THE OTHER CUSTOM-ERS.
GOD-DESS !!?
LILLY TOO !!!
!!
NOW I REMEMBER! THE MEN'S AND WOMEN'S BATHS ALTERNATE ACCORDING TO THE TIME...
THE MANAGER FORGOT I WAS STILL IN HERE!!
WHAT DO I DO !?
I'VE GOT TO GET OUT OF HERE BEFORE ...
ジャバ...
JYABA (SNEAK)
ポヨン
POYON (JIGGLE)
HUH ...?
SOFT ...?

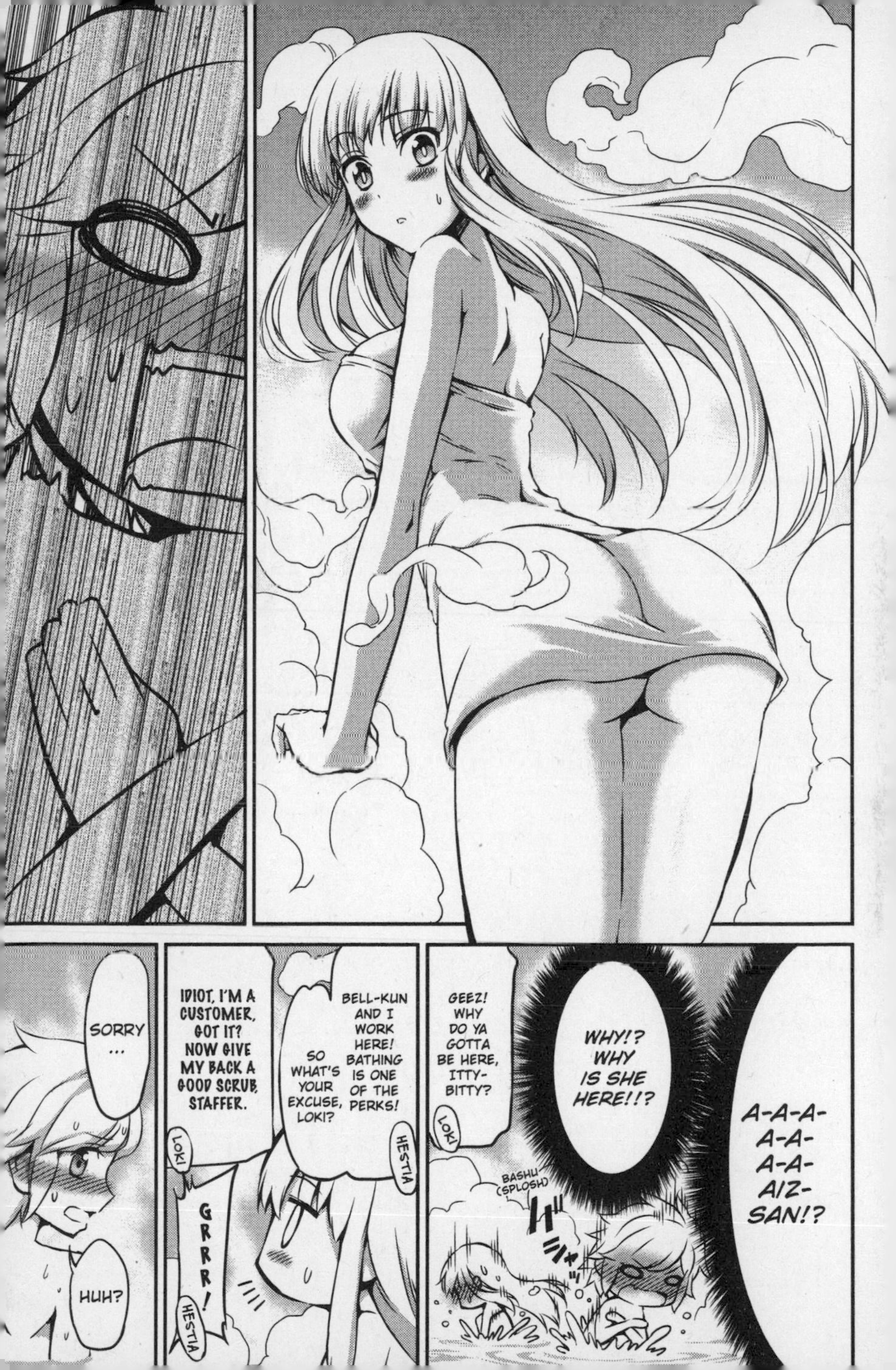
A-A-A-A-A-A-A-AIZ-SAN!?
WHY!? WHY IS SHE HERE!!?
BASHU (SPLOSH)
GEEZ! WHY DO YA GOTTA BE HERE, ITTY-BITTY?
LOKI
BELL-KUN AND I WORK HERE! BATHING IS ONE OF THE PERKS!
HESTIA
SO WHAT'S YOUR EXCUSE, LOKI?
IDIOT, I'M A CUSTOMER, GOT IT? NOW GIVE MY BACK A GOOD SCRUB, STAFFER.
LOKI
GRRR!
HESTIA
SORRY ...
HUH?

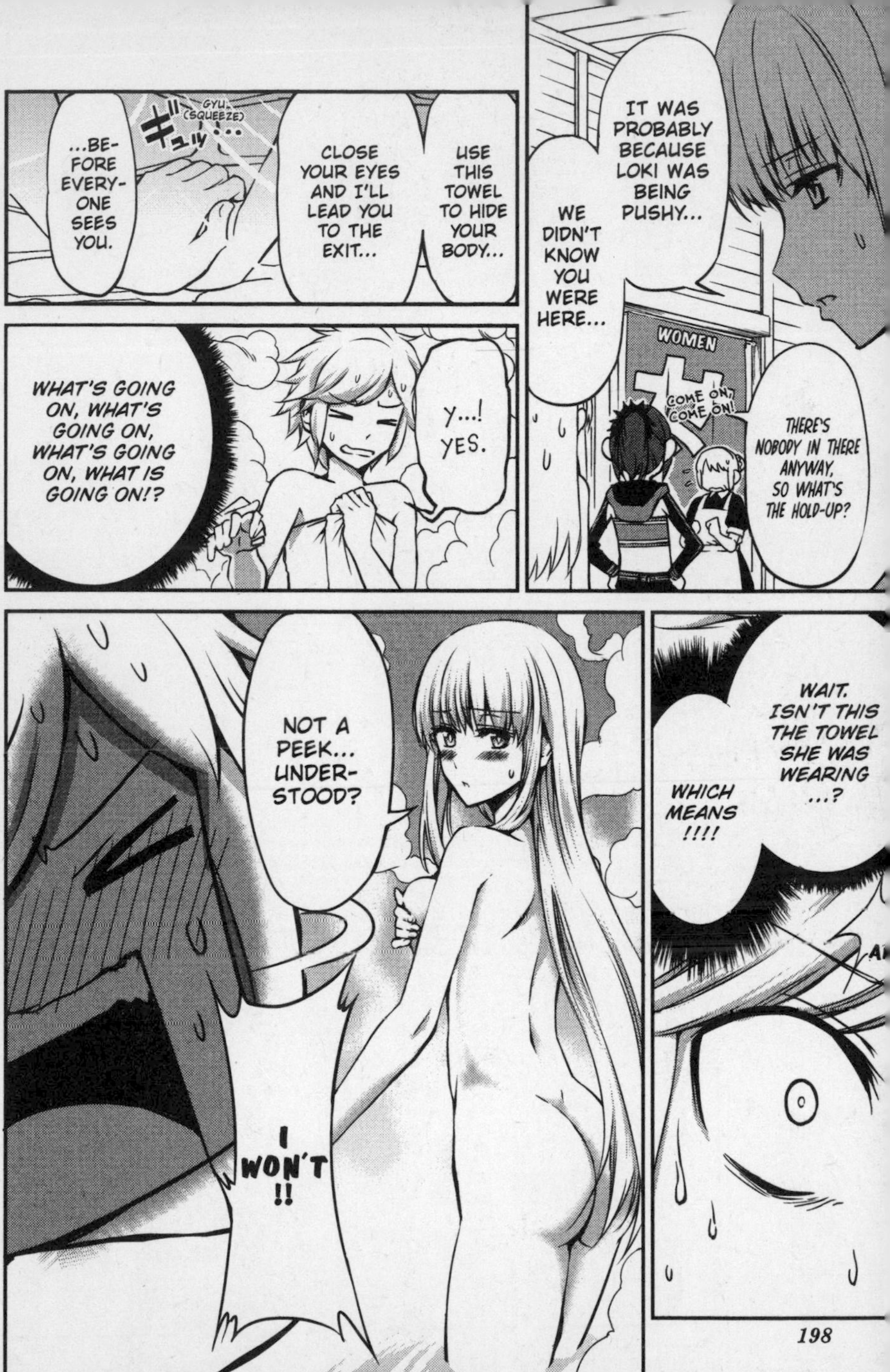
IT WAS PROBABLY BECAUSE LOKI WAS BEING PUSHY...
WE DIDN'T KNOW YOU WERE HERE...
WOMEN
COME ON, COME ON!
THERE'S NOBODY IN THERE ANYWAY, SO WHAT'S THE HOLD-UP?
USE THIS TOWEL TO HIDE YOUR BODY...
CLOSE YOUR EYES AND I'LL LEAD YOU TO THE EXIT...
GYU (SQUEEZE)
...BEFORE EVERYONE SEES YOU.
Y...! YES.
WHAT'S GOING ON, WHAT'S GOING ON, WHAT'S GOING ON, WHAT IS GOING ON!?
WAIT. ISN'T THIS THE TOWEL SHE WAS WEARING ...?
WHICH MEANS !!!!
NOT A PEEK... UNDERSTOOD?
I WON'T !!

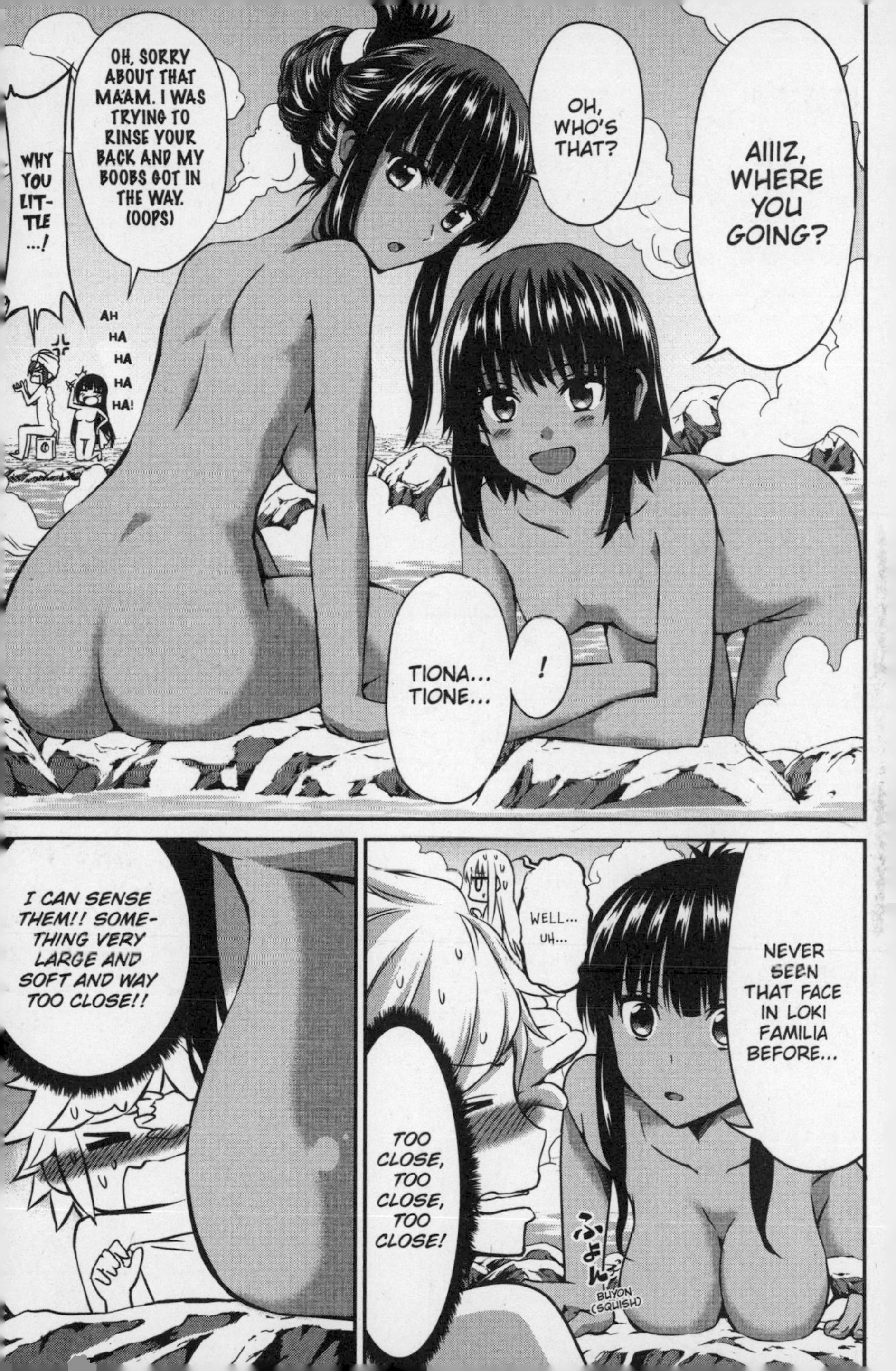
AIIIZ, WHERE YOU GOING?
OH, WHO'S THAT?
OH, SORRY ABOUT THAT MA'AM. I WAS TRYING TO RINSE YOUR BACK AND MY BOOBS GOT IN THE WAY. (OOPS)
WHY YOU LIT-TLE ...!
AH HA HA HA HA!
!
TIONA... TIONE...
NEVER SEEN THAT FACE IN LOKI FAMILIA BEFORE...
WELL... UH...
TOO CLOSE, TOO CLOSE, TOO CLOSE!
ふよん
BUYON (SQUISH)
I CAN SENSE THEM!! SOME-THING VERY LARGE AND SOFT AND WAY TOO CLOSE!!

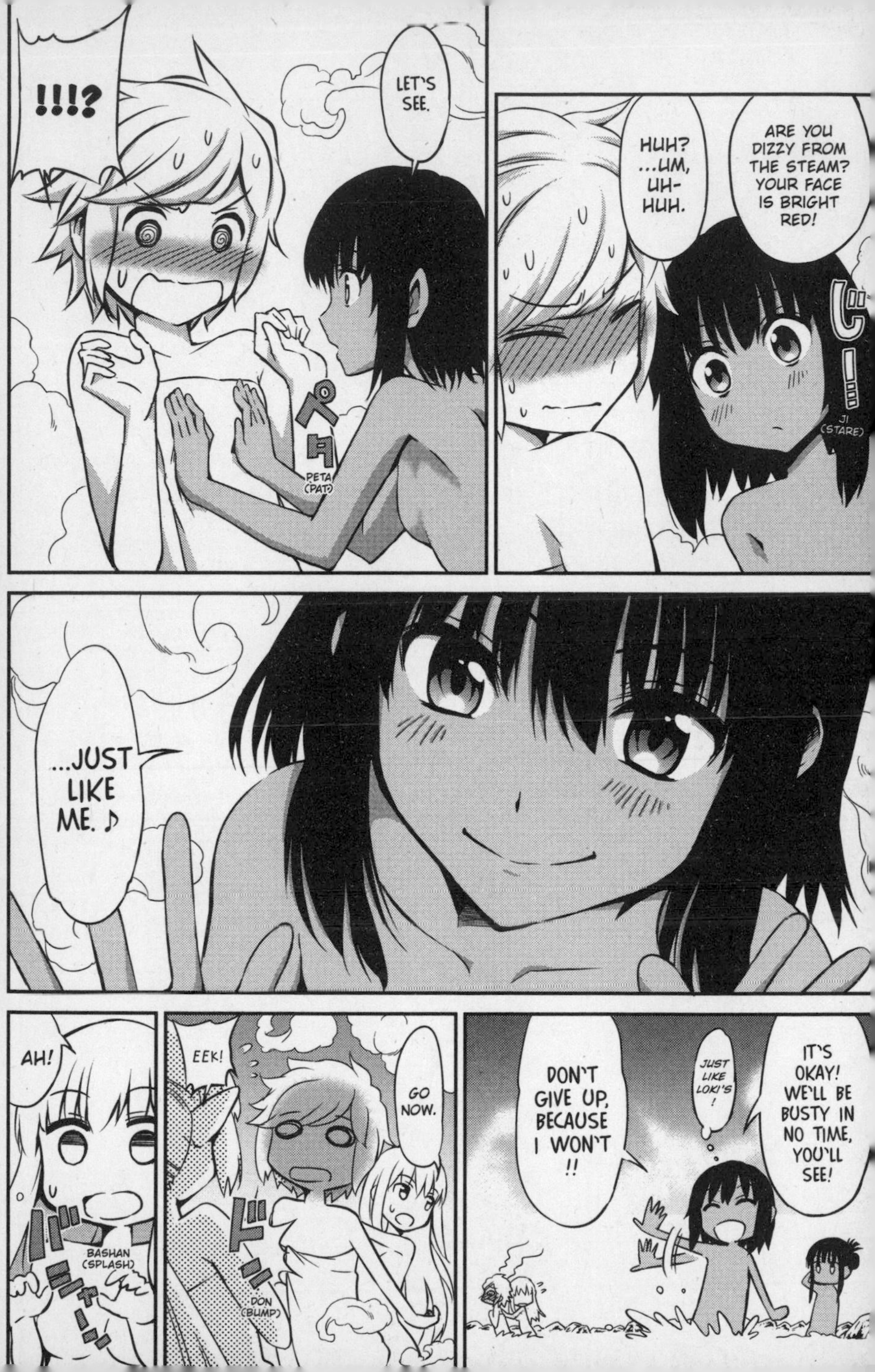
ARE YOU DIZZY FROM THE STEAM? YOUR FACE IS BRIGHT RED!
HUH? ...UM, UH-HUH.
JI (STARE)
LET'S SEE.
!!!?
PETA (PAT)
...JUST LIKE ME. ♪
IT'S OKAY! WE'LL BE BUSTY IN NO TIME, YOU'LL SEE!
JUST LIKE LOKI'S!
DON'T GIVE UP, BECAUSE I WON'T !!
GO NOW.
EEK!
DON (BUMP)
AH!
BASHAN (SPLASH)

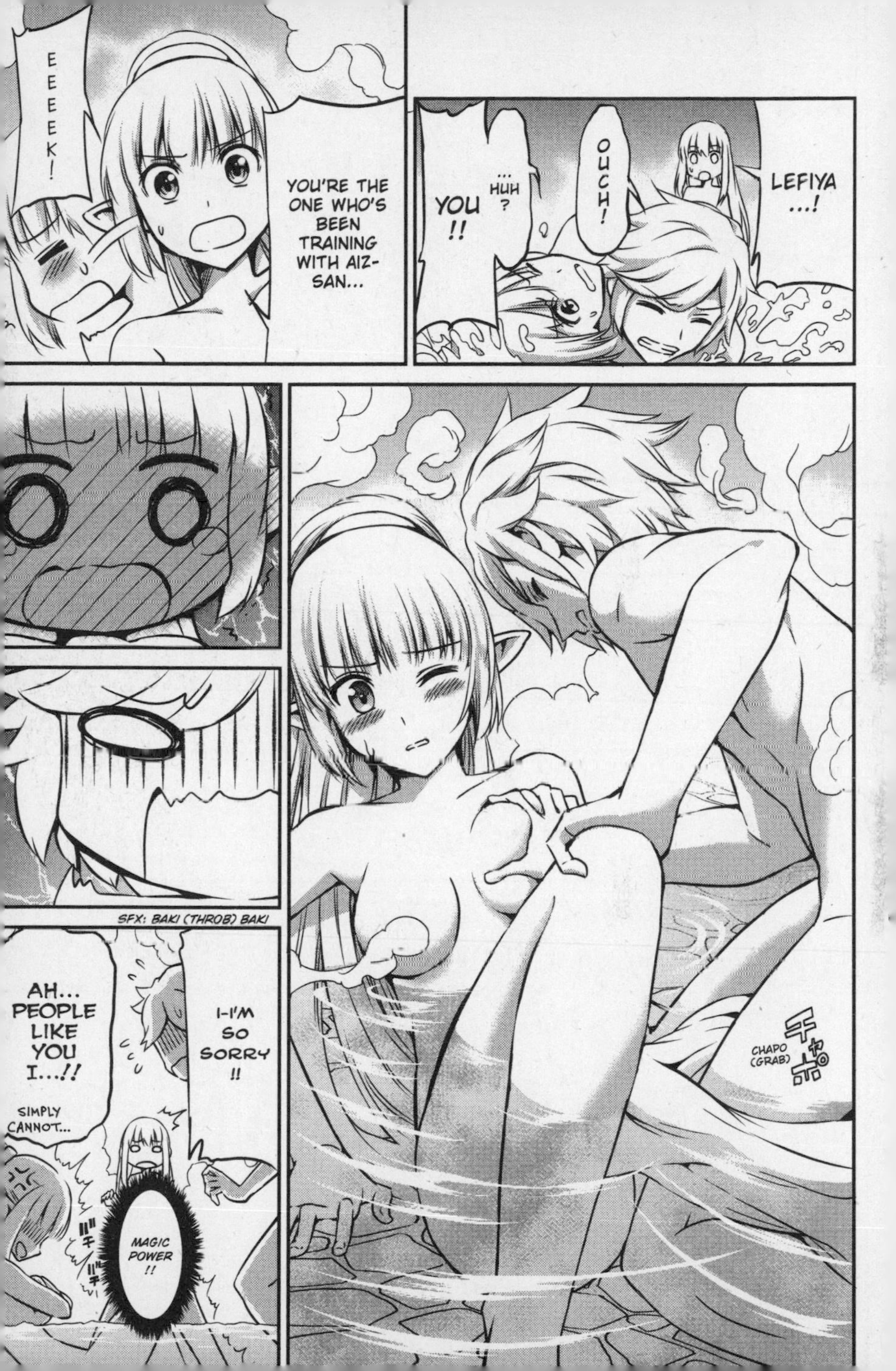

LEFIYA ...!
OUCH!
... HUH?
YOU!!
YOU'RE THE ONE WHO'S BEEN TRAINING WITH AIZ-SAN...
EEEEK!
CHAPO (GRAB)
SFX: BAKI (THROB) BAKI
I-I'M SO SORRY!!
AH... PEOPLE LIKE YOU I...!!
SIMPLY CANNOT...
MAGIC POWER!!

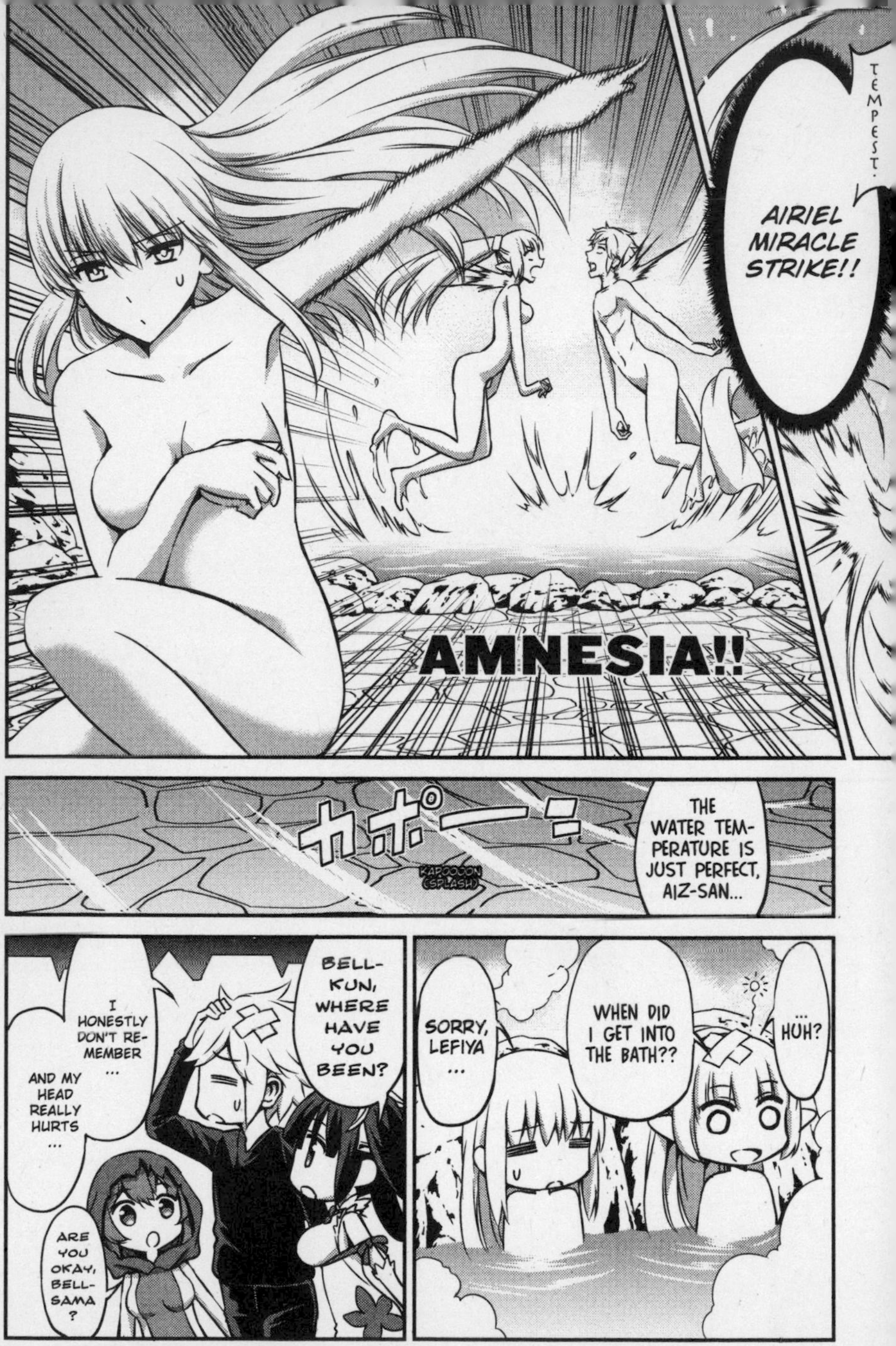
TEMPEST.
AIRIEL MIRACLE STRIKE!!
AMNESIA!!
THE WATER TEMPERATURE IS JUST PERFECT, AIZ-SAN...
カポーン
KAPOOOON (SPLASH)
... HUH?
WHEN DID I GET INTO THE BATH??
SORRY, LEFIYA ...
BELL-KUN, WHERE HAVE YOU BEEN?
I HONESTLY DON'T REMEMBER ...
AND MY HEAD REALLY HURTS ...
ARE YOU OKAY, BELL-SAMA?

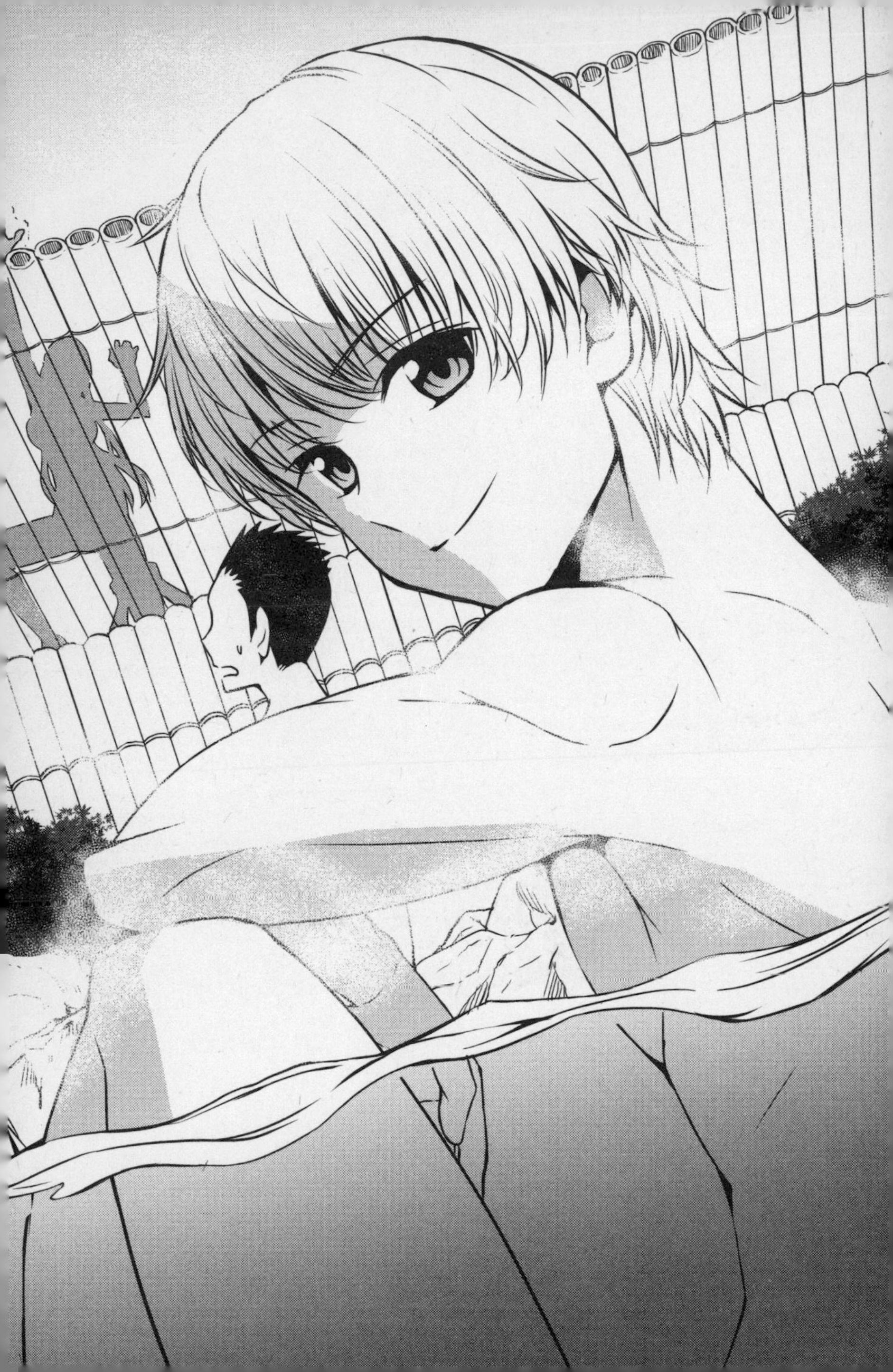

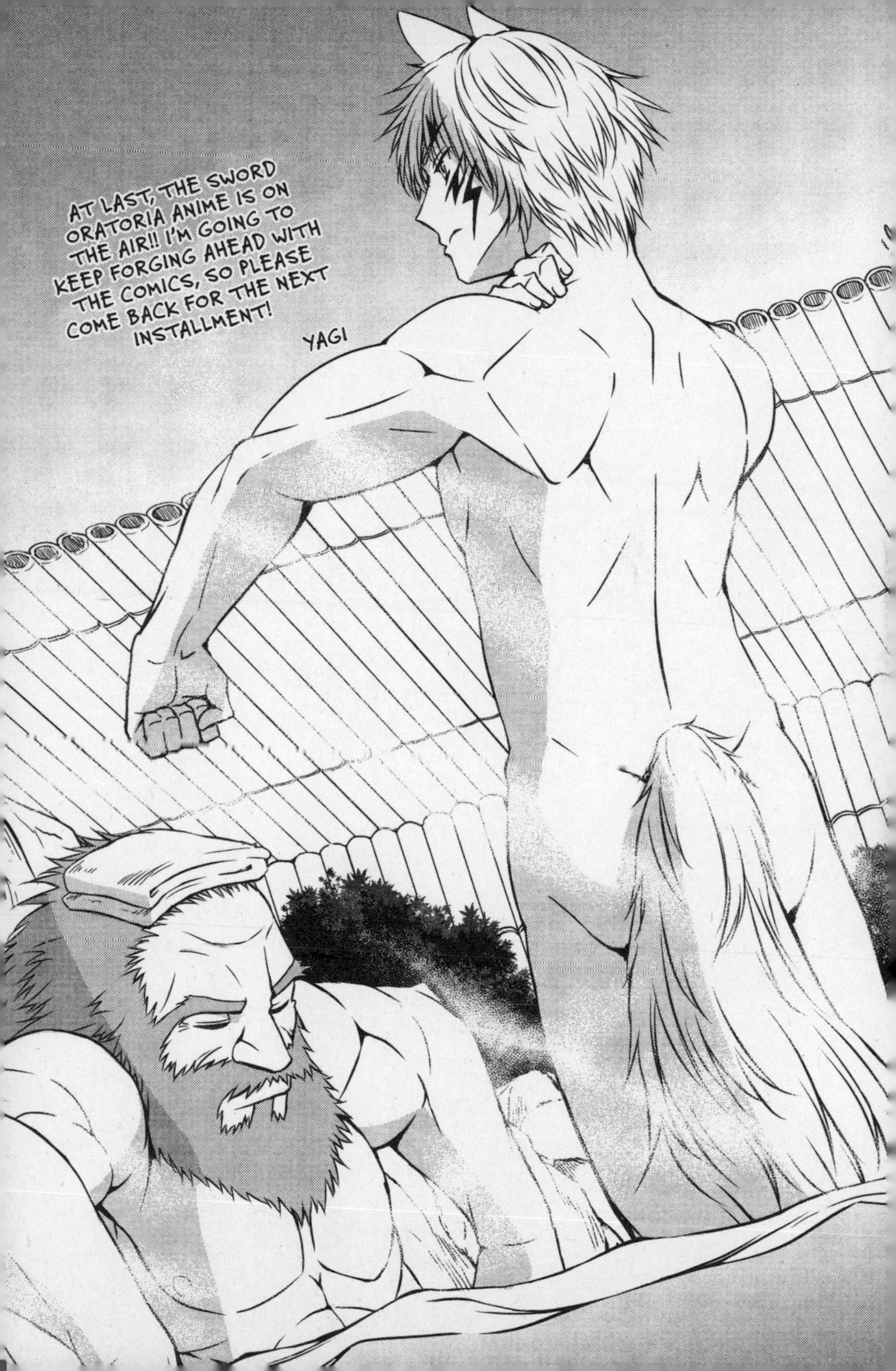
AT LAST, THE SWORD ORATORIA ANIME IS ON THE AIR!! I'M GOING TO KEEP FORGING AHEAD WITH THE COMICS, SO PLEASE COME BACK FOR THE NEXT INSTALLMENT!
YAGI

Coming up...

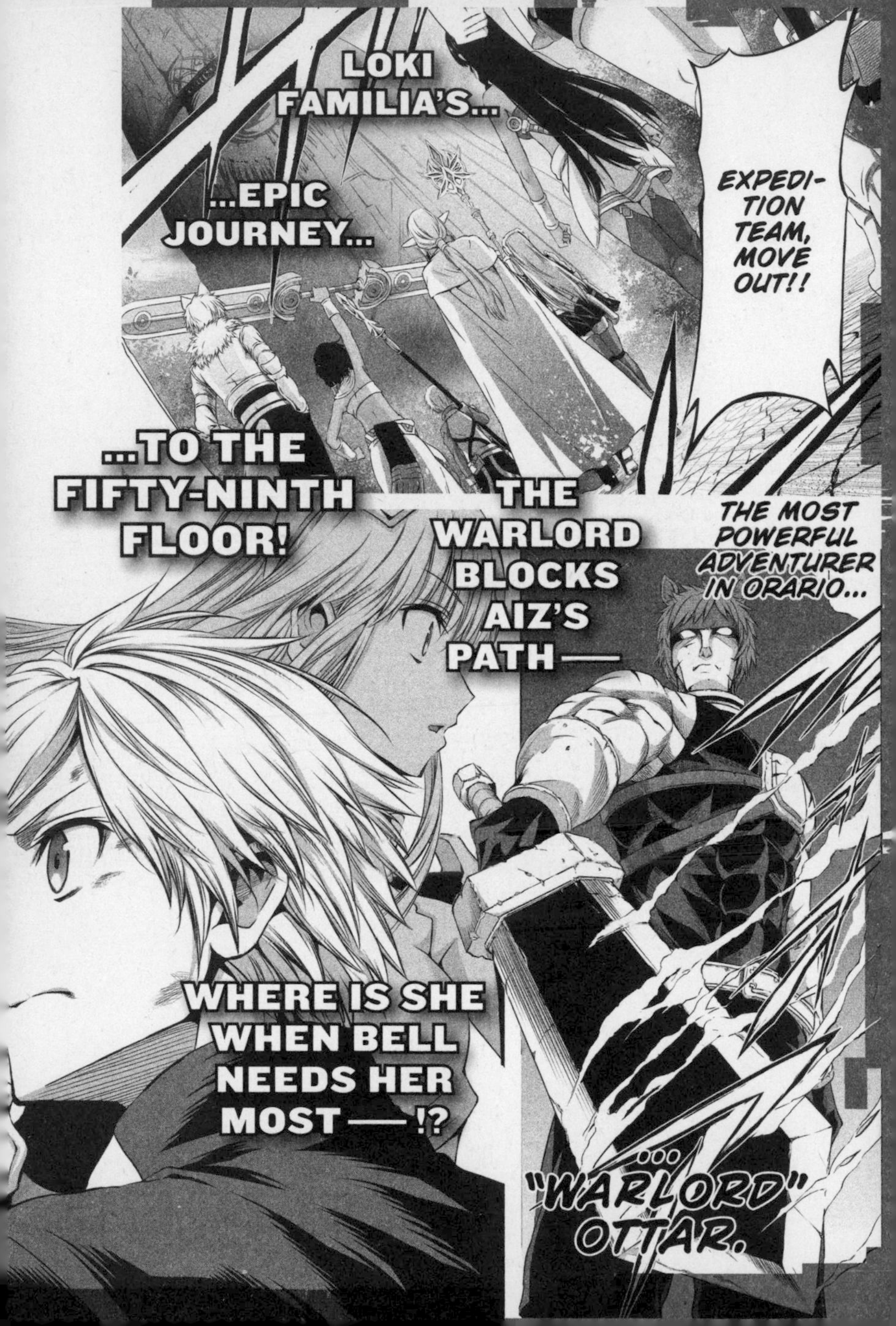
EXPEDITION TEAM, MOVE OUT!!
LOKI FAMILIA'S...
...EPIC JOURNEY...
...TO THE FIFTY-NINTH FLOOR!
THE MOST POWERFUL ADVENTURER IN ORARIO...
..."WARLORD" OTTAR.
THE WARLORD BLOCKS AIZ'S PATH——
WHERE IS SHE WHEN BELL NEEDS HER MOST——!?

IS IT WRONG TO TRY TO PICK UP GIRLS IN A DUNGEON? ON THE SIDE: SWORD ORATORIA 8

Fujino Omori
Takashi Yagi
Haimura Kiyotaka, Yasuda Suzuhito

Translation: Andrew Gaippe • Lettering: Barri Shrager

DUNGEON NI DEAI WO MOTOMERU NO WA MACHIGATTEIRUDAROUKA GAIDEN SWORD ORATORIA vol. 8
© Fujino Omori / SB Creative Corp. Character design: Haimura Kiyotaka, Yasuda Suzuhito
© 2017 Takashi Yagi / SQUARE ENIX CO., LTD.
First published in Japan in 2017 by SQUARE ENIX CO., LTD.
English translation rights arranged with SQUARE ENIX CO., LTD. and Yen Press, LLC through Tuttle-Mori Agency, Inc.

English translation © 2019 by SQUARE ENIX CO., LTD.

Yen Press
150 West 30th Street, 19th Floor
New York, NY 10001

Visit us at yenpress.com
facebook.com/yenpress
twitter.com/yenpress
yenpress.tumblr.com
instagram.com/yenpress

First Yen Press Edition: July 2019

Yen Press is an imprint of Yen Press, LLC.
The Yen Press name and logo are trademarks of Yen Press, LLC.

Library of Congress Control Number: 2016946068

ISBNs: 978-0-316-44813-0 (paperback)
       978-0-316-44814-7 (ebook)

10 9 8 7 6 5 4 3 2 1

WOR

Printed in the United States of America